East Asia in Crisis

Until the middle of 1997 the record of sustained rapid growth for the economies of East Asia was outstanding. Their performance was widely branded a miracle, and much discussed as a model for others. With the recent turmoil, however, the achievements of decades are now in jeopardy.

McLeod and Garnaut have brought together some of the world's leading experts on Asian economies in order to shed light on East Asia's crisis. The book includes case studies of thirteen countries in the region (including Thailand, Malaysia, Indonesia, Korea, Japan, China, Hong Kong, Taiwan and Singapore), examining these countries' experiences, how their governments and the international community reacted, and why some states weathered the storm better than others.

With these case studies as background, lessons are drawn from the ways in which the crisis unfolded to suggest how similar crises might best be handled – and, ideally, how they might be avoided in the future. The book's insights therefore have strong policy relevance in the region and beyond, at a time when upheavals in East Asia threaten the stability of the global economy.

East Asia in Crisis presents a comprehensive survey and analysis of the most dramatic development in the world economy for decades. It should be of considerable interest, not only to economists, but also to the business community and policymakers who need to make sense of these events.

Ross H. McLeod is Fellow and **Ross Garnaut** is Professor in the Department of Economics, Research School of Pacific and Asian Studies, at The Australian National University.

East Asia in Crisis

From being a miracle to needing one?

**Edited by Ross H. McLeod
and Ross Garnaut**

London and New York

First published 1998
by Routledge
11 New Fetter Lane, London EC4P 4EE

Reprinted 1999 ,(Three Times), 2000

Simultaneously published in the USA and Canada
by Routledge
29 West 35th Street, New York, NY 10001

Routledge is an imprint of the Taylor & Francis Group

Typeset in Garamond and Helvetica by
Japan Online, Canberra, Australia
Printed and bound in Great Britain by
TJ International Ltd, Padstow, Cornwall

British Library Cataloguing in Publication Data
A catalogue record for this book is available from the
British Library

Library of Congress Cataloging-in-Publication Data
A catalog record for this book is available on request

ISBN 0-415-19831-3 (hbk)
ISBN 0-415-19832-1 (pbk)

Contents

Figures

Tables

Contributors

Ross H. McLeod is Fellow in the Indonesia Project, Department of Economics, Research School of Pacific and Asian Studies, at the Australian National University. He has been working in and on Indonesia in various capacities – postgraduate student, consultant and academic researcher – since 1978, and is a fluent Indonesian speaker. Prior to joining the Indonesia Project in 1992, he worked as a private consultant based in Canberra, focusing primarily on banking and finance in Indonesia. His consulting work has been mainly for Indonesia's central bank (Bank Indonesia), its state-owned banks, and its Department of Finance. He is Editor of the ANU's *Bulletin of Indonesian Economic Studies*, a journal which has been in continuous publication since 1965. He has also been a regular contributor to the Asia Pacific Economics Group's *Asia Pacific Profiles* series.

Ross Garnaut has been a Professor of Economics at the ANU's Research School of Pacific and Asian Studies since 1989. His previous appointments include Australian Ambassador to China (1989–94), Chairman, Primary Industry Bank of Australia, Chairman, Bank of Western Australia and Chairman, Western Australia China Economic and Technical Research Fund. Professor Garnaut is the author of numerous books, monographs and articles in scholarly journals on international economics, public finance and economic development, particularly in relation to East Asia and the Southwest Pacific.

Prema-chandra Athukorala: Senior Fellow, Department of Economics, Research School of Pacific and Asian Studies, Australian National University.

Leilanie Basilio: Research Analyst, Philippine Institute for Development Studies.

Yuk-shing Cheng: Assistant Professor, Department of Economics, Hong Kong Baptist University.

George Fane: Senior Fellow, Department of Economics, Research School of Pacific and Asian Studies, Australian National University.

Christopher Findlay: Associate Professor, Department of Economics, and Co-director of the Chinese Economies Research Centre, University of Adelaide.

Brian Gray: Chief Manager, Risk Analysis and Research, Bank Supervision Department, Reserve Bank of Australia.

David Gruen: Chief Economist, Economic Analysis Department, Reserve Bank of Australia.

David D. Hale: Global Economic Strategist for the Zurich Group, and member of several major US government and private sector policy committees.

Akiyoshi Horiuchi: Professor of Economics, University of Tokyo.

Ponciano Intal Jr.: President, Philippine Institute for Development Studies.

Sisira Jayasuriya: Reader in Economics, La Trobe University, Melbourne.

Shirley W.Y. Kuo: Minister of State in charge of financial and economic policies, and Professor of Economics, National Taiwan University.

Le Dang Doanh: President, Central Institute of Economic Management, Hanoi.

Suiwah Leung: Director, Graduate Studies in Economics of Development, National Centre for Development Studies, Research School of Pacific and Asian Studies, Australian National University, and Convenor of the AusAID–NCDS Vietnam Economic Research Project 1995–8.

Christina Y. Liu: Professor, Department of Finance, National Taiwan University and Board Member, Board of Directors, Taiwan Stock Exchange.

Warwick J. McKibbin: Professor of International Economics and Head of Department of Economics, Research School of Pacific and Asian Studies, Australian National University. Also non-resident Senior Fellow, Brookings Institution, Washington DC, and President, McKibbin Software Group Inc.

Melanie Milo: Research Associate and member of the Macroeconomics Group at the Philippine Institute for Development Studies.

David C.L. Nellor: Assistant Director, International Monetary Fund Regional Office for Asia and the Pacific, Tokyo.

Celia Reyes: Research Fellow and member of the Macroeconomics Group at the Philippine Institute for Development Studies.

Heather Smith: Research Fellow and Coordinator of the Korea Economy Program, Department of Economics, Research School of Pacific and Asian

Studies, Australian National University, and Associate Director of the Pacific Trade and Development (PAFTAD) Secretariat.

Hadi Soesastro: Director, Centre for Strategic and International Studies, Jakarta.

Ligang Song: Fellow, Australia Japan Research Centre, Research School of Pacific and Asian Studies, Australian National University.

Glenn Stevens: Assistant Governor (Economic), Reserve Bank of Australia.

Sir Alan A. Walters: Vice-Chairman and Director of AIG Trading Group Inc.

Peter G. Warr: John Crawford Professor of Agricultural Economics, Department of Economics, Research School of Pacific and Asian Studies, Australian National University.

Wong Marn-heong: Director, Public Affairs, Pacific Economic Cooperation Council International Secretariat, Singapore.

Foreword

Ross McLeod and Ross Garnaut have performed a great service in offering this timely and thoughtful review of the East Asian financial crisis. What began as a currency crisis in Thailand has since enveloped many of the region's banks, and has slowed the growth trajectories of all countries in the region. While the crisis has affected the entire region, the nature and severity of its impact has varied greatly from country to country. This superb collection of case studies underscores both the interdependence among Pacific Basin countries and the diversity and heterogeneity of the Asia Pacific economy.

But this is more than a collection of case studies. The volume offers timely reflections on how East Asian economies have been affected by the volatile movements of global financial flows. It assesses the role of the IMF in responding to challenges confronting the most distressed of the region's economies. It examines what can be learned from the experience of other regions confronting similar crises. It does not merely analyse problems; it suggests practical remedies for them. And it offers thoughts on the long-term implications of this crisis for the future of Asia, the prospects for developing economies and the role of international financial institutions.

Thus there is something in this volume for virtually everyone concerned about Pacific Asia and the need for a closer 'fit' between the economic forces that are reshaping the region and the regimes that must absorb and accommodate the impact of global markets on the collective aspirations of Asia's peoples.

Ambassador Michael H. Armacost
President, The Brookings Institution
July 1998

Acknowledgments

The Reserve Bank of Australia and the Australian Agency for International Development (AusAID) both provided financial support for this book, without which it would not have been produced. Additional support is also gratefully acknowledged from the United States Information Service; Deutsche Bank Australia; Cathay Pacific Airways; the Embassy of the Republic of Indonesia in Australia; and the Research School of Pacific and Asian Studies, Division of Economics, comprising the Department of Economics, the Australia Japan Research Centre, and the National Centre for Development Studies.

A number of individuals have assisted us greatly in bringing the book to fruition. Marilyn Popp of the Australia Japan Research Centre effectively handled the organisational burden of conducting a conference to discuss chapter drafts at the Australian National University on 4–5 May 1998, assisted by Hilda Heidemanns, Carol Kavanagh, Sonya Bodger, Lim Poh Ping, David Tierney, Chatib Basri, Chang Hsiao Chuan and Renuka Mahadevan. Production of the manuscript was efficiently managed under demanding circumstances by Denise Ryan of the Australia Japan Research Centre, ably assisted by Raylee Singh, Rebecca Crannaford, Beth Thomson, Minni Reis and Beatriz Waddell. Victoria Smith at Routledge was an enthusiastic supporter of the project from its inception, and we thank her for her efforts.

We are grateful also to those who gave comments on the chapter drafts, including Heinz Arndt, Peter Drysdale, Ron Duncan, Bob Gregory, Stephen Grenville, Ian Harper, Hal Hill, Huang Yiping, Helen Hughes, Neil Hyden, Kali Kalirajan, Kwon Jae-jung, Peter McCawley, Bhanupong Nidhiprabha, On Kit Tam, Graeme Wells and Yang Yongzheng. To the authors who have contributed to this book, we offer our thanks for responding to our pleas to put other things aside in the interests of helping us to meet a most ambitious publication deadline.

Finally, particular thanks are due to Prapti and Dian McLeod, who have had to put up with a husband and father who spent most of the last few months glued to his computer.

Ross H. McLeod and Ross Garnaut
Canberra, June 1998

Abbreviations

A$	Australian dollar
ADB	Asian Development Bank
ANU	Australian National University
APEC	Asia Pacific Economic Cooperation
APEG	Asia Pacific Economics Group
ASEAN	Association of South East Asian Nations
ASEAN-ISIS	ASEAN Institutes of Strategic and International Studies
BAP	Bankers Association of the Philippines
BIBF	Bangkok International Banking Facility
BIS	Bank for International Settlements
BNM	Bank Negara Malaysia
BOJ	Bank of Japan
BOK	Bank of Korea
BOT	Bank of Thailand
BSP	Bangko Sentral ng Pilipinas
CAR	capital adequacy ratio
CD	certificate of deposit
CEPD	Council for Economic Planning and Development
CPI	consumer price index
DIC	Deposit Insurance Corporation
DOSRI	directors, stockholders and related interests
EMEAP	Executive Meeting of East Asia and Pacific (central banks)
ERM	exchange rate mechanism
FCDU	Foreign Currency Deposit Unit
FDI	foreign direct investment
FDIC	Federal Deposit Insurance Corporation
FIDF	Financial Institutions Development Fund
FY	fiscal year
G10	group of 10

GATS	General Agreement on Trade in Services
GATT	General Agreement on Tariffs and Trade
GDP	gross domestic product
GNP	gross national product
HK$	Hong Kong dollar
HKMA	Hong Kong Monetary Authority
HSI	Hang Seng Index
IEDB	International Economic Data Bank
IMF	International Monetary Fund
KLSE	Kuala Lumpur Stock Exchange
KSE	Korea Stock Exchange
LIBOR	London Inter-bank Offered Rate
LPEM-UI	Lembaga Penelitian Ekonomi Masyarakat–Universitas Indonesia (Institute for Economic and Social Research–University of Indonesia)
MAS	Monetary Authority of Singapore
MEFP	memorandum of economic and financial policies
MNE	multinational enterprise
MOF	Ministry of Finance
NAFTA	North American Free Trade Agreement
NBER	National Bureau of Economic Research
NBFIs	non-bank financial institutions
NPA	non-performing asset
NTB	non-tariff barrier
NT$	New Taiwan dollar
ODA	overseas development assistance
OECD	Organisation for Economic Cooperation and Development
Q	quarter
RBI	Reserve Bank of India
RER	real exchange rate
RM	ringgit
RMB	renminbi
Rp	rupiah
RPI	retail price index
Rs	rupees
S$	Singapore dollar
SBI	(Bank of Indonesia) certificate of deposit
SEC	Securities Exchange Commission

SMEs	small and medium-sized enterprises
SOEs	state-owned enterprises
T-bonds	Treasury bonds
UK	United Kingdom
US	United States
USAID	US Agency for International Development
W	won
WEF	World Economic Forum
WPI	wholesale price index
WTO	World Trade Organisation

Part I

Overview

1 The East Asian crisis

Ross Garnaut

INTRODUCTION

There never was such a thing as an East Asian 'miracle'. There was, however, an East Asian phenomenon of sustained rapid growth, as one economy after another in East Asia began to accumulate capital, apply improved technology, and utilise human resources more effectively for economic development.

Through the 1990s the international community came to expect the continuation of sustained, rapid growth in the developing economies of East Asia. These expectations were shattered by the sudden emergence of financial, economic and even political disruption throughout the region in the second half of 1997. This book documents the evolution of the East Asian crisis, and seeks to answer some big questions raised by this dramatic episode.

What were the causes? What sense can be made of the coincidence in timing of the onset of crisis in many countries and, in particular, of the phenomenon that came to be described as 'contagion'? Why did the crisis first appear in Thailand, and have its most costly expression in Indonesia? How did some economies with close ties with the most troubled countries avoid severe consequences from the East Asian crisis, at least through its first year? How was the evolution of crisis in each country affected by the character of the financial system and its regulatory framework?

A second set of issues involves the immediate policy response to the crisis. How much was the path and eventual severity of the crisis affected, ameliorated or exacerbated by the policy responses in individual economies? And how were they affected by the international policy response – in particular, by the IMF-led programs in Thailand, Indonesia and Korea?

Finally, the volume seeks to draw lessons from this remarkable and unhappy episode. How are short- and long-run growth prospects affected? Does the crisis mark the end of sustained rapid growth in East Asia, or in individual economies in which it had appeared well established? What have we learned about the relative merits of various types of exchange rate regimes, and about macroeconomic management more broadly in rapidly growing and increasingly outward-oriented economies? About the priority of liberalisation of capital flows in the sequence of related reforms? About the type of financial systems and regulatory regimes that are most helpful to sustaining growth in economies becoming deeply integrated into the international economy? About domestic and international policy adjustments that can contribute to avoiding financial crises in the future? Most fundamentally, how does the crisis of 1997–8 affect thought about economic development and economic policy in East Asia and beyond?

STRUCTURE OF THE BOOK

This introductory chapter sketches some of the main features of the crisis, its origins and its evolution, and some preliminary thoughts about its implications for policy and development. It summarises some basic economic data for the 13 economies covered in the case study chapters that comprise Parts II to IV, for purposes of comparison and easy reference. And it begins to address questions that are dealt with in detail in subsequent chapters.

The core of this book, and its distinctive feature, is the set of twelve chapters in the form of country case studies. Four of these concern the economies that have been most troubled by the crisis (Part II). Why did the crisis first appear in Thailand? Why was it so severe in Malaysia and Korea – economies apparently with great underlying strength? And why did Indonesia – at first appearing to have the least problematic macroeconomic fundamentals of the troubled four – experience the greatest and least tractable damage?

In Part III the Vietnam case study raises the question of whether the absence of convertibility on the capital account was a help in avoiding contagion. Perhaps more importantly, it discusses the conditions under which Vietnam might have benefited from more openness to capital flows, while keeping the risk of financial instability to a manageable level. Vietnam's huge current account deficit raises a question about whether capital account controls have simply enabled necessary adjustments to be postponed. China also administers heavy controls on capital movements, but this is rendered less central to China's story by a strong current account and high foreign exchange reserves, price stability, massive direct foreign investment inflows, and a well-established reform momentum.

The chapter on India provides another perspective on capital controls. This country is linked less closely to East Asian trade and investment than any of the East Asians themselves, but may be exposed to 'contagion' through competition with East Asian economies in global markets, and through the pulling back of Western investors from Asia as a whole. Here the questions include why India and other South Asian economies appear to have been able to withstand the growth-depressing effects of the crisis, and whether this may turn out to be a temporary respite.

The five other case studies, in Part IV, examine six economies that, so far, have avoided exceptionally large set-backs to economic growth. The Philippines, long the 'sick man' of Southeast Asia, weathered initial shocks comparable to those felt by Indonesia, Thailand and Malaysia far more successfully. Taiwan in one chapter, and Singapore and Hong Kong together in another, provide additional examples of very open economies, closely linked to the troubled four and receiving large initial shocks from them, but which nevertheless had avoided financial crisis up until June 1998. Examination of these important cases leads into an examination of the value to sustainable economic growth of relatively transparent regulatory regimes and competitive, open financial systems. The treatment of Singapore and Hong Kong within a single chapter also allows comparison of the effects of highly contrasting exchange rate regimes – the former, a managed float; the latter, a rate firmly fixed against the US dollar and incorporating major elements of a currency board system.

Australia is in some ways similar to Taiwan, Hong Kong and Singapore, and in other ways different. Far-reaching financial deregulation in the mid-1980s abolished capital controls, floated the currency, removed direct controls on interest rates and lending, and increased the level of competition between banks and amongst financial institutions more generally. By the time of the East Asian crisis, financial institutions and regulatory authorities had learned how to make the new arrangements work – not least through the bitter lessons from Australia's own currency crisis of 1985 and 1986, and the banking crisis it experienced in the early 1990s. The Australia chapter asks whether there were lessons in the currency and banking instability in the eight years following financial deregulation that, if heeded by the East Asian developing economies, might have helped them to avoid the worst of the current crisis.

The case study of Japan describes a country that had been having its own, slow-burning financial problems for some years before the East Asian crisis began, and in which some of the same contributory factors are evident – such as a boom-and-bust cycle in asset markets, and weakness in the financial system and its regulatory regime. The decline of the yen has been gentle by comparison with that of the currencies of the troubled four, although in total magnitude over the three years to mid-1998 it is about as large as that of the baht, ringgit and won. At the heart of the Japanese stagnation is weakness in the banking system – the focus of this chapter – and there are lessons in the Japanese experience for financial reform in developing East Asia. The Japanese case is important, moreover, because Japan's dominant role in regional trade and capital flows meant that its own slow growth and currency weakness helped it to trigger the East Asian crisis, and now adds to the difficulty of recovery in the region.

Eight other chapters in Parts V, VI and VII step back from the country detail to analyse more general issues and to draw more general conclusions.

Warwick McKibbin applies a dynamic intertemporal general equilibrium model to simulate the East Asian crisis, focusing on the impact of a sudden increase in the perceived risk of holding assets in the countries of the region. He emphasises the importance of taking into consideration the changes in international capital flows that necessarily accompany – indeed, drive – changes in the pattern of international trade, rather than simply assuming that it is possible to estimate the impact on trade flows resulting from the observed realignments of exchange rates without doing so.

David Nellor describes the policy reform packages that were negotiated as a condition of International Monetary Fund (IMF) financial support for three of the troubled economies – Thailand, Indonesia and Korea – and the rationale for their various components. There has been extensive criticism of the IMF's approach, especially in Indonesia, against which a vigorous defence is presented in this chapter.

David Hale compares the Mexican crisis of 1994 with the East Asian crises. The latter are distinguished by financial excess and miscalculation within the private sector rather than the public sector. This required different domestic and international policy responses – a lesson that was learned late, and imperfectly, in East Asia. The Mexican economy recovered quickly and strongly from 1995. Hale examines the conditions under which East Asian economies might enjoy a similarly impressive return to good health.

George Fane looks at the roles that weaknesses in the financial system and in prudential regulation have played in the crisis. He points out the near impossibility of persuading depositors that governments will not bail them out if banks fail, and argues that this implies that a moral hazard problem is therefore unavoidable. The important need, then, is to adopt policies that will optimally reduce and offset problems of this kind.

Alan Walters examines the choice of exchange rate regimes in the light of the recent experience. The hybrid regimes that were present in the four troubled economies – with a fixed but adjustable peg against the US dollar – contributed to the emergence of financial crisis. This raises an old question: whether genuinely fixed and freely floating rates are more conducive to stability than the hybrids in between.

Hadi Soesastro looks beyond the immediate issue of restoring financial stability and economic growth to focus on what is likely to be the most important legacy of the East Asian crisis – namely, the changes in ideas about development-oriented economic policy it will stimulate. He examines the lessons to be drawn, and the changes in perceptions that are likely to result, from the crisis, and asks what effects these are likely to have on the future path of development.

Finally, McLeod draws upon the book as a whole in his discussion of the new era of financial fragility, and Garnaut looks at economic lessons from the crisis.

The remainder of this introductory chapter sketches important features of the East Asian crisis, and provides statistical reference points for the case study chapters that follow.

EAST ASIAN ECONOMIES ARE NOT ALL ALIKE

The East Asian economies in their years of sustained high growth seemed to have much in common, at least to distant observers. The World Bank's *East Asian Miracle* (1993) drew attention to common features contributing to growth across economies as diverse as Korea, Indonesia, Singapore, Malaysia and Thailand. The common features were said to include high rates of saving and investment, a strong focus on investment in education, sound macroeconomic policy generating reasonably stable macroeconomic conditions, and good economic governance.

In the unhappy times since mid-1997, differences have been more obvious than similarities. In the 'contagion' that followed Thailand's abandonment of the dollar peg, domestic and international financial markets raised the risk premia on investment throughout developing East Asia. A largely undifferentiated initial shock had extraordinarily different effects, depending crucially on the nature of political systems, policy responses and financial institutions in the countries concerned.

While the expression 'Asian financial crisis' appeared frequently in the world's newspaper headlines in the third quarter of 1997, at that time it was a misnomer. Then, it would have been more accurate to confine the term 'financial crisis' to Indonesia, Korea, Thailand and Malaysia. There had been virtually no 'crisis' in South Asia. A number of the other economies in East Asia – the Philippines, Singapore, China and, more problematically, Hong Kong – were expected to grow in 1998 and 1999 at rates below the average of recent years, but well within the range of their own experience over the past two decades. Through 1998, however, economic contraction, currency depreciation and reduction in imports in some major economies have been transmitted to others. Social disorder and political instability in Indonesia in May, and the realisation that Japan was in recession in June, sent new negative shocks through the region, generating intensive international discussion as it became clear that widespread economic recession through East Asia and beyond was a real possibility.

Still, by June 1998, there were only four countries in which serious economic dislocation had occurred, markedly more damaging than any since the beginning of the era of rapid, internationally-oriented growth. These countries contain about one-tenth of Asia's population and one-sixth of East Asia's. The one-tenth and the one-sixth matter a great deal. And for the 200 million people of Indonesia, the proliferating problems are of immeasurable consequence. Other countries and people remain vulnerable to further complications from the forces tending to recession unleashed in the first year of the crisis.

A STATISTICAL SKETCH OF THE CRISIS

This section presents a statistical sketch of macroeconomic conditions in the years preceding the crisis in each of the economies covered in case studies, to introduce the data, and for convenient reference throughout the book.

The first manifestation of crisis was in exchange rate movements (Figure 1.1). Indonesia stands out as having experienced by far the greatest fall in the value of its currency since mid-1997. At the other extreme, China, Vietnam, India and Hong Kong have seen little or no change in their exchange rates during the crisis period. Taking a longer-term perspective, it can be noted that all of this group other than Hong Kong had devalued their currencies by large amounts during the early and mid-1990s (although, in China's case, the devaluation of the official exchange rate was in the context of unification of official and market rates that had little effect on the prices at which the majority of foreign trade was transacted). Of the remainder, Thailand, Malaysia and Korea have been hard hit; the Philippines, Taiwan, Australia and Singapore less so. The currencies of most of this group bounced back quite strongly during March and April 1998, but weakened again in May and June as a result of the political turmoil in Indonesia and the increasingly obvious weakness of Japan's economy.

As we examine the other macroeconomic data, we learn to be wary of simple generalisations across the troubled economies and the others in our case studies. There are some general patterns linking macroeconomic conditions to the crisis. But they are complex, depending on the interaction between general economic factors, weaknesses in financial institutions, and policy and political responses.

The troubled economies had all grown rapidly at rates of the order of 8% per annum for several years prior to the crisis (Table 1.1). (The tables for Chapter 1 are collected at the end of the chapter, on pages 22–7.) Growth throughout East Asia other than the three Chinese economies was especially strong in 1995. Inflation at 3.5–6.5% per annum in the troubled economies in 1996 was not in itself an obvious precursor to crisis, but the persistence of rates above the contemporary international norm posed problems for economies with exchange rates pegged to a US dollar that was appreciating strongly against most other currencies (Table 1.2). A strong nominal exchange rate and inflation above international levels led to a significant appreciation of the real exchange rate through most of the East Asian developing economies after 1995, and notably in what became the troubled economies.

A severe slowdown in export growth in 1996 was experienced by most of East Asia. This was most apparent in Japan, Thailand, Korea and Malaysia,

Figure 1.1 Nominal US$ exchange rate (1990 = 100)

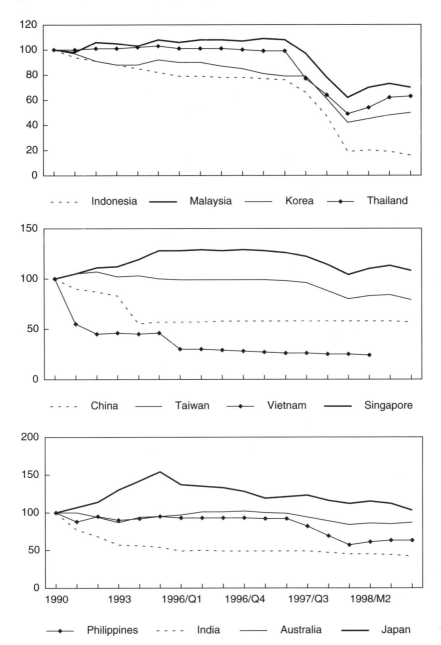

Note: Data are period averages, except for the last point, which is for 29 May 1998. The exchange rate is expressed as US$ per local currency. Hong Kong is not included in Figure 1.1 because there was virtually no change in its exchange rate during this period.
Source: IMF 1998d; IEDB, ANU. Data for Taiwan are from CEPD (various years). Data for Vietnam are from APEG 1998.

but was far less prominent in the fourth troubled country, Indonesia (Table 1.3). The Philippines, Singapore, Hong Kong, Taiwan and India all experienced significant reductions in export growth in the same year. Import growth declined in most East Asian countries (Table 1.4). Notably, Japan's imports grew by only 3% in 1996, compared with 22% in the previous year.

The troubled economies had relatively large current account deficits in the two years prior to the crisis (Table 1.5). Thailand became famous for its average deficit of around 7% of GDP in the first half of the 1990s, rising to 8% in 1995–6. Malaysia's current account deficit soared to over 10% of GDP in 1995 before falling back to about 5% in 1996, a little lower than the average for the previous six years. Korea's deficit jumped to nearly 5% in 1996, having been much lower previously, while in Indonesia the level was lower – just 3.5% – in the two years prior to the crisis. Among the other countries, the deficit in the Philippines was also close to 5% in 1996, while Vietnam stands out with its high deficits in the mid-1990s, rising to over 16% in 1996. Hong Kong went from a strong surplus of 7% of GDP in 1993 to a deficit of about 2.5% in 1995 and 1996.

The data on governments' fiscal positions prior to the crisis do not reveal significant concerns (Table 1.6). Budget surpluses, or small deficits, were the norm in the troubled countries. Thailand ran quite substantial surpluses, averaging 3.1% of GDP in the first half of the 1990s. Amongst the other countries, only Vietnam and India (and Japan and Australia) ran sizeable deficits.

Investment growth was more rapid in the troubled countries than elsewhere for most of the period prior to the crisis, though not as rapid as in China (Table 1.7). India registered similar investment growth. There was a significant slowdown in Thailand, Korea and Malaysia in 1996, and in Taiwan and China as well, though not in Indonesia. Investment growth accelerated, however, in the Philippines and Singapore in 1996.

Data on the growth of broad money supply (M2) provide a measure of conditions in the banking sector. A rapid rate of increase (in the absence of high inflation) indicates that intermediation of funds by the banking system is increasing in importance – and may suggest that too little attention is being paid to the risks involved in lending. Rapid growth was evident in all the troubled countries (Table 1.8), especially Indonesia. But even more rapid growth occurred in China and Vietnam, while the Philippines and India exhibited growth similar to that in Thailand, Korea and Malaysia. The economies of Singapore, Hong Kong and Taiwan all had slower rates of money growth.

Another possible indicator of vulnerability to financial crisis is the level of external indebtedness, and changes therein (Table 1.9). Again, the picture is very mixed. Vietnam's debt, as a percentage of GDP, was huge relative to all the other countries considered here. Two of the troubled countries – Indonesia and Malaysia – had relatively high debt, but not Thailand or

Korea. The Philippines had high foreign debt. Indonesia's debt seemed to have been falling prior to the crisis, though this seems in retrospect to reflect inadequacies in the data. Neither Thailand's nor Malaysia's foreign debt appears to have been rising.

It has been common practice for decades to measure the adequacy of countries' international reserves in terms of their equivalence in months of imports. A lesson from the current crisis is that this is very much an outdated way of seeing things. Potential shocks to the balance of payments arising from sudden, unexpected capital flows are far greater than the shocks that might be expected to arise from disturbances to trade flows. Nevertheless, for comparative purposes it is necessary to use some scaling factor to convert the absolute level of reserves to a common basis, and its equivalence in months of imports serves this purpose reasonably well (Table 1.10). Amongst the troubled countries, only Korea showed a relatively low, but fairly stable, level of reserves, while Malaysia's had fallen somewhat since the early 1990s. The Philippines and Vietnam also had low levels of reserves, Indonesia and Thailand somewhat higher, and Hong Kong, Taiwan and China significantly more.

BACKGROUND TO THE CRISIS

Macroeconomic policy was complicated in the 1990s by greatly increased international capital mobility and the business exuberance accompanying the advanced stage of long, strong economic expansion. Capital mobility had been greatly enhanced by dramatic reductions in transaction costs, with technological change in communications and the management of information. Policy reform had reduced official barriers to international capital movements, most importantly in the 1980s in developed economies, and continuing through the 1990s for East Asian developing countries.

Conventional international financial mediation through banks was encouraged by the deregulation of the 1980s, which had gone furthest in the English-speaking countries. The North American banks had been caught in the Latin American crisis of the 1980s. These, and British and Australian banks, had also learned severe lessons about the management of lending risks in their domestic banking crises of the early 1990s. Banks operating within the less competitive and less transparent systems of Japan and continental Europe played larger roles in the extension of bank credit to the booming East Asian developing economies of the mid-1990s.

Institutional innovation in higher-income countries – that saw banks playing a steadily diminishing role relative to newer types of financial intermediaries – also played a part. Investment funds grew rapidly in importance, operating under great competitive pressures to earn high returns. These funds became major investors in developing countries for the first time in the 1990s; unlike banks, they were little constrained by the need to maintain carefully nurtured relationships with firms that had turned to them for finance, and could exit the scene at any hint of trouble.

The rapid expansion of trade, at rates well in excess of production growth, also widened the channels of international capital mobility. With high trade volumes, large capital movements could be effected through modest adjustments to the timing of payments for export and import transactions.

Years of virtually unbroken high growth made a special contribution to the origins of the crisis. After 1987, growth was high and relatively steady for most of the East Asian countries, remaining near 8% per annum in most years in the countries most deeply affected by the subsequent crisis – Indonesia, Thailand, Korea and Malaysia. Such steadiness in growth has been rare, even in East Asia. By the mid-1990s, the usual visitation of years of slower growth, let alone recession, was a distant memory. Financial institutions and the corporate sector more generally had been lulled into an unrealistic view of fluctuations in economic activity. Enterprises that gambled on continued expansion were consistently rewarded, increasing their command over assets and attracting reputations as competent investors. Large increases in stock market and real estate values inevitably came to contain elements of speculative excess.

Increased international capital mobility and the escalating speculative content of the long boom helped to expose flaws in the systems of macroeconomic management, however, first of all in exchange rate management. There are two polar types of exchange rate regime. One is the rate that is fixed firmly against some external currency or basket of currencies (or, as in the old gold standard, gold). The other is the freely floating rate. Between the two extremes is a wide variety of hybrids. The fixed rate regime has some advantages. First, if the currency against which the rate is fixed is of major importance for external transactions, then stability in that rate can reduce the costs of international trade and investment; this is said to be a reason for monetary union in Europe. Second, if the authorities are firmly committed to maintenance of the fixed rate, that commitment can provide an anchor for macroeconomic stability, assisting with the maintenance of fiscal and monetary discipline.

But a fixed rate regime runs into problems when the authorities are unable to constrain monetary growth within the limits required to validate the rate, or where inflexibility in the economy prevents downward adjustment of prices when validation of the rate requires contraction of domestic demand. The consequence in either case is a misaligned real exchange rate. If the exchange rate is fixed at too low a level, the misalignment is inflationary. If it is fixed at too high a level, in the absence of a sufficient degree of price flexibility, it will cause unemployment and low growth, and may be associated with speculative capital outflow and financial instability. A floating rate is not vulnerable to the same extent to large and sustained misalignment. There is a concern, however, that it might be susceptible to short-term misalignment, or overshooting, that it may be associated with higher costs of international trade and investment transactions, and that it may provide less effective support for disciplined expenditure policy.

Greater international capital mobility in recent times has made it more likely that misalignment with a fixed rate will be converted into a crisis by speculative capital flows, and has compressed the time within which such a crisis can develop. If the monetary authorities have sought to maintain a fixed rate in the past and failed, the credibility of the firmly fixed regime is weakened for a long time. As a result, the economic costs of measures designed to maintain a fixed rate are increased. A country that has demonstrated that it is unable to hold growth in demand within the limits required by a fixed rate has little choice but to opt for a highly flexible rate. There is a great deal of evidence that it is easier to operate the exchange rate near the extremes of the firmly fixed and the floating regimes than in the hybrid positions in between.

In the modern world, the only fixed rate regimes that seem to survive over long periods are those supported by passive monetary policy, where money supply is driven by the balance of payments. This is the 'currency board system', in which base money is backed by foreign exchange reserves. It may impose large costs of domestic adjustment on inflexible economies, but the case of Hong Kong shows that a firmly fixed rate accompanied by (more or less) passive monetary policy can work well if there is sufficient price and structural flexibility.

Current account deficits in Thailand, Malaysia and Indonesia had been the subject of concern for several years prior to the crisis. In all three cases, economic analysts drew some comfort from the fact that external deficits were associated with reasonably strong fiscal positions and adequate foreign exchange reserves. The current account deficit resulted from private investment exceeding private savings, and private domestic savings were reasonably large. The deficits could be seen, therefore, as the response to high levels of international direct and portfolio investment, encouraged by perceptions of high prospective profits and yields. The contribution to those perceptions of implicit guarantees of various kinds (including the promise of a steady relationship between the domestic currency and the US dollar) was rarely acknowledged. Nor was the potential for rapid change in perceptions about prospective returns on investment.

Thus was the scene set for the dramatic events of 1997. Once anxieties about asset prices and exchange rates began to precipitate a reversal of the large inflows of capital, the change of sentiment fed upon itself, eventually forcing the movement to floating rates and large depreciations.

THE ONSET OF CRISIS: THAILAND

In all of the troubled East Asian economies, there was much discussion of problems of economic governance in the year preceding the crisis. But these issues were rarely recognised as major risks to macroeconomic stability and growth except in the longer term. Worries about the financial and macro-economic environments began to weigh on the perceptions of investors in Thailand (and Korea) from early 1996. Through 1996, economic commentary in Thailand focused on the slowdown in export growth and the effects of over-borrowing by some Thai financial institutions (Warr 1997). As a prominent indicator of concern, the Thai – and, to a lesser extent, the Korean – stock market indexes moved downward from the second quarter (Figure 1.2). By contrast, the stock market index continued to rise in Malaysia until late in the first quarter of 1997, by which time investment behaviour was being influenced by speculative capital outflow in Thailand. The Indonesian index continued to rise for longer, until a few days after the floating and collapse of the Thai baht in July. Market indexes for the other countries are also shown for comparative purposes in Figure 1.2; the rapid increase in China's index throughout 1996 and, to a lesser degree, Taiwan's, is as noteworthy as the declines during this period in Thailand and Korea.[1]

The Thai currency crisis thus actually began in 1996, interacting with the stock (and property) market slump, and influenced by the marked slowdown in export growth. Rumours of possible baht devaluation circulated from May 1996; by May 1997, speculative outflow was threatening the convertibility of the baht, and prompting a strong effort to defend the established exchange rate against the US dollar. This speculation quickly overwhelmed the monetary authorities.

CONTAGION

The term 'contagion' came into frequent use in the third quarter of 1997, to describe the rapid spread of financial instability through East Asia. Stock market indexes fell sharply in all East Asian economies. Floating currencies fell in value. Currency pegs to the US dollar were tested severely, and successively abandoned in all East Asian economies other than China, Vietnam and Hong Kong.

'Contagion' had three sources (Garnaut 1998). One was the realisation that presumed government guarantees of currency parities, and in various ways of bank solvency and the profitability of other enterprises, could not be taken at face value. If they could be withdrawn in Thailand, they could be withdrawn elsewhere. This was important for domestic and international investors alike.

The second source of contagion was the realisation by investors that they had a poor understanding of the workings more generally of the economies to which they were exposed. Investors had been surprised by the dramatic falls in currency and asset values in Thailand. If they knew so little about Thailand, how much did they not know about conditions in neighbouring

Figure 1.2 Stock market performance (31 March 1997 = 100)

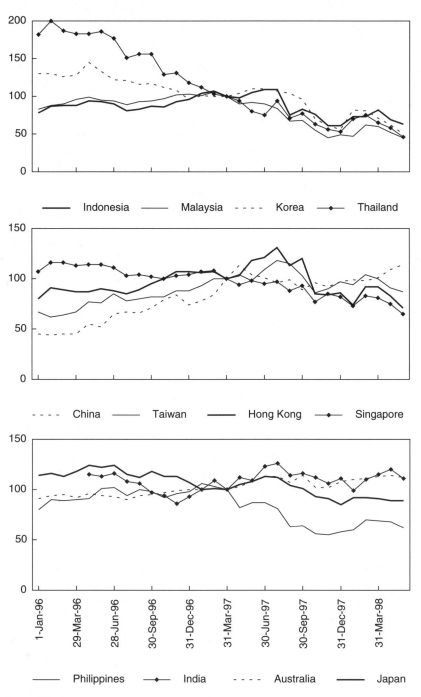

Source: Datastream.

economies? This concern was strongest in Thailand's own region, Southeast Asia, but important throughout Asia – a tendency reinforced by early popular reference to the 'Asian' financial crisis. This source of contagion was most important amongst distant international investors, whose ignorance was greatest. This caused a sudden and large increase in the required risk premia on investment throughout developing East Asia. It gradually eased in economies with more transparent and effective corporate and financial regulatory systems, such as Hong Kong and Singapore.

The third source of contagion was the diminished opportunities for gains from trade with, and investment in and by, regional economic partners. Throughout the long boom from the mid-1980s, the large majority of the increase in trade and direct investment for developing East Asian economies was within East Asia; in 1996, about half of East Asian exports were to other countries in the region (Figure 1.3). Economic crisis in the region would lead to slower intraregional trade growth. In addition, real depreciation in some East Asian economies meant greater competition in third country markets for others. For all East Asian economies, the falls in value of regional currencies and assets pointed immediately to slower expansion of trade and investment, lower economic growth, and domestic currency and asset values lower than they otherwise would be.

Each of these sources of contagion contributed to the pressure on fixed exchange rates and, after the abandonment of established pegs, to the large falls in currency values.

PRESSURE ON FINANCIAL INSTITUTIONS

Falls in asset values in all East Asian economies, and in currency values in most, put pressure on financial institutions. In cases where this exposed underlying weaknesses, it disturbed the flow of funds to potentially profitable business, and compounded the reduction in real economic activity. In turn, falls in economic activity gave rise to a proliferation of non-performing loans, even in well-managed banks. When borrowers default, banks must rely on the value of their security. But in the context of falling asset values, deficiencies emerge in the security backing for loans. In well-managed banks, depositors and other creditors are protected by a high ratio of equity capital to risk assets, which allows bad loans to be written off without threatening the solvency of the bank; a soundly based and transparent system of prudential regulation and supervision reinforces good banking practice such as this. Transparency generates confidence in sound financial institutions, providing assurance to depositors and other creditors that their assets (the banks' liabilities) are safe. Events in the second half of 1997 revealed crippling weaknesses, however, in regulatory systems and financial institutions, in Thailand, Korea and Indonesia in particular.

A conspicuous feature of the East Asian financial crisis is the extent to

Figure 1.3   Export destination shares, 1996 (% of total exports)

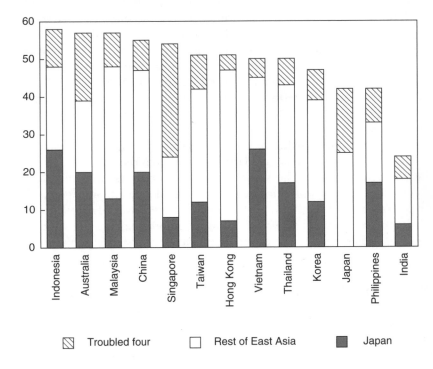

Troubled four   ▨   Rest of East Asia   □   Japan   ■

Source: Direction of trade, IMF; IEDB, ANU.

which financial institutions and other enterprises were exposed to foreign exchange risk. A high proportion of foreign liabilities had relatively short maturities. In normal conditions of continuing growth and economic stability, such loans would easily have been rolled over, but in the crisis conditions of the second half of 1997, lenders insisted on immediate repayment at the crisis exchange rates. (The Philippines had one advantage over its Southeast Asian neighbours in this respect. It came later to internationally oriented reform and high levels of capital inflow and, as a latecomer, it had a smaller accumulation of foreign liabilities.) Uncovered foreign liabilities generated immense losses as exchange rates fell in the most deeply troubled economies. Soesastro (1998) estimates, for example, that with an exchange rate of Rp10,000 to the US dollar, currency losses had entirely wiped out the aggregate net assets of all companies listed on the Jakarta Stock Exchange. Large, uncovered foreign currency liabilities can bankrupt a business if the exchange rate moves far enough. Many firms were rendered insolvent in this way. And, even if not holding exposed positions themselves, banks incurred additional losses on loans to enterprises that were themselves exposed to exchange rate risk. The accumulation of large, uncovered foreign liabilities reflected imprudence on the part of several parties: borrowers and their owners; domestic banks and other lenders; and foreign lenders and portfolio investors. How was imprudence possible on such a large scale? Lack of transparency about corporate financial affairs and the ineffective prudential supervision of banks both contributed. So did the presence of implicit official guarantees on exchange rates, bank safety, and sometimes other business parameters. 'Moral hazard' might have played a role, influenced by an expectation that public international support would become available to offset losses that might be incurred in the worst of circumstances.

Differences in the quality of the financial systems and institutions across East Asian economies generated large differences in the economic impact of the contagion shocks. The weaknesses in financial systems, and the economic consequences of the shocks, were moderate in Singapore, Hong Kong, Taiwan and the Philippines, somewhat greater in Malaysia, severe in Thailand and Korea, and catastrophic in Indonesia. Financial systems in other countries less open to capital flows were not tested in the same way.

PRESSURE ON ECONOMIC POLICY

The crisis demanded policy decisions in three areas as matters of great urgency: the exchange rate and external payments regimes; the settings of macroeconomic policy; and the management and rehabilitation of the financial system. The pressure of capital outflow forced Malaysia, the Philippines, Indonesia and Korea to follow Thailand in floating their currencies, at least for the time being. Choices as to the most appropriate exchange rate regimes for the future have yet to be made.

There is now widespread debate about free convertibility on the capital account (Jomo 1998; Montes 1998). In Malaysia and Thailand, capital account liberalisation in the early 1990s is seen as having facilitated both the speculative inflows of the boom times and the panicky outflows of the crisis. Both countries briefly reimposed elements of controls at the onset of crisis – but to no avail, and possibly exacerbating outflows by further raising risk premia. Korea found that capital controls were of minimal assistance in stemming the inflow in good times or the outflow in crisis: there were enough open channels to facilitate large movements of capital in response to changes in perceptions of opportunity and risk. For the time being the regional crisis has increased the desire for caution in relation to capital account liberalisation in China and Vietnam.

The second area for urgent policy decision was the setting of macroeconomic policy. If inflation, relatively large current account deficits, and recent real exchange rate appreciation had required some contraction of demand and nominal depreciation in the troubled countries, the crisis delivered a great deal of both. The huge currency depreciations reduced the real exchange rates of troubled countries to the lowest levels they had seen since rapid growth began. Private consumption fell sharply, through the wealth and income effects of the crisis. Private investment collapsed, with high risk premia and disruption of the financial system. Monetary policy was tightened within IMF packages, or independently, with rising interest rates intended to stem capital outflow.

The main unresolved questions of macroeconomic policy relate to adjustments of the fiscal settings. There seemed to be discordance between good policy, on the one hand, and international market perceptions of good policy, on the other (Jomo 1998). With rapid demand growth prior to recession mostly having its origins in private activity, there seemed to be a strong economic case for letting the automatic stabilisers work – that is, allowing budget revenues to fall as incomes began to fall.

A contrary view was that fiscal policy in reality had not been as trim as it appeared at first sight. Governments' contingent liabilities arising from explicit and implicit official guarantees to banks and other entities were not recorded – much less quantified – in conventional budget accounts. Notwithstanding the prevalence of balanced or surplus budgets, governments were becoming increasingly more heavily exposed to potential high outlays in the future as a result of such guarantees; this became painfully obvious as the crisis evolved and banks and other enterprises began to be propped up with government funds. The appropriate remedy in this case, however, was not to cut actual spending or raise actual revenues, but to minimise contingent liabilities by the denial of guarantees for private entities of all kinds.

Whatever the requirements of good policy, the financial markets reacted negatively to fiscal deficits during the crisis. The Malaysian stock market and currency fell in response to an October budget that was thought to be insufficiently contractionary (Jomo 1998). Failure of the first Indonesian budget in January 1998 to meet an IMF surplus target, and criticism to that effect, precipitated the sharpest and largest rupiah depreciation of the crisis period; a revised budget had to be formulated almost immediately.

The third area of urgent policy decision, the management and rehabilitation of financial systems, was critical to recovery. In particular, greater transparency, better regulatory arrangements, and quick action in relation to unhealthy financial institutions were all important to restoring the confidence of depositors and other creditors, at home and abroad. These were major elements of the three IMF country programs, and some steps along these lines were taken in Malaysia as well. Where failures of financial institutions were extensive, it was necessary to facilitate the injection of new equity, including from foreign sources. The effectiveness of government response in this third area of policy decision became a principal determinant of the severity of economic decline. The response was least effective in Indonesia, and the consequences of inappropriate policy response have been severe.

ECONOMIC CONSEQUENCES

The individual country case study chapters tell widely different stories about the effects of financial disturbance on economic activity, and about future prospects. Recovery in the troubled countries will be led by the tradable sectors, which have received a huge boost in competitiveness from currency depreciation; the scope for growth in net exports has also been encouraged by weakness in domestic demand. But the timing and strength of the anticipated tradables-led recovery will be constrained by the process of financial system rehabilitation. Export-oriented firms are now potentially much more profitable than ever before, but the breakdown of the banking system has severely constrained the availability of working capital finance to them, especially if they are heavily reliant on imported inputs.

Where early progress is made on financial rehabilitation – and in mid-1998 there was promise of this in Malaysia, Thailand and Korea amongst the troubled economies – the recovery led by net exports is likely to be powerful, although there are risks of delay in the continued stagnation and decline of activity and imports throughout East Asia. The combination of enhanced competitiveness and weak domestic demand in East Asia, and continued economic expansion and an extremely strong dollar in the United States, is bound to generate large trade and current payments surpluses across the Pacific. Although these will necessarily be accompanied by an offsetting worldwide shift of new investment activity, there is a danger that this will generate negative political responses in the United States, complicating the task of maintaining an open framework for Asia Pacific trade relations.

Recovery can be expected to be accompanied by a reduction of risk premia on investment, some renewal of capital inflow, and substantial real appreciation of exchange rates back towards pre-crisis levels; indeed, as already noted, a partial recovery of nominal rates had already been observed in several countries, although this process was interrupted in mid-1998 by political events in Indonesia and continuing economic woes in Japan. In the meantime, recession in some economies and slow growth in others will reverse the reductions in poverty that were associated with the years of rapid growth, and place great strain on social and political systems. In countries in which this strain generates political instability or lurches in economic policy, recession may worsen as in Indonesia, or give way to stagnation rather than recovery.

What effect will the crisis have on longer-term economic growth and structural change? The crisis has disrupted the use of resources, but it has not negated the years of human and physical capital accumulation and institutional development. Although it is impossible to make confident predictions in relation to Indonesia, given the political upheaval it has been going through, in the other countries many of the conditions that supported sustained rapid growth are likely to remain in place: high savings and investment; a strong emphasis on education; acceptance of a major role for markets in resource allocation; deep integration into the international economy; and, after a while, the self-reinforcing character of internationally-oriented growth across neighbouring economies.

It is possible, but not certain, that the international orientation of East Asian economies will have been enhanced by the crisis. The initial round of crisis-induced policy reform, reinforced by the IMF programs, will make markets more effective in allocating resources. In Indonesia in particular, the market-oriented reforms within the IMF agreements are far-reaching – although, of course, it remains to be seen to what extent they will be implemented. And even if reforms are carried out, the question then is whether they will survive recovery, or whether they will be discredited as arrangements imposed from outside when the East Asian developing economies were in a position of weakness.

Two of the preconditions of growth in the old East Asian style obviously have been lost for the time being: a reasonable degree of macroeconomic stability; and political coherence around the growth objective. If the current stabilisation programs are successful, the prospects for future economic stability will have been enhanced. Exactly the same mistakes will not be made again. There will be greater caution at signs of asset booms, and there will be a re-evaluation of alternatives to the hybrid exchange rate regimes that were in place at the onset of crisis. Restoration of political coherence and stability around the growth objective is facilitated by constitutional and political arrangements that support reasonably smooth political change in Thailand, Korea and Malaysia. The challenge is far greater in Indonesia.

The shock of 1997 is a defining event in the economic history of East Asia. Like the Great Depression in the West, it has the capacity to change thought about economic development and economic policy in fundamental ways. The lessons that will be drawn from the crisis depend on whether the current stabilisation programs in Thailand, Korea and Malaysia lead to early recovery and to restoration of strong growth. If they do not, the recent commitments to competitive markets and transparency will be viewed sceptically. For the whole of Southeast Asia, the future of political cohesion and economic development in Indonesia will strongly influence the lessons that are drawn from the crisis of 1997–8; but that big story is still unfolding.

Now it is time to look more closely at particular countries and issues.

NOTE

1   From the point of view of foreign investors, the US dollar values of shares are of greater interest. A summary of movements in these values from the beginning of 1996 through to mid-1998 is presented in Table 1.11.

Table 1.1 Real GDP growth (% p.a.)

	1990	1991	1992	1993	1994	1995	1990–5 avg.	1996	1997	1998
Indonesia	9.0	8.9	7.2	7.3	7.5	8.2	8.0	8.0	5.0	−10.0
Thailand	11.7	8.0	8.1	8.3	8.8	8.7	8.4	5.5	−0.4	−1.5
Korea	9.7	9.2	5.0	5.8	8.4	9.0	7.5	7.1	5.5	−2.5
Malaysia	9.7	8.8	7.8	8.4	9.4	9.4	8.7	8.6	8.0	3.0
Philippines	2.7	−0.2	0.3	2.1	4.4	4.8	2.3	5.5	5.1	3.3
Singapore	8.7	6.7	6.3	10.4	10.3	8.9	8.5	6.9	7.8	2.8
Hong Kong	3.4	5.1	6.3	6.1	5.4	4.6	5.5	4.7	5.5	2.5
Taiwan	5.4	7.6	6.8	6.3	6.5	6.0	6.6	5.7	6.8	6.5
China	3.7	9.5	14.6	13.9	13.0	10.7	12.3	9.6	8.8	8.0
Vietnam	4.5	6.0	8.6	8.1	8.8	9.5	8.2	9.4	9.0	7.0
India	5.6	0.5	5.3	4.0	6.3	6.1	4.4	7.5	6.0	6.0
Australia	−0.8	0.2	3.3	4.9	4.2	3.3	3.2	3.6	3.1	3.0
Japan	5.1	4.0	1.0	0.1	0.4	0.9	1.3	3.6	0.9	1.0

Source: Data for 1996 and 1997 and estimates for 1998 are from APEG 1998. Data for 1990–5 are from World Bank 1997b. Taiwan data are from CEPD (various years).

Table 1.2 Inflation (CPI, % p.a.)

	1990	1991	1992	1993	1994	1995	1990–5 avg.	1996	1997
Indonesia	7.8	9.0	8.3	9.3	8.5	9.3	8.7	6.5	11.6
Thailand	5.9	6.0	3.8	3.6	5.3	5.0	4.9	5.8	5.6
Korea	8.6	9.0	6.4	5.2	5.7	4.7	6.6	4.5	4.7
Malaysia	2.7	4.0	4.8	3.7	3.5	6.0	4.1	3.5	2.6
Philippines	14.2	19.0	8.4	7.8	9.4	7.9	11.1	8.4	5.1
Singapore	3.4	3.0	2.9	1.9	3.7	0.9	2.6	1.4	2.0
Hong Kong	9.8	11.0	9.9	8.2	9.1	9.0	9.5	6.0	6.8
Taiwan	4.1	3.6	4.5	2.9	4.1	3.7	4.0	3.1	0.9
China	3.1	4.0	5.8	14.5	24.6	16.6	11.4	8.3	2.8
Vietnam	60.0	67.5	17.6	5.2	14.4	12.7	29.6	4.5	4.0
India	8.9	14.0	11.4	6.3	10.4	10.1	10.2	9.4	7.0
Japan	3.1	3.0	1.9	1.0	0.9	0.0	1.7	0.1	1.8
Australia	7.3	3.0	1.0	1.9	1.9	4.6	3.3	2.6	0.3

Source: Data for 1996 and 1997 are from APEG 1998. Data for 1990–95 are from World Bank 1997b. Taiwan data are from CEPD (various years).

Table 1.3 Export growth (US$, % p.a.)

	1990	1991	1992	1993	1994	1995	1990–5 avg.	1996	1997
Indonesia	15.8	13.4	16.6	8.4	8.8	13.4	12.7	10.4	11.6
Thailand	14.9	22.9	14.4	13.2	22.7	25.1	18.9	−1.3	3.5
Korea	4.2	10.6	6.5	7.3	16.8	30.3	12.6	5.3	7.3
Malaysia	17.1	16.7	18.7	15.7	24.7	26.0	19.8	6.7	−7.2
Philippines	4.0	8.7	11.2	13.8	19.9	31.6	14.8	17.5	12.2
Singapore	18.1	11.7	7.6	16.5	30.8	22.2	17.8	2.9	3.4
Hong Kong	12.4	20.0	21.2	13.2	11.9	14.8	15.6	4.0	4.2
Taiwan	1.4	13.3	6.9	4.4	9.4	20.0	9.2	3.8	5.3
China	18.1	15.0	20.5	7.1	33.1	22.9	19.4	17.9	20.9
Vietnam	23.1	−12.9	23.4	15.7	20.7	39.5	18.3	34.0	23.9
India	13.9	−1.7	10.7	10.0	16.3	22.7	12.0	4.1	4.2
Japan	5.1	9.4	7.9	6.5	9.7	11.6	8.4	−8.7	−0.1
Australia	7.3	5.3	2.1	−0.2	11.3	10.8	6.1	4.3	8.3

Source: Data for 1996 and 1997 are from APEG 1998. Data for 1990–5 are from World Bank 1997b. Taiwan data are from CEPD (various years).

Table 1.4 Import growth (US$, % p.a.)

	1990	1991	1992	1993	1994	1995	1990–5 avg.	1996	1997
Indonesia	32.9	18.8	5.4	3.8	12.9	27.9	17.0	11.1	7.7
Thailand	29.5	12.6	8.2	13.5	17.9	30.0	18.6	11.6	−13.1
Korea	13.5	16.8	0.4	2.4	22.1	32.0	14.5	12.2	2.4
Malaysia	30.2	24.9	9.0	14.5	30.4	30.5	23.3	1.3	−6.7
Philippines	16.1	−1.5	20.3	22.1	19.9	25.7	17.1	20.9	3.1
Singapore	22.5	8.9	8.9	18.0	20.5	21.3	16.7	4.9	8.3
Hong Kong	14.3	21.2	23.0	13.0	16.5	19.0	17.8	3.0	5.2
Taiwan	4.7	14.9	14.6	7.0	10.8	21.3	12.2	−1.1	11.8
China	−10.1	19.2	28.7	27.9	12.2	11.6	14.9	26.1	2.6
Vietnam	7.0	−14.9	8.5	54.5	27.4	45.4	21.3	48.0	7.7
India	15.1	−13.6	15.7	−3.4	17.7	28.6	10.0	6.0	4.9
Japan	11.9	0.9	−1.7	3.9	13.6	22.1	8.5	3.0	2.0
Australia	−6.5	−0.7	5.0	4.1	17.1	14.8	5.6	4.4	4.3

Source: Data for 1996 and 1997 are from APEG 1998. Data for 1990–5 are from World Bank 1997b. Taiwan data are from CEPD (various years).

Table 1.5 Current account (% of GDP)

	1990	1991	1992	1993	1994	1995	1990–5 avg.	1996	1997
Indonesia	−2.6	−3.3	−2.0	−1.3	−1.6	−3.5	−2.4	−3.4	−3.6
Thailand	−8.5	−7.7	−5.7	−5.1	−5.7	−8.1	−6.8	−7.9	−2.2
Korea	−0.7	−2.8	−1.3	0.3	−1.0	−1.8	−1.2	−4.8	−3.2
Malaysia	−2.0	−8.9	−3.8	−4.5	−5.9	−10.2	−5.9	−4.9	−4.7
Philippines	−6.1	−2.3	−1.9	−5.5	−4.6	−2.7	−3.8	−4.7	−4.0
Singapore	8.5	11.6	11.3	7.3	16.2	18.0	12.2	15.0	15.2
Hong Kong	4.7	2.9	5.8	7.2	2.3	−2.6	3.4	−2.5	−6.8
China	3.1	3.3	1.3	−1.9	1.4	0.2	1.2	0.9	2.1
Vietnam	−5.6	−1.9	−0.7	−8.3	−6.9	−9.8	−5.5	−16.2	−8.6
India	−3.4	−0.7	−1.8	−0.8	−1.1	−1.8	−1.6	−1.0	−1.2
Taiwan	7.0	6.8	3.9	3.1	2.6	2.0	4.1	3.8	2.6
Japan	1.2	2.0	3.0	3.1	2.8	2.2	2.4	1.4	2.0
Australia	−5.4	−3.8	−3.9	−3.6	−5.2	−5.5	−4.6	−4.0	−3.4

Note: Negative values represent deficits.
Source: Data for 1996 and 1997 are from APEG 1998. Data for 1990–5 are from World Bank 1997b. Taiwan data are from CEPD (various years).

Table 1.6 Government budget surplus (% of GDP)

	1990	1991	1992	1993	1994	1995	1990–5 avg.	1996	1997
Indonesia	−1.1	−0.6	−0.4	−0.6	0.2	0.3	−0.4	0.0	1.0
Thailand	4.5	4.7	2.8	2.1	1.8	2.6	3.1	2.3	−1.5
Korea	−0.7	−1.6	−0.5	0.6	0.3	−0.2	−0.4	−0.2	0.3
Malaysia	−4.8	−4.4	−4.2	0.2	2.4	1.0	−1.6	0.7	1.8
Philippines	−3.5	−2.1	−1.2	−1.5	1.1	0.6	−1.1	0.3	0.1
Singapore	10.6	8.8	12.6	15.5	12.1	13.3	12.2	13.9	2.8
Hong Kong	2.2	3.5	0.9	−0.2	0.7	2.6	1.6	1.5	2.6
Taiwan	5.5	2.6	4.5	5.0	4.6	2.8	4.2	1.6	2.2
China	−2.1	−2.4	−1.0	−1.0	−0.5	−1.0	−1.3	−0.8	−0.7
Vietnam	−6.4	−2.0	−2.7	−6.0	−4.5	−3.8	−4.2	−0.1	0.2
India	−8.1	−5.8	−5.7	−7.4	−6.1	−5.5	−6.4	−4.9	−4.9
Japan	−1.6	2.9	1.4	−1.6	−2.1	−3.1	−0.7	−3.9	−3.7
Australia	0.4	−2.6	−4.6	−3.8	−2.7	−1.5	−2.5	−0.3	1.0

Note: Negative values represent deficits.
Source: Data are from APEG 1998. Taiwan data are from CEPD (various years).

Table 1.7 Investment growth (% p.a.)

	1990	1991	1992	1993	1994	1995	1990–5 avg.	1996	1997
Indonesia	20.2	14.2	15.5	4.3	22.1	22.2	16.4	17.7	n.a.
Thailand	37.2	18.2	6.7	14.4	15.8	21.4	19.0	8.3	−2.1
Korea	39.8	24.6	6.0	9.5	13.7	17.6	18.5	9.4	−16.6
Malaysia	24.7	28.5	5.2	25.0	20.5	23.3	21.2	12.1	n.a.
Philippines	29.2	0.4	13.1	23.9	14.2	5.8	14.4	20.2	n.a.
Singapore	14.1	16.3	15.0	14.2	10.7	10.5	13.5	20.1	n.a.
Hong Kong	13.2	15.6	20.2	14.5	22.9	9.3	15.9	13.7	20.7
Taiwan	7.8	9.0	13.9	8.6	5.7	5.5	8.4	2.4	10.9
China	9.1	25.5	40.0	56.1	29.9	18.7	29.9	15.4	10.3
India	20.6	10.1	16.4	10.2	22.3	26.3	17.6	12.7	n.a.
Japan	11.6	5.5	−0.3	−2.2	−2.2	−0.4	2.0	8.3	n.a.
Australia	−5.2	−9.1	2.1	5.9	12.0	4.0	1.6	4.0	7.2

Source: IMF 1998d. Taiwan data are from CEPD (various years). Data for 1997 are from APEG 1998.

Table 1.8 Money supply (M2) growth (% p.a.)

	1990	1991	1992	1993	1994	1995	1990–5 avg.	1996	1997
Indonesia	44.6	17.5	19.8	20.2	20.0	27.2	24.9	27.2	23.2
Thailand	26.7	19.8	15.6	18.4	12.9	17.0	18.4	12.6	8.3
Korea	17.2	21.9	14.9	16.6	18.7	15.6	17.5	15.8	15.4
Malaysia	10.6	16.9	29.2	26.6	12.7	20.0	19.3	22.9	19.2
Philippines	22.5	17.3	13.6	27.1	24.4	24.2	21.5	23.2	11.8
Singapore	20.0	12.4	8.9	8.5	14.4	8.5	12.1	9.8	10.3
Hong Kong	n.a.	n.a.	8.5	14.5	11.7	10.6	11.3	12.5	9.9
Taiwan	11.0	19.4	19.1	15.4	15.1	9.4	14.9	8.1	8.0
China	28.9	26.7	30.8	42.8	35.1	29.5	32.3	26.0	17.3
Vietnam	32.4	78.7	33.7	19.0	21.3	30.2	35.9	28.0	n.a.
India	15.1	18.3	16.9	17.0	20.3	11.0	16.4	15.9	17.0
Japan	8.2	2.5	−0.1	2.2	3.1	2.8	3.1	2.3	4.0
Australia	12.6	0.7	7.6	6.0	9.7	8.6	7.5	9.7	8.1

Source: Data for 1996 and 1997 are from APEG 1998. Data for 1990–5 are from World Bank 1997b. Taiwan data are from CEPD (various years).

Table 1.9 External debt (% of GDP)

	1990	1991	1992	1993	1994	1995	1990–5 avg.	1996	1997
Indonesia	50.9	50.9	50.5	45.3	45.2	43.4	47.7	38.9	n.a.
Korea	9.5	9.7	10.5	10.5	10.7	9.4	10.0	11.2	15.0
Malaysia	33.2	33.4	29.0	32.1	31.9	32.2	32.0	28.8	29.1
Thailand	23.2	23.8	22.4	20.9	22.2	20.1	22.1	19.8	25.0
Philippines	57.1	58.2	50.3	54.6	50.7	50.9	53.6	n.a.	n.a.
Taiwan	0.5	0.5	0.3	0.3	0.2	0.2	0.3	0.1	0.1
China	12.9	12.3	14.7	13.5	17.5	15.3	14.4	15.0	14.0
Vietnam	237.3	224.6	159.4	178.8	138.3	122.5	176.8	n.a.	n.a.
India	23.7	29.2	32.1	32.8	29.6	29.2	29.4	24.5	22.7
Australia	42.2	44.9	46.3	50.3	45.9	46.8	46.1	n.a.	n.a.

Source: Data for 1996 and 1997 are from APEG 1998. Data for 1990–5 are from World Bank 1997b. Taiwan data are from CEPD (various years).

Table 1.10 International reserves (months of imports)

	1990	1991	1992	1993	1994	1995	1990–5 avg.	1996	1997
Indonesia	5.3	6.1	7.5	7.9	6.4	5.6	6.5	6.1	4.5
Thailand	5.8	6.4	7.0	7.5	7.5	7.0	6.9	6.6	5.3
Korea	2.7	2.2	2.7	3.1	3.2	3.1	2.8	2.8	2.0
Malaysia	4.5	3.9	5.6	7.6	5.5	4.2	5.2	4.3	3.8
Philippines	2.0	4.4	4.4	4.0	4.0	3.5	3.7	4.4	3.6
Singapore	5.9	6.7	7.0	7.2	7.2	7.0	6.8	7.0	7.4
Hong Kong	8.0	8.2	8.6	10.1	10.0	9.1	9.0	10.9	n.a.
Taiwan	16.7	16.5	14.5	13.8	13.8	11.8	14.5	10.3	8.7
China	3.1	5.2	3.6	2.9	6.5	8.0	4.9	9.1	11.8
Vietnam	0.2	0.2	2.2	1.4	2.1	2.2	1.4	2.1	2.3
India	1.1	3.5	3.5	7.8	8.9	5.6	5.1	7.0	8.3
Japan	4.9	4.6	4.6	6.1	6.7	7.8	5.8	8.5	7.6
Australia	5.9	6.0	4.0	4.0	3.4	3.1	4.4	2.5	2.9

Source: Data for 1996 and 1997 are from APEG 1998. Data for 1990–5 are from World Bank 1997b. Data for Hong Kong are from Hong Kong Monetary Authority. Taiwan data are from CEPD (various years).

Table 1.11 Stock market price indices (US$)

	1 Jan 1996	28 Jun 1996	1 Jan 1997	30 Jun 1997	1 Jan 1998	30 Mar 1998	1 Jun 1998
Indonesia	100	114	120	133	30	28	17
Thailand	100	97	64	42	15	24	15
Korea	100	89	68	74	19	31	21
Malaysia	100	116	125	109	38	51	35
Philippines	100	127	122	108	46	62	52
Hong Kong	100	109	133	151	106	114	85
Singapore	100	104	98	88	64	68	51
Taiwan	100	125	131	160	121	124	100
China	100	145	166	226	216	226	257
India	n.a.	100	82	104	86	89	81
Japan	100	104	84	90	59	63	58
Australia	100	108	117	126	104	111	103

Note: 1 January 1996 = 100, except India, 28 June 1996 = 100.
Source: Datastream.

Part II

Case studies: the troubled economies

2 Indonesia

Ross H. McLeod

MACROECONOMIC FUNDAMENTALS IN THE LEAD-UP TO THE CRISIS

In the first half of 1997, the Indonesian economy seemed to be performing very well. Inflation, having averaged a moderate 9% per annum since the early 1980s, had been reduced to 6% in 1996 and to 5.1% in the year to June 1997. Output grew rapidly in the year to June 1997, by 7.4%, and investment grew by 16.5%. The budget had been managed in a conservative manner for years – so much so that the government had built up a nest egg estimated at US$11 billion (before the float) in banking system deposits (McLeod 1997b: 12–13), and was able to prepay a small but significant amount of its outstanding debt in 1996.

Concerns were often expressed about 'overheating' but, if this term is taken to mean excessive aggregate demand leading to rapid increases in prices of goods and services and declining net exports and international reserves, this was not the case. Growth had been sustained at around 8% per annum on average since the late 1980s. Inflation was falling, not rising, and the relatively large current account deficit – a little less than 4% of gross domestic product (GDP) – was more than covered by high capital inflow. Private capital inflow was spread over direct foreign investment, portfolio investment in both shares and bonds, and direct lending by foreign institutions. A large proportion of lending was in short maturities, including some in the form of three-month commercial paper.

Throughout the 1990s, the values of exports and imports of goods and services had each been equivalent to roughly a quarter of GDP. According to the national accounts data, exports grew in constant rupiah terms by 3% in the year to June 1997, by comparison with 14% on average over the 1990s. Imports grew by 10%, compared with the average of 15% previously. These movements were well within the range of Indonesia's experience in the previous decade, and there was more than enough capital inflow to cover the current account deficit, despite the relatively larger decline in export growth. Indeed, the balance of payments was so strong that international reserves – already high – increased by no less than 38% in the ten months prior to the crisis, to some US$28 billion. Foreign debt, high in absolute terms at around US$135 billion, was only about 55% of GDP – by no means unmanageable. In recent years most of the growth in foreign debt had been generated by the private sector; public sector foreign debt was beginning to decline.

At the macroeconomic level, then, there seemed to be little or no sign of the turmoil that was to emerge in the second half of the year, although some commentators had warned of the vulnerability of the economy to various shocks (see, for example, Montgomery 1997: 18). With the benefit of hindsight, it appears that investment and financing decisions had become too much driven by the euphoria engendered by years of largely uninterrupted expansion, and too little by careful analysis of business prospects and risks. In other words, Indonesia seems to have been in the advanced stage of an economic boom, in which growth momentum relied increasingly on continued business optimism.

ASSET MARKETS AND THE FINANCE SECTOR PRIOR TO THE CRISIS

Foreign exchange market

For most of the 1970s, the rupiah was fixed against the dollar. In 1978 it was devalued by 33%, in order to improve Indonesia's competitiveness, and the government announced that henceforth it would follow a policy of managed floating against a basket of trading partner currencies; in practice, the US dollar has had a weight of approximately 100% in this basket. For most of the subsequent period the rupiah was caused to depreciate slowly against the dollar, although there were two further large depreciations of the order of 30% in March 1983 and September 1986, in response to large falls in oil prices (Indonesia being heavily dependent on oil exports during the 1980s).

During the 1990s the rupiah tended to appreciate, but this was prevented by more or less continuous purchases of foreign exchange by the central bank, Bank Indonesia (BI). This caused problems for monetary management (see below), to which BI reacted by progressively widening its foreign exchange market intervention band. The exchange rate continued to push against the strong side of the band, nevertheless, right up until the crisis began to break in July. Indeed, there seemed to be some support within the government for the idea of floating the rupiah, which could have been expected to result in appreciation (McLeod 1997b: 7, 22).

Share market

The Jakarta Stock Exchange (JSE) was still in an early phase of development when the crisis struck. Although it had been operational since 1977, it was not until deregulatory reforms were implemented late in 1988 that it began to take off (Cole and Slade 1996: ch. 6; Noerhadi 1994: 212–13). The JSE was not a place for faint-hearted investors: the composite share price index bounced its way to a new record high of 637 at the end of 1996, up from only 514 at the end of 1995, after peaking previously at 624 in April 1996 and bottoming at 533 in July 1996. Further impressive gains continued to be registered in the first half of 1997, and the index peaked in July 1997 at 720.

An interesting feature of the market was that listed companies remained tightly controlled; few if any had issued sufficient shares to the public to cause their founders to relinquish their majority position. It may also be noted that foreigners had been major investors in the market. Indeed, the take-off did not occur until most of the constraints on foreign participation had been removed. Finally, the quality of corporate financial statements – essential to a well functioning stock market – left a great deal to be desired, not least because the accounting profession in Indonesia was protected from foreign competition.

Financial institutions

Although the stock exchange was becoming increasingly important, the financial sector was still dominated by banking, which underwent a remarkable transformation following an era of significant reform stretching from 1983 to 1991 (Cole and Slade 1996: ch. 2; McLeod 1998c). Until 1983, banking had been dominated by state-owned institutions, and by the central bank – a highly significant source of subsidised funds, and the administrator of interest rate and lending controls. The industry was closed to entry, branch expansion was heavily constrained, and market shares of existing banks were effectively determined bureaucratically. There was therefore little competition between existing institutions, and no threat of it from new ones.

In just a few years, the combination of two major deregulatory reform packages (in June 1983 and October 1988) took the banking system from struggling under state bank dominance and bureaucratic suffocation to being an effervescent, private sector driven collection of institutions, remarkably free of government intervention. The banking industry grew much faster than the rest of the economy, and there was a dramatic decline in nearly all measures of market share of the state banks as their private sector competitors proliferated and expanded rapidly.

Rapid expansion of the industry necessarily implied a need for large-scale recruitment of managerial personnel. Given the relatively small pool available, lack of management skills and experience was bound to be a problem. Moreover, the relative ease with which the privately owned segment of the banking market was able to expand no doubt created a temptation for banks to engage in various forms of potentially profitable but excessively risky behaviour. Prudential regulations brought in with the second major reform package attempted to guard against such practices, but the central bank proved ineffective as supervisor.

One private bank wiped out its capital by speculating in foreign exchange in 1990, but was saved by fresh injections of capital contributed by certain business associates of President Soeharto, so there were no losses to its depositors (Soesastro and Drysdale 1990: 21–2). Another failed in 1992 and had to be liquidated because of heavy exposure to property development projects within its own group. In this instance, small depositors were paid out almost immediately, but larger depositors did incur some losses (Marshall 1994: 199). Yet another banking scandal emerged in 1994, involving one of the state banks, Bapindo (Cole and Slade 1996: 137–8; Fane 1994: 31). Losses of some hundreds of millions of dollars were incurred as a result of defaults on large, unsecured loans it had made to a relatively unknown entrepreneur. These cases need to be kept in perspective, however, as there were well over 200 banks in all.

Property market

A surge in property development had continued unabated for many years prior to the crisis. Observers had been worrying for years about supply outpacing demand and possibly leading to a slump in property values and a flow-on to the banking sector. The volume of new office and apartment space soon to come onto the market made it hard to dismiss these fears. Occupancy rates for office buildings were slipping a little at the beginning of 1997, although rents were fairly stable; apartment blocks were faring less well. On the other hand, the retail sector was still strong, and hotel room rates had continued to rise in 1996 (McLeod 1997b: 20). In short, although there were strong concerns about the level of investment in property in the first half of 1997, the long awaited shake-out of this sector had yet to materialise.

IMPACT OF THE CRISIS

Real sector

Indonesia's crisis began to emerge in July 1997, following the float of the Thai baht and the Malaysian ringgit. Although purely a financial phenomenon initially, it began to have a severe impact on the real sector before long – not least because of a range of counterproductive policy decisions by the government (discussed below), and because of growing political instability associated with the presidential succession issue. Despite a huge improvement in competitiveness by virtue of devaluation, exports failed to take off as might have been expected. Moreover, the sudden negative shock to private sector wealth arising from the increase in value of foreign debt caused firms to postpone or cancel investment spending, while individuals reacting to growing uncertainty cut back on discretionary consumption. Finally, the government cut back its own spending, adding to the general reduction in aggregate demand.

As a consequence, unemployment soared into the millions as the crisis spread. The slowdown in economic activity gave rise to fears of falling profits, and the increased likelihood of corporate failures made debt roll-overs more difficult. This added to net capital outflow, put downward pressure on share prices, and further weakened the rupiah, as investors sought safer places to hold their wealth.

Notwithstanding the spreading recession, inflation began to accelerate rapidly towards the end of 1997 and early in 1998, as a result of upward pressure on the rupiah price of tradables, combined with a significant loosening of monetary policy in December and January. Food prices also rose because drought had reduced agricultural production. For the six months through May 1998, the CPI increased at an annual rate of about 104% per annum.

Financial sector

The banking system suffered terribly through all of this. First, it had to contend with a drastic reduction in its reserves by virtue of a severe liquidity squeeze implemented by the government. Second, the government closed down some sixteen private banks at the end of October, leading to a sudden and widespread loss of confidence on the part of the general public in the safety of their deposits with the banking system as a whole.

The government responded by promising that no more banks would be closed, but the public were not fully reassured and continued to make withdrawals, mainly from the private banks. Eventually, a blanket guarantee to all creditors of the banks was announced (excluding holders of subordinated debt). Fears that many more banks were in poor condition were borne out in April 1998, when the government froze the operations of seven more private banks and purged the managements of another seven, including one state-owned bank.

Contagion

Although it was the sudden fall of the Thai baht that triggered Indonesia's crisis, the latter is best described as a disaster waiting to happen, and would have occurred sooner or later, whatever happened in Thailand. There had been a fundamental shortcoming in Indonesia's macroeconomic policy stance throughout the Soeharto era that had caused problems from time to time, and was principally responsible for setting off the current crisis. A complex set of microeconomic policy concerns and political considerations then began to interact with this macro policy-induced problem so as to turn what initially seemed a minor financial disturbance into an economic catastrophe, resulting ultimately in the demise of the 32-year-old 'New Order' regime of President Soeharto. This macroeconomic weakness was the failure to accept the empirical reality, supported by theory, that governments cannot simultaneously control more than one of the nominal macroeconomic variables (the price level, the money supply, the nominal exchange rate and the nominal interest rate) – at least, not in the long run.

Indonesia has nearly always tried to control at least two, and sometimes three or all four, of these variables. First and foremost, it has tried to control the nominal exchange rate. Second, it has tried to control the price level (usually indirectly, by controlling the money supply, but also by direct controls over the prices of certain goods and services). Third, to a lesser extent, it has also tried to control interest rates. At times, of course, it has seemed possible to control all four variables, if the targeted values have happened to be consistent with those that would have emerged from the relevant markets. But in these cases 'control' has been illusory, serving only to give the authorities an exaggerated sense of their real influence.

Because of the policy of steady depreciation of the rupiah against the dollar, the balance of payments was nearly always in surplus during the last decade and, as a result, money grew too rapidly to be compatible with the government's inflation targets. Nevertheless, inflation would have been much higher but for the fact that the government sterilised much of the monetary impact of its exchange rate policy. This was achieved in two main ways. First, the government managed its budgetary operations so as to build up large deposits with the central bank. Second, the central bank engaged in open market operations, issuing its own certificates of deposit (SBIs) in order to soak up liquidity.

Net foreign assets of the central bank grew by a factor of nine from June 1990 to June 1997, while base money grew by less than four times. For the first sub-period through 1993, sterilisation involved issuing some Rp23 trillion (US$11 billion) of SBIs. In the following sub-period, it involved reducing net claims on government by over Rp21 trillion (US$10 billion). It is especially noteworthy that net foreign assets increased by Rp20 trillion in the year to June 1997 alone, while both kinds of sterilisation operations combined to offset some Rp14 trillion of this.

This policy was argued previously to be unsustainable (McLeod 1997a: 401; McLeod 1997c: 37) because losses incurred by the central bank as a consequence of the large negative interest spread between its rapidly increasing rupiah liabilities and foreign assets would eventually cause it to modify its policies. As it turned out, these policies were indeed unsustainable in the long term. But the manner of their demise has been quite different from what had been envisaged by the writer.

A consequence of the twin policies of controlling the nominal exchange rate and controlling money growth through open market operations and budget surpluses was that the private sector was crowded out of the domestic financial market. BI borrowing (the issue of SBIs) and budgetary cash flow surpluses forced many private firms to go offshore for funds, building up a large stock of foreign debt in the period 1989–97. Moreover, because the government was promising to maintain a slow and steady rate of depreciation – and because it had done so successfully throughout the previous decade – most borrowers did not bother to hedge the foreign exchange risk.[1] The same was true of foreign investors in rupiah-denominated financial assets.

When the baht was unexpectedly floated and quickly devalued, it became clear to borrowers and to offshore investors that there was a substantial exchange rate risk that could not safely be ignored. They responded by rushing to buy foreign currency in order to protect themselves against a possible currency devaluation, such as had occurred in Thailand, and their fears quickly became a self-fulfilling prophecy.

In turn, this brought to the surface concerns about various other kinds of risk, particularly those relating to inadequate prudential supervision of the banking system and the speculative nature of many property development projects. Indonesia very quickly began to succumb to this crisis of confidence, and its prolongation and deepening were surely related to perceptions of the way the Indonesian economy and polity were being managed. At the back of many people's minds was a concern that the long wait for a presidential successor, and thus for a more democratic style of government and a lessening of abuses of power for economic gain (see, for example, McLeod 1997b), may be in vain – that ultimately the first family would somehow find a way to ensure there would be no diminution of its power and influence in the future. There is little doubt that these concerns are an important explanation as to why the crisis in Indonesia became so severe relative to the crises in other economies in Asia.

POLICY RESPONSES

The crisis has involved several significant policy misjudgments. The government's policies helped create the preconditions for the crisis, and the incoherence of the government's response to the sudden devaluation of the rupiah and subsequent events made the crisis much more severe than it need have been. The lack of a clear and consistent strategy for dealing with the precipitate change in business sentiment may be explained by various factors: genuine confusion as to how to handle a crisis of a kind not previously experienced;[2] divisions within the government, given the President's reliance on economic policymakers who themselves were becoming increasingly concerned about the steady stream of privileges extended to his family and business associates, and his continued support for the high technology visions of former Research and Technology Minister, B.J. Habibie; a strong tradition of economic nationalism within the community, reflected in the views of some ministers and their departments; ethnic and religious tensions between the numerically dominant indigenous community and the economically dominant ethnic Chinese; increasingly widespread concern about the President's intentions regarding the succession; and a general lack of sympathy for the private sector and for market processes within large sections of the bureaucracy. We will now consider some of these issues.

Exchange rate regime

The government seemed to have been moving towards floating the currency prior to the crisis by steadily widening its exchange rate intervention band. This may have reflected recognition of the theoretical proposition mentioned above – that it is not possible in the long run to control both the nominal exchange rate and the level of prices – and the fact that the policymakers' inclination was to accord a higher priority to controlling inflation than hitherto. The negative impact on the central bank's own profitability of having to sterilise persistent payments surpluses probably was also an important consideration.

After the baht and the ringgit were floated, the rupiah moved quickly to the weak side of BI's intervention band, for the reasons just mentioned. The government reacted almost immediately by widening the band, but further heavy speculation soon ensued. This was all that was needed to push the government at last to take the step of floating the currency. By contrast with Thailand, there had not been much loss of reserves, since the government had determined quickly that it would not play the speculators' game.

Notwithstanding the decision to float, it was stated at the time that the government retained the option of intervening in the market from time to time should this be considered necessary. This ambivalence was apparent subsequently in occasional central bank forays into the foreign exchange market, which created considerable doubt as to whether the government actually had any coherent exchange rate policy at all.

Monetary and fiscal policy

The government's lack of commitment to the float at an intellectual level quickly became obvious when it saw the immediate large depreciation of the rupiah. In what appears in hindsight to have been a panic reaction, it chose to sacrifice its monetary targets in order to try to regain control over the exchange rate.

It imposed a severe liquidity squeeze in order to raise interest rates and attract capital back into the country – a strategy it had employed to defeat currency speculators in 1984, 1987 and 1991 (Binhadi and Meek 1992:

115). But previous success had been achieved in the context of a quasi-fixed exchange rate policy. Now things were different: the markets had only just been told that the official policy was to float the rupiah. They could see the possibility of further depreciation and were not about to be swayed even by very high interest rates. Thus, whereas on the earlier occasions the squeeze did not last long, this time it was maintained for many weeks, rather than a few days, and was more severe. Bank reserves were cut by two-thirds and were not replenished by the authorities for more than three months.[3]

Although the liquidity squeeze may have slowed the rupiah's fall, it failed to return the currency to its earlier level. Accordingly, the government decided that further belt-tightening, in the form of a cutback of government spending, was necessary. In September it announced a list of major infrastructure projects that would be cancelled, postponed, or reviewed. As a result of these spending cuts and severe monetary tightening, the construction and property development sectors in particular were hit hard. Regular workers started being laid off, while those who ordinarily sought work on a daily basis began to find no one to employ them.

Financial sector policy

With their reserves cut drastically, banks had no choice but to raise interest rates substantially in an attempt to maintain liquidity. The government seems to have realised that it was guilty of overkill in depriving the banks of reserves but, rather than simply correct its mistake, it effectively reduced the banks' need for reserves by overlooking breaches of its minimum reserve requirements – such has been the quality of policymaking in the midst of crisis![4] Nevertheless, the banks' vulnerability to being accused of ignoring these requirements made it virtually impossible to write new loans and, although most existing loans had variable interest rates, it was difficult to pass on large increases to borrowers in the midst of spreading recession. Doubts quickly emerged about banks' soundness in view of the severe decline in their interest margins, and in light of their heavy exposure to the now especially vulnerable property sector.

In early October the government called on the International Monetary Fund (IMF) for help. An assistance package was announced at the end of the month, after difficult and protracted negotiations. This required that the government immediately close some sixteen private banks, as already discussed. Deposits of up to Rp20 million were guaranteed by the government and were paid out without incident during the next two weeks.

The abrupt closure of this group of banks was disturbing to depositors at other banks, not least because of rumours that as many as 40 banks initially had been listed for closure. The government was obliged in the weeks that followed to assure the public that there would be no further bank closures, but by then there was a significant credibility problem; there ensued a large-scale flight of deposits from many of the private banks.[5] Funds were shifted to both the state banks, regarded as being implicitly guaranteed by the government, and to foreign banks, viewed as inherently more sound. Although no announcement was made, it is clear that BI pumped a great deal of funds into the private banks to keep them liquid in the months that followed.[6]

The IMF packages

The announcement of the first IMF package brought about an immediate strengthening of the rupiah in the first days of November. The package promised financial assistance of US$10 billion from the IMF itself plus US$8 billion from the World Bank and the Asian Development Bank (ADB) combined. These amounts were supplemented by stand-by loans from several governments, totalling something of the order of US$20 billion. In an attempt to make the overall package seem more impressive than it was, a further US$5 billion of Indonesia's own funds was also tacked on, such that the total amount was variously reported as anything up to US$43 billion. The notion of providing financial assistance to oneself is an oxymoron, of course, but the media have been happy to ignore this, by and large.[7]

There was never a clear statement of what these funds were to be used for. There was no suggestion of any increase in government spending: indeed, both the government and the IMF were keen on fiscal austerity, to varying degrees. The funds could not have been intended to provide subsidies (for example, for food, energy and fuel), since the IMF was set firmly against such subsidies and only grudgingly conceded later that they might be necessary to soften the impact of the crisis on the poor. Moreover, the budget had been in good shape previously and, if a deficit emerged because of falling incomes, this would have provided a helpful automatic spending stimulus to the economy. Nor could the funds have been used for bailing out the private sector, since this would be outside the realm of IMF operations. The only other possibility was potential or actual intervention in the foreign exchange market.

Presumably the mere announcement that the government now had more than US$40 billion extra at its disposal was hoped to dissuade the markets from further speculation against the rupiah. Yet there was no attempt to convince them that the government had decided to defend any particular exchange rate: officially, the policy was still to float. If the hope was that the government could actually use the funds to intervene in the market to defend the rupiah, it did not take participants long to realise that: the IMF funds were to be disbursed only in tranches over a period of several months; the World Bank and ADB funds were slower-disbursing loans that could not be used for this purpose; and the supplementary funds from other countries were to be drawn on only after the IMF funds had been fully disbursed – and then only if Indonesia had done everything asked of it by the IMF. In practice, the authorities appear to have had access to nothing more than the US$3 billion released by the IMF in November to use for defence of the rupiah in the short term – a trivial amount in the circumstances. In short, notwithstanding the considerable effort involved in putting together a package of the order of US$35–40 billion, it seems that there was simply no coherent strategy for using these funds.

It is not surprising that the rupiah soon resumed its slide, which again became rapid in early December. Concerns about the President's health came to dominate market sentiment after he decided, on medical advice, not to attend two overseas meetings to which he had been committed. This was the first occasion on which he had been prevented by ill health from carrying his normal workload, and it crystallised concerns about what the future might bring if he were suddenly to depart the scene, as he had been in office for over three decades without preparing anyone to take over. The rupiah slumped to around Rp6,000 per US dollar before recovering to around Rp5,000 as the President later began to be seen carrying out his normal duties. By late December it was fluctuating in thin trade within a wide range of around Rp5,000–6,000, more than twice its level in July.

It was not just the President's health that rendered the IMF package ineffective. After the initial positive reaction of market participants – that probably reflected mere relief that some agreement had at last been reached – they began to analyse the package more carefully and found its details wanting. Three aspects stood out. First, it called for increased fiscal and monetary austerity, notwithstanding the conservatism that had characterised fiscal and monetary policy previously and the fact that belt-tightening policies seemed likely to worsen the crisis by amplifying the fall in demand that was already apparent; this caused considerable damage to the IMF's credibility. Second, the package was strongly focused on a number of structural reforms that were bound to be difficult to implement for political reasons, and had little or no obvious connection with the sudden decline in the value of the rupiah.[8] Third, the package said virtually nothing about how the rupiah might be restored to a realistic level at which Indonesian borrowers might be able to meet their obligations and the wheels of finance might start turning again.

Subsequent policymaking showed little coherence, and the economy suffered accordingly. The budget brought down on 6 January 1998 had been prepared weeks earlier on the basis of projections for the exchange rate and rates of inflation and growth that had been overtaken by events. The government made no attempt to modify the budget documents, nor even to concede that rapidly changing circumstances made significant revisions – that might have been presented, say, as a supplementary annex – necessary. This inflexibility made the government appear quite out of touch with what was happening. To make matters worse, the form in which the budget was presented made it difficult for less well-informed analysts to interpret because it differed in important respects from what is conventional elsewhere.

The initial negative market response to the budget, and to earlier signs of backsliding on the reforms in the first IMF package, was greatly compounded by obvious signs of displeasure on the part of both the IMF and the World Bank in Washington. The markets marked the rupiah down savagely, and urban consumers responded by rushing supermarkets and shops to buy up essential items such as food. Indonesia's plight became front page news around the world, and the government had little option but to quickly reopen negotiations with the IMF. The latter modified its earlier insistence on strong fiscal austerity, but in respect of structural reforms it drew up a much longer list of demands.

ECONOMIC RESPONSE TO POLICY ADJUSTMENTS

Exchange rate movement

The astonishing decline in the value of the rupiah most clearly encapsulates the course of Indonesia's economic crisis. The sudden depreciation between July and October 1997 (from Rp2,430 to the US dollar to Rp3,600) seemed horrendous at the time, but this was dwarfed by subsequent movements. From Rp3,600 to the US dollar in October and Rp6,000 by the end of the year, the currency plummeted to Rp17,000 at its lowest ebb in January, following the budget debacle and the President's implicit near-repudiation of the second IMF agreement almost before the ink was dry. There was then a period of recovery, especially following the re-election of the President and the announcement of his new cabinet in March.[9] Following a third IMF agreement in April the rupiah settled for some time at Rp7,500–8,000 to the US dollar – three times higher than prior to the crisis, or half as high as the January peak, depending on one's point of view. But there was a new slide in May to about Rp10,000, following rises in the administered prices of fuels and electricity, which resulted in many street protests and, in some places, the return of violence against ethnic Chinese shops and businesses such as had been witnessed in the tense weeks that preceded the presidential election in March.

Significant declines in the value of companies listed on the stock exchange were also posted. Movement of the share price index followed that of the rupiah for the first few months of the crisis. After peaking in July 1997, the share price index had fallen by more than half by mid-December. By mid-February there had been a somewhat surprising recovery; by the latter part of March the average loss had been cut to around 20% in rupiah terms. But, as a result of the spread of social unrest and violence in May, share prices fell again. By May 1998, the dollar values of shares were only about 15% of their levels of mid-1997.

Macroeconomic conditions

By mid-1998 inflation was still not under control and unemployment still appeared to be growing. Life had become extremely difficult for the poor, in particular, ensuring that the possibility of widespread social unrest remained a threat. Although imports had declined drastically as a result of price increases and falling demand, the boost to exports that should have accompanied the rupiah's heavy fall remained muted because of financial bottlenecks that deprived export firms of the working capital needed to purchase inputs, especially imports. More than half of Indonesia's initial international reserves had been frittered away by the central bank's sporadic attempts to support the rupiah.

IMPACT ON DOMESTIC POLICY DEBATE

Opinions differ as to the cause of the sudden loss of confidence in the value of the rupiah. Culprits abound in popular commentary, and include excessive investment in property development, made easier by poor supervision of the banking system; the supposed unsustainability of the current account and allegedly excessive foreign borrowing; and governance problems, including corruption, cronyism and nepotism, and the related succession issue.

Although BI had been putting pressure on the banks to cut their lending for property development for some time before the crisis, there is little to suggest that investors and financiers precipitated the financial crisis by suddenly pulling out of this sector. Even by late October 1997 there had been no significant fall in selling prices for the stock of new property already on the market or soon to be completed. This is not to deny that previously latent concerns about this sector eventually had an important impact, after the bubble of confidence had been pricked. But the policy-induced liquidity squeeze and the severe recession that began to engulf the economy after the crisis emerged also certainly resulted in the postponement of many projects, including those already under construction, and this makes it difficult to disentangle cause and effect.

It has been argued elsewhere (McLeod 1994a: 272–4; McLeod 1996; McLeod 1997c: 38–44) that the popular preoccupation with the size of the current account deficit and the foreign debt is misplaced. Provided the investments financed by foreign borrowing are sound, debt service will not be a problem: by definition, sound investments cover their financing costs. Since most new foreign borrowing in recent years was attributable to the private sector, and took place in the absence of widespread corporate distress, it would appear that past returns must have been satisfactory on average. On the other hand, to the extent that past success created an atmosphere in which all kinds of risk began to be underestimated – if not ignored altogether – it is likely that the average rate of return would have fallen in the future. But this is a concern about the quality of investment decisions, not about foreign borrowing per se.[10]

The assertion that the crisis resulted from governance problems is similarly unconvincing. Corruption has been a perennial issue for decades, and probably the majority of complaints about Indonesia's microeconomic policies in recent years have reflected concern about the continuing, and apparently increasing, abuse of power for the benefit of the first family and the President's close business associates. But few observers would maintain that there had been any drastic turn for the worse such as to warrant the astonishing decline of the currency, notwithstanding a few notable aberrations (McLeod 1997b: 25–42). Nevertheless, it seems that once the crisis was underway and people started examining the future prospects of the economy more carefully, concerns about governance began to be given a much heavier weighting than previously. In particular, entities that had chosen to take on first family members and cronies as business partners as the 'price of admission' to lucrative fields of business – and institutions that had financed the enterprises in question – would have had good reason to be worried about the trend of events.

There are no obvious means of discovering the extent to which any of these kinds of issues had a negative impact on investors' perceptions and thus contributed to capital flight. Perhaps of greater interest, therefore, is the question as to whether the government's response to the crisis was helpful or counterproductive. Two aspects are considered in the concluding sections of this paper. First, did the government overreact initially, compounding private sector concerns and thus turning what might otherwise have been a minor burst of financial turbulence into a deep crisis? Second, were the reforms demanded by the IMF essential to recovery from the initial shock, or did they also have a perverse impact?

Did the government overreact?

The government reacted to the initial rapid decline of the currency rather as it might react to a disaster such as a large fire – seeing it as a threat of mortal and material danger that had to be fought. This was a misconception: there was no reason for the government to change either its fiscal or its monetary policy settings when the rupiah began to fall. Specifically, the economy would have been best served by holding base money growth roughly constant and allowing both the exchange rate and interest rates to be determined by the markets.[11]

Prices, including exchange rates, do not threaten wellbeing. They are signalling mechanisms that reflect how the state of the world is changing, and suggest responses to such change. To control a price because it moves unexpectedly is analogous to censoring the reporting of a fire. Distorting or suppressing information does not change what is happening, but hinders the process of dealing with it.

A fire left unattended can destroy a neighbourhood. The fall in the currency, if left 'unattended', would not have 'destroyed' the rupiah. If the supply of rupiah (or its targeted growth rate) had remained constant, the foreign currency price of the rupiah would have stabilised to reflect the changed demand for it that had resulted from the sudden new awareness of the risks posed by potential devaluation. In order to generate a current account surplus to match the sudden capital outflow, it was necessary for exports to expand and imports to contract. But such adjustments are extremely difficult in the very short run, for logistical reasons. Clearly, with the exchange rate floating, it was bound to move a great deal before a new equilibrium could be reached in the foreign exchange market.

Governments inevitably come under great pressure in such circumstances to 'do something', yet very often it is best to do nothing. If the government had kept its nerve, sticking to its monetary targets and allowing the rupiah to float, the currency might well have fallen further than it actually did in August and September. But it could have been expected to recover much of the lost ground in time, because the elasticities of supply of exports and demand for imports are much higher in the longer run. Moreover, it would have been unrealistic to expect capital outflow to remain high indefinitely. Once the rupiah fell, domestic assets of all kinds became more attractive, creating an incentive for funds to return and capture the bargains on offer. Choosing to suppress information contained in the exchange rate did nothing to alter the changed risk perceptions which drove the sudden capital outflow, but merely sought to compensate them with much higher interest rates.

How far back would the rupiah have bounced? The question is impossible to answer. The world investment community would probably have decided that Indonesia was a more risky place than it had thought previously, for the various reasons already discussed, and capital inflow would have resumed at a lower level than before, resulting in some sustained devaluation. But there was no reason for the government to have opposed such an outcome. On the contrary: if Indonesia's external circumstances were now different, the exchange rate should have moved so as to signal that fact.

In short, the government should not have responded as it did to the fall in the rupiah. It did not need to cut its own spending, and it did not need to drain liquidity from the system. In doing both these things it not only heightened the sense of crisis in the private sector, but created real – as distinct from financial – effects that resulted in an extraordinarily severe recession. Moreover, as discussed already, the contractionary impact of fiscal and monetary belt-tightening was compounded by the drastic decline of confidence in the banking system as a result of the poorly planned moves to deal with its problems. In the final analysis, the whole range of government policy responses left the economy a shambles, and failed signally to achieve the central objective of stopping the rupiah from falling.

Were structural reforms a prerequisite for recovery?

It seems clear that Indonesia's economic policymakers saw the emerging crisis less as a problem to be dealt with, and more as an opportunity to accelerate the flagging progress of reform, by using it to persuade the President of the urgency of changing certain microeconomic policies. The main focus was on the domestic economy (including banking), and involved an attack on the privileged position of the President's family and his business associates. When the IMF was brought in, it prosecuted this same strategy with considerable vigour.

The early decision to cut government spending was supposedly made to support macroeconomic objectives. But these cuts were heavily concentrated on certain infrastructure projects, especially toll roads, many of which had first family members as principals. Next, the first IMF agreement introduced moves to abolish a number of monopolies that benefited various presidential offspring and cronies. The second IMF agreement significantly augmented the scope of such reforms, and extended the attack to the domain of presidential protégé, B.J. Habibie, by removing financial support from his aircraft development projects and requiring all government funding vehicles to be brought explicitly into the budget.

The list of reforms contained in the third and current IMF agreement was so extensive that reformers would have virtually nothing more to talk about if they were all implemented.[12] Were this to happen, the economy would be on a very firm footing for future progress – once the crisis had been overcome. The interesting analytical issue, however, is whether these extensive reforms could have been expected to contribute to overcoming the crisis, or whether they in fact compounded it.

Of itself, the funding component of the IMF assistance package was of marginal importance, for reasons already explained. But it seemed clear that Indonesia's recovery could not occur until capital flight could be turned around: physical capital cannot be fully productive when financial capital is absent. Moreover, it appeared that investors were likely to continue to take their cue from the IMF's assessment of the government's commitment to, and progress regarding implementation of, the reform package. The IMF's leverage over Indonesia thus stemmed not from its own command over resources but from the potential impact of withholding its imprimatur.[13] Would the structural reforms have been essential to recovery if the IMF had not made them so by demanding them, knowing that the world markets would follow its lead?

In the view of the writer, they would not have been. The existence of anti-competitive policies designed to enrich the favoured few was deplorable, but the fact that these policies had been compatible with high growth that delivered immense material benefits to most segments of the population over a long period cannot be ignored. To put it bluntly, there is little evidence to support the view that these policies caused the crisis.

It may be objected that by implementing the reforms the government would restore Indonesia's attractiveness to the owners of capital – and indeed make it even more attractive than before. But implementing even a single microeconomic reform is never easy. The IMF packages amounted to an increasingly vigorous attack on policies that had served the President and his supporters well. They could only have succeeded if the President had been persuaded that they were genuinely necessary for recovery and ultimately in his own interest. Clearly, he was never persuaded of this. As a consequence many of the reforms were unlikely to be implemented, and this fact itself greatly amplified the initial loss of confidence.

The lesson to be learned from this, to paraphrase Grenville (1998: 18), is that when the emergency room is full of train crash victims it makes good sense to give top priority to those in mortal danger, leaving those with minor lacerations for later. To this we might add that the doctor will have better things to do than haranguing those present about smoking and drinking to excess. The IMF would have done well early on to pare down drastically its wish-list of reforms and measures to those unambiguously relevant and necessary for Indonesia's recovery from crisis. Nirvana could well have waited.

Ironically, it was the government's move to reduce subsidies on fuel and electricity on 1 April 1998 that provided a strong impetus to student protests that had been building for weeks. In turn, this led to the shooting of several students by the military, setting off devastating riots that claimed many lives and caused enormous material damage. As before, the ethnic Chinese community bore the brunt of the violence, causing many to flee the country of their birth – at least, temporarily. Ultimately, the widely despised President was forced to step down. But the change of regime did not bring any solutions to Indonesia's economic misery and, by mid-1998, recovery seemed just as distant as ever.

NOTES

1   This is not to say there was no awareness of the possibility of a devaluation. On the contrary, few had forgotten that the government had implemented devaluations of the order of 30% three times in the period 1978–86, as a result of which occasional bursts of speculation against the rupiah – based on the flimsiest of rumours – were not uncommon, despite high and rising international reserves. The fear of devaluation is one reason why Indonesian interest rates were much higher than foreign rates. Thus many Indonesians were prepared to hold US dollar bank deposits rather than rupiah deposits paying much higher rates, and many firms were prepared to borrow at high rates in rupiah rather than risk taking on foreign currency liabilities.

2   Hal Hill has drawn the writer's attention to the contrast between the successful handling of the mid-1970s Pertamina crisis and the mid-1980s oil price crisis, on the one hand, and the blundering that has characterised the present upheaval, on the other. One explanation, presumably, is that these earlier problems were single issues that directly concerned only the government, not the private sector.

3   An alternative view is that interest rates should have been raised even higher.

4   Unfortunately, BI's monthly report provides no less than three – quite different – sets of figures for the banks' reserves.

5   It may be argued that if many more banks had been closed at the outset there would have been greater confidence in those that remained. This will remain a matter for conjecture.

6   In BI's monthly report (*Indonesian Financial Statistics*), BI's balance sheet shows an increase from Rp23 trillion to Rp37 trillion in its claims on commercial banks between June 1997 and April 1998. The consolidated balance sheet for the commercial banks presented in the same document shows an increase in commercial banks' borrowings from BI from Rp15 trillion to Rp92 trillion during the same period. It is not possible, therefore, to know the true extent of BI's liquidity support for the banks from its own report.

7   It is likely that the World Bank and ADB contributions included significant amounts that they would have loaned to the government in any case; these also were not genuinely additional resources.

8   Some argue that a clear and genuine commitment to implementing such reforms was needed to restore investor confidence and pave the way for a return of capital. Unfortunately, it is inherently difficult, if not impossible, to prove or disprove this proposition. In other words, it is in the nature of an article of faith.

9   At about this time, the President seriously considered the introduction of a currency board system as a means of putting an end to the crisis. This presumably contributed to the recovery of the rupiah at that time, as the consensus view was that if such as system was implemented the peg rate would be close to Rp5,000 per US dollar. The idea was strenuously opposed by the IMF, and was eventually dropped. Some argue that Indonesia lost valuable time in coming to grips with the crisis while this idea occupied the minds of policymakers. By mid-1998, however, the issue had resurfaced in public debate (see, for example, Ch. 18 for arguments in favour of such a system).

10   The only sense in which foreign borrowing was 'excessive', therefore, was in that it was artificially large by virtue of the private sector's being crowded out of the domestic market as a result of the government's exchange rate and monetary policies, as already discussed.

11   If the central bank stays out of the foreign exchange market at times when speculation causes depreciation of the currency, and keeps base money growth constant, tradables' prices will rise and non-tradables' prices will fall (assuming the transactions demand for base money is roughly unchanged). There is therefore no presumption that a reduction of base money growth is needed in order to prevent inflation of prices overall.

12   The reforms included accelerated tariff reductions; discontinuance of local content policies; abolition of import and domestic trade monopolies; removal of special tax privileges for the 'national car' project, taxes on various exports, and restrictions on foreign investment in certain sectors; and attention to a range of governance issues. (Greater detail is contained in McLeod 1998d.)

13   The question of whether the founders of the IMF intended that it should use its influence virtually to blackmail a sovereign government into implementing a set of economic policies not of its own choosing is not addressed here.

3 Thailand

Peter G. Warr

In early 1996 Thailand seemed to many to be a model of developmental success. Over almost a decade the Thai economy had been the fastest grow-ing in the world, with moderate inflation, a stable exchange rate, seemingly healthy foreign exchange reserves and a rapidly declining incidence of absolute poverty. Many observers expressed misgivings about the apparent increase in income inequality, but in macroeconomic terms Thailand's per-formance seemed exemplary. For many years the World Bank, the Interna-tional Monetary Fund (IMF) and the United Nations Development Program had been praising Thailand's stable macroeconomic management as an example that other nations might follow. The central bank, the Bank of Thailand (BOT), was regarded as a bastion of financial soundness.

By early 1998 all that had changed. The economy was in disarray. The exchange rate had collapsed following the decision to float the currency in July 1997, a humiliating IMF bailout package had been agreed to, and con-fidence in the country's economic institutions – especially the BOT – was shattered. Both rich and poor Thais were experiencing genuine economic hardship.

Internationally, Thailand had been identified as the initiator of a 'conta-gion' that had infected the financial markets of Southeast and Northeast Asia, destroying confidence, undermining economic and political stability, and bringing hardship to millions of people. Countries as far away as Aus-tralia and the United States nervously anticipated the inevitable negative ef-fects on their exports. Japanese banks dreaded the prospect of massive provisions for bad loans. The very commentators who previously had been so impressed by the Thai experience now cited it as an example to be avoided. Something had gone really wrong, but few if any of the profes-sional observers had seen it coming. What was it?

The core of this chapter, an analysis of the long-term factors that made Thailand vulnerable to a financial crisis, is contained in the next section. The following section identifies the short-term trigger that led to the ex-pectation of the devaluation that in turn produced the crisis, while the next section describes the crisis itself. The implications the crisis may have for poverty incidence in Thailand are then discussed. The final section reviews the prospects for the Thai economy in the wake of the crisis.

THE BOOM

Thailand's crisis was the culmination of a long period of economic boom, unprecedented in its vigour and duration not only in Thailand's economic history, but in that of almost any country. It is not possible to understand the crisis of 1996 and 1997 except in the context of the boom which preceded it. Real gross domestic product (GDP) had grown at close to 10% per annum from 1988 to 1996. What fuelled this extraordinary growth? Growth of this magnitude does not result from a sudden, enormous and exogenous increase in productivity; to explain the boom we must examine the growth of the factors of production.

Explaining the boom

The source of the boom did not lie in improvements in the quality of the labour force. The performance of Thailand's educational sector is among the weakest in East Asia. Secondary school participation rates are lower than in Indonesia and have not improved greatly in the past two decades (Khoman 1993). The answer, therefore, must lie with the capital stock. This grew dramatically in the years after 1987. Both foreign direct investment and domestic investment contributed, but the acceleration of foreign direct investment occurred first and was proportionately larger (Warr 1993).

Studies of total factor productivity growth in Thailand reveal a crucial point. Over the twenty-year period ending around 1987, and therefore preceding the economic boom that began in 1988, growth was explained reasonably well by growth accounting methods. The unexplained residual growth, known as total factor productivity growth, was less that 1% per annum. But over the period of the boom of the late 1980s and the first half of the 1990s, the unexplained residual increased dramatically to around 5% (Warr 1993). Growth of factor supplies, as conventionally measured, did not account for the growth that was occurring.

A clue to the difference between these two periods is found in the data on incoming foreign direct investment, which increased dramatically from 1987. From annual levels ranging between US$100 and US$400 million over the previous fifteen years, the rate of inflow rose more than fivefold to over US$2 billion per year, and remained at roughly this level over the next eight years. Rates of domestic saving and investment were also high, but the stock of capital represented by direct foreign investment was increasing much more rapidly than the stock represented by domestic investment. The proportion of the total capital stock represented by direct foreign investment was thus increasing significantly.

The way the capital stock is measured in total factor productivity studies involves adding the value of capital from all sources, foreign and domestic, but the Thai experience exposes a flaw in this procedure. Suppose foreign capital embodies forms of technological know-how which domestic capital does not: then the two forms of capital are imperfect substitutes for one another. According to my econometric estimates, the elasticity of substitution between the two is about 0.45 – certainly not infinity, as implied by the usual aggregation. This implies that an increase in the stock of foreign capital will *increase* the productivity of domestic capital. Simply adding them is inappropriate, because it will miss this effect.

If this is true, then when the foreign component of the total capital stock is increasing rapidly, increases in the productivity of the domestic capital stock will in fact be occurring in a way that the conventional approach does not recognise. Increased foreign investment induces increases in the level of domestic investment because it raises the productivity of the domestic capital stock. When these two components of the capital stock are separated, the total factor productivity growth becomes much smaller. Therefore, to explain the boom we must take note of the massive inflow of foreign capital and abandon the notion that foreign and domestic capital are perfect substitutes.[1]

Bank of Thailand response: sterilisation and liberalisation

Thailand has a long and proud history of stable monetary policy and low inflation. The operations of the BOT have been seen as an important contributor to that record. The BOT sees its major role as controlling inflation. As foreign investment poured in, the BOT attempted to sterilise its impact on the money supply. Domestic interest rates were bid up, despite the increased openness of the capital market, implying that foreign and domestic assets were imperfect substitutes. The result was an increased level of foreign portfolio investment, which entered the country in response to the increased rate of return. At the same time, the BOT was relaxing its controls on capital movements. Although financial capital movements into and out of Thailand had been subject to extensive controls prior to 1990 (Warr and Nidhiprabha 1996), these controls were greatly relaxed during the early 1990s. The hope was that Bangkok might replace Hong Kong as a regional financial centre following the restoration of Chinese sovereignty in Hong Kong in 1997. Following the liberalisation of Thailand's capital controls, both the entry and exit of foreign funds had become very much easier.

Now suppose an inflow of foreign capital occurred. If there were no sterilisation, the nominal prices of traded goods would not be affected – since they are determined (with lags) by international prices and the fixed exchange rate – but non-traded goods' nominal prices would be bid up by the increased domestic demand. That is, the capital inflow would produce a real appreciation – an increase in domestic non-traded goods' prices relative to domestic traded goods' prices. This is the phenomenon known as the 'Dutch disease' (Corden 1984). The current account deficit would increase, preventing any increase in foreign exchange reserves.

The outcome would be much the same if the monetary authorities were attempting to sterilise under a fixed exchange rate, if capital movements were unimpeded, and if foreign and domestic assets were perfect substitutes. Any attempt to sterilise by raising domestic interest rates (through sale of bonds) would be defeated, because it would produce an inflow of portfolio investment sufficient to drive the domestic interest rate down to its previous level. Nominal demand would be increased by the monetary consequences of this inflow. This is the Mundell-Fleming model (Mundell 1962; Fleming 1962; Taylor 1993).

If sterilisation had been complete, the monetary effects of the capital inflow would have been exactly offset by the sale of bonds. The money supply would not have increased, and relative domestic prices would not have been affected. It should be recognised that in an economy like Thailand's, however, complete sterilisation would be highly improbable, because by the mid-1990s capital movements had been liberalised significantly.

Incomplete sterilisation implies an intermediate outcome. This might be observed if the monetary authorities were attempting to sterilise where domestic and foreign assets were imperfect substitutes, leading to portfolio capital inflows that only partially offset the attempts to sterilise, or where some residual controls on capital movements were limiting mobility. We would then expect coexistence of the following phenomena, relative to what would otherwise have occurred:

1   increased levels of foreign exchange reserves;
2   high current account deficits;
3   increases in prices of non-tradables relative to tradables (a real appreciation); and
4   increased inflows of foreign portfolio investment.

This is what happened. Items 1 and 2 are straightforward: reserves increased steadily during the 1990s, from US$14 billion in 1990 to US$39 billion in 1996; the current account deficit averaged 7% of GDP during the same period. We can therefore concentrate on items 3 and 4.

Real appreciation

A dramatic real appreciation was occurring throughout the 1990s (Figure 3.1). This figure updates a calculation presented in Warr and Nidhiprabha (1996), which used monthly domestic price data for Thailand to calculate an index of prices of 'traded goods' (using 33 individual wholesale prices for goods that approximately match the analytical concept of traded goods) relative to 'non-traded goods' (using 42 individual consumer prices for goods

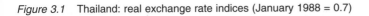

Figure 3.1   Thailand: real exchange rate indices (January 1988 = 0.7)

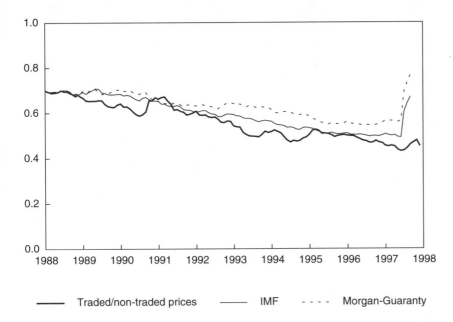

——— Traded/non-traded prices   ——— IMF   - - - - Morgan-Guaranty

and services that approximately match the analytical concept of non-traded goods).[2] In the previous study, data were presented for the twenty years from 1968 to 1988. Over this period the index took values between a maximum of 1.7 and a minimum of 0.68 (indexed to August 1973 = 1). At the end of the data series (January 1988) the value of this index was 0.7.

For comparison with the earlier series, Figure 3.1 is indexed to begin at 0.7 in January 1988, and the composition of the index shown is identical to the one used in the earlier study. Short-term fluctuations aside, the index declined steadily from 1990 onwards. By April 1997 its value was just 0.43; a very large real appreciation had occurred.[3] The real exchange rate, as measured, had fallen to 37% less than its lowest value over the two decades prior to the boom. Do external exchange rate changes explain this outcome? The question arises because it is now well understood that the depreciation after 1995 of the Japanese yen and other currencies relative to the US dollar meant that any currency pegged to the dollar would suffer a real appreciation. But the answer is no.

The real appreciation demonstrated in Figure 3.1 was not at all confined to the period after 1995, when the US dollar was appreciating. A large real appreciation can also be seen in the first five years of the 1990s, when the dollar was depreciating relative to the yen and other currencies. Most of the real appreciation from 1990 to mid-1997 was already evident by mid-1994, well before the appreciation of the US dollar began. External exchange rate changes were clearly relevant, but they were not the main causal factor.

The principal cause of the real appreciation resided in forces operating within the Thai economy – not external exchange rate adjustments. The principal factors were the demand effects of large foreign capital inflows, only partially sterilised. The real appreciation undermined the competitiveness of Thailand's traded goods industries, by which I mean their capacity to attract resources within the domestic economy in competition with nontraded goods sectors.

Portfolio capital inflow

The longer the boom continued, the greater the accumulated stock of short-term, mobile funds became. Such funds are highly volatile, so these developments had significant implications for Thailand's vulnerability to a financial crisis. The BOT was attempting to maintain a (nearly) fixed exchange rate relative to the US dollar.[4] Figure 3.2 shows two measures of reserve adequacy. The conventional measure – the number of months of imports that reserves could finance – relates a financial stock (reserves) to a trade flow (the average monthly value of imports). This measure reveals no problem at all regarding reserve adequacy at the time of the crisis, but why should it? This indicator is conceptually of almost no relevance as an indicator of vulnerability to a financial crisis.

What is much more relevant is the stock of financial capital that could be presented to the central bank at short notice for conversion from domestic currency to foreign currency, relative to the stock of foreign currency available to the central bank to finance these transactions – that is, foreign exchange reserves. The accumulated stock of foreign portfolio capital is one component of the former – not the only component, but one of the most volatile. The second indicator shown in Figure 3.2 is thus the stock of reserves relative to the accumulated stock, since 1972, of foreign portfolio capital. This indicator reveals a significant increase in vulnerability to a crisis in the years of the 1990s leading up to the crisis. The ratio falls from an index of around five in 1991–2 to less than two in late 1996.[5] In other words, the value of Thailand's reserves was declining dramatically relative to the stock of volatile funds that could be presented against these funds in the event of a loss of investor confidence.

What had caused the massive inflow of foreign portfolio investment? The attempted sterilisation undertaken by the BOT caused foreign portfolio investment to be greater than it would otherwise have been, but this explains only a small part of the inflow. Euphoria resulting from an extended boom is a more significant part of the answer. Large returns were being made by investing in Thailand, and this had been the case for several years. Not to participate was to miss out. The government was assuring everyone that reserves were adequate to maintain the fixed exchange rate. The IMF also seemed satisfied, judging from its public statements. Investing in Thailand seemed both safe and profitable. But scarcely anyone was looking at

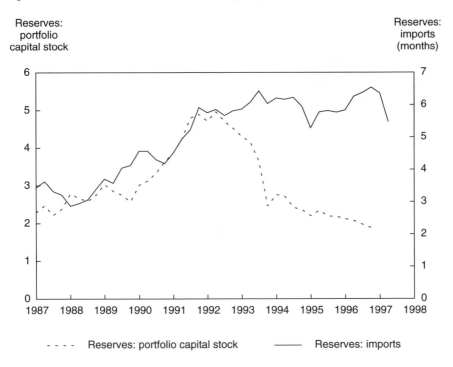

Figure 3.2   Thailand: indicators of reserve adequacy

the appropriate indicators. The growth of volatile portfolio capital relative to reserves left Thailand increasingly vulnerable to a speculative attack on its currency.

THE TRIGGER

The underlying causes of the crisis were therefore long-term. The trigger that actually undermined confidence sufficiently to set in process a speculative attack on the baht was the collapse of export growth in 1996. This provoked capital outflow and speculation against the baht because it produced the expectation of a devaluation. Once this expectation developed and portfolio capital headed for the exit, the process was unstoppable. The subsequent slowdown in exports was widespread among Thailand's export destinations, but was greatest in exports to Japan and the North American Free Trade Agreement (NAFTA) and Chinese economies. By looking at the composition of exports by commodity (Table 3.1), it can be seen that the slowdown was concentrated in manufactured exports from labour-intensive industries.[6]

Observers of the Thai economy have identified several factors which

Table 3.1　Thailand: major exports and export growth by commodity

	1994	1995	1996
Total exports (billion baht)	1,138	1,406	1,401
Overall growth rate (%)	20.9	23.6	−0.35
Growth rates by commodity (%)			
Computers and parts	44.9	38.7	31.3
Garments	12.4	1.3	−21.9
Rubber	43.3	46.5	1.4
Integrated circuits	27.5	28.4	3.4
Gems and jewellery	8.3	11.5	8.4
Rice	18.9	24.1	8.4
Sugar	41.2	67.2	11.7
Frozen shrimps	29.9	2.3	−17.8
Television sets and parts	26.2	12.7	14.1
Shoes and components	40.5	37.0	−40.9
Canned seafood	24.7	4.1	−0.3
Air conditioners and parts	62.1	49.6	33.6
Plastic products	−29.1	102.2	51.4
Tapioca products	−13.6	−2.8	16.7
Textiles	4.5	22.1	−4.4
Total commodities (billion baht)	612	766	741
Growth rate (%)	20.7	25.2	−3.27
Share in total exports (%)	53.8	54.4	52.9

Source: Bangkok Post 1996.

contributed to the export slowdown, including: the political events of the previous two years; monetary policy; the congestion of industrial infrastructure; the falsification of export data to receive value added tax rebates; increasing competition in international markets from China after China's currency devaluation in 1994; effective appreciation of the baht through pegging to the dollar while the latter appreciated relative to the yen from late 1995 through 1997; and a slowdown in demand among importing countries. But two other factors were particularly important: the long-term real appreciation resulting from the demand effects of foreign capital inflow discussed above, and a closely related phenomenon, a large increase in real wages.

Real wages

Data on real wages provide a powerful explanation for the export slowdown and its concentration in labour-intensive industries. Research at the Thailand Development Research Institute has recently produced a reliable series of real wage data for Thailand's manufacturing sectors. These data are

Figure 3.3   Thailand: real wages in manufacturing (1982 = 100)

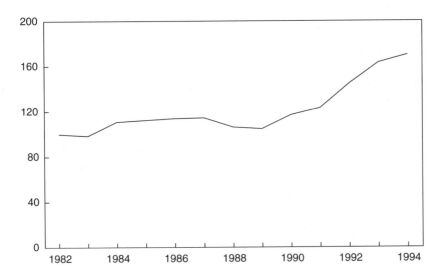

Source: Thailand Development Research Institute.

reproduced in Figure 3.3 for the years 1982 to 1994. The data describe average nominal wages in manufacturing deflated by the consumer price index, with a base of 100 in 1982. Over the thirteen years from 1982 to 1994, real wages increased by 70%, but this increase was heavily concentrated in the years after 1990. Over the years 1982 to 1990 the compound average annual rate of increase was 2%, but over the following four years to 1994 the real wage increased at an average annual rate of over 9%!

Both supply- and demand-side forces played a role in real wage increases. First, consider the supply side. During the early stages of Thailand's economic development the rising industrial and services sector demand for labour could be satisfied from a very large pool of rural labour with relatively low productivity. The potential supply of unskilled rural labour was so large and so elastic that, as workers moved from agriculture to more productive jobs in the manufacturing and services sectors, it was possible for these sectors to expand their levels of employment without significantly bidding up real wages. But as this process continued the pool of cheap rural labour was largely used up, so that by the early 1990s labour shortages were becoming evident and the labour supply was no longer as elastic as it had been. Agricultural industries were themselves experiencing serious problems of seasonal labour shortages. Further increases in the demand for labour outside agriculture led to rising wages.

Changes in the demand for labour also played a role. Non-tradables are on average more labour-intensive in production than tradables. As non-tradables' prices rise, wages are bid up relative to both tradables' and non-tradables' prices – the Stolper-Samuelson effect (Stolper and Samuelson 1941; Ethier 1995). Wages therefore rise relative to the consumer price index.

With the end of the era of 'cheap labour', Thailand's labour-intensive export industries faced the prospect of declining competitiveness. The importance of this point is confirmed by the fact that the export slowdown in 1996 shown in Table 3.1 was concentrated in labour-intensive industries such as garments, footwear and textiles.[7] Thailand's export industries were especially vulnerable to increases in real wages for two basic reasons. First, many of its most successful export industries are highly labour-intensive, implying that a given increase in real wages has a large impact on their costs. Second, these export industries face highly competitive international markets for their products, where they must act as price-takers. This means that export producers cannot pass on cost increases in the form of increases in product prices, whereas producers for the domestic market may have greater scope for doing so.

THE CRISIS

Through late 1996 and the first half of 1997 the BOT struggled against speculative attacks on the baht. Despite the insistence of the government and the BOT that the exchange rate could be defended, market participants did not believe this. They were right. The level of officially declared foreign exchange reserves declined from US$40 billion in January 1997 to well under US$30 billion six months later. On 2 July, the BOT announced the floating of the currency. The rate moved immediately from 25 baht per US dollar to 30 baht. By January 1998 it was 55 baht, recovering by February to 45 baht. Late in 1997 the government sought and obtained the assistance of the IMF, which required a package of stringent financial measures to be implemented in return.

The politics

The crisis had political casualties. In November 1997, a year after it came into government, the administration of Prime Minister Chavalit Yongchaiyudh was forced to surrender office as its coalition of political parties unravelled. It was replaced by a new coalition government led by Democrat Party leader and former Prime Minister Chuan Leekpai, who had led the parliamentary opposition to the Chavalit government. The latter had comprehensively lost public confidence, appearing quite unable to cope with the developing crisis.

The change of government gave Thailand a major advantage in responding to the crisis that some of its neighbours lacked. The new government carried no baggage of having to defend itself against blame for the crisis. Notwithstanding the parliamentary efforts of the new opposition, now led by General Chavalit, there seemed little political necessity for debate as to whether ultimate responsibility for the nation's problems lay with foreigners, domestic businessmen or the government. Full attention could be given to instituting a reform package that might resolve the emergency.

There was considerable debate as to what the most appropriate reform package would be. The government felt bound to implement the IMF package and to announce publicly its commitment to it. The package was widely criticised within Thailand, however, and behind the scenes the government lobbied to have it modified. The economic crisis had produced a contraction of domestic demand that was much larger than expected, as private consumption and investment spending had declined dramatically. Inflation remained low, in spite of the mid-year depreciation of the baht.

The IMF package had seemed a copy of packages the IMF had previously devised for Latin American countries burdened with external imbalances associated with massive public sector debt, hyperinflation and low rates of private saving. The external imbalance in Thailand, like that in most of its neighbours, lacked any of these features. Inflation was relatively low, foreign debt was held primarily by the private sector (US$72 billion out of US$99 billion in total) and saving rates remained high. The crisis quickly produced a massive contraction in private spending. The IMF package added a public sector contraction, by requiring a budget surplus equivalent to 1% of GDP. Moreover, at a time when confidence in the financial sector was essential, the IMF required that problem institutions be closed. Given the circumstances of the time, this requirement seemed to many observers to be as irresponsible as crying 'Fire!' in a crowded theatre.

While the IMF rescue package was handled poorly, this was not the main failure. The main failure occurred before the crisis, not after it, in that the developing crisis was apparently not foreseen in time, and was thus not averted. Some IMF officials have suggested subsequently that the government was indeed properly warned about the impending danger during 1996. If this is true, the warnings were made only in secret and cannot be verified. Moreover these warnings, if they were given, were inconsistent with published IMF commentary of the time, including that contained in the IMF's *Annual Report 1996* and its special 1996 report on the Thai economy (IMF 1997a; IMF 1996).

The bubble economy

Through the first half of the 1990s, investment in real estate and commercial office space soared. Much of this investment subsequently proved to be financially non-performing, destroying many of the companies that had undertaken it and others which had provided the finance. Why had investors acted so imprudently? Euphoria induced by almost a decade of high growth was a major reason, but the underlying real appreciation was another. The classic bubble economy is one in which real estate prices continue to rise well beyond levels justified by the productivity of the assets, but so long as the prices continue to rise, existing investors are rewarded and collateral is created for new loans to finance further investment, and so on – until the inevitable crash. Unrealistic expectations of continued boom are the underlying fuel for this process. These expectations generally arise only after several years of sustained boom; the boom therefore provides the mechanism for a crash. This is why economic booms almost never peter out gradually, but collapse. In these respects, Thailand's financial panic was similar to many previous examples around the world, including the Mexican crash of 1994.

In the Thai case, there was another, less well-understood cause for over-investment. Banking licences in Thailand are highly profitable, since the issuance of new licences is tightly controlled by the BOT. It had become known that the number of licences was to be increased significantly, and Thai finance companies immediately began competing with one another to be among the lucky recipients. To project themselves as significant players in the domestic financial market, many companies were willing to borrow large sums abroad and lend domestically at low margins, thereby taking risks they might not ordinarily have contemplated. With lenders eager to provide vast sums, real estate was a favoured investment, because purchasing real estate requires almost no specialist expertise, only the willingness to accept risk.

Capital mobility

The economic boom since the late 1980s had encouraged the BOT to remove almost all of its earlier restrictions on the movement of financial capital into and out of Thailand. What surprised all observers was the rate at which funds could flow out of the country in response to what seemed small changes in market sentiment, putting irresistible pressure on the BOT's foreign exchange reserves. The crucial point was the very large volume of short-term capital that had entered Thailand during the boom. To attract this capital it had been necessary to demonstrate not only that entry was open, but that exit was unobstructed as well, so the government had removed most of the capital controls that had made maintenance of its fixed exchange rate policy consistent with a degree of monetary independence. This liberalisation meant that speculative attacks on the baht became much easier. When the market began to expect a devaluation, the rate of financial outflow became so great that depreciation became inevitable. In January 1998 the influential *Bangkok Post Year-end Economic Review* commented that 'liberalised capital flows but a fixed exchange rate proved to be the undoing of the Thai economy' (*Bangkok Post* 1998:18).

THE POOR

During the economic boom from the late 1980s to 1995 it was frequently said that the boom was failing to produce benefits for the poor. The faster the growth, it seems, the more it is despised.[8] When growth stops, however, these statements are not heard. But if economic growth really offered little for the poor, as claimed, the reverse would surely apply as well: the cessation of growth, as in the present economic crisis, would present few if any hardships for poor people. The evidence clearly indicates otherwise.

As the crisis developed, money wages for unskilled workers actually fell for many of those fortunate enough to retain their jobs, while food prices continued to rise. For the hundreds of thousands who lost their urban sector jobs, the immediate prospects were grim. Many returned to rural areas, but continued drought, agricultural mechanisation and the presence of vast numbers of illegal immigrants from Burma and Laos meant that the prospects in rural areas were not promising either. The rich were seriously affected as well, especially by the collapse in asset values, increased interest rates and the increased cost in domestic currency of servicing foreign debt. In Bangkok, a Sunday market quaintly called 'the market for the formerly rich' developed in what is normally a busy street, in which upper income and middle income people devastated by the crisis could sell off personal possessions acquired in happier times.

In terms of the systematic study of poverty incidence and inequality, the periodic Socio-Economic Surveys (SES) conducted by the National Statistical Office (NSO) are virtually the sole source of reliable data that are comparable over time. Despite the limitations of the data, a clear picture emerges. Although relative inequality increased during the period of rapid growth, the incidence of absolute poverty fell dramatically, from almost 30% of the total population in 1986 to less than 10% in 1994, the latest year for which data are currently available (Table 3.2). This decline was not confined to the capital, Bangkok, or its immediate environs, the Central Plains. In fact, the largest absolute decline in poverty incidence occurred in the poorest region of the country, the North East.

Did economic growth contribute to poverty reduction? It is obvious that, over the long term, sustained economic growth is a necessary condition for large-scale poverty alleviation. No amount of redistribution can achieve this. But what does the evidence indicate about the short-run relationship between aggregate economic growth and poverty reduction? The data summarised below cover the period 1975–6 to 1994, for which data on poverty incidence are available for seven rounds of the SES survey. When the rate of economic growth during the intervals between SES data points is graphed against measured changes in poverty incidence over the same periods, we obtain the relationship shown in Figure 3.4.

Although the number of data points is small, the implications seem clear. Economic growth was strongly associated with reduced levels of absolute

Table 3.2 Thailand: poverty incidence and income distribution (%)

	1981	1986	1988	1990	1992	1994
Absolute poverty incidence						
Head count ratio	23.0	29.5	22.2	16.6	13.1	9.6
Relative inequality						
Income share by quintile						
Quintile 1 (poorest)	5.4	4.6	4.6	4.2	3.9	4.0
Quintile 2	9.1	7.9	8.1	7.4	7.0	7.3
Quintile 3	13.4	12.1	12.5	11.5	11.1	11.6
Quintile 4	20.6	19.9	20.7	19.3	19.0	19.6
Quintile 5 (richest)	51.5	55.6	54.2	57.7	59.0	57.5
Ratio of income share of						
Quintile 5 to Quintile 1	9.5	12.2	11.8	13.7	15.0	14.4
Gini coefficient	0.453	0.500	0.485	0.522	0.536	0.525

Source: Bangkok Post 1996: 22.

poverty incidence. Rapid growth from 1976 to 1981 coincided with de-clining poverty incidence. Reduced growth caused by the world recession in the early to mid-1980s coincided with worsening poverty incidence in the years to 1986. Finally, the economic boom of the late 1980s and early 1990s coincided with dramatically reduced poverty incidence. The evidence pro-vides no support at all for the notion that economic growth is bad for the poor in absolute terms. On the contrary, the data show that the rate of ag-gregate growth is an important determinant of the rate at which absolute poverty declines, even in the short run. Reduction of poverty incidence must obviously depend on more than just the aggregate rate of growth, but the evidence shows clearly that faster growth has been associated with faster reductions in absolute poverty.

Figure 3.4 reveals a further significant point. The rate of economic growth at which poverty incidence remains constant is not zero, nor is it the rate of population growth, currently around 1% per year. According to the data, the rate of growth at which poverty incidence is stationary is at least 6%. With growth above that level, poverty falls; when growth falls below 6%, poverty incidence rises. This empirical observation has major implica-tions for the way the present crisis will affect the poor.

In 1997 Thailand's real GDP growth rate was almost zero (minus 0.4%) and the National Economic and Social Development Board projects growth of minus 3.5% in real terms in 1998. Extrapolating the relationship be-tween growth and annual changes in poverty incidence, as shown in Figure 3.4, we obtain an estimated increase in poverty incidence over these two years of 12% of the total population (just over 5% in 1997 and just under 7% in 1998). If these calculations are roughly correct, they mean that over

Figure 3.4 Thailand: poverty reduction and growth

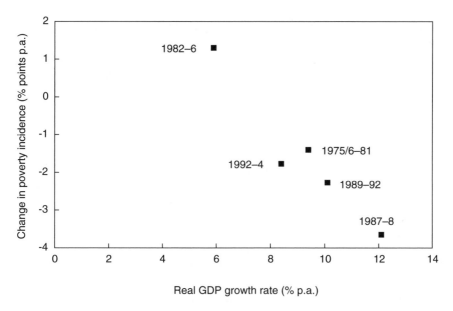

Source: Poverty data from Table 3.2 and Warr 1993; GDP data from World Bank, *World Tables*.

seven million people will have moved from incomes above the poverty line to incomes below it, in just two years. Whereas poverty afflicted around 8% of the population in 1996, by the end of 1998 it could be 20%, eliminating almost all of the dramatic reductions in poverty incidence achieved since 1981. If growth remains below 6% beyond 1998, poverty incidence can be expected to rise even further.

THE FUTURE

The increase in real wages described above reduced the competitiveness of Thailand's labour-intensive exporters. The massive depreciation of the baht will reverse that decline, at least temporarily. The depreciation means a major reorientation of domestic prices, with tradable goods prices (exportables and import substitutes) rising relative to non-tradables, especially services and construction. The more rapidly resource allocation can adjust in response, the smaller will be the unemployment and consequent human suffering that results. Resources will be released by the services and construction sectors and absorbed by exporters. It remains to be seen to what extent resources can be moved efficiently from the services sectors that are now laying off workers to the export industries that are now becoming much more profitable. The less flexible is resource reallocation, the greater will be frictional unemployment. The flexibility of the Thai economy is now being tested.

There is no doubt that 1998 will be a very difficult year. Financial reform and facilitation of the response of exports to the increased profitability created by the depreciation are the priority areas for policy. Like the Indonesian government, the Thai government has expressed an interest in establishing a currency board, but there seems no prospect of that shift of policy being implemented at least until the stability of the banking system is restored. Increased inflation in response to the devaluation seems inevitable. Poverty incidence will increase at a rate heavily influenced by the rate at which labour can relocate from the contracting services and construction industries to the now more profitable export industries. Financial reform will be an important determinant of the success of this adjustment.

Closer examination of certain aspects of the economy raises doubts about the restoration of sustained strong growth. First, the domestic resource which fuelled the boom, cheap unskilled labour, will no longer be abundant once the unemployed workers released by the current recession have been reabsorbed. Once these workers re-enter the work force the era of cheap labour will be over for Thailand. The evidence supporting this view includes the dramatic increase in real wages during the early 1990s described above. The failure of the education system to supply the skilled labour required for more skill-intensive modes of production, especially for export, will then be critical. The problem is the low rates of secondary school participation in Thailand, rather than shortcomings at either the primary or tertiary levels.

Second, foreign investment also fuelled the boom because it brought with it advanced technology and skills. It seems doubtful that foreign investment will return to anything like the levels experienced during the boom, because investors will surely be more cautious. In early 1998 there were promising signs of a recovery of foreign direct investment, but it was still too early to distinguish adequately between temporary bargain-seeking in asset markets and a long-term commitment to introducing new capital.

Finally, public infrastructure, especially transport, was badly congested by 1996. The severe cutbacks in public investment now in place will mean that after the recovery that constraint will be present again.

There is every reason to expect that Thailand will return to moderate rates of growth, potentially in the neighbourhood of 6% or even 7% per annum if all goes well, and possibly even slightly more during the recovery phase. But the heady growth that Thailand experienced during the boom will not be repeated – and that may be just as well.

NOTES

Discussions with Prema-chandra Athukorala and George Fane, the comments of Bhanupong Nidhiprabha and the able research assistance of Agus Setiabudi and Prem J. Thapa are gratefully acknowledged. The author is responsible for all defects.

1   The treatment of the public sector capital stock is also potentially important in this respect, but in the Thai case the really important distinction appears to be between the private domestic and private foreign capital stocks.

2   For a full discussion of this index and its composition, see Warr and Nidhiprabha (1996: 221–6).

3   Figure 3.1 also shows two other measures of real exchange rates. These are the Morgan-Guaranty index (the export share-weighted sum of trading partner wholesale price indices, each multiplied by the bilateral exchange rate divided by the domestic wholesale price index) and the IMF index (which has the same numerator but the denominator is the domestic consumer price index). For the reasons demonstrated in Warr (1986), both these measures understate the magnitude of a real appreciation. Both also greatly exaggerate the gain in export competitiveness resulting from a depreciation, and distort the pattern of its changes over time.

4   See Warr and Nidhiprabha (1996), Chapter 9, for a detailed discussion of exchange rate management over the period ending in 1991, and also Robinson, Byeon and Teja (1991).

5   A fuller discussion of measures of vulnerability to a financial crisis is contained in Athukorala and Warr (1998).

6   The fifteen commodities represented in Table 3.1 comprised between 52% and 54% of total exports in each of the three years shown.

7   The frozen shrimp industry is a special case, where US import restrictions were important, effectively banning imports of non-farm shrimps from Thailand. These restrictions were lifted in the following year.

8   An example is a review article entitled 'Growth hides rising poverty', appearing in the December 1995 edition of the influential *Year-end Economic Review*, an annual magazine supplement to the *Bangkok Post*, Thailand's principal English language newspaper. The article begins: 'While politicians claim credit for Thailand's buoyant economic growth, the poor have little to applaud. Only the rich are getting richer ...' (*Bangkok Post* 1995: 63). The data on poverty incidence analysed in the present chapter are identical to those reported in the article concerned.

4 Korea

Heather Smith

INTRODUCTION

The origins of Korea's financial crisis predate 1997. Administrative guidance and state-directed lending, which had appeared to work in the early stages of industrial development, created an industrial structure characterised by highly leveraged firms and a banking sector with little experience in managing risk. Against this backdrop, in the early 1990s the government embarked on a program of financial liberalisation, without simultaneously strengthening prudential standards. Confident that the state would always bail them out, banks and companies piled up debt through imprudent and barely monitored lending. Under such circumstances Korea was always vulnerable to any internal or external shock that might alter the fragile balance. That catalyst emerged in 1995–6, when an adverse terms of trade shock affected firms' ability to service their huge build-up of short-term debt commitments, triggering a series of corporate bankruptcies and banking defaults. If, as this chapter argues, the causes of the crisis were systemic, the appropriate policy response was not simply the provision of funds to accommodate short-term liquidity constraints and the restructuring of debt. Rather, a commitment to fundamental structural and institutional reforms was necessary as a precondition for reviving access to international capital.

Korea's economy prior to the crisis

The real economy grew strongly in the first half of the 1990s, with annual growth averaging 7.7% between 1990 and 1996 – close to the average sustained for more than 30 years. The driving force was the growth of exports of goods and non-factor services, which averaged 15.3% per year in US dollar terms between 1992 and 1996. This in turn was made possible by growth in facilities (fixed) investment, with the share of gross fixed capital formation in gross domestic product (GDP) averaging nearly 37% in the five years to 1996.[1] Unlike in the strong growth cycle of the late 1980s, inflationary pressures were largely absorbed in producer margins, although inflation remained above Organisation for Economic Cooperation and

Development (OECD) levels, contributing to real exchange rate appreciation during the mid-1990s (Garnaut 1998).

While macroeconomic indicators appeared healthy, conditions had been deteriorating since 1996. Industrial output growth had slowed from an annual growth rate of 14% in mid-1995 to 8.4% in 1996. The growth rate of manufacturing sales fell abruptly from 20% in 1995 to 10% in 1996. The financial health of the industrial conglomerates (*chaebol)* was increasingly shaky, given very high debt-to-equity ratios and falling profitability. In 1996, 20 of the largest 30 *chaebol* showed a rate of return below the cost of capital (Corsetti et al. 1998: 6). Major financial institution bankruptcies were also beginning to emerge in 1996. Reflecting these weaknesses, the share market fell by 35% during 1996 as the slowing economy affected corporate profitability. Corporate bankruptcies in turn led to serious difficulties for the banks – especially merchant banks that had borrowed heavily abroad to finance the investment projects of the *chaebol* (Corsetti et al. 1998: 57). All of this was occurring well before the float of the Thai baht in July 1997.

The current account deficit – which was low in the early 1990s (at 1–3% of GDP) – widened in both 1995 and 1996, reaching US$23.1 billion (4.8% of GDP) in 1996, the highest level ever recorded. The widening of the deficit, stemming primarily from the trade accounts, led to an increased dependence on net capital inflows and, in turn, to a doubling of the deficit on investment income between 1993 and 1996 (OECD 1996).

Measures to liberalise long-term capital inflows were taken between 1990 and 1993 as the current account moved into deficit. Rather than rely on public sector borrowing, as was done in the early 1980s, the government opened the domestic equity market and eased the regulatory environment for foreign direct investment (FDI) in Korea. At the same time, Korea's gross external liabilities began to rise more quickly as the government encouraged the country's banks and *chaebol* to borrow heavily abroad to finance rapid industrial expansion.[2]

By the end of 1996, Korea's gross external liabilities totalled US$158 billion. Still, at around 30% of GDP, external liabilities were not high by historical standards. Korea has always relied on external borrowing to finance its investment. The problem was not the absolute size of the debt but its term structure. Except for Taiwan, Korea by mid-1997 had the highest amount of short-term debt among borrowers in Asia, Latin America and Eastern Europe. The increase in the share of short-term debt in external liabilities was dramatic – rising from 34% in 1992 to 63% by the end of 1996. Foreign reserves had grown substantially over the 1990s, from US$14 billion in 1990 to US$34 billion in 1996, but were still lower than those of many other East Asian economies. By June 1997 Korea's short-term debt was more than three times the size of its reserves, a higher ratio than for any other country in the region.

While, on a net basis, the increase in the external borrowings was equal to the current account deficit, the increase in the gross external liabilities was much larger in the 1990s as large short-term capital inflows were also accompanied by very large capital outflows. Although Korea financed only a small fraction of the increasing current account deficits with FDI (10% in 1996), FDI outflows were in fact greater than inflows throughout the 1990s, as the *chaebol* expanded offshore. A large portion of the gross capital inflows and outflows were intermediated through the banking sector, with domestic banks increasing their foreign short-term liabilities to international banks much faster than their foreign assets. Between the end of 1993 and the first half of 1997, the net liability position of the Korean banking system went from US$21 billion to US$57 billion (Corsetti et al. 1998: 66).

Declining competitiveness

In the first half of the 1990s Korean exporters were able to maintain high rates of volume growth largely because of two factors: the geographical diversification of exports, particularly to China and Southeast Asia; and a high degree of competitiveness relative to Japan in third markets, owing to the depreciation of the won against the yen during the first half of the 1990s. Exports to Southeast Asia grew at annual rate of 37% between 1990 and 1995, boosting their share of Korea's total exports from 14% to nearly 33%. Exports to other markets grew at only 11% annually.

The strong yen made Korea's key exports, such as steel, semiconductors and cars, especially competitive. Taken together these three items accounted for nearly half of merchandise exports in 1996. The semiconductor industry, in particular, had been the driving force of Korea's export growth in the first half of the 1990s, accounting for nearly 20% of exports in 1995, compared with 13% in 1994. But by August 1995, as the yen began to fall against other currencies, Korea's price advantage over Japanese competitors diminished. In the second quarter of 1996, Korea suffered a sharp fall-off in the prices of its main export products, notably semiconductors, just as new production facilities were coming on stream. Merchandise export growth slowed sharply to 5% in 1996 from 32% in 1995. Following the slowdown of the export boom in 1995, the ratio of ordinary corporate income to sales fell below 1% in 1996 – the lowest level ever recorded. The squeeze on profits put an increasing strain on companies' – and ultimately the banking sector's – ability to repay short-term debts.

Relative to those of major competitors, Korean exports showed no advance in dollar value during the first half of the 1990s. Although this was partly attributable to a decline in traditional labour-intensive export lines, Korea had been losing competitiveness since the early 1990s. Despite strong export growth, indicators of Korea's international competitiveness show a deterioration in cost factors from 1993–4 (Figures 4.1 and 4.2): the real effective exchange rate appreciated, prices of major export items fell and

Figure 4.1 Korea: competitiveness indicators (1991 = 100)

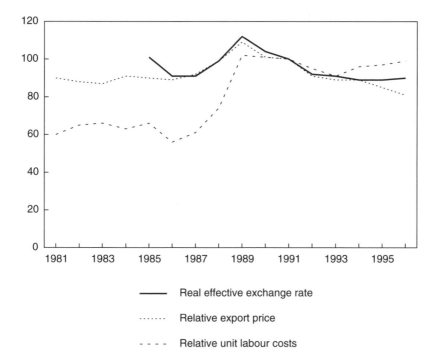

    Real effective exchange rate

    Relative export price

    Relative unit labour costs

Note: Indicators are expressed in a common currency and concern manufactured goods. The indices take into account both export and import competitiveness. For details on method of calculation, see section on effective exchange rates and competitiveness indicators in OECD 1997.
Sources: OECD 1998: Annex tables 38, 43 and 44.

relative unit labour costs increased. Korea's increasingly inflexible labour market was undermining competitiveness. Labour costs had been rising significantly since the mid-1980s, and although the rate of increase had slowed by the early 1990s, real average monthly earnings in manufacturing still grew by an average of 7.8% per year between 1992 and 1996, while productivity growth lagged.

Failure to maintain competitiveness relative to its major rivals in technologically advanced product lines was also an important factor, suggesting that Korea's industrial structure was increasingly hindering competitiveness. Korea was finding it hard to compete with lower-cost producers of low-margin manufacturing products such as steel and memory chips. Korea had been slower than Taiwan, Singapore and Japan to shift into the more sophisticated segments of these industries. Korean firms were also being squeezed by countries with low labour costs, including China and some Southeast Asian countries. Korean firms were relatively slow to relocate investment to low-cost areas of East Asia, thereby allowing themselves

Figure 4.2   Korea: relative export prices, Korea and major competitors (1991 = 100)

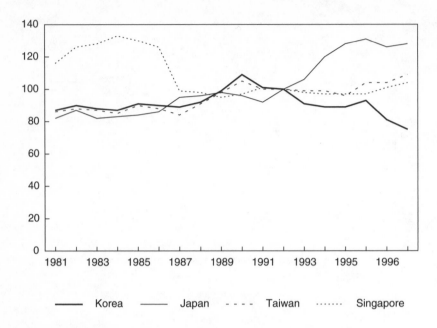

Korea ——— Japan - - - - Taiwan ⋯⋯ Singapore

Source: OECD 1998: Annex table 44.

increasingly to be priced out of the market in industries that had migrated to cheaper labour locations earlier.

While early industrial strategies and structures had enabled the *chaebol* to mobilise large amounts of resources and to cross-subsidise risky activities, this approach increasingly became a liability, preventing firms from competing at the innovation frontier. The scale-intensive approach of the *chaebol* contrasted sharply with those of Korea's major competitors. Taiwanese firms, for example, innovated across niche markets, on a much smaller scale (Hobday 1995). A flexible, diversified production base meant firms were able to respond more quickly to rapidly changing markets and unexpected shocks such as the fall in export prices in 1996. Free of huge debts, firms in Taiwan and Singapore were also better placed to respond to the changing currents of the global marketplace, and were more effective in neutralising the effects of the yen's movements. Most Korean companies do not have a long-term exchange rate strategy – when the yen has been strong they have tended to expand capacity, assuming the cost advantage will continue indefinitely.

Backsliding in reforming the *chaebol*

Reforming the industrial system has always been complicated by the fact that Korean companies have been highly leveraged and highly interdependent financially. Over the years, the socialisation of bankruptcy risk, combined with low interest rate ceilings, has made the cost of debt financing cheap, encouraging the *chaebol* to take on excessive levels of debt and expand outside their core competencies (Huh and Kim 1994: 26). From 1963 to 1971, the debt-to-equity ratio of the manufacturing sector increased more than fourfold, from 92% to 394%, increasing further to 488% by the end of the 'Heavy and Chemical Industry Drive' in 1980. The ratio fell during the 1980s but, by 1996, the debt-to-equity ratios of companies listed on the Korean Stock Exchange (KSE) still averaged over 300%.

In an attempt to slim down the *chaebol* the Kim Young-sam administration, which came to power in 1992, initiated investigations into the complex system of cross-shareholdings among parent companies and their network of subsidiaries, and sought to limit the amount of credit available to these groups. But the impetus for reform began to wane during 1994 because of concern that restrictions on the activities of the *chaebol* could impact adversely on growth, given their large share in domestic production and trade. Rather than scaling back, the *chaebol* actually grew during the 1990s, expanding their core business and branching out into new sectors. The top 30 *chaebol* increased their aggregate number of subsidiaries from 616 to 696 between 1994 and 1996 (*Korea Herald* 1 July 1995: 8). By early 1998, they had 819 subsidiaries. Of these, only 184, or 22% – presumably the more profitable – were listed on the KSE.

Korean firms, like those in Japan, have long used property as the main collateral for their borrowings, and banks base their lending decisions mainly on the size of collateral, not on the merit of investment proposals. Moreover, practices such as cross-loan guarantees continued to be widely used. Among units of a *chaebol,* such guarantees enabled individual companies to obtain credit guaranteed by the assets of the entire group. The practice facilitated easy access to loans but also left the *chaebol* dangerously exposed to chain bankruptcies involving subsidiaries within the same group. Transparent accounting would have revealed the extent of the problem, but because the *chaebol* did not produce consolidated accounts, they were able to hide their financial weaknesses, pledging the same assets as collateral many times over. The true level of corporate debt still remains concealed by opaque accounting, although estimates by the Korea Development Institute in March 1998 put the figure at between 900–1,000 trillion won (US$600–700 billion) (*Reuters News Service* 16 March 1998).

Corporate financing

Korean firms rely almost exclusively on external finance, while corporate investment in most OECD countries is funded to a larger extent from retained earnings. The bulk of funding during the 1990s was used to expand manufacturing capacity, as distinct from the property sector expansion seen in Southeast Asia. The distinctive feature has been the emergence of direct financing as an important source of funds relative to indirect financing. In the 1990s, firms have relied heavily on issuing high-cost financial instruments such as unsecured commercial paper and corporate bonds to finance growth. Merchant banks and insurance companies, in particular, were the major sources of short-term liquidity for corporations. By mid-1997 there were 30 merchant banks, many established during 1994–6. These institutions undertook large amounts of short-term borrowings in international capital markets and then re-lent to firms on a long-term basis, taking advantage of differences in short- and long-term rates.

The resulting shortened debt profile reflects several factors: reduced availability of other funding sources; higher demand for foreign currencies for hedging or speculative purposes; the rolling over of existing credit lines into shorter-term facilities; and perceived arbitrage opportunities between domestic and international interest rates. During the first half of 1997, corporate sector fundraising through the financial markets continued to rise rapidly. This expansion, which occurred despite the deceleration in growth of fixed investment, was bought about by an increased demand for operating funds in response to the slowdown of sales and profitability.

Between 1992 and 1996, international lending to Korea surged by 158%, outpacing the 44% rise in total lending from G10 banks to other developing countries. Outstanding claims on Korean borrowers amounted to just over one-quarter of all loans to East Asia, and 10% of total international claims, at the end of 1996. Loans to the Korean banking sector accounted for 66% of all lending by international banks, while 28% went to the non-bank private sector and 6% went to the public sector. Thus much of the borrowing from foreign banks (at floating rates) was intermediated through the domestic banking sector. Korean banks also invested in foreign assets with funds borrowed from foreign banks and were major investors in the bond markets in Southeast Asia, Russia and Latin America (*Chosun Ilbo* 8 January 1998).

Korean firms and banks had little trouble obtaining international finance. It may be that government bailout promises to domestic financial institutions were perceived by foreign creditors as a form of collateral guaranteeing the safety of their loans. Meanwhile, restrictions on lending at home, by raising the domestic cost of finance, saw firms take advantage of lower interest rates overseas. OECD membership, while largely symbolic, significantly strengthened Korea's credit rating in international financial markets. Between 1994, when Korea passed its first entry test, and December 1996, when it officially joined the OECD, foreign banks more than doubled their lending to Korea, from US$47 billion to US$85 billion (Mo and Moon 1998). Korean banks' spreads over the London Inter-bank Offered Rate (LIBOR) narrowed during 1995–6.

DEVELOPMENTS IN ASSET MARKETS AND THE FINANCIAL SECTOR PRIOR TO THE CRISIS

Financial institutions

There have been significant structural changes in the financial system over the past fifteen years. The market share of banking institutions has shrunk considerably while that of non-bank financial institutions (NBFIs) has grown rapidly. The market share of banking institutions for Korean won deposits fell from 71% in 1980 to 32% in 1996, while that of NBFIs increased from 29% to around 68%. Banking institutions' share of loans and discounts contracted from 63% to 42% between 1980 and 1996, while that of NBFIs expanded from 37% to 58%.

These large shifts in market share were caused by differences in regulatory treatment. NBFIs were established in the 1970s when the government attempted to reduce the importance of the informal credit market by allowing the creation of new institutions. NBFIs were favoured by the regulatory regime. They were allowed greater freedom in their management of assets and liabilities, and could apply higher interest rates on deposits and loans than could banking institutions. The higher returns allowed in the non-bank sector supported substantial gains in market share in the 1980s and 1990s. As a result, NBFIs have a markedly different portfolio structure from that of banks. By the beginning of 1993, NBFIs had invested 30% of their assets in securities (other than equities) – three times as much as banks (OECD 1994: 104).

In 1992, the government outlined a new blueprint for the comprehensive liberalisation of the financial sector. The so-called '1993–97 Financial Sector Reform Plan' was designed to overcome inefficiencies introduced by the non-price allocation of credit in the economy, by opening the financial sector to foreign participation and gradually removing controls on long-term, and later short-term, international capital movements. By the end of 1995, the deregulation program had given almost complete freedom to the domestic financial system to determine its lending and borrowing rates.

But reform of the financial sector was complicated by the fact that the banking system had not adequately dealt with the losses it had suffered during earlier periods of more pervasive government-directed lending. While the government now allowed banks greater discretion in setting interest rates and allocating loans, government control of the banking sector persisted. The asset portfolios of commercial banks were still constrained by specific limits on lending to large companies, and subsidised lending from the central bank still distorted credit markets. Although the commercial banking sector had been largely privately owned since the mid-1980s, the government did not allow it to have full managerial autonomy. As a result, banks continued to have little discretion or incentive to control risk by screening projects and monitoring corporate performance. Insider relationships between banks and borrowers still resulted in lending without regard for rates of return, and at rates below the cost of funding.

Prudential standards

If the banking sector had always been weak, why were the banks not a problem before 1997? Much of the explanation lies with the implicit coinsurance scheme existing among government, banks and industry, and with the lax prudential supervision standards that allowed a sharp deterioration in the quality of the loan portfolios of financial institutions. New lending opportunities for banks and non-banks resulted in a rapid expansion of credit in the first half of the 1990s, with rates of growth of lending to the private sector averaging 17% annually between 1990 and 1996 – well in excess of nominal GDP growth (Corsetti et al. 1998). Korean merchant banks became highly exposed to foreign currency loans in the absence of any prudential regulations regarding their foreign currency operations.

In practice, the government averted the periodic bankruptcy of large enterprises by directing banks to provide relief loans or rescheduling debt (Huh and Kim 1994: 26). To avert bank insolvency, the Bank of Korea (BOK) compensated banks for some of their losses through subsidised rediscounts. Special allowances in financial reporting were often made, creating difficulty in comparing performance with previous years: for example, by not requiring banks to make full provisions for investment securities losses, and by allowing the deferral of foreign exchange losses for Korean corporate accounts.

After the introduction of the financial reform plan, investors probably perceived banks as having become less risky. The plan strengthened prudential controls in various ways. In particular, the 8% BIS capital adequacy ratio for commercial banks was to be compulsory by the end of 1995, and the Office of Bank Supervision announced a new reporting system for commercial banks, designed to give an early warning of emerging problems. While commercial banks had accumulated provisions that exceeded the value of their bad loans by 36% at the end of 1995, and the capital adequacy ratios of commercial banks were two percentage points above the Bank for International Settlements (BIS) requirement, standards of disclosure of non-performing loans were much weaker, and the definition of 'bad loans' was much narrower, than in many OECD countries (OECD 1996: 78–80). By the Korean definition of bad loans, which included only 50% of unrealised securities losses, 22 of its 26 banks met the BIS ratio as of the end of 1997. However, on the assumption of full provisioning for loan losses and marking securities to market, the average capital ratio was 7% at that time. In this case, twelve banks were over the minimum standard and the remaining fourteen (including Korea First Bank and Seoul Bank) were under it.

At least during 1994–6, there was little evidence of banks undertaking cosmetic adjustments to increase their capital ratios by shifting activities off-balance sheet, revaluing reserves, and so on (Song, I. 1998: 30–1). Lending continued to increase, with banks choosing to maintain their traditional support for the expansion of business corporations rather than strengthening their credit evaluation criteria. In addition, banks were constrained in shrinking their loan portfolios as a way of increasing capital adequacy because the domestic loan sale market was not well-developed. Implicit guarantees that banks would not be allowed to fail created an incentive for them to take excessive lending risks, and the introduction of a deposit insurance scheme in 1992 effectively removed the need for depositors to monitor the health of banks. In fact, credit conditions deteriorated after 1992, as indicated by the default rate in the unsecured note market, which rose to a pre-crisis high in 1995 – almost double the level seen in the early 1990s (OECD 1996: 79–80).

Capital markets

Although the share market is well-developed, debt has remained the primary source of external funds, partly reflecting the low default risk perceived by firms which could generally count on government assistance in times of distress. Korea's long-term corporate bond market is active and liquid, being the second-largest in East Asia, behind Japan. However, past administrative controls have led to a lack of innovation in other capital markets. For government bonds, the primary market has been based on administrative allocation rather than competitive bidding, while the small size and heterogeneity of the bond issues has not allowed the development of an efficient and liquid market (OECD 1996: 49–50). This in turn has inhibited the development of innovative financial instruments such as bond and interest rate futures.

Share market capitalisation is higher than in many OECD countries. Prior to the crisis, government controls had resulted in an equity market that was segmented between residents and non-residents, given that direct access by foreigners to the share market was allowed only from 1992. By 1996 foreigners owned 11.6% of stocks listed on the KSE, compared with 4.1% in 1992.

International capital flows

The pace of deregulation of international capital flows has been slower, proceeding in a manner closely linked to macroeconomic developments. In this way, the government has been able to maintain some control over domestic monetary aggregates while achieving a relatively stable exchange rate. The government has always been reluctant to allow the liberalisation of Korea's financial system to proceed too fast, fearing that an inflow of foreign funds would push up the nominal and real exchange rates and undermine competitiveness.

Nonetheless, by the end of 1995, three principal changes to regulations governing long-term capital flows implemented between 1993 and 1995 had generated considerable net capital inflows. The limit on foreign owner-ship of the stock of a company was raised to 15%; companies were permit-ted to borrow from international banks for the purposes of financing capital goods imports (both directly, and through authorised Korean banks); and constraints on the ownership of foreign currency deposits were eased.

Despite progress in the deregulation of capital flows, Korea's regulations remained extensive for a country whose share in international trade was so large. For instance, investments in foreign bond markets were restrained, and non-residents had limited access to domestic bond markets and were subject to equity ownership ceilings in listed Korean companies. These re-strictions have meant that Korean interest rates have remained well above world market rates.

Controls on short-term capital flows remained more strict than those on long-term capital transactions. In general, the won could only be purchased for approved purposes – primarily, current account operations and permit-ted capital transactions (OECD 1996: 55).

Exchange rate regime

The exchange rate system has been modified several times. In 1981 the pegged rate against the dollar was replaced by a system relying on a basket of currencies, with a heavy weighting for the US dollar and the yen. In March 1990, the government moved to a more flexible 'market average sys-tem', whereby the official won/dollar rate was determined by market forces in the interbank foreign exchange market. The new rate was a weighted average of the market exchange rates used in all transactions of the previous day, with the weight being the volume of each transaction. Under this sys-tem, the exchange rate was allowed to fluctuate within ±0.4% of the previ-ous day's market average rate. Since then the daily fluctuation band has been gradually widened, such that prior to the crisis the exchange rate was allowed to fluctuate by up to 2.25% per day.

Official intervention, combined with changes to the capital flow regula-tions during the past decade, has resulted in stability of the US dollar ex-change rate. Between 1981 and 1995, this remained within ±10% of its average in that period (OECD 1996: 73). The won depreciated in nominal terms from 1990 until the beginning of 1993 (from 700 to almost 800 won per US dollar), then traded in a very narrow range of 800 to 770 won per US dollar between 1993 and mid-1996. From mid-1996 to October 1997, just prior to the crisis, the won had depreciated gradually from 800 to around 900 won per US dollar.

IMPACT OF THE CRISIS

Even in mid-July 1997, Korea's broad macroeconomic indicators appeared favourable. Real GDP growth had averaged more than 6% annually during the first half of 1997; the current account deficit had narrowed and would fall to 2% of GDP in 1997; and fiscal policy remained prudent, recording only a small deficit. However, operating in a slowing economy and unable to generate sufficient cash flow to service their short-term debts, eight of the top 30 *chaebol* had effectively become insolvent by July 1997. In the first six months of 1997, net earnings of companies listed on the stock exchange fell 28%. Following the collapse of Hanbo Steel in January, the interest rates over the LIBOR that banks and firms had to pay in the international money market rose – albeit slightly – to 0.20%, from an average of 0.15–0.18% in the previous December. A series of corporate bankruptcies and corruption scandals – combined with industrial unrest in January, as workers protested against a new law making it easier to lay off staff – saw consumer and business confidence fall throughout 1997. The effects eventually spilled over into the real sector. By the last quarter of 1997, growth had slowed to 3.9%.

Financial sector

Reflecting the debt servicing difficulties of the corporate sector, ten of Korea's 26 commercial banks posted losses in the first half of 1997. In response, the government announced a reform package for the financial sector in July that included a government injection of US$4.4 billion into the banking system. By the end of October 1997, the total amount of bad loans held by suspended merchant banks was US$4.2 billion, or 51% of their total loans. Corporate failures prompted the banks to begin redeeming commercial paper discounted by merchant banks, which in turn called in their short-term loans to companies. To offset the impact of these moves, banks were instructed by the government to extend the maturity of commercial paper from merchant banks and provide call loans.

Exchange rate

Prior to the crisis the won was not fully convertible, making it harder for investors to sell Korean assets. Onshore trading of the won had to be backed by real economic transactions such as settlements of import bills, and the currency was only tradable among Korean domestic entities. The won started to weaken rapidly in October as corporate failures continued to mount. Market nervousness about the true level of the central bank's net foreign exchange reserves, combined with a contagion effect from Southeast Asia, also prompted selling of the currency. Official reserves stood at US$31 billion at end-October, slightly below the level recommended by the

International Monetary Fund (IMF). Unofficially, though, the central bank had been buying won with forward contracts since February. In October and November the government spent close to US$15 billion to prop up the won in foreign exchange markets. When Korea called in the IMF on 21 November, dollar reserves had fallen to just US$7.3 billion. By the time stand-by credit negotiations were concluded on 4 December, Korea's 'useable' reserves stood at only US$5 billion.

It is difficult to tell whether Korea would have ended up in a crisis without the contagion from Southeast Asia. After starting the year at 844 won to the US dollar, the exchange rate fell to 915 by September, a depreciation of only 8%. But by October, with six major currencies in the region having devalued by an average of 40%, the won could not maintain a parity that had become out of line with fundamentals. Moreover, Singapore and Taiwan had allowed their currencies to depreciate, rather than defend their parities, putting Korea at a serious competitive disadvantage (Corsetti et al. 1998: 62–3). Concern about debt servicing might explain why the Korean government did not devalue earlier. At the height of the crisis in December, the proportion of non-performing loans in the banking system was estimated to be 15–18%, or 7.5% of GDP (IMF 1997b).[3] The falling exchange rate caused banks to struggle to roll over huge amounts of short-term debt denominated in US dollars.

By early November the markets were speculating that Korea would have to go to the IMF if it continued to expend reserves defending the won. In response to further downward pressures on the currency, the BOK widened the trading band from 2.25% to 10% on 19 November, and finally scrapped the limit on 16 December. However, during this period the biggest sellers of the won were not speculators but local firms trying to hedge or repay debts denominated in US dollars. In addition to having sold forward a large portion of its reserves, the BOK had run down reserves by extending support to banks experiencing difficulties borrowing abroad.

Between 21 November, when the IMF was called in, and the signing of an agreement on 3 December, the currency continued to fall as doubts arose about the authorities' commitment to making needed adjustments. Some of the first measures implemented under the IMF agreement were the suspension of the activities, and later closure, of fourteen merchant banks; the raising of the limit on aggregate foreign ownership of listed stocks to 50%; and the tightening of monetary policy, on 22 December, which involved raising the cap on interest rates from 25% to 40%.

The rise in interest rates occurred after the fall in the won had already increased the external liabilities of borrowers, and increased the level of non-performing loans. In the end, corporate Korea faced a classic liquidity crunch – a bunching of foreign loan repayments without the foreign currency to meet them. The burden of debt servicing among banks and non-banks was worsened by the depreciation of the currency: financial institutions began to go bankrupt, and a financial panic ensued. An increasing flow of information about the size of foreign liabilities and the extent of non-performing loans made it clear that implicit guarantees of a bailout were no longer credible. All of this, combined with the disclosure of statistical information that revealed that the financial problems faced by firms and financial institutions were much greater than originally believed, saw foreign banks starting to refuse to roll over loans that otherwise would have been renewed automatically. This led to financial panic wherein the currency collapsed by 40% between mid-December and the end of the year (Corsetti et al. 1998: 66). The share market, which had declined by a modest 15% between January and October, had fallen 50% by the end of December.

Political instability

These events coincided with the lead-up to a presidential election on 18 December, which meant that the system was paralysed just when some of the toughest decisions in the country's history were required. In the months prior to the election, the government's complacency in the face of corporate bankruptcies and mounting bad debts had exacerbated market jitters. During November it attempted to smooth over the crisis by raising the foreign share ownership limit marginally from 23% to 26%, raising the ceiling on foreign ownership of corporate bonds to 30%, widening the currency fluctuation band, and establishing a bailout fund to purchase bad loans from banks. The government was also paralysed by bureaucratic infighting between the Ministry of Finance and Economy and the BOK regarding control over monetary policy and the supervision of financial institutions. The parliament's failure to pass a major financial reform bill on the last sitting day before the election became a crucial turning point for the markets, which had been looking for government action. Then, just prior to the election, candidates Kim Dae-jung and Rhee In Je declared their intention to renegotiate the terms of the IMF agreement if they were elected. This caused the won to dive by 10% on two consecutive days, prompting President Kim Young-sam to seek written commitments from all election contenders to uphold the IMF agreement.

After Kim Dae-jung's election the currency and the share market continued to plummet, as markets remained nervous about his stated intention to renegotiate the terms of the IMF agreement. On 23 December, the won fell to an historic low of 1,962 to the US dollar, less than half its value only two months before. The share market index plunged 7.5% to a record low of 366. The circuit breaker was Kim Dae-jung's eventual clear signalling of his intention to support the US$57 billion IMF package. Kim then launched a personal diplomacy drive, promising wide-ranging reform in return for increased investment.

ECONOMIC RESPONSE TO THE POLICY ADJUSTMENT

The situation eased at the end of December when the National Assembly passed key financial reform bills and, faced with the prospect of a default by an OECD economy, international banks jointly agreed to negotiate the rolling over of US$24 billion worth of short-term loans due by March 1998. Earlier, on 22 December, the US Federal Reserve had called in leading US banks and urged them to coordinate a program of short-term loan rollovers and longer-term debt restructuring among European, Japanese and US banks, warning that a debt moratorium in Korea would pose a systemic risk to the world financial system because of the perceived high exposure to Korea of Japanese banks (P. Lee 1998). By the end of January 1998, international banks had agreed to exchange their loans to commercial, and certain merchant, banks for one- to three-year loans carrying Korean sovereign guarantees. Importantly, Korean officials then embarked on a global road show, selling the government's commitment to the reform task as it sought to roll over its debt. Around mid-February, Korea's sovereign credit rating was raised to one notch below investment grade. As a result, foreign lenders began to resume credit lines to a few healthy institutions. By mid-April the exchange rate had stabilised at 1,400 won to the US dollar, and foreign reserves had increased to US$30 billion. After rebounding sharply in the first quarter of 1998, the share market then slumped to an eleven-year low by the end of May. Periodic corporate debt crises and the fallout from financial sector restructuring will result in further volatile movements in the share market index.

Real sector

Growth will turn negative in 1998 in response to subdued demand in Japan and the rest of East Asia, which takes about half of Korea's exports. A severe contraction in consumption and investment will outweigh the gains from a weak won. Reflecting this, output fell by 3.8% in the first quarter of 1998. Private consumption fell by −10%, while fixed capital formation recorded negative growth of −23%.

If the exchange rates of May persist, the current account surplus could exceed 5% of GDP in 1998. While the weak currency should substantially boost competitiveness, to date the surplus is being driven by sharply falling imports and invisibles rather than strong export growth. Imports began to decline during the third quarter of 1997, when the deepening business slump put a brake on fixed investment. Merchandise imports were down by more than 50% in the first quarter of 1998, compared to the same period in 1997, also reflecting the reluctance of banks to accept letters of credit. While merchandise exports grew by 30% in volume terms in the first quarter of 1998, weak prices for Korea's key items, such as steel and semiconductors, resulted in only single-digit growth in value terms. The slump in domestic demand, a curtailing of imports of materials required by export industries, and the domestic liquidity crunch are all impacting on exports. The weak yen will also undermine an export recovery, given that Korea and Japan compete in third country markets.

The weakened won is giving rise to considerable inflationary pressures, given Korea's heavy reliance on imports of raw materials and food. In the first quarter of 1998 consumer price inflation was around 9%, while over the same period in 1997 producer prices had increased by 17%. Manufacturing plants that were operating at 83% of capacity in April 1997 had slumped to 65% by April 1998. The sectors most affected by the slowdown were steel, petrochemicals, machinery, automobiles and consumer electronics. These sectors have completed large-scale facility investments, have considerable excess capacity, and are the most highly geared.

Monetary and fiscal policy

Monetary policy will be kept tight in the short term, to attract capital and to keep inflation below the target of 9%. This places great pressure on a weak corporate sector. High interest rates in particular are squeezing the small and medium-sized business sector, with the BOK reporting 10,000 bankruptcies in the first quarter of 1998, compared with nearly 14,000 for all of 1997. By April, interest rates on three-year bonds had fallen to 18%, from 29% at the end of December, while call rates had fallen to 18% from 31%.

Although initially contractionary, fiscal policy progressively became more flexible to support financial and corporate sector restructuring. The IMF agreement initially called for offsetting measures, amounting to about 1.5% of GDP, to achieve a balanced budget or a small surplus for 1998. The Korean government itself initially insisted on an even tighter fiscal policy, with 1998 budget expenditure rising by only 3.3%, the lowest increase in 25 years. In May 1998, the fiscal deficit was raised to 1.2% of GDP from 0.8%. Despite the substantial costs of financial sector restructuring, Korea's past fiscal prudence means there is considerable scope for fiscal expansion in order to cushion the social adjustment that is going to accompany reform. Rising unemployment is emerging as a major economic and social concern: it had more than doubled from 2.6% in 1997 to 6.7% by April 1998. In a country without a well-developed social welfare system, the social and political ramifications of this could be far-reaching.

Korea's last experience of negative growth was also preceded by overheating resulting from an investment boom, wage pressures, and problems in the financial sector. The government's initial response to this 1980 crisis was the opposite of its response to the current one, and was at odds with IMF advice at the time, which recommended contractionary fiscal and monetary policy during 1980–2 (Haggard and Collins 1994). Interest rates were first raised to dampen inflationary pressures, but then gradually reduced from June 1980 to counteract the effects of recession. The money supply was expanded and the corporate tax rate was cut. Fiscal policy was strongly expansionary in 1981, with the budget deficit at 4% of GDP. It was not until 1983–4 that the government resumed stronger stabilisation policies and accelerated structural reform. An important difference between 1980 and 1997 is that in 1980, Korea, having ample foreign exchange, had little problem servicing its debt: in 1979, short-term borrowings comprised only 27% of the total. In the current crisis there is also greater doubt about the strength of export recovery, given Korea's heavy reliance on the international economy.

Financial sector

The requirement that the commercial banks meet the BIS risk-adjusted capital adequacy ratio of 8% before June 2000 is adding a new dimension to Korea's credit squeeze. At the end of 1997, fourteen of the commercial banks did not meet this ratio. In order to meet the target, banks will have to increase their equity capital, issue subordinate bonds and/or increase capital through asset revaluation. Mergers and acquisitions will also play an important role in recapitalising viable banks, although this is likely to meet with considerable resistance from both management and labour.

The capital account is to be dramatically liberalised. All restrictions on foreign access to the short-term capital market were lifted as of 1 January 1998. Restrictions on long-term capital flows will be liberalised throughout 1998. The opening of financial markets to greater foreign participation will improve their functioning, reduce long-term real rates, and add to the financial stability of the business sector by reducing its dependence on debt finance.

Korea is now entering a new era of monetary management. Before the crisis, the authorities had been able to combine some control over domestic monetary growth with stability of the US dollar exchange rate by means of sterilisation. The opening of the capital account will present new challenges to the government in its efforts to maintain export growth if this results in significantly increased capital inflow. Short-term interest rate developments will influence movements in the exchange rate to a much greater extent than they have in the past. In particular, the transmission mechanism will change as price becomes a more important consideration than the availability of rationed credit. The IMF requirement that the central bank shift from monetary targeting towards a medium-term inflation objective would seem appropriate, given that the demand for money had become increasingly unstable as competition among financial institutions intensified, contributing to volatile short-term interest rates.

IMPACT ON DOMESTIC POLICY DEBATE

Korea's commitment to the IMF package has clearly been crucial in restoring confidence. Korea differs from its Southeast Asian neighbours in that the US–Korea security alliance, along with Kim Dae-jung's close ties with successive US administrations, has been an important factor reinforcing Korea's commitment to the IMF package.

Provided reform proceeds relatively smoothly, Korea's economy should return to stable growth more quickly than the other troubled economies. Despite the crisis, Korea's economy has great underlying industrial strength, and one of the most highly educated and motivated workforces in the world. There are no guarantees that the reforms will proceed smoothly, however. They involve an overhaul of the financial system, austere fiscal and monetary measures, an opening of business operations to external scrutiny, reform of the labour market, and the removal of barriers to domestic markets. There are real risks of increased economic nationalism as reforms continue to bite, and of large-scale labour unrest in response to lay-offs and foreign takeovers. There are also doubts about Korea's ability to sustain a political consensus on reform. In particular, the alliance of convenience between the coalition ruling parties could easily unravel and see the economic restructuring process lose momentum.

The transition process is likely to be characterised by large-scale corporate and financial bankruptcies. However, the key to restoring confidence lies in the rapid restructuring of the financial system. This, in turn, requires both a clear signal from the government that it will cease providing emergency loans towards failing banks and firms, and stronger enforcement of bankruptcy laws. Big business is also likely to resist pressure to restructure – especially calls for dilution of family control. The *chaebol* are required to sell marginal subsidiaries and focus on their core businesses. They are also required to lower their debt-to-equity ratios, to concentrate on profitability rather than expansion, and to adopt internationally accepted accounting practices. Kim Dae-jung's major challenge will be to ensure that the *chaebol* do not back away from these commitments to reform.

While the arrival of the IMF in Seoul was viewed by many Koreans as 'capitulation to IMF trusteeship', most of the key reforms contained in the IMF agreement have been on the economic agenda of the Korean government for years – notably, cleaning up the financial system, slimming the *chaebol*, and introducing greater transparency in corporate governance. While the seeds were sown in the early 1970s, in the final analysis, blame for the crisis is likely to rest with Kim Young-sam. In almost every area of reform his administration oscillated between pursuing reform and maintaining the status quo.

While there may be 'overkill' in the IMF agreement, the need to entrench reform overrides such concerns, for two reasons. The first is the need to finally restructure the financial and industrial system that is stifling Korea's international competitiveness: Korea needs a new economic paradigm to sustain its competitiveness into the next century. The second reason involves North Korea. Regardless of the form unification may take, Korea needs to put more effort into preparing its economy for the impact of unification. This requires substantial fiscal and financial sector restructuring and reform.

The hardest reforms involve changes in culture and in processes that have been fundamental to the Korean way of doing business, and building institutional structures supportive of growth. These will include developing standards of disclosure that prevent future problems from building up undetected, and investing in the training of a new generation of Korean officials. For now, Kim Dae-jung has credibility with the groups most severely affected by the crisis, but he is likely to encounter considerable resistance from the two groups upon which Korea has been built, namely the *chaebol* and bureaucracy.

NOTES

The author is grateful to Dr Jae-Jung Kwon for helpful comments and suggestions.

1   By the beginning of 1995, the share of business sector non-residential investment in GDP had reached a record high of 25%, well above even Japan's record in the high-growth period of the 1960s (OECD 1996: 18).
2   As part of the IMF agreement, Korea changed its definition of external liabilities to include the foreign borrowings of overseas branches and subsidiaries of financial institutions, and the offshore borrowings of financial institutions.
3   If calculated on a six-month rather than three-month non-payment basis, at the end of 1997 non-performing loans of commercial banks without collateral represented 2.7% of all loans, or 6% if those with collateral are included.

5 Malaysia

Prema-chandra Athukorala

INTRODUCTION

Malaysia did not look especially vulnerable when the floating of the Thai baht sparked the financial crisis in East Asia in July 1997. The Malaysian economy had experienced virtually full employment for the previous six years and modest inflation (4.5%). The country's foreign currency sovereign credit rating was an A+, in the same league as Hong Kong.[1] It also had a continuing high inflow of long-term capital, as opposed to Thailand's short-term capital inflows. With a very low non-performing loan ratio and a high capital adequacy ratio, the Malaysian banking system looked fairly robust. In terms of political stability and policy continuity, Malaysia appeared much better off than Thailand and the other crisis economies.

Yet the crisis hit Malaysia with ferocity. Its currency, the ringgit, recorded a loss of almost 50% of its exchange value against the US dollar at its lowest point (7 January 1998), compared with the average value for June 1997. The stock market experienced the biggest plunge of the crisis countries, losing over 65% of its capitalisation during this period. The currency and the stock markets began to recover from about mid-January, but the full impact of the blow to the real economy was yet to be felt by May 1998. The official growth forecast for 1998 has been revised downward three times since the onset of the crisis; the latest forecast is between 2% and 3%, compared with an average growth rate of over 8% for the past nine years.

What happened to Malaysia? Did it simply fall victim to a wild speculative attack in the wake of the Thai crisis, or were there some fundamental weaknesses in the pre-crisis Malaysian economy that made it vulnerable to the Thai contagion? What has been the role of policy in the recovery process, and what triggered particular policy responses? Has recovery been delayed by inappropriate policy responses? What are the future growth prospects? This chapter sets out to answer these and related questions, while laying the groundwork for deriving general lessons for other countries from the Malaysian experience.

SIGNS OF VULNERABILITY

An international financial crisis occurs when foreign asset holders try to dump assets, usually securities or bank deposits denominated in a given currency (Kindleberger 1992). A country succumbs to such a crisis from a situation of vulnerability, in which there is real room for a difference of opinion about its ability to defend the currency in the event of a speculative attack (Dornbusch et al. 1995; Dornbusch 1997). A state of vulnerability by itself does not give rise to a crisis. There needs to be a certain disturbance – a trigger – that will convert a vulnerable situation into an actual collapse. Some likely disturbances are policy errors, such as a minor devaluation in the context of a significant and persistent overvaluation of the real exchange rate, depletion of reserves after a prolonged period of backing the currency, failure to implement a promised policy reform, or simply contagion – investor panic spreading from a neighbouring crisis country. It is possible for a currency to come under speculative attack despite sound domestic economic fundamentals, because of speculators' wrong market calculations or because of other arbitrary and unpredictable factors that cause a shift in expectations (Kindleberger 1989; Obstfeld 1994a). However, a country is able to shrug off such an attack if it is not in a state of vulnerability – assuming of course that the unexpected attack does not cause panic, resulting in serious policy errors.

There is a sizeable body of literature on vulnerability to financial crises,[2] and when Malaysia's macroeconomic performance prior to the recent crisis is closely examined in the light of this literature, there is considerable evidence that it succumbed to the Thai contagion because its economy had developed considerable vulnerability to speculative attack. There were a number of clear signs of vulnerability: a significant appreciation of the real exchange rate (suggesting a deterioration in international competitiveness), a build-up of short-term foreign borrowings, a low level of reserves, and some fundamental weaknesses in the financial system.

Real exchange rate

Persistent appreciation of the real exchange rate (adjusted for fundamentals) has been identified as a major factor in setting the scene for a crisis (Goldfajn and Valdes 1997b; Kaminsky et al. 1997a; Sachs et al. 1996). Such appreciation implies that a country's economic fundamentals may not allow a successful defence of its currency in the event of a speculative attack.

There is no unique way of measuring the real exchange rate. Three alternative indicators are presented in Figure 5.1. The first (RER1) is the JP Morgan index, which measures changes in non-food producer prices in Malaysia's trading partners relative to producer prices in Malaysia, as measured in a common currency. It is an indicator of the international

Figure 5.1   Malaysia: alternative real exchange rate indices, 1984–98Q1 (1990 = 100)

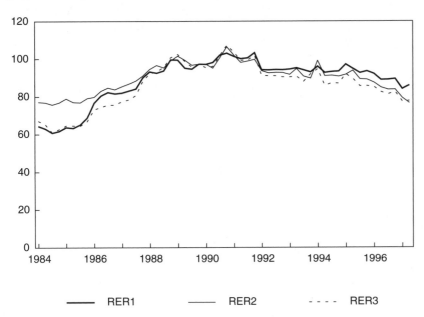

Notes:
RER1: J.P. Morgan Index: non-food producer price in Malaysia's trading partners in ringgit relative to producer price in Malaysia.
RER2: Producer price in Malaysia's ten leading trading partners in ringgit relative to consumer price in Malaysia.
RER3: Price of traded goods relative to that of non-traded goods, derived from Malaysian CPI sub-indices.
Source: RER1: J.P. Morgan web site <http://www.jpmorgan.com>; RER2 and RER3: author's computation based on data from IMF, *International Financial Statistics* (various issues) and BNM, *Monthly Bulletin of Statistics* (various issues).

competitiveness of traded goods produced in Malaysia. The second index (RER2) differs from the first in that domestic prices are measured in terms of the consumer price index (CPI). It is therefore a rough proxy of the price ratio of traded goods relative to non-traded goods. The third index is similar to the second, but it has been derived directly from the sub-indices of the CPI (as the ratio of the composite price index of non-food traded goods to that of non-traded goods). All three indices have been constructed in such a way that an increase implies a real depreciation (i.e. an increase in competitiveness).[3]

All tell a similar story: the real exchange rate has steadily appreciated over the past three years or so. And the degree of appreciation is sharper in terms of RER2 and RER3, which are better measures of the resource allocation implications of macroeconomic imbalance than RER1. In terms of all three measures, by the first quarter of 1997 the real exchange rate had reached a level lower than that which prevailed in 1987, when the recent high-growth phase of the Malaysian economy began. The observed difference in relative price shifts reflected in RER1 compared with that of RER2 and RER3 can be explained in terms of the ongoing process of trade liberalisation and increased foreign investment. With the rapid integration of the economy with the world economy because of these forces, RER1 (which compares world and domestic tradable prices) has begun to move closely with world prices, while RER2 and RER3 (which compare world tradable prices with combined domestic tradable and non-tradable prices) are driven predominantly by the behaviour of non-tradable prices, reflecting changes in domestic demand.[4]

Of course, a real appreciation during a given period should not be confused with exchange rate overvaluation (misalignment). If a country borrows to invest and/or attracts significant foreign direct investment (FDI), such capital inflow naturally strengthens the currency in real terms – which is the expected effect of an inward transfer. An appreciation can also be a reflection of deep reforms that open up large and lasting opportunities for economic expansion. The 'Balassa-Samuelson' effect – long-term improvement in productivity which normally has a greater cost-lowering effect on tradables than on non-tradables – can be another factor. Real appreciation due to these factors should not cause concern about the macro-economic health of the economy. But in the Malaysian case, there are clear indications that the interaction of exchange rate policy and fiscal expansion, rather than these 'natural' factors, bears much of the responsibility for the recent real exchange appreciation.

In the area of foreign exchange management, throughout the post-independence period (from 1958), Malaysia has maintained a unified exchange rate and free convertibility of the ringgit on current account transactions. Notwithstanding the demise of the universal fixed exchange regime of the Bretton Woods system in the early 1970s, it continued to maintain a fixed parity against the US dollar for over five years. In 1978, in response to large fluctuations in the dollar vis-à-vis other industrial country currencies, Malaysia (following similar moves by Thailand, Korea and Indonesia) switched its peg from the dollar to a currency basket. As part of a macro-economic adjustment package introduced in 1986, greater flexibility was introduced to the basket peg. This policy change, coupled with better macroeconomic management and the rapid appreciation of the yen against the US dollar (the intervention currency in the managed float), was reflected in a significant depreciation of the real exchange rate in the late 1980s, aiding the process of FDI-led export-oriented industrialisation (Figure 5.1).

From about mid-1994 until July 1997, there was a gradual nominal appreciation of the ringgit (on a trade-weighted basis), for two reasons. One was the intensification of foreign exchange market intervention by Bank Negara Malaysia (BNM, the central bank) in the hope that it would provide a quick-fix solution to inflation. The other was the recent appreciation of the US dollar (the dominant currency in the basket of currencies to which the ringgit was pegged) against the other major currencies – in particular, the yen and the deutschmark.

The impact of nominal exchange rate appreciation on the real exchange rate was compounded by increases in prices of non-tradables caused by domestic demand pressure, emanating largely from massive government expenditure on infrastructure projects.[5] Over many years (except during the period 1981–6 when Malaysia experienced a major macroeconomic crisis, triggered by a public investment boom), the government has maintained a reputation for sound fiscal policies. However, the period following Prime Minister Mahathir's Vision 2020 statement early in this decade has been characterised by some fiscal excesses, the intensity of which has increased over the years. Reflecting the 'big growth push' to propel Malaysia to developed-country status by the year 2020, public investment expenditure surged, pushing the total investment to gross domestic product (GDP) ratio to 46% in 1997, the highest in the region. Throughout the 1990s, there has been a continuous increase in the share of investment in domestic aggregate expenditure, from about 35% early in the decade to over 46% in 1997. The public sector contribution to the annual increase in total investment jumped from 3.5% in 1996 to over 32% in 1997. Given the increased emphasis on construction and infrastructure projects, the non-tradable component of these expenditures is likely to have increased over the years.

Short-term foreign borrowings

There has not been a massive build-up of overseas debt in Malaysia. Unlike in Thailand and Indonesia, foreign capital inflows to Malaysia over the past ten years have been dominated by foreign direct investment rather than short-term private sector borrowings and other portfolio investment. However, prior to the onset of the financial crisis, there was a significant increase in the net inflow of private short-term capital (Table 5.1). These inflows, which were driven primarily by the boom in the Malaysian share market, accounted for 43.3% of total annual capital inflow by the end of 1996, compared with 13.2% in the previous year. Increased reliance on short-term capital naturally increases the vulnerability of a currency to speculative attack, because such investments can turn around very quickly and leave the country facing pressure for devaluation.

Foreign exchange reserves

The amount of foreign exchange reserves at hand is a key determinant of a country's ability to fight a speculative run on its currency. In the context of

Table 5.1 Malaysia: components of net capital inflow, 1986–97 (%)

	1986–9[a]	1990–4[a]	1995	1996	1997
Official long-term capital	39.4	18.5	32.1	3.1	115.4
Private capital	60.6	81.5	67.9	96.9	−15.4
Direct foreign investment	24.7	72.7	54.7	53.6	271.0
Private short-term capital[b]	35.9	8.8	13.2	43.3	−286.4
Total	100.0	100.0	100.0	100.0	100.0
Total (US$ billion)	0.2	6.7	7.7	9.5	1.7

Notes:
a Annual average.
b Including portfolio investment.
Source: BNM, *Annual Report* (various issues).

a financial crisis, not only do gross capital inflows dry up but also holders of liquid domestic liabilities try to convert them into foreign exchange and flee the country. In any analysis of a country's vulnerability to a panic, the strength of its reserve position has, therefore, to be assessed against a broader measure of liquid money assets. Of various such measures, M2 (currency plus demand, time and savings deposits in commercial banks) is considered to be a 'compromise' measure of liquid money assets for this purpose (Calvo 1995; Sachs et al. 1996).[6]

Figure 5.2 depicts the M2–reserve ratio ('reserve inadequacy index') for Malaysia for the period 1985–June 1997. An increase in this ratio points to a decrease in the country's ability to defend its currency or an increase in the currency's vulnerability to a speculative attack. By June 1997, the ratio stood at 4.7, compared with around 3.0 at the beginning of the decade. The increase was particularly rapid in the years immediately prior to the crisis. The most important factor behind the increase in the ratio was rapid growth in M2, which in turn was largely a reflection of rapid expansion of back credit to the private sector. At the same time, the growth of the country's foreign reserves (measured in US$) was constrained by rapid import growth fuelled largely by massive construction projects, a slowing of export growth (from the latter half of 1995) reflecting the adverse demand conditions faced by electronics exports, and a rapid expansion of investment overseas. The last factor was perhaps the most important. From a modest start in early 1990, total FDI outflows from Malaysia increased to over US$3.5 billion (more than 50% of total FDI inflows) by mid-1997. This was predominantly, if not solely, the outcome of an aggressive investment promotion campaign by the Malaysian government (with direct involvement by the prime minister), rather than a reflection of local firms expanding their operations overseas as a 'natural' response to global business opportunities (Athukorala 1997).

Figure 5.2   Malaysia: ratio of M2 to foreign reserves, 1985–June 1997

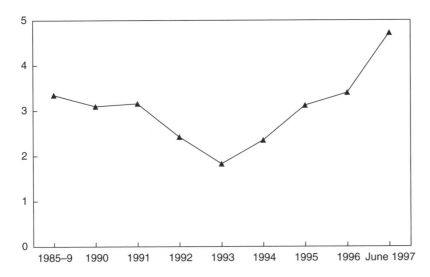

Source: BNM, *Annual Report* (various issues).

Financial sector problems

The Malaysian banking system is generally sturdier than most in the region (BNM 1994; Yusof et al. 1994). From lessons learnt from the mid-1980s economic crisis (when there were some bank failures), BNM has developed an early warning system to detect troubled banks and to police the banking system. Thanks to these measures, non-performing loans (those three months or more in arrears) in the banking system fell from 5.5% in 1995 to 3.9% in 1996, far below the critical level of 15–16% used by the Bank for International Settlements (BIS) to identify troubled banking sub-systems. (Banking systems in Indonesia, Thailand and Korea had surpassed this limit at the time of the onset of the currency crisis.) Capital adequacy ratios maintained by the Malaysian banks are the highest in Southeast Asia, other than Singapore. BNM also requires banks to maintain a general loss reserve amounting to 1% of total outstanding loans, in addition to provisions made for specific problem loans. By mid-1997, the average capital adequacy ratios for commercial banks, merchant banks and finance companies were 11.8%, 13.3% and 10.6% respectively, compared with the BIS international standard of 8% for the overall financial system.[7]

Despite this apparent soundness, the Malaysian banking system had developed two signs of weakening prudential norms during the three or four years prior to the onset of the crisis: rapid expansion of bank loans, and heavy exposure to the property sector (broadly defined to include real estate, construction and share trading).

Figure 5.3   Malaysia: bank credit to the private sector[a] relative to GDP (%) and
growth (% p.a.), 1985–June 1997

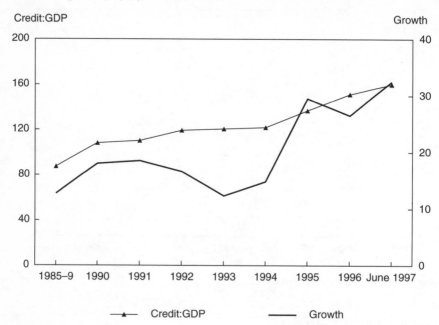

Note:
a End of year balance.
Source: BNM, *Annual Report* (various issues).

The annual rate of growth of bank lending to the private sector increased
continuously, from 18% in 1990 to 33.5% in 1997 (Figure 5.3). The level
of outstanding credit relative to GDP increased from an average of 85%
during 1985–9 to 120% in 1994, and then to over 160% at the time the
financial crisis broke in mid-1997. At that time, Malaysia had the highest
credit build-up among the four crisis countries.[8] Speculators consider a
massive credit build-up of this nature as an indicator of policymakers'
reluctance to use interest rates as a policy tool in the event of a speculative
attack on the currency. Also, rapid build-up of credit in a short period may
imply a growing share of lending to less creditworthy borrowers, and therefore a sign of weakening in the banking system.

Rapid credit expansion was accompanied by a sharp increase in the share
of total credit going to the property sector. By the end of 1996, this sector
accounted for over 45% of total outstanding bank credit. It is believed that
this share would be much higher (around 55%) if unclassified loans to conglomerates, which are often used to finance property, were taken into account. The increased exposure to the property sector eventually weakened
the financial position of the banks, as this lending led to a property glut.[9]
BNM began to pay attention to this sign of vulnerability in the banking sys-

tem only about three months before the crisis. In March 1997, Dr Ahmad Don, the governor of the bank, warned that rapid credit expansion to the sector was a clear threat to the stability of the banking system. He further noted that this 'concern is predicated on the lessons of the last recession in the region in the mid-1980s, as well as recent developments in the region, in particular Thailand'. In the same month, BNM imposed a limit of 20% on the share of new lending for property and share market transactions in total new lending as a pre-emptive prudential effort to prevent a Thai-style banking collapse (*Far Eastern Economic Review* 10 April 1998: 60).

The long silence of BNM on this issue is presumably related to the fact that much of the recent expansion of bank lending to these activities had taken the form of 'connected (state-directed) lending' rooted in the long-standing intimate link between the government and business. As part of the strategy of restructuring business ownership under the New Economic Policy (introduced in 1970 and replaced by the National Development Policy in 1986), the Malaysian government has throughout influenced bank lending activities (Gomez and Jomo 1997). Such influence gained added impetus under Dr Mahathir's 'big push' towards the year 2020. Off-budget financial support, mostly in the form of government-sponsored bank loans, has been a key element of the incentive package offered to industrialists, property developers and Malaysian companies investing overseas, as part of this ambitious growth strategy (Holloway 1997).

Quite apart from the massive credit accumulation with an increased exposure to the property sector, the ability of the Malaysian banking system to face a crisis had presumably been weakened over the years because of the growing dominance of local, relative to foreign, banks. It has been national policy that local banks should dominate. Several decades ago, BNM ruled that only local banks could open new branches in the country. With the foreign banks' network frozen, new deposits gravitated towards their local competitors. Consequently, the share of foreign banks in total bank deposits declined from over 80% in the early 1970s to a mere 30% by the mid-1990s.

There had been a rapid expansion in the share market in Malaysia from the late 1980s. By the mid-1990s, with a market capitalisation of around US$200 billion, the Kuala Lumpur Stock Exchange (KLSE) was the third largest in the Asia Pacific region, after Tokyo and Hong Kong. In relation to the level of GDP, stock market capitalisation (over 300% of GDP) was substantially higher than anywhere at any time (Henderson 1998: 21). Rapid expansion of the share market has not been matched, however, by initiatives to redress underlying weaknesses of corporate governance.[10] Most of the listed companies in Malaysia are tightly controlled by a handful of powerful families. Moreover, in many cases the interests of company bosses and politicians are closely interwoven. The manipulation of inter-company share transactions in order to augment profit in privately owned companies at the expense of listed companies has been a common occurrence in the

Malaysian corporate world. Such malpractice makes share trading vulnerable to financial panic because unconnected (minority) shareholders have every reason to worry about how they would be treated in the event of a market downturn.

ONSET OF THE CRISIS

For over five years prior to the onset of the East Asian crisis, the exchange rate of the ringgit varied in the narrow range of 2.36 to 2.51 ringgits per US dollar. When the Thai baht came under heavy speculative attack in mid-May 1997, the ringgit also experienced heavy selling pressure. BNM responded with massive foreign exchange market intervention, selling close to US$1.5 billion to prop up the currency. The bank also orchestrated a liquidity squeeze in the swap market to stem short-selling of the currency. The intervention was successful, and the ringgit appreciated to 2.47 by the end of the month.

BNM held the ringgit firmly through continued market intervention for another week, but then gave way to market forces on 14 July by floating the currency. By that time, the ratio of money supply (M2) to foreign reserves had increased to a historical high of 6.25. Moreover, the mid-May intervention caused BNM to soak up an estimated 3.5 billion ringgit, causing a significant jump in interest rates: the one-month interbank lending rate, usually around 5%, reached a high of 9%. As the ability to defend the currency dramatically declined, and without any indication as to the depth of the impending crisis, 'unleashing the cavalry' seemed sensible policy. Between the first week of July 1997 and 7 January 1998 when the slide finally halted (at RM4.88 = US$1), the ringgit depreciated by almost 50% against the dollar.

The stock market collapse was even sharper. Between July 1997 and mid-January 1998, the all-ordinaries index of the KLSE fell by over 65%, wiping almost US$225 billion off share values. This massive slump cannot be explained in terms of the run on local stocks by foreign stockholders alone. At the time of onset of the crisis, foreign investors accounted for only 30% to 40% of activity in the market. Many sellers were therefore local players. Analysts see this massive panic by locals as reflecting underlying weaknesses of corporate governance in Malaysia and, in particular, defects in the way bourses and listed companies treat investors. When the economy was growing strongly, even foreign investors were prepared to ignore lax stock market oversight and patchy enforcement of rules. In a bear market, such shortcomings became a powerful inducement to sell. Because of past experience, minority shareholders were naturally concerned that in troubled times they might be the hardest hit. A number of murky share market dealings immediately after the onset of the crisis compounded this suspicion, and thus aggravated the share market slide (based on *The Economist* 20 December 1997: 111).

POLICY RESPONSE

The initial response of the Malaysian government to the outbreak of the currency crisis was one of denial. Given the perceived soundness of economic fundamentals and the earlier success of BNM in repelling speculators in May, Malaysian policymakers acted as if the country were in a different economic league from that of Thailand and Indonesia. When speculative waves actually hit the economy a month later, this was considered to be the work of speculators who totally ignored the underlying health of the economy. The immediate reaction of the prime minister was to attack (in particular, American financier George Soros). At the International Monetary Fund (IMF) and World Bank meeting in Hong Kong on 20 September 1997, Dr Mahathir remarked that currency trading (beyond the level needed to finance trade) was 'unnecessary, unproductive and immoral', and that it should be made illegal.[11] He called for international cooperation to tame speculators, and to control the activities of hedge funds. Subsequently, in a number of domestic and international policy forums, he tried to promote the idea of a new global initiative to protect developing-country financial markets from these 'ferocious beasts'. At the same time, he reiterated that 'there will be no slow down' in his 'Year 2020 development drive', adding to the worry that he would continue to stretch the country's resources through large economically dubious projects. But almost every attack by Mahathir against perceived enemies precipitated further sliding of the ringgit.

More damaging to investor confidence than the prime minister's attacks on speculators were several initiatives to intervene directly in the share market operations with a view to punishing speculators. On 27 August, the KLSE had banned the short-selling[12] of 100 blue-chip stocks, and rules were introduced to discourage the selling of stocks: sellers were required to deliver physical share certificates to their brokers before selling, and the settlement period was reduced from five to two days. On 3 September, the prime minister unveiled a plan to use funds from the Employees Provident Fund to prop up share prices by buying stocks from Malaysian shareholders – but not foreigners – at a premium to prevailing prices. These moves backfired, triggering a massive sell-off of stocks on the KLSE, and undermining sentiment on other regional bourses. Ironically, government-sponsored share purchases were seen by market participants, both local and foreign, as an opportunity to get rid of Malaysian shares (rather than a reason for holding onto them). Moreover, attempts to boost the share market through non-market means amounted to political violation of the autonomy of the central bank. This presumably raised doubts among market participants about BNM's ability to manage the crisis. As already noted, BNM had introduced a curb on bank lending for the purpose of share market trading earlier in the year.

In his usual leadership style, Dr Mahathir was pragmatic enough to reverse his 'unorthodox' policy posture when occasion demanded. The ban on short-selling was lifted on 4 September. In the same month, the government announced the postponement of some grandiose projects – the huge and controversial Bakun dam, a new airport, and part of a new administrative capital – amounting to almost US$10 billion in aggregate investment commitments.

The government failed to come up with a coherent program of reforms to deal with the crisis in its budget for 1998, unveiled on 17 October. It seemed that, even three months after the onset of the crisis and after the ringgit had already lost about 25% of its value, the government continued to consider the crisis as a passing phenomenon that required only some tinkering with policy.[13] The major focus of the proposals was on reducing the current account deficit through selective import duties and a 'buy Malaysia' campaign. There were no proposals to redress domestic macroeconomic imbalances. Some budget proposals (such as a two percentage point cut in corporate taxes and new incentives for exporters) were inappropriate to the new economic circumstances. Apart from a restatement of the commitment to postpone the implementation of a few large infrastructure projects, there were no concrete measures to cut government expenditure with a view to restoring macroeconomic stability. The budget projected government spending to grow by 1.9% in the coming fiscal year. Nor were there proposals for the monetary restraint needed to avert the currency slide, other than a restatement of ceilings on property lending introduced by BNM earlier in the year. A growth rate of 7% (only one percentage point lower than the 1997 rate) was predicted for 1998, at a time when market participants were predicting a growth rate below 5%. This gave the impression that the government was not prepared to stick to the promise of fiscal prudence or to increase the interest rate if need be to support the currency. On the first trading day after the budget, the ringgit fell by 3% and the composite index of the KLSE sank by 4%.

During the first speculative attack on the ringgit in mid-May, BNM made no attempt to sterilise the liquidity squeeze resulting from its massive market intervention to defend the currency, so interest rates increased. The correct approach would have been to continue with this tight monetary policy until the wild currency slide came to an end. However, the bank soon began to inject liquidity through its agent banks to keep debt-laden firms afloat and to avert an increase in non-performing loans in the banking system. In this context, many companies continued to borrow at a feverish pace until late 1997. By the end of the year, total domestic loans stood at around 160% of GDP, the highest level of domestic indebtedness in South-east Asia. Money supply (M2) increased by over 30% between July and December 1997.

As the financial turmoil continued to escalate, Dr Mahathir announced on 22 November the formation of a National Economic Association Council (NEAC) to act as the pivotal body in economic policymaking (under the leadership of Daim Zainuddin, Malaysia's most powerful behind-the-scenes economic powerbroker). In terms of its significance, Mahathir compared the NEAC to the National Operations Council appointed to run the country after the bloody May 1969 race riots. On 5 December, the deputy prime minister and finance minister, Anwar Ibrahim, unveiled a major economic policy statement involving a series of fiscal austerity measures, amounting to abandonment of the aggressive high-growth policies pursued over the previous five years. The key elements of the package included cutting government spending by 18%, postponing indefinitely all public sector investment projects which were still in the pipeline, stopping new overseas investment by Malaysian firms, freezing new share issues and company restructuring, and cutting the salaries of government ministers by 10%. With these measures, the previous budget forecast for economic growth (7%) was lowered to 4–5%.

This statement undoubtedly marked the most important economic policy shift in the decade. It was a clear admission of the severity of the crisis and the need for drastic measures. As part of his speech, Anwar presented position papers dating back to 1995 to support the view that the financial crisis was not simply a sporadic speculative attack, but that both BNM and the finance ministry had repeatedly warned of impending economic problems.

Judging from commentaries in the financial press, market participants applauded these significant fiscal measures, yet the slide of both the ringgit and the share price index continued unabated for another month or so. There are two possible explanations of this inconsistency. First, it may be that restoring shattered market sentiment involved a time lag. Second, the 5 December package had a key missing element (which the IMF had been advocating since the onset of the crisis): raising domestic interest rates to support the currency and to tame inflation. While it is not possible to assess the former explanation using the available (secondary) information, market developments following the policy statement are quite consistent with the latter.

Despite the government's apparent reluctance to use interest rate policy to support the currency, interest rates soon started increasing as a natural market response to the continuously weakening currency and tightening liquidity in the economy as a result of the share market slump. By early February 1998, the interbank one-month rate stood at 12.2%, up from 9% in July 1997. The average base lending rate of commercial banks and finance companies increased from 10.2% and 12.1% to 13.2% and 15.3%, respectively, during the same period. It was only after these significant interest rate adjustments that the ringgit and the share price index began to record significant improvements.

Why did the policymakers attempt to delay the inevitable interest rate increases for so long? The obvious answer is that policy choice was constrained by the excessive reliance of the economy on bank credit. In that context, an increase in interest rates was bound to have a severe contractionary effect on debt-ridden private sector firms – and the viability of their banks – which were already suffering from the burst real estate bubble and the share market crash. Thus, the Malaysian experience is consistent with the prediction of the currency crisis literature that excessive credit growth is a source of vulnerability to a financial crisis. Of course, in the Malaysian case, there was an additional political dimension. Given the intimate link between business and government forged under the NEP, the positive stabilising impact on the ringgit from the use of interest rates as a policy instrument had to be weighed against the negative effects that action would have on politically connected business groups.

In recent months, BNM has taken some initiatives to restructure the financial system. On 2 January, it advised the country's 39 finance companies to begin merger talks, so that smaller companies join one of the five or six largest ones. A similar restructuring initiative is believed to be under consideration for the banks. However, unlike Thailand and Korea, the Malaysian government has so far shunned financial sector liberalisation (including relaxing restrictions on the entry of foreign banks), which would seem to be the most appropriate step to rejuvenating the system. The government seems to be of the view that the fragmented domestic financial system needs to be strengthened before it is forced open next year under the World Trade Organisation commitments.

As the combined outcome of the property market crash and massive capital outflows, non-performing loans in the banking system have increased. According to BNM, the ratio of non-performing assets stood at around 6.5% by the end of April 1998, up from the pre-crisis level of around 3%. Market analysts believe that the problem is much more severe than the official figure suggests, however, as many companies have begun to roll over debt as part of their survival strategy. Independent estimates of the non-performing loan ratio range from 10% to 30% (Hiebert 1998). As yet no concrete policy initiative has been taken to avert the potential threat to the viability of the banking system. BNM's approach to the issue so far has been to temporarily cushion the banking sector and debt-ridden companies against the liquidity squeeze (caused by the share market crash and capital outflow) by trying to hold down interest rates and injecting liquidity into the system by printing money. On 9 February, BNM lowered the statutory reserve requirement ratio of the commercial banks from 13.5% to 10% to help check the rise in lending rates – a controversial move in a context where the currency still remained highly undervalued.

AFTERMATH OF THE CRISIS

The run on the ringgit and the stock market seems to have come to an end. However, it is too early to assess the overall implications of the crisis for the performance of the economy. As already mentioned, in October 1997 the government forecast a growth rate of 7% for 1998, but subsequently adjusted it downward to 4–5% in December, and to 2–3% in March 1998.

Domestic market-oriented industries, and the construction and services sectors, are going to be affected by the contraction in domestic demand resulting from the negative wealth effect of weaker stock prices and property market slump, and the net contractionary impact of the significant currency depreciation.[14] On the other hand, the traditional export industries (that account for 10% of GDP) and export-oriented manufacturing (30% of GDP) seem to have promising growth prospects. As the banking system has not been severely disrupted, exporters are unlikely to face a credit squeeze. Apart from significantly increased competitiveness because of the real exchange rate appreciation, export-oriented manufacturing is well placed to benefit from the strong links forged through FDI with the booming US economy. The recovery of the world electronics trade since late 1997 is another positive factor on the export side.[15] A new product cycle has emerged in the computer industry, fuelling demand for PCs and related products, thus boosting exports from Malaysia and other electronics producers in the region. Lately there has been a clear shift in consumer preference for mid- and low-end PCs, and Malaysia is a major producer of disk drives for such computers.

Although there has been a significant shift in Malaysia's trade flows away from the traditional European markets and towards the Asia Pacific region, the country still depends heavily on markets in North America and Europe for manufactured exports. In the case of electronics, the major export category, this figure was as high as 70%. ASEAN (Association of South East Asian Nations) accounts for about one-quarter of Malaysia's exports and one-fifth of its imports. Malaysia also has an edge over other countries because of its intra-firm trade links forged through FDI. Given these export patterns, slow growth in crisis-affected Asian countries is not going to be a significant constraint on the ongoing process of export-led recovery in Malaysia.

The recovery process will depend crucially on whether multinational enterprises (MNEs), which account for over 45% of Malaysia's manufacturing production and over 75% of total manufactured exports, continue to treat Malaysia as a preferred location for international production. Some observers have cast doubt on this possibility, simply by referring to the massive capital outflows following the onset of the crisis. This view is based, however, on a false aggregation of FDI with portfolio investment and short-term bank credits. FDI flows are determined by long-term considerations governing the international production decisions of MNEs, not by financial panics and related short-term economic changes. In fact, according to the Malaysian Industrial Development Board, there has not been a noticeable decline of FDI in export-oriented ventures following the crisis. Indeed, the crisis may have ushered in an era of greater – not less – MNE participation in the Malaysian economy; it has been the experience of other crisis-affected countries that there tends to be an 'FDI surge at a time when foreign capital in general is fleeing a country' (Krugman 1998b).

An issue of great immediate importance for the crisis-affected Asian countries is the maintenance of social and political stability in the face of economic dislocations. This risk appears to be low in Malaysia. Given the favourable prospects for export growth and the fact that nearly 25% of the work force consists of foreign workers who can easily be repatriated, it is unlikely that the rate of unemployment will become a significant destabilising factor. Rapid economic growth and a dramatic reduction in poverty over the past ten years have brought about social peace and political stability. There is always the danger that, should things go wrong on the policy front, old dangers will arise anew. But judging from the unfolding policy scenario, this possibility seems remote.

In sum, the financial crisis is not a sign of the end of the Malaysian (or Asian) miracle. As policymakers have finally decided to swallow bitter reform medicine (after a period of almost six months of policy indifference), and given the prospects for a rapid export-led recovery, Malaysia is likely to resume rapid growth by early 1999. The structural adjustments triggered by the crisis – in particular the rationalisation of the public investment program – are likely to provide further impetus for recovery. This scenario hinges, however, on the assumption that the Malaysian authorities will take appropriate initiatives to restructure the debt-ridden domestic banking system, and to ensure the orderly functioning of the share market. Otherwise, there is a potential danger that massive private sector debts will give rise to a vicious circle of slow growth, failing banks and contracting credit, plunging the economy into a prolonged slump.

NOTES

Comments from Ross McLeod, Peter McCawley and Peter Searle are gratefully acknowledged.

1   Standard & Poor's ratings for the other crisis countries as at the end of May 1997 were: South Korea AA-, Thailand A, Indonesia BBB and the Philippines BB+ (*Far Eastern Economic Review* 29 May 1997: 60).
2   See Kaminsky et al. (1997) for a comprehensive survey.
3   The original J.P. Morgan index has been inverted to make it consistent with this interpretation.
4   The degree of real exchange rate appreciation would have been much greater had it not been for the massive influx of migrant workers as the economy

approached full employment. By the early 1990s, foreign workers accounted for over 25% of a local work force of 8 million. The presence of foreign workers, by limiting rapid wage growth, mitigates relative increases in non-tradable prices. Perhaps reflecting differences in the degree of dependence on foreign workers, the average annual growth rate of real wages in Malaysia during 1990–6 was a mere 6% compared with over 15% in Thailand.

5   The consolidated government budget of Malaysia has been in surplus since 1993. However, the surplus has basically been a 'revenue surplus', a reflection of the expansion of revenue at a faster rate than expenditure.

6   The conventional yardstick for the adequacy of reserves used in the literature on balance of payments issues is the import-month equivalent of reserves (the ratio of reserves to one month's worth of imports). This measure is not appropriate for the present analysis because a run against a currency is rarely associated with an import spree (Calvo 1995).

7   The IMF head, Michel Camdessus, when visiting Kuala Lumpur in early November 1997, admitted that Malaysia's financial system was sound.

8   Note that financier George Soros pointed to massive private sector credit accumulation as the main weakness of the Malaysian economy. See note 11.

9   By the end of 1997, more than 5.8 million square feet of new office space was under construction in the Kuala Lumpur metropolis, in addition to the 5.6 million square feet of space available at the time (*Far Eastern Economic Review*, 10 April 1998, 60).

10   This policy indifference is not surprising given the fact that, ever since the introduction of the New Economic Policy, the stock market has been a key instrument used by the Malaysian leadership to achieve the political goals of restructuring wealth ownership in the economy. (I owe this point to Peter Searle.)

11   George Soros responded to Mahathir, saying that 'interfering with the convertibility of capital at a moment like this is a recipe for disaster' and that Dr Mahathir was 'a menace to his own country'. He dismissed as totally unfounded the allegation that he was responsible for the fall of the ringgit, and pointed to 'excessive credit expansion' as the source of Malaysia's troubles. For excerpts from statements made by Mahathir and Soros at the IMF meetings, see *FPB* (1997).

12   The selling of shares not yet owned, with the intention of buying them later at a cheaper price to enable completion of the deal at a profit.

13   One important indicator of this optimistic view is Malaysia's significant financial commitment to IMF-sponsored rescue packages for Thailand and Indonesia. In the last week of October 1997, Malaysia offered RM3.4 billion (about US$1 billion) to each country.

14   Note that real depreciation first depresses demand via the income effect before stimulating demand through the substitution effect (Diaz-Alejandro 1965).

15   The electronics industry accounts for over 35% of manufacturing output and over 66% of total exports.

Part III

Case studies:
safe behind closed doors?

6 China

Ligang Song

INTRODUCTION

The Chinese economy has not suffered from the financial crisis that has afflicted many economies in the East Asia region. This chapter examines the
characteristics of China's economy which prevented it from sharing the
damage experienced by the countries in crisis. The chapter goes on to identify the systemic weaknesses that remain in China's economy, then suggests
directions the ongoing reform of China's economy will need to take if
growth is to continue and exposure to any future crisis is to be avoided.

MACROECONOMIC FUNDAMENTALS FOR PREVENTING
FINANCIAL CRISIS

Why not China?

The commonly cited reasons for China's avoiding the crisis include the
following.

First, China's economy has been experiencing an economic soft landing
amid the general financial turmoil. Real gross domestic product (GDP)
grew at 8.8% with an inflation level below 3% in 1997. There was no sign
of economic overheating at the time of the onset of the crisis in Southeast
Asia and Korea. This laid a foundation for resistance to external shocks.

Second, China's balance of payments has been in a good shape since the
early 1990s. There have been current account surpluses in most years. Exports were US$182.70 billion in 1997, up 20.9%, while imports were up
only 2.5% over 1996, at US$142.36 billion.

Third, the continued current account surplus had added to China's substantial international reserves, which reached US$140 billion by the end of
1997. This provided the capacity to smooth out any imbalances between
foreign receipts and payments and to stabilise the domestic economy in the
presence of external shocks.

Fourth, China had only a moderate level of foreign debt (US$131 billion) by the end of 1997, compared with its capacity for repayment. The bulk of China's foreign debt (above 80%) is of long maturity, with about half consisting of borrowings from international organisations and foreign governments. Judged by the measures of debt service ratio (12%), liability ratio (14%) and foreign debt ratio (74%) for 1997, China's foreign debt is at a moderate level.[1]

Fifth, the Chinese currency (RMB) has maintained a stable exchange rate against major currencies since the exchange rate system was dramatically re-formed in 1994. The yuan closed at 8.2796 yuan per US dollar at the end of 1997, representing an appreciation from the rate of 8.7 yuan per US dol-lar which was in place when the unified system was introduced in 1994. This strong showing is due mainly to an excessive market supply of foreign exchange resulting mainly from China's persistent increases in trade surplus in recent years. Furthermore, RMB is convertible only on current, and not on capital, accounts and control is still strictly applied over capital flows. This has essentially insulated the economy from financial shocks flowing through exchange and capital market channels.

Finally, foreign capital continued to pour in – mainly in the form of di-rect investment, albeit at a decelerating rate – for new investments for 1997. Total foreign capital utilisation reached US$62 billion for the whole year, up 13% over 1996, of which US$43 billion was foreign direct investment. A large volume of export-oriented foreign capital substantially enhances China's export capacities as marked by the large contribution of these firms to China's total export increase (above 40% in recent years).

Policy factors

The benign macroeconomic environment outlined above follows the im-plementation of moderately tight monetary policy since 1993, targeting especially the high investment in real estate sectors, which had increased by 118% in 1992 and 165% in 1993 (Yi and Zhao 1998: 2). Growth in the supply of broad money (M2) fell from an annual growth rate of 43% in 1993 to 17% in 1997.

Investment growth also slowed due to tight administrative controls on investment by state-owned enterprises (SOEs), as the government sought to encourage an 'intensive' rather than 'extensive' development strategy. An-nual growth in total investment in fixed assets fell from 59% in 1993 to 9% in 1997.

In response to the rapid expansion of the stock market in 1996 and early 1997, the government adopted effective measures to prevent an overheating of the stock market which could cause significant market risks. Those mea-sures included strengthening the supervision and management of the secu-rity markets; educating the public on the risks associated with investment in stock markets; and banning banks from providing loans to securities companies.

The government has effectively reduced the risk of 'bubbles' in the economy. Inflation has subsided since it peaked in 1994 (at 22%). By the time the financial crisis in East Asia emerged in 1997, the government had succeeded in engineering a soft landing for the Chinese economy, reducing inflation without a severe reduction in growth. China's inflation came down further in 1998. For example, inflation fell for five consecutive months from October 1997 to February 1998, playing a positive role in stabilising the RMB and the Hong Kong dollar (both of which, but especially the latter, were facing pressure for depreciation).

EXISTING PROBLEMS AND POTENTIAL RISKS TO STABILITY

The financial crisis in Asia sounds an alarm to the policymakers in China, although the economy has escaped the crisis relatively unscathed. The government has good reasons to worry about the structural problems in the economy and the damage that they may cause if not dealt with properly. These problems include the following.

Weak market demand

There has been a slowing-down in the growth of domestic aggregate demand, partly reflected in a shift from a sellers' to a buyers' market, which has raised market competition and put more pressure on inefficient enterprises (see Table 6.1). This shift marked the end of the 'shortage economy' which had characterised the economy under the planning system and the economy in the early reform period.

The retail price index (RPI) increased only 0.8% in 1997. The consumer price index (CPI), which also covers prices for services, was up by only 2.8% for the whole year. This trend continued into 1998. The official figures show that the RPI dipped 1.5% and the CPI inched up only 0.3% in the first quarter of 1998. Mirroring the weak market demand conditions of recent years, there is excess supply in both producer and consumer products; increasing inventories; underutilised productive facilities; widespread enterprise losses; and weak import demand.

The weak market demand reveals the longstanding problems of irrational economic structure and inefficiency among SOEs. More importantly, it may also indicate that the tight macroeconomic policies implemented since the early 1990s have come to a kind of limit, beyond which there is a real danger of disinflation which would have negative effects on the reform process.

Danger of disinflation

There is potential for disinflation, caused by the high real interest rates which have arisen from the tight monetary policies of recent years. Since the

Table 6.1 China: changes in domestic aggregate demand, 1992–6 (%)

	1992	1993	1994	1995	1996
Aggregate demand	17.1	12.3	15.4	8.8	8.5

Source: Yi and Zhao 1998: 3.

end of the 1980s, there have been wide fluctuations in inflation levels, but nominal interest rates have remained fairly stable. This has led to large swings in real interest rates. In particular, a rapid increase in real interest rates in recent years, due to declining inflation levels, has increased enter-prises' interest payments to unprecedented levels, providing a more strin-gent financial environment for industrial enterprises (Yi and Zhao 1998: 5).

This changing environment has two implications from a macroeconomic perspective. One is that the increasing financial burden on enterprises might cause a reduction in investment. The other is that it might lead to a further slowdown in the total money supply, which in turn would have even more contractionary effects on domestic aggregate demand and create more difficulties for enterprises. This situation demands that the central bank ease its monetary policy, since recession could increase such financial risks.

Rising unemployment

China has experienced worsening unemployment in recent years, resulting mainly from the measures taken to restructure SOEs. The total number of laid-off workers reached 11.5 million in 1997, up by 41% over 1996. Among them were 7.9 million retrenched by the SOEs, accounting for 68% of the total. It is estimated that the ongoing reform process will add about a million workers per year to the army of the unemployed.

A slowdown in the economic growth rates of township and rural enter-prises may also worsen the rural employment outlook. Township industries accounted for two-thirds of the country's rural output and one-third of the country's GDP in 1996. More significantly, they have created substantial employment opportunities, growing from 28 million workers in 1978 to 135 million by 1996. At current rates of growth, these township enterprises are generating more than two million jobs each year and provide social wel-fare coverage for a large proportion of the rural labour force.

But, with poor management and low productivity, many township en-terprises are unable to compete and face tremendous challenges to restruc-ture successfully. As a result, the government has lowered its growth target for the township industries. Similar reform measures to those used for SOEs – such as enterprise regrouping and the formation of holding companies and cooperatives – are now being applied to the township enterprises.

The official goal of keeping unemployment under control while restructuring the country's state sector can be achieved only by maintaining relatively high economic growth; developing the tertiary sector; sustaining the growth of township and village enterprises; building a unified social security system; and enhancing external trade. But success in the latter task has been under threat from the Asian crisis.

Losing competitiveness

It is widely believed that weak currencies in Southeast Asian countries may significantly reduce the competitiveness of China's exports and threaten the growth of China's exports in 1998 and beyond. There are increasing difficulties for exports, which already are showing signs of slowing.

There are difficulties associated with the strategy of maintaining the current exchange rate, and the consequences of slowing exports could be far-reaching for the domestic economy.[2] First, falling export competitiveness may affect those foreign investors – particularly in small and medium-sized firms – who use China mainly as an export production base. As a result, inflows of foreign investment may slow down. Second, with a drop in export revenue and a slowdown in capital inflows, supporting an overvalued exchange rate could be costly and result in a substantial reduction in official exchange reserves. Third, a setback to export growth is likely to cap economic growth in the next two years, making the current structural adjustments even more difficult to implement.

Without depreciation of the RMB, China's export performance could rely heavily on its ability to keep domestic costs low and to provide further incentives to exporters through policy measures.

Bad loans and financial risks

There are hidden financial risks in the economy, reflected mainly in the appearance of bad loans in the banking system. The main cause of bad loans in China, apart from poor financial management and lack of regulation and surveillance, stems from banks' relationships with SOEs, with which state banks still have extensive links. Because of the reforms, mechanisms for allocating funds have come to rely on bank lending rather than the state budget.

The high economic growth rates achieved during the past two decades have been sustained partly through bank loans provided by the state banks to domestic enterprises. A main feature characterising this relationship between banks and enterprises has been that any gains from successful investments have accrued to enterprises, while failures have ended up on banks' balance sheets as bad loans. Since 70–80% of total bank lending went to relatively inefficient SOEs, a large number of bank loans cannot be recovered. Under this circumstance, part of households' claim on bank deposits has ceased to exist, causing significant financial risks in the banking system (Zhang et al. 1998: 9).

Institutionally, the banking system in China is highly concentrated. The four big state commercial banks handle about 90% of total credit funds. Of these funds, 90% has been lent to SOEs, which account for only about one-third of the total economy. Since about 45% of SOEs are still making losses, banks with high concentration ratios are competing with each other to provide loans to efficient enterprises. There have been significant increases in the allocation of credit to those efficient enterprises, but the banks have refrained from lending to inefficient firms (Zhang et al. 1998: 10). As a result, the state commercial banks did not use up their lending quotas in 1997, reflecting the fact that budgets have been hardening for SOEs. This may be one of the reasons for the low growth rate of investment in recent years.

Three categories are used to define bad loans in China. The first category represents 'unrecoverable' loans, which account for between 5% and 6% of all domestic bank loans. Loans in the second category are referred to as 'non-performing' loans and constitute about 20% of loans made by Chinese banks. The third category covers those loans which are more than two years overdue and represents 8% to 10% of all bank loans. These figures reflect the seriousness of bad loan problems in China's banking system.

Bad loans, like fiscal deficits, could be sustained for a while but not indefinitely, especially now that the Chinese government has obliged banks to impose stronger repayment disciplines. This government requirement is equivalent to gradually reducing state subsidies to investment (Yi and Zhao 1998: 6). The government has dealt with the problem of banks' bad loans by further reforming the banking system, enforcing financial regulations and writing off some loans. For example, China plans to write off more than 50 billion yuan (US$6 billion) in bad loans in 1998 and another 60 billion and 70 billion yuan (US$7.1 and US$8.6 billion) in 1999 and 2000 respectively. But the government's plan to write off bad loans may create a 'moral hazard' problem, which would not be conducive to ongoing SOE reform.

Declining share earnings

There is no apparent link between stock market movements in China and the performance of the real sector. Several booms and busts in the stock markets in recent years have mainly been due to activities of excessive speculation and market manipulation. A lack of regulation and surveillance, combined with market irregularities, should also bear some of the blame.

Furthermore, since there have been no fundamental improvements in the industrial structure and performance of domestic enterprises, earnings per share and rates of return on equity for listed companies have shown signs of declining in recent years (see Table 6.2).[3]

Table 6.2 China: stock earnings for listed companies, 1993–6

	1993	1994	1995	1996
Shanghai Stock Exchange				
Net assets per share (yuan)	2.09	2.10	2.21	2.33
Earnings per share (yuan)	0.25	0.27	0.24	0.22
Earning rate of net assets (%)	12.00	12.90	10.90	9.40
Shenzhen Stock Exchange				
Net assets per share (yuan)	3.07	2.61	2.50	2.53
Earnings per share (yuan)	0.55	0.41	0.26	0.25
Earning rate of net assets (%)	17.90	15.70	10.40	9.90
Total				
Net assets per share(yuan)	2.40	2.26	2.31	2.41
Earnings per share (yuan)	0.35	0.32	0.25	0.23
Earning rate of net assets (%)	14.60	14.20	10.80	9.50

Source: Li et al. 1998: 11.

Although the stock markets in Shanghai and Shenzhen listed shares worth 30 billion yuan (US$3.6 billion) in 1997, they are still a long way from becoming full-scale capital markets. SOE mergers and acquisitions are hard to realise through standard capital market practices because only small numbers of companies are currently listed. The relatively short supply of publicly circulating shares also makes them vulnerable to speculators with large sums of money.

This vulnerability is exacerbated by the fact that 90% of the investors in these markets are individuals, far above the 30% found in developed countries. The many small, separate investments by individual investors seem to contribute to the frequent fluctuations in, and speculative pattern of, the stock market in China. As a result, China will continue to depend on Hong Kong as the financial centre for economic development of the mainland. As China began listing some of its enterprises abroad in the 1990s, Hong Kong became the biggest external fund-raising market (producing H-shares) for China-incorporated companies, followed by New York and London.

Weak institutions

Among the biggest impediments to sustained economic growth in China are its inadequate institutions: weak and inefficient banking and tax systems; complex relationships between central and provincial governments and between the government and SOEs; and weak legal and social security systems (Oksenberg et al. 1997: 26). Reforms in these areas – particularly the reform of SOEs and of the financial sector – will become increasingly necessary if China is to achieve its growth potential in the future.

POLICY ADJUSTMENTS

The Chinese government now has to implement its macroeconomic policies in an environment in which there is an oversupply of commodities (largely due to duplicated investments); a lack of aggregate demand, bringing with it a danger of disinflation; and tougher competition for China's exports, due to its strong currency. Policies also have to be implemented in the absence of well-developed money and security markets. Under this circumstance, finetuning in implementing its macroeconomic policies will be crucial for China if it is to avoid the double squeeze of weak domestic demand and a deterioration in its external trade environment.

Monetary policy

In the past few years, China's monetary authorities have moved further away from direct credit allocation and towards market-based mechanisms for monetary control, making increasing use of indirect instruments such as rediscount, interest rates, reserve requirements and open market operations to regulate the money supply. China relinquished the credit quota system governing state-owned commercial banks from the beginning of 1998.

To boost economic growth, the government reduced interest rates five times between 1996 and the first quarter of 1998. The rate cuts encouraged bank lending to enterprises (total bank loans reached US$905 billion in 1997, an increase of 17% from the previous year); lessened the burden of debt repayments on enterprises (it is estimated that about US$8 billion was saved on annual interest payments); and sustained an increased consumption level (total retail sales reached US$329 billion in 1997, up 9% from 1996). However, room to further reduce interest rates is limited, since to do so would be incompatible with the current policy of holding the RMB exchange rate unchanged.

Although the rate reductions led to some discontent among households over the returns on bank deposits, domestic household saving was not in fact discouraged by the cuts. This was due in part to an improvement in the real interest rate, which continued to rise due to reduced inflation. Total accumulated household savings reached US$560 billion in 1997, an increase of 19% from 1996. Transferring this huge pool of savings into productive investments remains a big task.

To date, the central bank has already abolished credit ceiling controls on cooperative financial institutions, shareholding commercial banks and other commercial banks. In the first half of 1996, China established a national interbank market and an open market operation network for trading treasury bonds (T-bonds). The final eradication of the credit quota system marks the completion of China's shift to indirect regulation of the country's money supply.

During the past several years – especially since the beginning of the

1990s – the central bank's asset structure has changed a great deal. A key factor behind the change has been a rapid increase in its foreign exchange reserves. For example, the ratio of the central bank's lending to commercial banks to its total assets went down from 75% at the end of 1993 to 52% by the first quarter of 1997. At the same time, its net foreign assets (mainly exchange reserves) increased from 12% to 41% of total assets during the same period (Yi and Fan 1997: 34).

This is because, in order to prevent the RMB from appreciating, the central bank has had to purchase US dollars. An increase in foreign exchange reserves at the central bank means an increase in its money supply. It is estimated that about 60% of the increase in money supply in recent years has resulted from the increase in foreign exchange reserves at the central bank. In order to control potential inflation, the central bank has tried to further reduce its relending to the commercial banks to offset the monetary expansion occurring through the purchasing of foreign exchange. But its ability to do so is limited as its assets structure continues to change in favour of net foreign assets (Yi and Fan 1997: 34).

In shifting from moderately tight to moderately loose monetary policies, the monetary authorities must always be alert to the possible dangers of inflation. Experience shows that rapid money growth and the overexpansion of credit through bank loans could fuel inflationary pressure which, coupled with a possible deterioration in the external balance of payments, could trigger another round of policy retrenchment (the last one started in 1994), which would pose severe threats to SOE and banking reforms and to the development of township industries.

On the positive side, it is likely that inflation will be controlled within target limits, at least in the short run. First, the change in market structure from a sellers' market to a buyers' market reduces the possibility of demand-pull inflation. Second, the soft budget constraints of SOEs are hardening as the reform process deepens. Third, prices for agricultural products are likely to remain stable. Fourth, the People's Bank Law prohibits the central bank from printing money to cover state budget deficits.

Exchange rate policy

The RMB exchange rate will remain at its current level of 8.27 yuan per US dollar, as promised repeatedly by the government, but pressure for devaluation will increase in the second half of 1998 due to the impact of the financial crisis on China's exports. In response, policy measures to boost domestic demand will be necessary to maintain the growth target for the remainder of this century, which will in turn be important to the success of the ongoing reform of SOEs and the banking sector.

On the plus side, without devaluation, China will become a stabilising force in the East Asian financial crisis. A strong yuan will help to keep the prices of imported goods down. Since about 50% of Chinese exports use

imported materials, this effect may partially offset any loss in export competitiveness. A stable Chinese currency will also help Hong Kong to keep its
currency and economy stable.

Fiscal policy

A new fiscal policy framework has been emerging in China against the
background of the granting of greater autonomy to SOEs, an expansion of
the role of market forces in determining resource allocation, and a tightening of the fiscal boundaries between central and provincial governments.
But China is yet to develop a unified and transparent tax system and tax
evasion and fraud remain widespread. Income taxes are not unified and
preferential tax policies are still applied in the special economic zones and
regions, with regard to income, import and circulating taxes. The share of
total government revenue in GDP stood at around 11% for the third consecutive year in 1997. While taxation revenues as a whole have been growing, the growth rates of some particular major categories of taxes showed
signs of decreasing in 1997.

The relatively low share of government revenue in national income has
limited the Chinese government's ability to use fiscal policy to influence the
macroeconomy, support structural reform, tackle the issue of regional income gaps through inter-governmental transfers and carry out public investment. Government investment in research and development, for
example, has accounted for a decreasing proportion of GDP, dropping from
0.7% of GDP in 1990 to 0.48% in 1996.

Despite problems on the revenue side, the fiscal position of the government continued to stabilise in 1997 as a result of a sweeping program of fiscal reform begun in 1994, which marked a shift from the 'fiscal contract'
system to a 'revenue sharing' system. Budget deficits persist, but their share
in GDP appears to be decreasing. Total deficits as a proportion of GDP for
1990, 1994, 1995 and 1996 were 0.8%, 1.2%, 1.0% and 0.8% respectively.
The figure for 1997 stood at 0.75% of GDP (*China Daily* 24 March 1998).
A balanced budget objective is even more pressing for local governments
than it is for the central government, since the former have been running
increasing budget deficits in recent years (China Statistical Publisher 1997).

Budget deficits have been financed mainly by the central bank and by domestic sales of bonds. External sources of financing have accounted for only
a small part of the total deficit. Bond financing has increased rapidly in
recent years. According to the 1998 budget, China plans to distribute 281
billion yuan (US$33.8 billion) of T-bonds in 1998 to cover 46 billion yuan
(US$5.5 billion) of projected fiscal shortfall and 235 billion yuan (US$33.8
billion) worth of matured T-bonds (*China Daily* 14 May 1998).

Initially, T-bonds were issued through mandatory placement with households and enterprises. Beginning in 1988, the government set up a secondary market for government bonds held by households, thereby

increasing their liquidity and attractiveness. The secondary market is expected to grow in 1998. This increased depth may help to stabilise the secondary market, which at the moment experiences considerable inflexibility due to manipulations and other irregularities.

Financial system reform

The government has recognised increasingly that reform of the financial sector, alongside the reform of SOEs, will be essential for maintaining macroeconomic stability and laying a more solid foundation for long-term growth. China's financial reforms have made some progress, reflected in the stability of the foreign exchange market and the exchange rate, the moderate size of foreign debt and the growing level of foreign exchange reserves.

But major problems remain, including bad loans, a lack of financial regulation and market irregularities. In particular, the reform of SOEs poses a dilemma for a banking system that is torn between the need to avoid heavy financial liabilities on the one hand and the burden of providing continued support to inefficient SOEs on the other.

While strengthening its financial system through tougher regulations and tighter controls over increases in capital investment and real estate, China may need to be more cautious about opening up its capital market and realising full convertibility of its currency in the near future. China currently exercises strict overall planning with regard to the scale, structure and destinations of overseas capital. It also closely monitors the raising of overseas loans while separating domestic and overseas investment in securities markets. It may not be wise for the government to remove the restrictions on the capital account at present, since the conditions for successful liberalisation do not appear to be in place. These conditions include having a central government that is able to effectively control the macroeconomy, enterprises that are highly adaptable to the market and a well-developed domestic capital market.

There are also serious challenges facing the central bank, which include removing controls on interest rates; coordinating interest rate and exchange rate policies; indirectly managing the macroeconomy using various monetary instruments; and providing incentives for banks to invest in credit assessment, monitoring skills and risk analysis, to help build banks' stocks of human and managerial capital during the reform process (Caprio et al. 1996: 419).

Export incentives

Maintaining China's export competitiveness while leaving the exchange rate unchanged will require a further boost in productivity, which might be achieved by upgrading China's industrial structure, encouraging technical improvement through new investments from both domestic and foreign sources, and lowering production costs. Domestic wages and prices will need to be more flexible. The government will have to make adjustments to its export tax rebate policy to enhance enterprises' export incentives.[4] It will also have to nurture the internal capital market to mobilise and utilise domestic resources more efficiently. Further reform of the state-owned sector is also needed, and monetary policy changes may be needed to boost domestic demand and offset some of the negative effects of the external economy. Finally, the government might be well advised to avoid a sharp devaluation but seek to depreciate the currency in a gradual manner, reflecting changes in the supply of and demand for foreign exchange.

A key question relating to the last policy measure is whether currency depreciation in China would lead to a new round of competitive depreciation in the region as each country struggles to maintain a competitive edge. A gradual adjustment in the Chinese exchange rate is unlikely to cause competitive depreciation, particularly given the fact that the currencies in the economies worst hit by the crisis have dropped to abnormally low levels. Those currencies are likely to appreciate rather than depreciate along the path to recovery over the next two to three years.

ECONOMIC RESPONSES

Against the backdrop of the Asian financial crisis and the widespread slowdown projected for the region, China's economic performance has become the focus of many economists and policymakers observing the region. China aims to keep its growth target of 8% while containing the RPI within 3% and the CPI within 5% in 1998. China's economy needs to grow at a high speed to create jobs for workers laid off in the restructuring of SOEs, which will be carried out on a massive scale in the next three years. To reach its growth target, China will launch a huge infrastructure building program and residential housing project to promote investment and consumption. To upgrade China's industrial structure, the government is also encouraging investments in high-tech industries.

The Chinese economy grew at an annualised rate of 7.2% in the first quarter of 1998, while inflation was almost zero (*China Daily* 25 April 1998). This means the economy must progress at a much more rapid pace in the next three quarters to reach the country's goal of 8% growth in 1998. As there is always a time lag between the announcement of a new kick-start policy and its effects, it is anticipated that the economy will pick up sometime later in the year.

China's exports increased by 13.2% to reach US$40 billion during the first quarter of 1998. The trade surplus during the period totalled US$10.6 billion. During the first four months of 1998, actual foreign direct investment in China edged up 0.07% compared to the previous year, to reach

Table 6.3 China: regression analysis for China's export supply, 1986–97
(quarterly data: 1986Q1–1997Q1)

Dependent variable	Coefficients of explanatory variables				F-statistic	Adj. R2	No. of observations
	Constant	ln(PIM)	ln(RER)	Dum94			
(1) ln(EX)	−10.6 (−12.1)[a]	2.36 (14.7)[a]	0.411 (2.19)[b]	n.a.	145.5[a]	0.87	45
(2) ln(EX)	−9.37 (−7.18)[a]	2.18 (10.28)[a]	0.32 (1.58)[c]	0.02 (1.26)	98.8[a]	0.86	45

Notes:
The t-values are shown in parentheses.
a Significant at the 1% level.
b Significant at the 5% level.
c Significant at the 10% level.
Source: Song, L. 1998, table 8.

US$11.7 billion (*China Daily* 20 May 1998). Although Asian countries were buying less from China, Chinese exporters expanded their business with other continents by 17% during this period.

The export growth figures in the first quarter of 1998 were better than many expected, but substantially lower than those for the same period of 1997. Many believe that competitiveness effects will begin to bite later in the year, causing China to lose billions of US dollars in exports in 1998. If that happens, China may need a real exchange rate adjustment for economic considerations.

The regression results (Table 6.3) show that the real exchange rate depreciations (RER) of the past twelve years, together with increases in world demand (PIM), have been two major driving forces behind the rapid growth of China's exports (EX).[5] However, the Asian financial crisis weakens both. Trade diversification may, to a certain degree, help China to maintain a sustained world demand for its exports, but the erosion of China's international competitiveness poses real threats to its exports and has a far-reaching effect on the ongoing trade reform and liberalisation program. An overvalued exchange rate combined with high real interest rates is not conducive to maintaining much needed growth momentum.

Even given the worst-case scenario – that is, a substantial drop in exports – there are still chances that the Chinese economy would be able to manage to overcome the negative external shock, given that such shocks are not permanent and other parts of the economy should maintain reasonably high growth as a result of policy measures adopted to boost domestic investment and consumption. China can help the East Asian economies most by maintaining its own economic stability.

CONCLUSION

The experience of the East Asian economies has taught us two important lessons with respect to the path towards development and modernisation. First, trade liberalisation leads to rapid economic growth and prosperity, as demonstrated by the remarkable performances of these economies in the past three decades or so. Second, profound structural reform and adjustment in industrialising economies cannot be delayed indefinitely, as shown by the financial crises some of the East Asian countries have been experiencing since mid-1997.

A related question is whether structural adjustment at deeper levels, or institution-building compatible with an open market system, can be implemented such that the countries concerned do not have to endure severe retrenchments and any negative impact on the global economy can be avoided. Addressing this question has profound implications for countries such as China.

China has learned the first lesson quite successfully, as reflected in the results of the reform and liberalisation carried out during the past two decades. But the second lesson is yet to be fully grasped and addressed in policy discussion and implementation. While invaluable lessons and experience have been gained in managing the transition, and remarkable macroeconomic performance has been achieved in recent years, immense difficulties remain in the economy with respect to the relationships between the government, its banking system and the SOEs.

China is facing the challenges and pressures of the global economy more than ever before, as the process of integration into the international economy proceeds. The government has increasingly accepted that external factors have to be taken into account in policy considerations to meet the new challenge of globalisation. The immense size of China's economy ensures that getting the integration process right will not only be vital for the Chinese economy in the long run, but will also have important implications for both the regional and the global economy.

NOTES

Comments made by Yiping Huang and other conference participants are gratefully acknowledged; any remaining errors are mine. I would also like to thank the Ford Foundation for its financial support for my joint appointment with Renmin University, which has allowed me to return to Beijing for teaching and research on a regular basis during the past three years. Figures used in this chapter (other than those referenced) are from APEG (1998, vol. 2: 105–32).

1   The debt service ratio refers to the ratio of the payment of foreign debts (principal plus interest) to exchange receipts in the current year; the liability ratio is

the ratio of the balance of foreign debts to GDP; and the foreign debt ratio is the ratio of the balance of foreign debt to exchange receipts in the current year.

2 On average, exports contributed 2.14 percentage points to the average real GDP growth of 11.47% for the period 1990–7 (Song, L. 1998).

3 Listed companies are expected to increase their profits in 1998 as the interest rate cut of 1997 lightens SOEs' interest burdens. The low interest rate for bank deposits is also encouraging more capital to flow into the stock market.

4 The State Administration of Taxation has raised the export rebate rate for textile products by 2 percentage points, to 11%, from January 1998. The rate increase means that the state will refund an extra 3 billion yuan (US$361 million) to textile exporters. China refunded a total of 82.8 billion yuan (US$9.97 billion) to exporters in 1996, and 43.2 billion yuan (US$5.2 billion) in 1997 (*China Daily* 23 February 1998).

5 The estimate for a slope dummy variable for RER shows that the policy measure for unifying the different exchange rates adopted in 1994 produced a weak impact on China's exports compared with the strong average impact on exports of changes in the real exchange rate during the period under study.

7 Vietnam

Suiwah Leung and
Le Dang Doanh

INTRODUCTION

Most analyses of the Asian currency crisis to date have identified the fragility of the banking systems in the crisis countries as a central factor (IMF 1997d; Krugman 1998a; Moreno 1998). The existence of rapid short-term capital inflows and pegged exchange rate regimes prior to the crisis meant that monetary policy was becoming increasingly ineffective, leading in various degrees to credit growth and inflation (Glick and Moreno 1994; Leung 1996). In an environment of poorly regulated financial intermediaries, moreover, this resulted uniformly in asset price inflation.

In the traded goods sector, the US dollar peg implied decreasing international competitiveness vis-à-vis Japan as the US dollar appreciated against the yen in 1995 and 1996. It also meant that the business sectors of the crisis countries paid little attention to exchange rate risks and, in fact, held large unhedged foreign currency debts. Indeed, the pegged exchange rate regime discouraged the development of forward markets in Asian currencies (Leung 1997). Therefore, when there were reassessments of exchange rate risks on the part of investors, large and rapid capital outflows occurred, causing large devaluations. Reversals of capital flows also brought down asset prices. A combination of capital losses from asset price deflation and unhedged foreign currency debts brought about sharp declines in the net assets of the business sector, increasing the bad debts of banks and making the already fragile banking sector even more vulnerable. Added to this were non-commercial lending practices on the part of some commercial banks in their loans to non-viable investment projects. Often politically inspired, these loans carried implicit government guarantees which, in the event, could not be honoured by the governments concerned.

Vietnam has a number of features in common with the crisis countries: namely, a crawling peg exchange rate regime and a fragile, largely state-owned banking sector – made particularly vulnerable by having 55% of total credit extended to state-owned enterprises (albeit down from over 90% in 1990). It also had a high growth rate of 9% in 1996, and a large current account deficit – 11.3% of gross domestic product (GDP) in 1996, reduced to about 8.6% in 1997 through severe import restrictions. Unlike those in the crisis countries, however, the capital inflows sustaining the current account deficit consisted principally of foreign direct investment (FDI) and overseas development assistance (ODA), rather than short-term portfolio investments and loans.

It is argued that the underdeveloped nature of Vietnam's financial system, together with the high degree of control exercised over the capital and the current account, has temporarily shielded the economy from speculative attacks.[1] Indeed, in 1996 and early 1997, a temporary relaxation of controls over the foreign borrowings of state-owned enterprises (SOEs) guaranteed by state-owned commercial banks fuelled real estate price inflation in Hanoi and Ho Chi Minh City, and resulted in a 'mini' financial crisis in the first half of 1997.

This incident shows that the underlying problems of moral hazard and adverse selection associated with asymmetrical information in financial sectors are certainly present in Vietnam. Suppression of these problems through administrative controls does not provide a sustainable solution, because such controls distort resource allocation and impede growth. They also tend to discourage much-needed long-term investment inflows.

The level of long-term investment in Vietnam began falling in 1996 because of an unfavourable domestic business environment. The Asian financial crisis has accentuated this decline, as well as resulting in a real reduction in aid flows because of the significant depreciation of the yen and the won vis-à-vis the US dollar. Aid funds from Thailand have ceased completely. Therefore, even with draconian administrative measures, Vietnam will probably face balance of payments constraints of 'crisis' proportions in the absence of structural changes that significantly enhance the competitiveness of its economy. Economic isolation is not a viable option, so the issue for Vietnam is how to continue liberalising its economy without running the risk of suffering a currency and banking crisis.

It is clear that continued economic liberalisation in Vietnam must involve comprehensive reforms in the SOE sector and in the international trading regime; the building of a strong and resilient domestic financial sector; and movement to greater flexibility in the management of exchange rates. This chapter concentrates on the last two items in the reform agenda, while recognising that successful SOE and trade reforms will considerably ease the burden on the banking sector.[2]

The following section discusses Vietnam's financial sector and exchange rate regime. We turn next to examine the 'mini' crisis of 1997 and the fragility of the banking sector, then discuss the policies required for building a strong and resilient financial sector. The concluding section emphasises the importance of institution building as opposed to administrative control, and draws some implications for the role of the state in moving from a command to a market economy.

FINANCIAL STRUCTURE AND EXCHANGE RATE REGIME

Prior to *doi moi* or 'economic renovation' in 1989, Vietnam's financial system had all the typical characteristics of a centrally planned economy: namely, a banking system consisting only of the government-owned State Bank, a totally accommodating or passive role for this bank in regard to credit for SOEs, and essentially a cash economy for households. Interest rates had virtually no role in allocating financial resources, and money was essentially a unit of account, with production and consumption decisions determined by credit and cash plans (Leung and Vo 1996).

In mid-1988, Vietnam moved to a two-tiered banking system. The State Bank is in the first tier, as the central bank. Departments within the old State Bank that had formerly performed commercial banking functions were transformed into four government-owned 'specialised' banks in the second tier. Then, in May 1990, two laws were enacted that set the basis for a market-oriented banking system. New joint stock banks (belonging to both the state and the domestic private sector), as well as foreign bank branches and foreign joint venture banks, have subsequently been set up in the second tier.

The current structure of the financial sector is depicted in Figure 7.1. Although this suggests a reasonable diversity of financial intermediaries, the banking sector dominates the financial system, and within that sector the four state-owned commercial banks hold 75% of total assets. This is not surprising, since banks generally tend to dominate the financial sector in developing countries. This is so because they are very efficient in handling the information asymmetry and adverse selection problems so prevalent in information-intensive industries such as finance (Mishkin 1996). Because of their confidential relationship with their customers, banks are better able to monitor and assess credit risks and to internalise the information they gather so as to avoid 'free rides' from their competitors. In the case of Vietnam, moreover, the state-owned commercial banks enjoy full government guarantees as well as protection from competition by foreign banks, which are not permitted to engage in deposit mobilisation. Development of securities markets is slow, as the lack of an adequate legal and commercial infrastructure means that reliable information on enterprises is scarce.

From the point of view of monetary policy, recent reforms include: rationalisation of the interest rate structure so that real interest rates are positive (although interest rate ceilings remain, and interest rate margins are large because of inefficiencies and lack of competition in financial intermediation); unification of reserve requirements (currently set at 10%) across all institutions and deposit types; cessation of concessionary central bank refinancing of lending to state-owned commercial banks (leading to reported falls in refinanced credit to these institutions); and a unified refinancing rate. Monetary policy is operated through bank-by-bank credit ceilings

Figure 7.1   Vietnam: structure of the financial sector

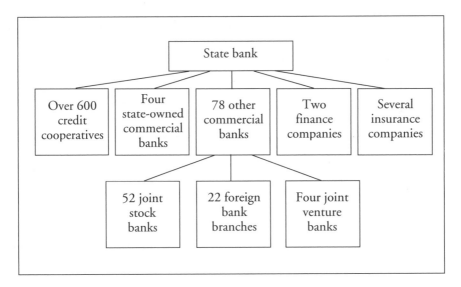

determined every quarter, applicable to the four state-owned commercial banks and 22 urban joint stock banks.

These reforms led to both an expansion of financial system assets and a significant change in their composition: lending to SOEs had fallen from 90% of total credit in 1990 to 55% by the beginning of 1997. However, the highly regulated nature of the domestic financial sector and Vietnam's poor legal and commercial infrastructure have meant that public confidence in banks has remained low. This is shown by the relatively low deposits: GDP ratio in Vietnam (16% in 1996, compared with 50% in China and 43% in the Philippines). The currency–deposits ratio, on the other hand, is very high (54% in 1996, compared with 16% in China, and even lower figures in the other Association of South East Asian Nations (ASEAN) countries) (World Bank 1997c). Furthermore, the use of US dollars in Vietnam, both in transactions and as a store of value, is significant (Ngo Huy Duc 1998).

On the foreign exchange policy front, exchange rates were unified in 1989. An official rate is now set by the State Bank, with upper and lower intervention bands within which the interbank market rate is determined. These rates, in turn, are set in relation to the dong/US dollar rate in the parallel market. Figure 7.2 shows that up to mid-October 1997, when the full impact of the Asian crisis was beginning to be recognised, the official and interbank exchange rates tracked the parallel market rate. Since then, however, there has been a sharp depreciation of the dong in the parallel market, followed by a widening of the intervention band (from 5% to 10%) in late

Figure 7.2   Vietnam: exchange rate movements during the crisis, 1997–8 (dong/US$)

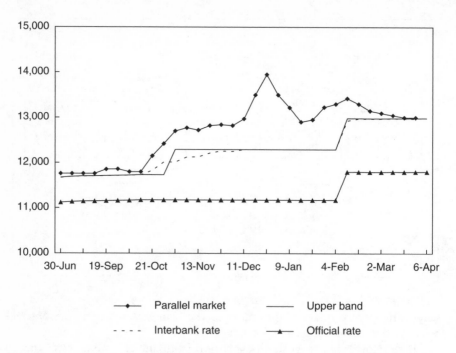

October 1997, and a devaluation of the official exchange rate by 5.3% in February 1998.

The reason the State Bank is able to maintain the official exchange rate – and, to some extent, manipulate the parallel market rate – lies in Vietnam's stringent controls over both the capital and the current accounts. All movements of capital into and out of the country have to be authorised. From 1994, all foreign currency deposits above a certain limit were required to be sold to the State Bank, and the use of foreign currencies in local transactions was made illegal.[3] More recently, following the February devaluation, all foreign currency holdings have been required to be deposited in banks, where they are subject to the rule concerning sale to the State Bank. Provisions have been made for repurchase for use in permissible activities, principally in payments for permitted imports. The introduction of this new control was probably responsible for the dip in the parallel market rate in March (Figure 7.2).

It has been argued that short-term capital had become much more mobile in the Asia Pacific region in the 1990s, even in countries where capital controls were still officially 'on the books' (Leung 1995). This was so partly because capital controls had been eroded through opening to international trade, since many of the techniques for evading capital controls are trade-related (Mathieson and Rojas-Suarez 1992). For example, capital can be transferred through the under- and over-invoicing of trade transactions; the leads and lags in commercial settlements; timing changes in the repatriation of foreign earnings; and forward exchange operations to cover trade transactions. By contrast, the fact that the government still exercises significant control over international trade in the form of trade licences and other regulations means that evasion of capital controls is more difficult in Vietnam than elsewhere.[4]

In addition, many Asia Pacific countries liberalised their domestic financial sectors in the 1980s, making apparent the large interest differential between domestic and world interest rates; this provided an incentive to evade capital controls. In Vietnam, however, domestic interest rate ceilings supported stringent controls over foreign borrowings, enabling the State Bank to regulate flows of short-term capital more effectively. However, the 'mini' financial crisis in the first half of 1997 demonstrated the fragility of Vietnam's internal and external financial sector, and underlined the importance of establishing and enforcing prudential regulations for the financial sector prior to interest rate and exchange rate deregulation (Villanueva and Mirakhor 1990).[5]

MORAL HAZARD IN THE BANKING SECTOR

Vietnam's dependence on controls can be best seen in the context of the 'mini' financial crisis, which arose after some elements of control were not implemented in 1996 and other elements were not imposed. This resulted in a 'letters of credit crisis' in the first half of 1997, the effects of which are still being felt.

As a result of tight domestic credit in 1996, interest rates on domestic currency loans rose sharply to about 1.7% per month for short-term loans and 1.6% for medium- to long-term loans. This compares with an average rate of 0.8% for US dollar loans from the Vietcombank, the largest government-owned commercial bank. The pegged exchange rate regime, supported by capital controls, gave rise to the belief that the government was willing and able to defend the dong against significant devaluation. There was a strong incentive, therefore, for enterprises to borrow in US dollars.

Prior to 1996, informal arrangements existed whereby some SOEs were able to obtain trade credit from their overseas suppliers. As discussed above, this is one of the most common ways of escaping capital controls, and it has been used in Vietnam to a limited extent. In 1996, however, SOEs were able to have their trade credit guaranteed by the state-owned commercial banks through letters of credit. This amounted to SOEs borrowing foreign currencies short-term through the state-owned commercial banks, so far as the risk to the banking system was concerned. The amount of these borrowings grew rapidly, both as a result of strong demand generated by the

Table 7.1   Vietnam: capital account (US$ million)

	1990	1991	1992	1993	1994	1995	1996 rev	1997 est
Capital account balance	122	188	656	107	1,363	1,837	1,908	n.a.
Disbursements	233	109	540	12	288	652	627	n.a.
Scheduled amortisations	−279	−104	−175	−695	−679	−826	−842	n.a.
Short-term loans (net)	48	19	-41	−133	124	−225	285	130
Direct foreign investment	120	165	333	923	1,631	2,236	1,838	1,930
Errors and omissions	−2	−4	−378	−397	−580	−393	286	n.a.

Source: World Bank 1997c: table 3.1.

interest rate differential mentioned above, and through increased willingness to provide credit resulting from the bank guarantees. As can be seen in Table 7.1, short-term capital inflows, after having been negative in 1992, 1993 and 1995, jumped to an estimated US$285 million in 1996.

In the event, a number of SOEs succeeded in channelling the borrowed funds into real estate investments, fuelling a real estate asset boom in the cities that faltered during 1995–7.[6] Others used the imported inputs in products where the market had declined. As a result, in early 1997, an estimated 40% of the guaranteed letters of credit (equivalent to 3% of GDP in value) became bad debts. Some commercial banks were not able to meet the external obligations they had guaranteed. The subsequent State Bank rescue reduced Vietnam's reserves to the equivalent of about five weeks of imports, and resulted in a downgrading of its sovereign credit rating from Ba3 to C (Thomson BankWatch Inc. 1997). Controls over state-owned banks' guaranteed letters of credit were subsequently imposed by the State Bank. This episode highlights the dangers of moral hazard problems in Vietnam's banking sector; the dangers of its crawling peg exchange rate regime; and its reliance on the successful implementation of controls to ameliorate the emerging financial crisis.

BALANCE OF PAYMENTS MANAGEMENT AND TRADE POLICY

Table 7.1 also shows that the bulk of Vietnam's capital inflow has been in the form of FDI and ODA, with the latter constituting most 'disbursements' shown in the table. Although these inflows are less subject to sudden reversals than short-term capital flows, both FDI flows and ODA flows are likely to decline in the near future. FDI approvals dropped by 50% in 1997, which will inevitably lead to a decline in actual inflows after a lag of one or two years. As for ODA flows, the large declines in the value of the yen and the won have meant that aid flows from Japan and Korea have fallen in US dollar terms. Given the expected loss of export markets as a result of both reduced growth in the region and Vietnam's appreciated real exchange rate, Vietnam faces severe balance of payments constraints. Increased reliance on import restrictions will not be wise, as reduced imports impact negatively on growth. A concerted effort to pursue export-oriented growth and restore foreign investor confidence would seem to be the only feasible strategy.

Vietnam has been artificially shielded from the Asian financial crisis through the successful imposition of controls over trade, capital flows and financial intermediation, all of which, however, prevent it from pursuing the strategy of export-oriented growth that has demonstrably brought economic prosperity to a large number of developing countries in the past four decades. In a number of Asia Pacific countries, to the extent that export-led growth had been successful, either capital controls were not imposed (as was the case in Indonesia, Hong Kong and Singapore) or their effectiveness was eroded (as in the Philippines and Thailand) (Leung 1995). It is clearly not a sensible option for Vietnam to stay 'behind closed doors'. Rather, the issue is how it can open its doors without exposing its economy to the severe instability that has been experienced recently by Thailand, Indonesia and South Korea. The lessons so far point to the need to have a strong and resilient financial sector and an appropriate exchange rate regime as the doors are being opened.

SEQUENCING IN FINANCIAL SECTOR REFORM

It is clear that financial sector and SOE reforms in Vietnam need to be conducted simultaneously, and that there are a number of elements common to both. The first step would be to incorporate all commercial banks (state-owned and private) and SOEs under the Company Law, and to institute standard systems of accounting and regular publication of audited financial statements.[7] It should be made clear that penalties under law would be incurred for non-compliance and for providing misleading information. In this way, the legal and commercial infrastructure would ensure a degree of transparency and accuracy of information for participants in the market. It is an appropriate role for government to institute disclosure requirements, as the 'free rider' problem otherwise discourages individuals from producing information on banks and enterprises (Mishkin 1996).

The incorporated banks should be charged with commercial, rather than social or political, objectives.[8] If the government wants social objectives to be met by the banks, it should reimburse them through budget transfers for efforts made in support of these objectives. In this regard, the recent decision to exempt large state corporations from needing to provide collateral for bank loans should be reversed, and commercial banks should be free to determine the kind and amount of collateral they require from each of their customers.

Even with regular publication of audited accounts, information on bank activities is incomplete and not entirely accessible, particularly for small, non-institutional savers. Monitoring by depositors cannot be relied upon completely to discourage irresponsible behaviour on the part of banks, so a case can be made for government regulators to impose restrictions on them. These restrictions might take the form of limiting the amounts of risky assets that banks can hold, and requiring banks to diversify their assets. Another possible restriction would require banks to have a higher level of equity capital relative to assets deposits, as a cushion against bad loans and so that bank owners would have more to lose if their banks failed. As soon as the authorities find any breach of regulations (particularly in relation to capital requirements), prompt corrective action is necessary to prevent any expectation of government bailouts (which cause moral hazard problems). Regulatory forbearance should be avoided at all times.

Universal deposit guarantees by the government tend to lessen the incentive for depositors to monitor and discipline their banks, and are therefore not recommended, since this can result in reckless behaviour on the part of bank management. A more effective approach would be for the government to lift restrictions on foreign joint venture banks, and allow them to take deposits from local residents, so as to provide competition for local banks.

With a more effective legal and commercial infrastructure in place, the government could proceed to abolish ceilings on credit growth and on domestic interest rates (Villaneuva and Mirakhor 1990).[9] Monetary policy could then be effected by influencing interest rates more generally in the economy, through open market operations, rather than by direct controls over banks. This has the advantage of allowing banks and non-bank financial institutions to compete on a more equal footing, and reduces the prospect of financial disintermediation.

As soon as the above reforms are in place, the government should move quickly to deregulate the capital account (McKinnon and Pill 1994). This means removing restrictions on short-term capital movements, as well as floating the exchange rate. As international trade is liberalised under Vietnam's commitments to ASEAN, and eventually as a result of its membership of the World Trade Organisation, capital controls will become increasingly difficult to implement. Besides – as has been the case in Australia, for example – capital account deregulation in the context of a floating exchange rate will encourage the growth of foreign currency hedge markets, and induce the business sector to become accustomed to managing exchange rate risk. With the necessary infrastructure in place, Vietnam could take advantage of the benefits of capital inflows whilst keeping the risks of overheating and instability to manageable proportions.

CONCLUSION

It has been argued that effective controls over trade, capital and financial intermediation in Vietnam have shielded the country, so far, from the serious instability affecting the region. However, administrative controls are not a sustainable solution, since they are not consistent with outward-looking growth. As has been the case in many Asia Pacific economies, increased international trade and investment will inevitably erode the effectiveness of such controls. In the longer term, Vietnam would best be served by undertaking comprehensive structural reforms – including building a strong and resilient financial sector – to enable it to take advantage of the benefits of international capital inflows while managing their inherent instability.

In a broader context, the issue strikes at the heart of the transition process. In a market economy where production and consumption decisions are decentralised, the primary role of the state lies in setting the framework in which markets operate. This encompasses the disclosure requirement and prudential supervision questions discussed above. Once an appropriate legal and commercial infrastructure is in place, competition rather than administrative control will bring the efficiency gains necessary for growth. Vietnam's commitment to the 'leading role of the state' therefore needs to be thought of in terms of instituting and maintaining such infrastructures.

Administrative controls give the illusion of providing a 'quick fix' when trouble strikes, whereas institution building necessarily takes time. Vietnam is still in the fortunate position of being able to choose a sustainable path without being in the midst of financial and currency turmoil. In addition, it has retained the strong support of the international donor community. However, such support will be quickly undermined if the international community is not convinced that the political will to undertake structural reforms exists. Although the crisis in the region has shortened the time frame in which Vietnam can choose to act, paradoxically, it also seems to have paralysed the policymaking process. Improving the legal and commercial infrastructure in the financial sector would appear to be an appropriate first step towards breaking the current standstill.

NOTES

1 Vietnam's economy is largely cash-based, as indicated by its very low M2:GDP ratio of 24%, compared with 54% in Indonesia, 50% in the Philippines, and 80% in Thailand.
2 On SOE reforms in Vietnam, see Leung (1998) and Mallon (1997). On trade reforms in Vietnam, see Kokko (1997).
3 It is widely acknowledged that the 1994 regulations against the use of US dollars in transactions were not strictly enforced. The February 1998 regulations

appear to be more draconian, and the government's determination to enforce them seems to be more apparent – a reaction, perhaps, to the Asian crisis.

4   Trade restrictions have been shown to be effective, as demonstrated by the fact that Vietnam's current account deficit was reduced from 11.3% of GDP in 1996 to 8.6% of GDP in 1997, largely as a result of restrictions on imports.

5   Otherwise, in the environment of a government deposit guarantee, banks will act as risk takers, lending to high-risk projects paying high interest rates on the expectation that they will profit if the projects succeed but taxpayers will bear the cost if the projects fail. This is the adverse selection–moral hazard problem facing banking regulators. Decisions to abolish government guarantees tend to suffer from credibility problems.

6   The real estate boom had already peaked in Ho Chi Minh City in 1995, but the downturn in small hotels and tourism facilities in which a large number of SOEs had invested did not occur until 1997.

7   The recently enacted Law on Credit Institutions should be changed substantially. This law provides for preferential bank credit for SOEs, cooperatives, and remote areas, thus undermining the commercial viability of banks and other financial institutions.

8   Two examples of major bank scandals point to the use of political influence over state-owned commercial bank lending. The TAMEXCO affair resulted in two senior officials of the Vietcombank being given long gaol sentences after large losses resulted from their loans to an import/export company owned by the Party Committee of the Tan Binh District. In another case, the Vietnam Industrial Development Bank (VIDB) lent the equivalent of 80% of the bank's capital to a joint venture between a private investor and the Party Committee of the 3rd District, Ho Chi Minh City. The joint venture collapsed and the VIDB was left crippled.

9   Privatisation of state-owned commercial banks could also be implemented at this point.

8 India

Sisira Jayasuriya

There have been few moments in recent decades when South Asians could look at East Asian economic performance with anything but envy.[1] After all, the South Asian economies have only just started to move along the path of rapid development that East Asians embarked on much earlier and, until this crisis, with such remarkable success. Since the middle of 1997, the almost unthinkable has happened. In contrast to crisis-ridden East Asia, South Asia seems a region of economic stability and of quite respectable growth: annual growth rates of 6–7% are accepted as 'normal', and the fabled 'Hindu rate of growth' (3.5% p.a.) apparently a fading memory. There has been a barely-concealed sense of relief among South Asian policymakers and technocrats that their economies have escaped contagion and experienced no major turbulence, despite some initial jitters. The more perceptive among them are aware, however, that the chill winds blowing from the East Asian crisis could spell trouble. Nevertheless, mixed with the worry and apprehension about what this crisis and its after-effects portend for their economies, many South Asians also feel an understandable, if not laudable, satisfaction at seeing the fast-running East Asians stumble and fall. The crisis raises many questions of profound importance for South Asia. How have its countries – poorer, more backward, far less dynamic and far more crisis-prone in the past – escaped the sickness that brought the tiger economies low? Are they really immune to the East Asian virus? What direct and indirect impacts will this crisis have on their economies? And how should they respond to the new challenges and opportunities?

This chapter attempts to provide some answers to these questions, by focusing on the experience of India, the largest South Asian economy. This is not to ignore the many, and important, differences among the countries of South Asia amongst their important similarities. A study of the Indian case can highlight some of the main reasons why the South Asian region escaped the contagion.

INDICATORS OF VULNERABILITY

India, the world's second most populous country after China, is also one of the poorest.[2] In the post-independence era, together with other South Asian economies, it followed inward-looking policies and emphasised the need for extensive state involvement in key economic sectors. Its growth performance was lacklustre (and punctuated by periodic crises): 3.6% per annum during the 1950s, 3.1% during the 1960s, and 3.6% during the 1970s. Improved performance during the 1980s (around 5.7%) – fuelled by large fiscal deficits and accompanied by large current account deficits – proved unsustainable, and paved the way for a major crisis in 1990–1.[3] In 1991, 'India was the most autarkic non-communist country in the world' (Joshi and Little 1996: 63). By 1991, India's share of world trade had fallen to 0.41%, from 2.4% in 1948 (Bhagwati 1993). The crisis proved to be a turning point. India made a decisive turn away from the previous policy stance and launched a major economic policy reform program. While there have been ups and downs in the pace and intensity of reforms since then, it has become clear that Indian policymakers across the political spectrum have embraced the international trend towards more liberal, open, pro-market policies.[4] The changes in India have been mirrored elsewhere in the subcontinent to varying degrees, with substantial progress in trade and exchange rate liberalisation, in scaling back the direct involvement of the state in economic enterprises, in developing a more welcoming attitude to foreign private capital inflows, and in making some progress with privatisation.[5] An example of this progress is that in 1994 all South Asian countries, with the exception of the tiny state of Bhutan, lifted exchange controls on current account transactions. As a result, by 1997 these economies were significantly better integrated with the global economy than during the 1980s, and therefore were also far more exposed to pressures emanating from disturbances in international markets.

To what extent, then, was India 'vulnerable' to a crisis in mid-1997? The literature on currency crises (and contagion effects) has been experiencing something of a boom recently.[6] Studies aimed at designing early warning systems based on leading indicators (factors that can foreshadow a crisis) conclude that the behaviour of a very large number of economic variables, in addition to country-specific political and other factors, warn of the onset of crises, and that the relative importance of different factors varies from crisis to crisis.[7] Each crisis throws up some unique features, however. Nevertheless, Kaminsky et al. (1997b: 12) identify a set of variables whose past behaviour (particularly during the 24 months preceding a crisis) seems able to provide some early warning:

> Currency crises seem to be usually preceded by multiple economic, and sometimes political, problems …

> *Those individual variables that receive ample support as useful indica-*
> *tors of currency crises include international reserves, the real exchange*
> *rate, credit growth, credit to the public sector, and domestic inflation.*
> The results also provide support for the trade balance, export per-
> formance, money growth, M2/international reserves, real GDP
> growth, and the fiscal deficit [emphasis in original].

In addition, analyses of the experience of Mexico in 1994 and recent work on the Asian crisis have emphasised variables reflecting the health of the financial sector, and the dangers of opening up a weak domestic financial system (particularly one with implicit guarantees for politically-favoured financial intermediaries) to international capital flows (see Krugman 1998a).[8]

THE INDIAN ECONOMY IN 1997: HOW VULNERABLE?

Historically, India (and other South Asian countries) have experienced balance of payments crises (in which it becomes difficult to finance imports for want of sufficient reserves), but not currency crises (in which capital flight leads to a collapse of the currency) or hyperinflation. This historical experience is important; agents instinctively respond to changes in the economic environment with historically-conditioned memories and reflexes. In the case of South Asia, it has been a history notable for its fiscal conservatism and for its prudent monetary policies implemented by conservative central bankers. This was the policy legacy that they had inherited from their ex-colonial masters, the British.[9] Hence, currency panics and generalised banking sector collapses are alien phenomena. Unless some key aspects of the monetary and financial systems had changed drastically in recent times, the most likely crisis, if there were to be one, would have been an 'old-style' balance of payments crisis of the kind that had regularly affected India and other South Asian countries.[10]

Let us begin with the variables whose behaviour has been important in past crises in India, and ignore, for the time being, the complications produced by large private capital flows and other financial sector issues. Joshi and Little (1994) identified four crisis episodes in India between the mid-1960s and early 1990s. All of them were balance of payments crises accompanied by some inflation. The first three (1965–7, 1973–5 and 1979–81) were caused primarily by adverse, unanticipated exogenous shocks, and the fourth (1990–1) was largely policy-induced, though triggered by an exogenous shock.[11] Harvest failures were a common and important factor preceding the first three crises. In each instance, an underlying poor macroeconomic situation was exacerbated by the unanticipated exogenous shock(s). The fragility of the pre-crisis economy in all cases was a reflection of India's external sector weaknesses. This was the product of inward-oriented protectionist policies, which had eliminated all so-called 'non-essential' imports but had also ensured that exports could not grow. As a result, India had chronic problems with low external reserves and very restricted capacity to finance any unexpected increase in imports. This made the economy vulnerable to any unanticipated shock, whether homemade (drought and harvest failure requiring food imports) or of foreign origin (oil price hikes generating sharply increased outward foreign payments).

But circumstances had changed in important ways by 1997. The post-1991 period was one of consolidation and growth for India, and by 1997 it had a cushion of comfort for dealing with shocks likely to exert pressure on the current account. The response to the policy reforms implemented in the midst of the crisis of 1991 was quick, and the economy was already in recovery mode by 1992–3, thereafter experiencing quite satisfactory growth by historical standards.

The achievements in the external sector were particularly impressive, given that in the 1990s India had to deal with the collapse of its traditional export markets in the former Soviet Union. Both exports and imports grew, so that, in 1997, the trade to GDP (gross domestic product) ratio was around 60% higher than the 1980s average. Higher export growth, helped by better export prices, raised the exports to GDP ratio by over 50%, despite the loss of East European markets. The current account deficit, which had been consistently over 2.5% of GDP during 1985–90, narrowed. Reserves increased to provide import cover for more than six months – something that had not been seen for many years. India seemed also to be more favourably placed in relation to international capital markets, with a relatively low debt service ratio (which had come down from 35% to 25%), and a sharp lowering of the ratio of foreign debt to annual current receipts from 3.3 years in 1990–1 to 1.6 years in 1996–7. The level of total foreign debt was a quarter of annual GDP, and around two-thirds was in the public sector – much of it on concessional terms from donors and multilateral lending institutions. While export growth slowed in 1996 (partly due to lower export prices), and the trade deficit widened, an increase in net invisible receipts led to a further narrowing of the current account deficit (see Chapter 1 tables).

The fiscal outcomes of the preceding period were also positive. The central government deficit declined from a high of 7.4% of GDP in 1993–4 to just over 5% in 1996–7; the combined gross fiscal deficit of the central and state governments also improved, from 7.4% of GDP in 1994–5 to 7% in 1996–7. While there was much room for further improvement, the direction of change was obviously in the direction of fiscal consolidation rather than looseness. There was no surge of domestic demand, and inflationary pressures were under control: average inflation during 1996–7 was 6.4%, down from 7.8% the previous year. Food grain production, a major influence on inflation, had experienced a 3% decline in 1995–6 (from a record figure in 1994–5), but recovered in 1996–7 to register a new record level of output (3% higher than 1994–5).

Thus, the Indian economy in mid-1997 was less susceptible to an old-style crisis. The outward-oriented policy reforms, despite their limited nature, had been effective in reducing vulnerability to a conventional balance of payments crisis. But did the post-1991 changes create the basis for a 'new-style' crisis?

The first point to note about India and other South Asian countries when assessing the potential for a new-style crisis is that, although their current accounts have been liberalised, their capital accounts have not. Capital movements remain subject to various restrictions, despite limited relaxation of some of them. India has accepted the goal of capital account convertibility as part of the ongoing liberalisation process, but has been proceeding in a very cautious manner. The Tarapore Committee, appointed to examine the issue of convertibility, recommended in May 1997 (RBI 1997) that capital account convertibility be phased in over three years, and be conditional on a set of stringent requirements, including fiscal consolidation, low inflation, strict supervision and regulation of financial institutions, and financial institution restructuring. The absence of a fully open capital account places limits on large-scale capital transfers within short periods of time. With these restrictions, the kind of currency switching that took place in East Asia, with domestic residents dumping their own currency in a wild scramble for foreign currencies, was far less likely in India. Further, firm action by the Reserve Bank in 1995, and again in 1996, had taught speculators that they should not underestimate its capacity to intervene.

However, the degree of insulation implied by the absence of full capital account convertibility should not be overstated. There are sources of volatility even when the capital account is not fully 'open'. Capital controls are never completely effective, and currency black markets are a ubiquitous feature of control regimes. Exporters can delay repatriation of export proceeds and thus affect foreign exchange flows. It has long been recognised that the maturity profile of foreign debt is important for the vulnerability of a country to capital flight: heavy dependence on short-term debt, or a large hump in the repayment schedule, are sources of potential difficulty. Portfolio capital flows are well known for their flightiness. What was India's situation in this regard?

Short-term debt was equivalent to only a quarter of foreign reserves – much lower than in most East Asian economies. But the post-1991 period has been characterised by a large surge of capital inflow, including both foreign direct investment and portfolio flows, with non-resident Indian deposits being an important source of such funds. These deposits have become an increasingly important, but potentially volatile, source of foreign financing.[12] Short-term debt of around US$7.5 billion, plus a stock of about US$6.7 billion of foreign portfolio investments by foreign institutional investors, plus about US$10 billion in non-resident Indian deposits that could be repatriated relatively quickly, constituted a total stock of volatile funds of about US$25 billion, which closely matched foreign reserves of some US$26 billion in mid-1997.[13] Looked at in this light, the possibility of a currency crisis in India brought about by changes in market sentiment should not be entirely ruled out, though its scope for damage may be more limited than in East Asian economies.[14]

The Indian financial system has long been recognised as being highly inefficient, and a major problem area. But without underestimating its weaknesses, it should be noted that at least there appears to have been some improvement as a result of financial sector reforms of recent years. According to the Reserve Bank, there has been a reduction in gross non-performing assets (NPAs) as a proportion of advances to about 18% in 1996–7 (RBI 1997). As is now well-recognised, rapid growth of credit to the private sector tends to lower the quality of bank loan portfolios, as more credit goes to poor-quality projects and creditors, and actual NPAs may increase without being immediately brought to light. But the growth of bank credit to the private sector did not accelerate; in fact, it fell in 1996–7 to 8.9%, from 17.7% in the previous year.

There was clearly no asset price boom, either in property or in the share markets. In any case, foreign capital accounted for only a small fraction of total Indian equity market capitalisation. While foreign capital inflows were up from 1995–6 levels, they were not large enough to generate serious inflationary pressures. Indeed, such pressures in the economy were moderating, and the inflation rate (at 6.4%) was not only below that of the previous year but also lower than the average of 8.6% during 1980–97. Broad money (M3) growth was slightly higher than the previous year, mainly because of an increase in time deposits, but at 15.9% was still a little lower than the average of 17.2% since 1980.

In these circumstances, India was unlikely to experience the real exchange rate appreciation that preceded the crises in Latin America and in Thailand, Malaysia and Indonesia.[15] There is evidence of some real appreciation from around March 1997, but by the middle of the year it was back to its January 1995 level.[16] Overall, the major indications were not suggesting that the economy was overheating; if anything, it was cooling down.

The Indian economy in mid-1997 differed, therefore, from the East Asian economies in a number of important ways. There was no panic, no contagion. India and the rest of South Asia escaped a crisis of either style, old or new.

REACTIONS TO THE CRISIS AND LIKELY IMPACTS

This did not mean that the East Asian crisis did not elicit any reactions in the South Asian region, however. The most visible reaction was some speculation against the region's currencies. In August 1997, comments by the deputy governor of the Reserve Bank of India (RBI) pushed the rupee down briefly, but it staged a relatively speedy recovery. It came under more sustained attack again later in the year, however, and, despite substantial RBI intervention, slipped below Rs40 to the US dollar in December 1997 (from around Rs35 in mid-year). In January 1998 the RBI implemented a series of measures to support the rupee, including an interest surcharge of 30% on import finance, and a domestic interest rate increase, which stabilised the currency.

The stock markets also peaked in August 1997 and were generally sluggish afterwards. Throughout the South Asian region, despite growing worries – particularly among exporters about the likely impact of East Asian currency depreciations on their competitiveness – the general response has been a cautious watchfulness, belied by occasional screaming headlines in the financial press, with central banks closely monitoring developments in the currency markets and attempting to ensure that there is no sudden collapse of their currencies.

What are the likely effects of the East Asian crisis on India, and more generally on South Asia? Of course, the magnitude of any impact depends very much on the way in which the crisis-affected economies evolve over time, and on the wider effects of the crisis on the global economy.[17] However, the nature of the impacts, the adjustment pressures that they will exert on the region's economies, and some of the ensuing policy issues are quite clear.

In principle, the East Asian crisis will have three effects on South Asia: the direct (negative) impact on South Asian trade and investment of economic recession in the crisis-affected economies; the competitive impact of devaluations by those countries in international markets; and the indirect effects that arise from the impact on the global economy. In practice, the trade and investment effects will be minor in absolute terms, though it should be noted that this region has been a significant outlet for growth for Indian exports in recent years; the share of East Asia other than Japan and China in South Asia's exports and imports is only around 15%, and in India's, around 16% and 11% respectively (Table 8.1). India competes globally with East Asian countries in a range of products but the enhanced competitiveness of East Asian exporters due to the currency depreciations will probably be felt most directly in manufactured exports to third-country markets, although cost-inflation, high interest rates and political turmoil will reduce the magnitude of this competitive edge.[18] The depreciation-induced export increases will tend to lower prices and intensify competitive pressure in labour-intensive manufactured exports markets. Exports of other goods and services, such as tourism, may also come under pressure. All these effects will be aggravated to the extent that the global economy is negatively affected.[19]

Intensified competition for diminishing flows of investment capital can

Table 8.1 South Asian direction of trade, 1995 (share of country's total trade, %)

	South Asia	Japan	China	Other Northeast Asia	Southeast Asia
Exports					
Bangladesh	2.7	3.3	0.6	4.1	1.3
India	5.0	7.0	0.9	8.1	7.4
Nepal	8.8	0.6	0.0	0.6	0.3
Pakistan	3.1	6.8	1.5	10.9	4.1
Sri Lanka	2.4	5.7	0.1	1.9	2.8
South Asia	4.3	6.5	0.9	7.7	6.0
Imports					
Bangladesh	17.7	9.2	9.3	15.7	9.2
India	0.5	6.5	2.4	3.8	6.6
Nepal	17.5	8.9	7.8	12.7	31.8
Pakistan	1.5	10.7	4.4	3.4	12.4
Sri Lanka	8.4	8.0	4.5	18.2	16.4
South Asia	3.6	7.8	3.8	6.6	9.3

Source: IMF Direction of Trade Statistics Yearbook (1996 and 1997).

also hurt South Asia. In principle, of course, there could be diversion of investor funds from crisis-affected countries to others, provided the others are seen as offering both safe and high returns to investment. In the current political climate, it is not clear that India (or any other South Asian country) stands to gain much through such investment diversion effects; and the outlook will have worsened as a result of US and Japanese sanctions after the nuclear explosions in mid-1998. Of course, one of the earliest casualties of the crisis has been East Asian investment flows into South Asia.

It is impossible to predict the magnitude of these impacts, or their time path. They most likely imply a reduced growth rate and a consequent excess of national expenditure over national income (relative to trend), leading to external sector imbalances.[20] By June 1998 it was too early for these effects to be fully felt but, as new Indian Minister of Finance Yashwant Sinha has pointed out, early indications are rather ominous:

> Overall economic growth has slowed to 5% in 1997/98, industry continues in the doldrums averaging only 4.6% growth ... exports have recorded negative growth in dollar terms in each of the three most recent months up to January 1998, for which data are available ... The capital market has been lacklustre and the fiscal situation is significantly worse than expected.[21]

These developments highlight the dangers that South Asian countries face: as Williamson (1998) has pointed out, the eruption of new-style crises in

East Asia has increased the vulnerability of South Asian economies to old-style crises.

The gradual but significant nominal depreciations of South Asian currencies, and a number of other initiatives either under consideration or being implemented, suggest that these danger signals are being heeded, at least by the monetary authorities. The RBI has signalled that it is likely to take firm steps to deal with weaknesses in the financial sector, and that it may go beyond the Basle recommendations in terms of capital adequacy. The crisis has also accentuated fears about the dangers and risks of integration with world markets, and made policymakers and administrators doubly cautious. India is certainly likely to heed the message from the East Asian crisis: that caution is needed in moving to capital account convertibility.[22] The RBI has indicated that it will not allow the banking system to take 'too much' short-term cross-border exposure, and has also halted the planned integration of foreign exchange and money markets. While it would be surprising if moves for greater openness and integration with global markets did not suffer some deceleration in the immediate future, it is unlikely that there will be a return to the old insular policies in South Asia, the source of slow growth and recurrent old-style crises. Avoiding a new-style crisis cannot be the sole objective of policy.

CONCLUSION

For a variety of reasons, India escaped the crisis that gripped the East Asian region in 1997–8. A more closed economy in the early stages of opening up, India had not experienced the sustained growth, the massive portfolio capital inflows, and the rising euphoria that, in combination with fundamental problems in the financial sectors, generated asset-market bubbles and precipitated the subsequent crises in East Asian countries. On the other hand, the limited reforms since 1991 had helped it to develop an external sector safety cushion, so that it was able to weather the initial impact. But it is already feeling the longer-term effects of the crisis. The policy response is unlikely to be a serious reversal of the opening-up process. But more than a refusal to return to insularity will be needed in the period ahead. The big lesson of the East Asian crisis and its aftermath for India (and South Asia) is the importance of following a path of fundamental and sustained reform, while paying due attention to their proper sequencing and timing.

NOTES

1   South Asia here includes Bangladesh, Bhutan, India, Nepal, Pakistan and Sri Lanka.
2   In 1995, its population was 930 million, with an annual per capita income of US$340 (below the low-income country average).
3   The crisis erupted in March 1991. For detailed analyses of Indian macroeconomic performance and policies, see Joshi and Little (1994, 1996).
4   Joshi and Little (1996) provide an analysis of the policy shift after the 1991 crisis and developments up to 1995. They also discuss the change in intellectual attitudes towards policy reforms, and the role played by the collapse of the Soviet model, and the East Asian and Chinese growth performance.
5   In fact, Sri Lanka was the first country to undertake policy liberalisation with a series of major trade and exchange rate reforms in 1977–8. It underwent a 'second wave' of reforms during 1989–90, spurred on by a crisis not very dissimilar to the Indian one of 1991. For discussions of the wider liberalisation process in South Asia, see, for example, Shand (forthcoming).
6   Recent models (e.g. Obstfeld 1986, 1994a) draw on and extend Krugman's (1979) seminal work. For a survey, see Kaminsky et al. (1997b).
7   Recent empirical studies of currency crises have adopted different approaches, ranging from single-country case studies (e.g. Leiderman and Thorne 1996), crises effects in a group of countries (e.g. Dornbusch 1997; Dornbusch et al. 1995), and the impact of a crisis in one country on a group of other countries (e.g. Sachs et al. 1996), to regression analyses of a large number of crisis episodes (e.g. Kaminsky et al. 1997b).
8   Again, as Indonesia's long experience with an open capital account demonstrates, this is not a sufficient condition by itself for a crisis.
9   As Little et al. (1994) point out, such policies have not been confined to ex-British colonies (cf Thailand), and have tended to weaken over time.
10   Williamson (1998) distinguishes between 'new-style' crises – such as the current ones in East Asia which are associated with collapsing asset-market bubbles, currency switching and capital flight, exchange rate depreciation and financial sector collapse – and 'old-style' or conventional balance of payments/exchange rate crises.
11   The 1965–7 period was affected by two bad harvests and unanticipated foreign aid problems; the second and third crises were related to the two oil shocks; and the fourth crisis was also triggered by the oil price hike in response to the Gulf conflict.
12   The Reserve Bank also includes the stock of US$5.4 billion in global deposit receipts (securities issued by Indian companies to raise funds in overseas markets) in evaluating the level of foreign reserves needed for exchange rate stability in the face of volatile capital flows (RBI 1997: para 6.26).
13   In March 1997, short-term debt was estimated at US$6.7 billion (RBI 1997). However, Bank for International Settlements (BIS) figures indicate that this had risen to US$7.7 billion by the end of June 1997.
14   The scope for 'outsiders' to mount speculative attacks on the Indian currency is much more limited, but the evidence on East Asia suggests that the crisis had

much more to do with domestic residents' loss of confidence in their own currencies than with speculation by outsiders.

15 Real exchange rate appreciation had not been identified as a major factor in the previous Indian crises analysed by Joshi and Little (1994).

16 Not too much should be read into this observed movement, since this measure has several weaknesses as a proxy for the price of tradables relative to non-tradables, and authorities are known to have been following a more flexible exchange rate policy to avoid any sustained real appreciation.

17 There is no consensus about the future evolution of the crisis, but this writer is less optimistic than many about a quick end to it. Conditions in the East Asian countries remain volatile in mid-1998, and there is a real threat of further deterioration and widening of the crisis; the impact on the real economy is only beginning to be felt. The full impacts on the long-stagnant Japanese economy, and on the slowing Chinese economy, remain to be seen, and the global consequences of a slide to crisis in either of these economies are not difficult to imagine.

18 It is unlikely that inflation will completely erode the competitive edge gained from currency depreciations, given that the drying-up of capital inflows will ensure cuts in their real expenditures, maintaining some degree of real depreciation (unless political turmoil, and dislocation in financial markets, destroy the capacity for supply-side responses).

19 A caveat is in order: it should be noted that falling oil prices are highly beneficial to the South Asian economies. While the current depressed oil prices cannot be attributed solely, or even mainly, to the Asian crisis, note that oil imports account for over a quarter of India's total import bill.

20 Even if the real exchange rate of these economies were in equilibrium prior to the East Asian crisis, the altered external circumstances imply that they would no longer be in equilibrium, and painful adjustments may be needed.

21 The fiscal deficit for 1997–8 expanded from a targeted 4.5% of GDP to 6.1% (*Economic Times of India* 1998). There are signs of slowing exports in other South Asian countries, but it is of course difficult to attribute these solely to the effects of the East Asian crisis.

22 Speech by Professor Joseph Stiglitz in New Delhi on 19 May 1998, reported in *The Business Line* (20 May 1998).

Part IV

Case studies: other countries' experience

9 The Philippines

Ponciano Intal Jr., Melanie Milo,
Celia Reyes and Leilanie Basilio

INTRODUCTION

The Philippine peso was one of the first currencies put under intense speculative attack after the devaluation of the Thai baht. Nevertheless, the Philippines has not been hit as hard by the East Asian 'crisis' as have Indonesia, Thailand or South Korea. A decade-long process of financial reform and rebuilding, in conjunction with economy-wide liberalisation and deregulation, have been major factors behind the country's greater resilience. The country's macroeconomic condition remains fragile, however, partly because the government's fiscal position is vulnerable to high interest rates because of the country's large public debt. At the same time, the El Niño phenomenon is wreaking havoc on Philippine agriculture, which remains an important sector of the Philippine economy. The longer currency instability in the region remains, the high domestic interest rate regime continues, and El Niño drags on, the greater will be the deflationary effect. That is, there will be adverse impacts on the investments and operations of Philippine businesses large and small, while the government will have to impose sharp cutbacks on its own discretionary expenditures. Thus it is critical for the Philippines that the regional currency situation stabilise in order that domestic interest rates can ease.

Many analysts and observers expect the Philippines to be one of the first countries in the region to grow out of the East Asian crisis. Nevertheless, the Philippines is still strengthening its foundations for a sustained and robust economic growth path, in contrast to the boom-and-bust cycle of previous decades. The crisis offers both challenges and opportunities. If the Philippines can further strengthen its economic fundamentals and continue its reform efforts, the country that was left out of the East Asian 'miracle' may yet embark on its own economic take-off in the near future.

THE FINANCIAL SECTOR: CRISIS AND REBUILDING

Finance in the East Asian crisis

There is a growing consensus that financial factors, both domestic and international, played a critical role in precipitating the East Asian crisis and in making it unexpectedly severe. On the domestic front, a number of the affected countries had weak prudential regulations and inadequate monitoring of financial institutions. These regulatory and institutional inadequacies were aggravated by moral hazard problems arising from implicit guarantees on the liabilities of banks (Krugman 1998a), leading to excessive risk-taking by domestic firms and lenders, and by problems of asymmetrical information (Stiglitz 1989), especially in relation to foreign lenders and investors.

The aggressive risk-taking of domestic firms was complemented by the 'irrational exuberance' and herd behaviour of foreign lenders and investors, facilitated in part by the revolution in telecommunications that allows international transfers of large volumes of funds to occur in seconds. Virtually all the affected countries had open capital accounts, with countries such as the Philippines facilitating access by domestic firms to foreign funds (largely short-term) – for example, through the Bangkok International Banking Facility (BIBF) in Thailand, and foreign currency deposit units (FCDUs) in the Philippines. Given domestic regulatory shortcomings and 'exuberant' local and foreign investors, the result was substantial asset inflation despite generally modest overall inflation rates. The eventual bursting of the bubble contributed significantly to the emergence of the crisis.

Financial crisis and reforms

The Philippine financial sector stood up relatively well during the crisis, in contrast to the large financial failures experienced in Indonesia and Thailand. Only one small and newly upgraded commercial bank failed, although two small development banks were taken over by two large commercial banks after the former experienced difficulties. Behind the relatively greater resilience of the Philippine banking sector are, on the one hand, the decade-long series of policy and institutional reforms in the financial sector and, on the other, the shorter period during which Philippine banks, in comparison with financial institutions in countries such as Indonesia and Thailand, had enjoyed liberal access to the international financial market.

The Philippines had already experienced a financial crisis, during the early 1980s. Some of the key causal factors were similar to those that helped bring about the more recent crisis in East Asia. The supervision and monitoring of banks by the Philippine central bank was weak, encouraging loose banking practices. Capital requirements were made less stringent; rules on credit to directors, stockholders, and related interests (DOSRI) were relaxed; political accommodation in lending was prevalent – especially at the two largest financial institutions, both government-owned; and negative real interest rates encouraged debt-financed investments (Intal and Llanto 1998; Nascimento 1991). In the non-bank financial institutions, such as investment houses, the central bank had little jurisdiction over transactions made on a 'without recourse' basis. A series of investment frauds and stockbroker failures, and the default and flight of a prominent businessman, eventually triggered the crisis (Laya 1982).

Financial reforms commenced in the early 1980s were extended during the late 1980s and early 1990s. Many of those reforms involved strengthening prudential regulations in relation to minimum capitalisation requirements; increasing compliance with the minimum capital to risk asset ratio, the single borrower limit, the limit on DOSRI loans, and the stipulations regarding interlocking directorships and management; making provision for loan losses or doubtful accounts; tightening audit and reporting requirements; and reviewing the bailout policy for problematic banks (Bautista 1992; Intal and Llanto 1998). The government also rehabilitated some ailing financial institutions including, notably, the government-owned banks and the rural banks. The central bank, which suffered massive losses in the early 1980s, was also eventually rehabilitated in 1993, with the creation of a new, independent Central Monetary Authority called the Bangko Sentral ng Pilipinas (BSP). Other banking reforms implemented in the 1990s included the deregulation of the entry of new domestic banks and bank branching in 1993 (further rationalised in 1995), and the easing of restrictions on the entry of foreign banks in 1994.

The required minimum capital for banks increased over time. For example, the requirement for universal banks increased from 500 million pesos in 1980 to 1 billion pesos in 1990, 2.5 billion pesos in 1995, 4.5 billion pesos in 1998, 4.95 billion pesos in 1999 and 5.4 billion pesos in 2000. The series of increases in bank capitalisation requirements and the easing of entry by foreign banks have proved to be important factors in light of the East Asian crisis. The capital adequacy ratio, defined as the ratio of net worth to risk assets, hovered between 16.9% and 20.2% between 1992 and June 1997 (Intal and Llanto 1998) – much higher than the Bank for International Settlements (BIS) requirement of 8%. The relatively high capital adequacy ratio of Philippine banks is one important reason why the Philippine banking sector has been able to weather the East Asian crisis relatively comfortably.

Reforms in other sectors of the financial system included efforts to develop equity markets, such as the unification of the Manila and Makati Stock Exchanges to form the Philippine Stock Exchange in 1994, and the liberalisation of the private insurance industry in 1995. The liberalisation of foreign investment and foreign exchange transactions had a significant impact on the development of the Philippine capital market. However, the ensuing large flows of portfolio capital posed macroeconomic problems and, as the East Asian crisis has shown, large capital movements can be destabilising.

Financial deepening

In terms of both assets and number of offices, the Philippine financial system stagnated during the early 1980s, expanded somewhat during the late 1980s, and surged during the 1990s – especially in the three years before the crisis (Figure 9.1). The earlier stagnation resulted from the financial and economic crisis of the period but, after reforms in the financial sector and the recovery of the economy in the mid-1990s, both total assets and the number of offices increased dramatically. The sharp expansion in the number of bank branches – from 2,698 in 1990 to 6,745 by June 1997 – is particularly noteworthy, and reflects the liberalisation of bank branching after 1994.

Despite the rapid growth of the banking sector in terms of assets and number of offices, the level of financial deepening remains fairly modest. Having stagnated for decades at around 20% prior to financial liberalisation, the ratio of M2 to gross domestic product (GDP) rose to around 26% in 1983, while the ratio of M3 to GDP increased to around 31%.[1] There was considerable financial shallowing during the mid-1980s, and a substitution away from deposits into secure, higher-yielding government securities. Significant financial deepening recommenced in 1993, with the M2 to GDP ratio increasing from 28% in 1992 to 43% in 1997.

Nevertheless, the ratios are fairly low compared to those in other countries in the region. This is partly due to the tight liquidity management policy pursued by the central bank to meet inflation targets agreed to with the International Monetary Fund (IMF). The high reserve requirement and the 20% withholding final tax on interest income resulted in low rates of return on deposits. As a result, there was a sharp increase, especially in the 1990s, in the off-balance sheet activities of commercial banks, which was facilitated by the easing of banking regulations. These included the use of FCDUs to fund foreign currency loans – which grew rapidly from just US$2.6 billion to US$17.7 billion in 1997 – and the use of trust accounts for securities investments. The latter did not become subject to the various intermediation taxes until 1993, and thus offered higher yields than traditional bank deposits. If the trust operations of banks were included in the measure of financial deepening (since banks were effectively using them in the same way and for the same purpose as deposits and deposit substitutes), the ratio of M4 to GDP would be 58%, which may be compared with the 44% ratio of M3 to GDP. If foreign currency deposits of residents were also included in the ratio – M5 to GDP – it would increase further to 76%.

The strengthening of the financial sector is indicated by a reduction in the role of wholesale debt as a source of funds for Philippine financial in-

Figure 9.1 Philippines: assets of the financial system by type of institution (billion pesos)

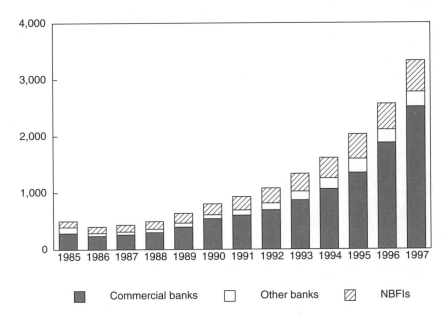

Commercial banks ▪   Other banks ☐   NBFIs ▨

stitutions, and a correspondingly greater emphasis on deposits. Commercial banks reduced their reliance on borrowings from 25% of total funds during the 1970s and early 1980s to less than 10% in the early 1990s; correspondingly, the share of deposits increased from less than 50% of total funds during the 1970s and early 1980s to about 67% by the early 1990s. The shift towards deposits as a source of funds was even more dramatic for rural banks and grew from less than 33% in the 1970s to 60% by the early 1990s. The increased reliance on deposits coincided with the rising financialisation of savings, as reflected in the increase in the ratio of total deposits to gross annual saving from a range of 33–5% during 1988–92 to an average of 54% during 1993–5. The liberalisation of bank branching and entry into the banking sector (especially by a limited number of large foreign banks) has resulted in greater competition for deposits. As a result, bank deposit concentration, as indicated by the top five banks' share of total deposits, has declined (Intal and Llanto 1998).

Financial vulnerability

Financial deepening in the 1990s coincided with two developments that, as recent experience has shown, could lead to a financial crisis if not managed well – namely, a significant increase in the foreign liabilities of banks, and a rise in lending to the non-tradables sector (especially the real estate sector). The total foreign exchange liabilities of private commercial banks increased

Figure 9.2   Philippines: foreign assets and foreign liabilities of commercial banks
(% of GDP)

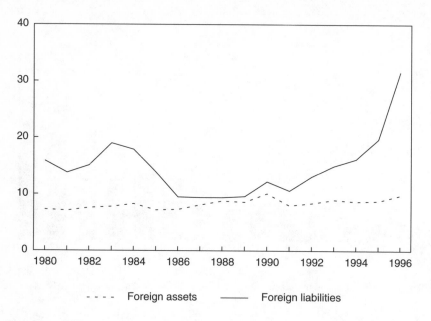

---- Foreign assets   ——— Foreign liabilities

Source: Bangko Sentral ng Pilipinas; National Statistical Coordination Board.

from US$0.52 billion in 1993, prior to the deregulation of foreign exchange transactions, to more than US$7 billion by the third quarter of 1997. As a percentage of the total foreign exchange liabilities of the country, the share of foreign liabilities of private commercial banks rose sharply from 1.5% to 15.2% during this period. Figure 9.2 shows the foreign assets and foreign liabilities of commercial banks expressed as a percentage of GDP. The gap between the two increased steadily from 1992 to reach almost 32% of GDP in 1996 – almost entirely because of the huge increase in foreign liabilities, which was especially rapid in 1996.

The rapid increase in commercial banks' foreign liabilities facilitated the lending boom of recent years. For instance, the contribution of foreign currency loans to the domestic lending of eight commercial banks that resorted to the international capital markets rose substantially, from 12% in 1993 to 40% in the first quarter of 1997. An increase in foreign liabilities is not necessarily a problem. What ultimately matters is how the funds were used; in the light of the East Asian crisis, this is clearly a source of financial vulnerability. Consider the distribution of FCDU loans, for example: while at least 50% went to exporters, the share going to non-exporters had increased from 4% at the beginning of 1994 to 30% by the third quarter of 1997.

The loan portfolio of the commercial banking system shifted increasingly

Table 9.1 Philippines: distribution of commercial banks' loans outstanding by sector
(% of total)

	Total (billion pesos)	Primary[a]	Manufacturing	Finance[b]	Other[c]
1981	87	21	30	17	32
1985	92	21	24	20	35
1990	240	14	39	17	31
1995	737	9	34	17	39
1996	1,120	7	32	22	40
1997	1,417	6	30	25	39

Notes:
a Agriculture, fishery, forestry; mining and quarrying.
b Finance, insurance, business services and real estate.
c Utilities, construction, wholesale and retail trade, transport, storage and communication, and community, social and personal services.
Source: Bangko Sentral ng Pilipinas.

towards the non-tradables sector during the 1990s. Table 9.1 shows that after the early 1990s there was a significant drop in the shares of the primary sector (comprising the agriculture, fishery and forestry sector and the mining and quarrying sector). The share of manufacturing, which increased during the economic recovery years of the late 1980s, also declined significantly during the 1990s. The sector that saw a substantial increase in its share was the finance, insurance, business services and real estate sector. Changes in the sectoral composition of the loans portfolios of commercial banks are significant because the commercial banks are the predominant source of funds, given that commercial banks' loans accounted for 86% of total banking system loans as of 1997.

THE EAST ASIAN CRISIS AND THE PHILIPPINE FINANCIAL SECTOR: RESILIENCE AND FORTUNE

Policy response

The Philippine peso was one of the first currencies to come under intense speculative attack after Thailand's property and financial crisis broke out in April 1997. The BSP allowed the peso to depreciate in mid-July, after spending around US$1.5 billion to keep the exchange rate at around 26 pesos per US dollar. The exchange rate breached that level in August, falling to over 45 pesos per US dollar in early 1998. The peso had recovered to around 38.50 pesos per US dollar by late April 1998.

The government's response to the crisis centred on tightening monetary policy, beginning in June. The central bank increased the requirements for bank reserves, including liquid reserves (i.e. funds required to be placed in short-term market instruments). The central bank closed the overnight lending window momentarily in August, and set stringent conditions on its use when it was reopened in October. The BSP also required banks to maintain a capital to asset ratio of not less than 10%. In January, it increased the cap on banks' real estate exposure to 20% of their total loan portfolios, and imposed a 30% liquid asset cover for dollar loans.

In addition to tightening monetary policy, the central bank imposed some new foreign exchange controls by placing a cap of US$100,000 on over-the-counter sales of foreign exchange for non-trade purposes at the end of June, which was lowered to US$25,000 at the end of July; this ceiling was partially lifted for residents in September. It also imposed a limit on commercial banks' oversold position (i.e. net foreign liabilities) of 10% of unimpaired capital, while their overbought position was set at 20%, with penalties and sanctions imposed on banks that exceeded these allowable positions.[2] The limits were later reversed and the overbought position of banks was lowered to 5%, but not allowed to exceed US$10 million in absolute terms, to force commercial banks to off-load their foreign exchange holdings. Tighter rules for computing banks' open positions were also implemented, in order to prevent banks from circumventing the regulations. The BSP and the Bankers Association of the Philippines also briefly entered into an agreement, in December 1997, to set daily quotas for the supply of dollars to be sold in the foreign exchange market at an agreed rate; in addition, the BSP undertook to provide forward cover to banks that had non-deliverable forward contracts with dollar borrowers.

Since the advent of the crisis, the monetary authorities have moved to implement stricter monitoring of the quality of bank assets. In particular, the BSP will be closely monitoring banks' compliance with prudential regulations, and banks' non-performing loans, exposures to real estate, and car and consumer loans. Further reforms in the financial sector are also being considered. These include: adopting and implementing international regulatory standards; improving supervision; rationalising taxation in the financial sector; allowing more liberal foreign investor participation in finance companies and investment houses; and facilitating the privatisation of pension funds.

In March 1998, the government approved a Memorandum for Economic and Financial Policies (MEFP), which placed the Philippines under a precautionary arrangement with the IMF for two years. The economic program specifically focused on banking sector reforms in light of financial crises in the region. The MEFP identified four banking reforms for implementation, namely: raising capital and encouraging some consolidation; reducing bank risks by tightening provisioning requirements and strengthening regulatory oversight; levelling the playing field between different types of institutions and instruments, especially with a view to reducing incentives for peso disintermediation; and the twin objectives of dealing expeditiously with individual problem banks while safeguarding the soundness of the banking system.

Impact on the financial sector

The government's tight monetary policy, used primarily to defend the peso, led to a sharp rise in domestic interest rates (Figure 9.3). The 91-day Treasury bill (T-bill) rate increased from 10% in April 1997 to 19.1% in January 1998. The rate subsequently fell to an eight-month low of 14.7%, on 27 April 1998, in response to increased stability in the regional currency markets and an improvement in the cash position of the government, in as much as April is the deadline for the submission of income tax. Nevertheless, the T-bill rate in April 1998 was still nearly 500 basis points higher than it had been a year earlier. In addition, the decline in lending rates has been slower – so much so that businessmen in the southern Philippines have staged demonstrations against the high interest rate regime.

Portfolio capital flows turned negative in May 1997. The negative portfolio flows and the high interest rate regime wreaked havoc on the stock market. The Philippine Stock Exchange composite index plunged from 3,171 points at the end of 1996 to 1,772 points – just slightly higher than its pre-boom level – by November 1997. Banking and property stocks were the worst hit. The composite index has been recovering more recently

Figure 9.3   Philippines: monthly 91-day T-bill rate and average lending rates (% p.a.)

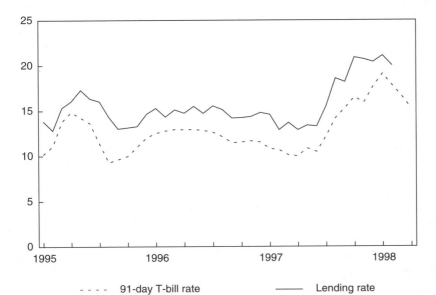

- - - - 91-day T-bill rate   ——— Lending rate

Source: Bangko Sentral ng Pilipinas.

(reaching 2,185 points by mid-April 1998), in part because foreign portfolio capital has started to return to the stock market.

The financial sector has largely weathered the regional crisis. Despite the minor failure and takeovers previously mentioned, the overall financial condition of the banking sector is manageable. The average capital adequacy ratio is substantially higher than legally required. The ratio of non-performing loans to total loans of commercial banks had increased to 4.7% by the end of 1997, as opposed to 2.8% in 1996. Nevertheless, this is much lower than it was during the mid-1980s, when the ratio reached more than 20%.

Resilience and good fortune

The Philippine financial sector weathered the crisis because of both resilience and good fortune. Its resilience stemmed from the experience of the financial crisis of the early 1980s and the reforms and rebuilding that had taken place since then. The reforms implemented during 1980–96 were quite far-reaching.

The current financial crises in Thailand and Indonesia are very similar to that which beset the Philippines in the 1980s, particularly in relation to the interplay of excessive risk-taking by banks and weak prudential supervision by the authorities. Indeed, another factor explaining the Philippines' relatively good recent performance may be that most weak and unstable banks and investment houses were weeded out of the system during the 1980s crisis. The banks that survived – and even thrived – during the crisis were the more conservative ones. Entry to the banking system has been tightly controlled, and the series of increases in minimum capital requirements for banks has made them financially stronger. Furthermore, the authorities have been more responsive and active than before, including in terms of monitoring both commercial banks' exposure to the real estate sector and levels of short-term foreign borrowings.

However, as discussed earlier, a number of worrying trends had begun to emerge in recent years. In particular, the commercial banking sector was beginning to manifest similar trends in lending activity and the accumulation of foreign exchange liabilities to those which were evident in Thailand. There had been a credit boom, although less pronounced than the boom in Thailand. Philippine commercial banks' total loans to the private sector rose from 19% of GDP in 1985 to 24% in 1994, whereas those in Thailand rose from 45% to 89% (IMF 1995). By the end of 1996, the Philippines' loan to GDP ratio had risen to around 63%, compared with Thailand's 114%.

Lending growth was concentrated in the financial and real estate sectors, although the magnitude of the property lending boom in the Philippines was smaller than that in Thailand. The BSP imposed a limit on banks' exposure to property loans in 1996, such that aggregate loans of commercial banks to the real estate sector were held to 11.8% of total loans in June

1997. However, as the case of the failed Philippine commercial bank clearly showed, there were some banks with significantly higher exposures. In Thailand, banks had actually extended only 9.4% of their total loans to the real estate sector at that time, but finance companies were a more important source of real estate lending, with real estate exposure estimated at 24% of total loans. The property boom in the Philippines has not been as strong as that in Thailand, and its duration has been relatively short. The vacancy rate in prime commercial districts in the Philippines was estimated at just 4% at the end of 1996, whereas Thailand's was 25%, which would seem to indicate the absence of any property glut in the Philippines prior to the current crisis.

A worrying trend that emerged in recent years was an increase in commercial banks' foreign liabilities, both in absolute terms and relative to their foreign assets. However, it has been noted that these were less susceptible to exchange rate movements and capital flight than Thailand's, since about 52% of the total foreign exchange liabilities of commercial banks in the Philippines was owed to residents, as against just 1% in Thailand, as of the first quarter of 1996. It was mostly the big universal banks, which had greater capacity to manage risks, that resorted to overseas borrowings in order to lengthen the maturity structures of their liabilities. Although there was an increase in short-term foreign liabilities, they accounted for only 19% of the Philippines' total outstanding foreign liabilities, around US$45 billion, as of June 1997. Thailand's short-term foreign obligations, by contrast, were estimated at 37% of the total at the end of 1996.

Simply put, there were signs of a potential financial crisis by the end of 1996, but these worrying trends were only just emerging. The case of Thailand has heightened awareness of the danger of allowing these trends to persist, and this should help the Philippines to avert any similar crisis.

MACROECONOMIC VULNERABILITY AND OUTCOMES

Vulnerability and contagion

Despite the prominence of financial market issues in the literature on the East Asian crisis, the macroeconomic environment and macroeconomic weaknesses have played a central role. There was, of course, a close connection between the macroeconomic environment and the state of the financial sector in the crisis-affected countries. For example, financial institutions were often an important conduit through which domestic firms tapped the international capital market: only a few large, internationally-known domestic firms would have direct access to this market.

Central to the crisis is the operation of the 'incompatible trinity': it is not possible to maintain internal consistency among an autonomous national monetary policy, free international capital flows, and fixed exchange rates

(Jager 1997). However, Indonesia and Thailand, amongst others, did attempt to control the money supply (to contain inflation) in the context of open capital accounts and essentially fixed (or steadily depreciating) exchange rates. The result was a large interest rate differential that motivated local firms to borrow in foreign currencies and, at the same time, encouraged foreign lenders and investors to provide funding offshore – or even onshore, through, for example, the BIBF. The emergence of the East Asian crisis underlines the notion of the 'incompatible trinity', but the severity of the crisis stemmed from various financial and regulatory shortcomings that deepened moral hazard problems and asymmetric information problems in the troubled countries.

Among the Southeast Asian currencies, the peso had experienced the largest real currency appreciation during the 1990s. The Philippines also had the highest merchandise trade deficit relative to GDP among the Association of South East Asian Nations (ASEAN) countries. Thus, the Philippines was vulnerable to any devaluation experienced by an important competitor country, such as Thailand. In addition, the Philippines had the lowest domestic saving rate among the ASEAN4 countries, implying that the country was dependent on foreign capital for a high investment rate and, at the same time, vulnerable to changed foreign investor sentiment in financing the country's current account deficits. Finally, the country had the highest ratio of public sector debt to GDP among the ASEAN4 countries, making its fiscal situation vulnerable to surges in interest rates.

Outcomes[3]

Table 9.2 presents selected macroeconomic indicators for the Philippines in 1996 and 1997. The impact of the crisis is clearly apparent in the balance of payments, which turned negative during the last three quarters of 1997, primarily because of the reversal of both portfolio and foreign direct investment. Both the trade and current account deficits also surged during the second and third quarters, although there was a significant reduction in these deficits in the fourth quarter. The latest estimates indicate that the balance of payments turned positive during the first two months of 1998, primarily because of a further sharp reduction in the trade deficit and a net inflow of portfolio capital.

The reduction in the trade deficit reflected the continued high growth of exports and the deceleration of import growth; indeed, during the first two months of 1998, imports declined marginally, while export growth increased slightly over the corresponding period in 1997. The recent decline in imports has concentrated largely on consumer durables (including cars) and mineral fuels, with the former resulting from the sharp rise in interest rates and the latter from the reduction in world oil prices. Imports of raw materials and intermediate goods – especially non-metallic, iron and steel products which are strongly linked to the construction sector – have also

Table 9.2 Philippines: macroeconomic indicators (% p.a.)

	1996	1997	1996				1997			
			Q1	Q2	Q3	Q4	Q1	Q2	Q3	Q4
Real GDP growth rates	5.7	5.1	5.1	6.1	6.1	5.4	5.0	5.8	4.9	4.7
Agriculture	3.1	2.8	1.9	5.9	3.6	1.6	3.7	2.9	0.7	3.4
Manufacturing	6.3	5.7	6.1	6.4	6.8	6.0	4.0	6.9	6.2	5.8
Services	6.5	5.6	6.1	5.9	6.7	7.1	6.4	6.2	5.6	4.5
Inflation	8.5	5.1	11.6	10.5	7.1	4.8	4.7	4.5	4.9	6.1
Unemployment rate (period average)	8.6	8.7	8.3	10.9	7.5	7.4	7.7	10.4	8.7	7.9
Balance of payments	4.7	−3.9	4.4	7.4	6.3	1.4	2.5	−3.4	−4.8	−10.4
Current account balance (% of GNP)	−4.5	−4.9	−3.8	−9.4	−0.2	−4.8	−2.3	−7.1	−6.9	−3.3
Trade balance (% of GNP)	−5.2	−6.2	−4.6	−10.1	−1.1	−5.1	−3.3	−8.2	−8.4	−4.7
Change in workers' remittances	11.3	33.3	n.a.	n.a.	n.a.	n.a.	29.3	5.8	29.0	76.1
Change in net foreign investments	118.6	−78.2	n.a.	n.a.	n.a.	n.a.	7.5	−128.2	−101.5	−98.2
Change in direct investments	−1.7	−16.5	n.a.	n.a.	n.a.	n.a.	10.6	−10.6	−46.5	−21.1
Change in portfolio investments	778.6	−116.1	n.a.	n.a.	n.a.	n.a.	3.8	−170.3	−147.7	−115.2

Note: Growth rates for quarters are on year-on-year basis.
Source: Intal and Medalla 1998.

declined since the last quarter of 1997. Remarkably, capital goods imports continued to grow strongly during 1997 and early 1998. Similarly, imports that were linked directly to exports grew robustly in this period, reflecting the continued healthy growth of exports relying on imported inputs.

While the financial sector has largely weathered the crisis, the fiscal situation has become precarious. The surge in interest rates has dramatically raised the government's projected interest payments for 1998 by nearly 50% compared with the original budget projections. The budget deficit during the first quarter of 1998 was more than double that of the corresponding period in the previous year, because of lower than expected revenues and higher debt servicing. Considering that there was only a small surplus in 1997, the sharp deterioration in revenue flows and interest payments implies a large budget deficit in 1998. In order to contain the projected deficit, the government imposed a mandatory 25% reserve on all expenditures other than personnel and debt servicing, and a deferment of 10% of the internal revenue allotment for local government units, as well as suspending all tax concessions to government agencies and corporations. Thus the continuation of high interest rates has a deflationary impact on the economy not only because it discourages investment and business activity, but also because it involves a reduction in government maintenance, operations and capital expenditures.

The economy slowed in 1997 – but the slowdown started before the crisis. It appears that the El Niño phenomenon had a greater impact than the crisis, resulting in a sharp reduction in agricultural output during the third quarter of 1997. Recent employment data corroborate the impact of El Niño. A rise in unemployment in January 1998 was caused largely by a decline in the number of people employed in agriculture. Press reports have starkly highlighted the severity of the drought in Mindanao, especially in early 1998, which has already claimed a number of lives among the upland population. Recent government estimates indicate that the production of two important agricultural crops, rice and sugar, might decline by 20% during the first half of 1998 because of the drought. Given that the agricultural sector still accounts for nearly 20% of GDP, substantial declines in crop production set back the overall growth performance of the economy significantly.

Nevertheless, the crisis has contributed to the slowdown. Interest-sensitive sectors – such as the automotive industry, appliance industries and real estate – were hit hard by the sharp rise in interest rates. Employment in the finance, insurance, real estate and business services sector declined by 4.6% in the first quarter of 1998 compared with the corresponding period last year. Department of Labor and Employment data show an increase during the first quarter of 1998 in the numbers of workers permanently laid off and workers temporarily retrenched. Poor industrial employment prospects and the decrease of employment in agriculture led to a significant increase in the urban unemployment rate, especially in Metro Manila, in early 1998.

The Philippines so far has not experienced a large jump in inflation, despite the substantial depreciation of the peso. This is quite unlike previous peso devaluations, which generally resulted in higher inflation. There are a number of reasons for this. First, the depreciation arising from the crisis was market-led and de-politicised – in contrast to previous devaluations, which were viewed as primarily policy decisions. Second, the peso depreciated when the country's international reserve position was relatively healthy, whereas previous devaluations occurred when international reserves were minimal implying that the devaluations were essentially measures of last resort. Third, food prices have been relatively stable: rice prices have been stabilised by way of substantial imports by the National Food Authority; fish prices have been kept from rising by the favourable impact of El Niño on domestic fish production (fish being an important food item in the Philippines); and greater domestic competition arising from more open consumer markets has put downward pressure on many food prices. Fourth, the world price of oil, an important import, has declined. Fifth, partly because of the relative stability of food prices, the minimum wage adjustments agreed upon in recent months have been small. Finally, the government has pursued tight monetary and fiscal policies in response to the crisis.

The relative stability of the price of rice, despite a substantial reduction in production, has had one important negative social impact: the incomes of farmers adversely affected by El Niño have declined significantly. Philippine poverty is largely rural; moreover, Mindanao, which was hit hard by El Niño, has a higher percentage of poor people than the national average. The combination of the national policy to stabilise food prices through imports and the decline in food production by already poor farmers has reduced the welfare of many of the very poor. Policymakers were preoccupied with the East Asian crisis, to the extent that the welfare of the rural poor was not adequately monitored and addressed. Indeed, it took the deaths of a number of tribal Filipinos in Mindanao's uplands to make the national government take serious notice of the adverse social welfare effect of El Niño on the rural poor. As Mindanao and the rest of the country are still reeling from the drought, the condition of the rural poor remains precarious.

In the face of slowing activity and rising unemployment, the foreign labour market provided an important safety valve. At the start of the crisis, there were worries about a massive repatriation of Philippine workers from countries adversely affected by the crisis, which would significantly worsen domestic unemployment. These worries proved unfounded. In fact, there was a sharp increase of 13.2% in the number of Philippine workers deployed abroad in 1997, as against a 0.9% increase in 1996. Interestingly, the increases in deployment were concentrated primarily in East Asia (e.g. in Japan, Hong Kong, Singapore, Taiwan and Malaysia). While poor employment prospects at home may be an important push factor (the Philippines has the highest unemployment rate in the region), it is likely that the substantial depreciation of the peso also provided a powerful incentive to seek employment overseas. Data on remittances from abroad show a marginal increase during the second quarter of 1997, but a massive increase during the fourth quarter, indicating the sensitivity of Philippine workers to developments in the foreign exchange market. Considering that a significant proportion of Philippine overseas workers come from the provinces (i.e. outside the Manila metropolitan area), the higher deployment of Philippine workers abroad and the sharply higher remittances earned last year provided an important safety net for hundreds of thousands of Philippine households in the provinces.

The nominal peso depreciation led to a significant real exchange rate depreciation of 30% between June 1997 and February 1998, although this was partially offset by nominal appreciation from March. This change has substantially wiped out the real appreciation that occurred during the 1990s, and thereby helped improve the competitiveness of exports. While exports grew by around 23% in 1997, much of the growth was accounted for by electronics and computer parts, for which the Philippines has developed a solid export platform because of its relative abundance of semi-skilled, readily trained, English-literate workers. By contrast, some traditional exports stagnated or declined. Traditional export industries that have not improved their efficiency (e.g. some segments of the garments industry) have been losing competitiveness as a result of rising labour costs and the appreciating peso. Other traditional industries that have been restructuring towards greater efficiency (e.g. parts of the textile industry) have registered moderate export growth.

The recent real depreciation will likely benefit the traditional industries by at least buying time for improvements in their efficiency and by improving their competitiveness in the world market relative to exports from China, Latin America and other regions. Although it is still too soon to be sure, the growth of 2% in exports of garments during the first two months of 1998, in contrast to declines in 1996 and 1997, may reflect the positive effect of the real peso depreciation. Simulations – based on the Medalla–Tan model – of the impact of the Philippine tariff reduction program, with and without exchange rate adjustment, demonstrate the significant role of real depreciation as a complement to that program (Medalla 1997; Tan 1997).

CONCLUSION

While the El Niño phenomenon wrought havoc on agricultural production and employment, the crisis prevented the industrial and services sectors from providing an employment safety valve to ameliorate problems in rural areas. The fiscal situation has become precarious because of the high interest rate regime and the economic slowdown. The crisis has also highlighted the importance of having healthy financial institutions and effective prudential regulations and supervision in the context of an open capital account. It has caused some worrying trends in the financial system – which, as the Thai case suggests, could eventually have generated a crisis – to be nipped in the bud. Finally, the crisis provided the first relatively successful market-led and de-politicised peso depreciation, which is an important complement to the ongoing tariff reform program.

Radelet and Sachs (1998b) state that the crisis is a 'crisis of success'. To a large extent this is true, and the Philippines has weathered the crisis relatively well partly because it was not experiencing economic 'success' in comparison with the very high growth rates of the previously high-performing East Asian economies. Before the crisis struck, the Philippine economy had been steadily on the mend for a decade, reforming itself by undoing the protectionism and crony capitalism of the 1970s and early 1980s to become one of the more open, transparent and deregulated economies in East Asia. The Philippines is following a path of development like other successful economies in Southeast Asia, but with a less imposing role for government. The process of industrial restructuring in an increasingly open economy has not been easy, as indicated by the mixed performance of the Philippine manufacturing sector during the past few years. In addition, the country still needs to raise its saving rate significantly; to reduce its fertility and population growth rate more appreciably; to increase its agricultural productivity; and to improve its infrastructure and transport systems. These fundamentals of the East Asian 'miracle', of course, are not achieved miraculously at all, but are the outcomes of consistent policy direction, well-directed investment, and persistence.

The East Asian crisis offers both challenges and opportunities for the Philippines. As its East Asian neighbours mend their economies, the country will face more formidable competition in international markets. At the same time, as the Philippines continues to improve its fundamentals for sustained robust growth, it may reap more benefits from its years of policy and institutional reform, eventually taking off economically and further strengthening its linkages with both the East Asian economies and the rest of the world.

NOTES

1. M2 is the sum of currency in circulation, demand deposits, and peso savings and time deposits. M3 is the sum of M2 and deposits substitutes of deposit money banks. M4 is the sum of M3 and trust accounts. M5 is the sum of M4 and FCDU deposits of residents.
2. 'Overbought' means that the bank's foreign exchange liabilities exceed its foreign exchange assets; 'oversold' means the reverse.
3. Parts of this section draw on Intal and Medalla (1998).

10   Singapore and Hong Kong

Yuk-shing Cheng,
Wong Marn-heong and
Christopher Findlay

INTRODUCTION

Singapore and Hong Kong are both now high-income economies and face similar challenges of structural change. They both present themselves as regional service centres and both face challenges in making the transition to that role. Although Hong Kong has made a sharper adjustment to the new external environment and experienced recession in the first half of 1998, both seem to have weathered the financial storms of East Asia better than most. Why is this? Are there lessons for other East Asian economies in this experience? These are the questions on which we focus in this chapter.

In terms of recent performance, Hong Kong's growth in the 1990s has been slower than Singapore's, and its inflation rate higher (see Table 10.1). The growth in Hong Kong's command over international resources has been comparable to Singapore's. Singapore has run persistent and substantial current account surpluses; Hong Kong in the last few years has run a deficit on the current account. Both run government surpluses, which are massive in Singapore's case. Both have enormous international reserves relative to the stock of money. The size of these reserves, and their scale relative to the stocks of both base money and narrow money, suggest why these economies came through the East Asian crisis reasonably well.

EXCHANGE RATE POLICY

The Monetary Authority of Singapore (MAS) manages the local currency within a flexible band against a trade-weighted basket of currencies. The width of the band was widened in response to shifts in regional currency markets in the second half of 1997. The International Monetary Fund (IMF) observed that 'monetary policy ... is the principal instrument of demand management and is centred on the exchange rate', which has implications for interest rate volatility (IMF 1998a).[1] The Singapore government, for example, permits the Singapore dollar to appreciate to reduce the rate of inflation that might otherwise be observed. At the same time it is sensitive to

Table 10.1 Hong Kong and Singapore in the 1990s

	Hong Kong	Singapore
Real GDP growth (annual)	1990–5: 5.5% 1996: 4.7% 1997: 5.5%	1990–5: 8.5% 1996: 6.9% 1997: 7.8%
Inflation (annual)	Moderate: in recent years between 6% and 7%; peak rate in the 1990s of 11%, in 1991	Low: less than 2% in the last three years; peak rate in the 1990s of 3.7%, in 1994
Current account	Shifting position: in surplus up to 1995; deficit of 6.8% of GDP in 1997	High surplus: 15% or more of GDP for the last four years
Government budget (relative to GDP)	Surplus: 1990–5: 1.6% 1996: 1.5% 1997: 2.6%	Surplus: 1990–5: 12.2% 1996: 13.9% 1997: 2.8%
International reserves	1997: over US$90 billion; ratio to M0 of 7.8:1; ratio to M1 of 3.8:1	1997: US$78.9 billion; ratio to M0 of 10.1:1; ratio to M1 of 3.9:1

Note: M0 is base money; M1 is narrow money.
Source: APEG 1998.

the effects of its choices on the competitiveness of Singapore's traded goods and services sectors. Singapore's policy could therefore be characterised as real exchange rate targeting (sometimes also called a 'dirty' float).

Singapore's goal is the gradual internationalisation of the local dollar, but this has occurred only at a rate which is thought unlikely to cause destabilising flows that could upset the domestic economy – that is, a rate which will not make the currency vulnerable to aggressive speculation. This constraint is imposed by intervention in capital markets, as discussed below.

Hong Kong adopted a fixed exchange rate system in 1983. The note-issuing system resembles that of a currency board, under which the US dollar equivalent (at the fixed rate of HK$7.80 per US dollar) has to be surrendered to the Exchange Fund for any issuance of Hong Kong currency. Three commercial banks are designated as note-issuing banks.

A true currency board system has a built-in arbitrage mechanism to defend the exchange rate. When the Hong Kong dollar is weaker than the official rate, market players can gain if they convert Hong Kong dollars back to US dollars at the official rate at the currency board. The money supply then contracts and domestic interest rates rise, inducing capital to flow in and restoring the official exchange rate.

In practice, the cash arbitrage mechanism does not function in this manner in Hong Kong. Any potential arbitrage has to go through the three note-issuing banks, which have no obligation to serve other parties free of charge. Unless the market rate deviated substantially from the official rate, other banks would not find it worthwhile to move large amounts of cash to the note-issuing banks for arbitrage purposes. In reality, there has been little arbitrage activity.[2]

The Hong Kong Monetary Authority (HKMA) does not buy and sell US dollars against Hong Kong dollar balances in the clearing accounts of the banks at the official rate. Instead, the rate is determined by demand and supply in the foreign exchange market. The exchange rate often deviates slightly from HK$7.80 per US dollar, and has stayed near HK$7.74 most of the time in recent years. In such a setting, interbank liquidity affects the exchange rate.

The HKMA's principal responsibility is to maintain exchange rate stability by influencing the level of liquidity in the interbank market through money market operations. Over the past decade, it has implemented a series of measures to strengthen the robustness of the linked exchange rate system. Its strategy has been to improve its capability to influence interbank liquidity and interbank interest rates. Since March 1990, a substantial volume of Exchange Fund bills and notes of various maturities has been issued to provide the instruments necessary for conducting open market operations.

A pure currency board is not a lender of last resort to banks. But in Hong Kong a liquidity adjustment facility was introduced at the end of 1996 and has been serving as the lender of last resort. There is debate about the requirement for such an institution, especially in an orthodox currency board system, as discussed further below.

IMPACT OF THE CRISIS

Singapore

On 2 July 1997, the Bank of Thailand announced a managed float of the baht and called on the IMF for technical assistance. The baht was immediately devalued, triggering crises in other East Asian economies. Central banks in Manila and Kuala Lumpur decided to intervene heavily to support their currencies. In Indonesia, the rupiah started to be affected, so the intervention band was widened from 8% to 12%. On 14 July the Malaysian central bank abandoned its defence of the ringgit.

The pressure placed on Singapore by these events among its trading partners became evident on 17 July, when the MAS allowed the depreciation of the Singapore dollar, which then fell to its lowest level since February 1995. Figure 1.1 shows the subsequent movement in the Singapore dollar compared with other East Asian currencies. The Singapore dollar moved along the same path as that of the Taiwan dollar. Both depreciated by less than the currencies of the other Southeast Asian economies shown in the figure and both recovered (as did the others shown in that figure) after January 1998.

Asset prices

Capital outflow was reflected in asset prices. In the six-month period from July to December 1997, the stock market index fell 23%. Its lowest point was reached on 28 October, when it sank to a four and a half year low. By the end of 1997, the total market capitalisation of the Singapore Stock Exchange was down 15.4% to S$218.3 billion (US$143.6 billion), and the number of listed firms in the 'billion-dollar club' had shrunk from 40 to 33. The stock market experienced wild fluctuations in early 1998. The Straits Times Industrials Index tumbled 29.8% over seven consecutive sessions at the start of the year, but improved sentiment led the index to post its biggest single-day gain, 173 points (13.7%), on 3 February 1998. These shifts after mid-1997 led to a cumulative bilateral depreciation against the US dollar of 12% through mid-February 1998, while the stock market index (in Singapore dollar terms) declined by about 20% over the same period.

Interest rates

Liquidity was tightened by the MAS's periodic intervention to support the weakening Singapore dollar. Local interbank rates, which had averaged 3% to 4%, soared in the second half of 1997. Risk premia rose along with the perceived risk of holding the local currency, with investors switching from Singapore dollar denominated deposits to US dollar denominated deposits. The three-month interbank rate reached a fifteen-year high of 10% on 18 December 1997 before tapering off to 7.25% at end-December. The rate shot up further in the new year, hitting the relatively high level of 20% on 15 January. These events were a consequence of the problems occurring in Indonesia at that time which, it was feared, would spill over to Singapore.

Weekly average rates are shown in Figure 10.1, which highlights a number of points. First, apart from the shocks in early January 1998, there was relatively little interest rate movement. Second, rates had returned to precrisis levels by the end of March. Finally, the yield curve implied by these data remained conventional (upward sloping), which was different from what happened in the troubled economies.

The prime lending rate, which had sat at an average of 6.26% since June 1995, was raised to 6.5% in November 1997. Persistently high interbank rates triggered further rounds of prime rate hikes, to 7% at the end of December 1997 and 7.5% in January 1998, for the four big local banks. The banks also scrapped their promotional rates for housing loans. Banks are turning to retail deposits as a cheaper source of funds, competing aggressively to attract new deposits. Fixed deposit interest rates have hit 7.5% for sums above S$100,000 (US$65,500), and over 5% for smaller deposits, from below 4% earlier in 1997.

Figure 10.1 Singapore: interbank interest rates, 3 October 1997–27 March 1998 (% p.a., weekly averages)

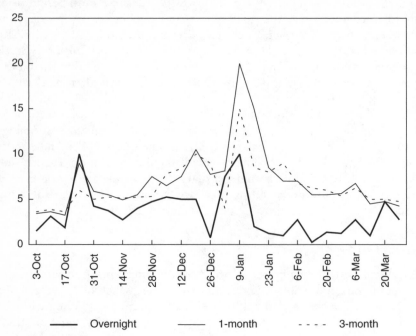

| Overnight | 1-month | - - - - 3-month |

Hong Kong

The Malaysian ringgit hit long-term lows about 24 July 1997, a week after the Singapore dollar started to lose value. Malaysian Prime Minister Mahathir started his attacks on 'rogue speculators' at this time. While the Hong Kong dollar remained steady, it was later reported that US$1 billion had been spent on intervention during a period of just two hours on an unspecified day in July. By 28 July, Thailand had called in the IMF.

It was not until October that the Hong Kong currency came under pressure again, when it was argued that the devaluation of the Taiwan dollar the previous week – the latest in a string of East Asian currency devaluations – had created concerns about the possibility of Hong Kong changing its long-standing peg to the US dollar. Investors were quoted as saying that Taiwan was a lot like Hong Kong, and noting that Taiwan had been unable to maintain its previous exchange rate.

Asset prices

Between 20 and 23 October 1997 the Hong Kong stock market lost nearly a quarter of its value, with the Hang Seng Index (HSI) down 23.3%. The fall was more severe than the 1987 crash. The HKMA fended off the attack of 23 October by squeezing liquidity, and the overnight interbank interest rate skyrocketed to 280%. Stock prices plunged, and the HSI bottomed at 9,060 points on 28 October 1997, compared with 15,128 points at the beginning of October. After recovering more than 2,000 points, the HSI dipped to a low of 8,121 points in January 1998 during another attack on the Hong Kong dollar. By March, some ground had been clawed back, with the index up to the 12,000 point mark – 20% below the October peak. As Figure 1.2 in Chapter 1 shows, the market in Hong Kong had much more of a roller-coaster ride than did the market in Singapore, where the index had been falling steadily for some time.

Interest rates

When speculators took a short position in Hong Kong dollars in October 1997, the HKMA warned the banks not to facilitate speculation against the currency. It then announced that 'repeated borrowers' in the liquidity adjustment facility would be charged a penalty rate. But the definition of 'repeated borrowers' and the level of the penalty were not specified, creating panic in the interbank markets and causing overnight interest rates to peak. Figure 10.2 shows interbank interest rates for the period from August 1997 to February 1998. On 23 October 1997, the overnight rate rose to over 280%.

It is important to note that the one-month and three-month rates rose for a longer time than the overnight rate did. In August 1997, these rates were around 6.5% (0.5 percentage points higher than the overnight rate). However, after the attack, the three-month rate stayed well above 10% for most of November 1997. To settle uncertainties in the interbank market, the HKMA announced on 12 November 1997 that 'repeated borrowers' were defined as those banks that had borrowed through the liquidity adjustment facility on eight occasions in any period of 25 days, or on four consecutive days on which the liquidity adjustment facility was open. The three-month rate then fell below 10% in December.

The rise in the interbank interest rate led to an increase in lending rates in late October 1997 and in January 1998. As a result, the bubble in the residential housing market burst. By the end of January 1998, prices of housing units had fallen by around 30% from their peak in the third quarter of 1997. However, the increase in the interbank interest rate was much milder during the currency attack in January 1998. Its peak at that time was 10–12%, in the middle of the month, but the three-month rate stayed above 10% for almost the whole month. These rises in interest rates were substantial.

POLICY RESPONSES

One of the most important lessons of the crisis of 1997 and 1998 has been that when an economy liberalises its capital account it must pay special

Figure 10.2 Hong Kong: interbank interest rates, 3 October 1997–27 March 1998 (% p.a.)

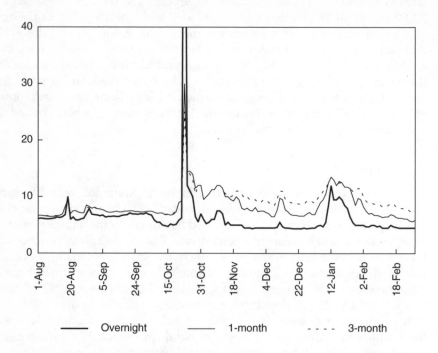

attention to its foreign exchange system. The majority of the exchange rate regimes in the region were hybrids – neither rigidly fixed, as in the currency board system, nor freely floating. The interest in the Hong Kong experience is the implication of its rigid rate. Singapore, on the other hand, appears to have operated a foreign exchange system that was not truly floating. How did it manage the impact of the crisis in that case?

The crisis also exposed fundamental weaknesses in the financial systems of some countries. Implicit guarantees that the government would bail out failed projects and banks encouraged imprudent lending. In some cases, lack of transparency in balance sheets and inadequate prudential controls have made it hard for investors to assess the status of the institutions to which they have lent. The paucity of credible information on private sector foreign liabilities has also complicated the task of domestic regulators and international watchdogs.

Financial system weaknesses affected not only the level of investment but also its composition. In a climate of easy credit, competition between financial institutions led to relatively high shares of lending into property and the stock market – relatively easy sectors of lending for newcomer financial institutions to enter. The ready availability of credit to these sectors led to a bubble in asset prices. Since a significant portion of bank lending was secured against these assets, banks were exposed to severe bad loan problems when the bubble burst. Again, there is interest in the status of the regulatory systems and the extent of exposure to bad loans (and in which sectors those bad loans occurred) in Singapore and Hong Kong.

In other economies, it has also been argued that the fiscal policy response to the crisis was not helpful. In circumstances of slowing activity, some governments cut back their spending where a fiscal loosening or at least a decision to let natural stabilisers operate might have helped. The pressure for tightening both fiscal and monetary policy was reinforced by the requirements of the IMF in the troubled economies. How did Singapore and Hong Kong manage fiscal policy in the context of the crisis?

FINANCIAL SYSTEM REFORM

Singapore

Years of strict supervision by the MAS and prudent and conservative accounting practices paid off. Local banks have capital adequacy ratios exceeding 12% – higher than those of most international banks. In a sign of confidence in the future, local banks are on the lookout for investment opportunities in the region; one of them recently acquired stakes in banks in Thailand and the Philippines. Banks in Singapore are facing rising bad debts from the troubled regional economies, but their 'classified' (questionable or uncollectible) loans are still within comfortable limits. As at the end of 1997, 5.7% or S$2 billion (US$1.3 billion) of the six major local banks' total loans in Malaysia, Indonesia, Thailand, South Korea and the Philippines were classified. Total classified loans to both local and overseas customers were 2.6% of their total loan portfolio and 2.3% of total global assets. The local banks have made provisions, both specific and general, for regional risk. As a result, their 1997 profits fell by an average of 30% – the first time earnings had fallen since the 1985 recession.

Standard & Poor's, while noting that the banks had recently publicly disclosed (for the first time) their levels of non-performing loans, stressed that the banks had not revealed their provisions for losses on their balance sheets (*South China Morning Post* 18 March 1998). The IMF argued that,

> given their exposure to the region and to the local property market, Directors noted that the financial position of Singaporean financial institutions would probably deteriorate in the near future as provisioning for classified loans increased. While the authorities remained confident that the financial system would weather the storm, Directors cautioned that timely monitoring would continue to be essential, in view of the risks of further declines in property prices and a deterioration in the quality of the regional portfolio. To enhance confidence, Directors urged that disclosure standards of individual banks be improved, including with respect to their regional

exposure, capital ratios, level of nonperforming loans, and level of
hidden reserves. In view of the strength of the banking sector, this
would reduce the risk of unwarranted contagion.

(IMF 1998a)

The MAS responded by pointing to a committee that it has working on
bank disclosure standards that should bring standards in Singapore into line
with those in 'developed countries'.

The banks' exposure to the property sector was also noted by the IMF.
The property market, which had experienced a boom from around 1993,
cooled in May 1996 when the government introduced measures to curb
property speculation. In hindsight, this was an astute move that prevented
the property bubble from growing and helped to avoid a severe correction
in the property market, with its attendant financial ramifications.

The government announced measures in November 1997 to ease the
property price slump, by suspending the 3% stamp duty on those who sold
within three years of purchase; postponing one-third of the 1997 supply of
land for private homes until 1998; and doubling the time developers were
allowed in which to complete their projects. The 1998 government budget
later cut land sales to about half the actual total supply in 1997. Interestingly, the IMF supported this operation. Its directors 'welcomed the new
package of measures introduced in November 1997 to help stabilize the
property and construction sectors. They encouraged the authorities to
closely monitor credit growth in these sectors' (IMF 1998a).

Hong Kong

When the attack on the Hong Kong dollar triggered a slide of property and
stock prices, there was concern about the impact on the financial sector. Although Hong Kong's banking sector is more robust than those of the troubled East Asian countries, its deep involvement in the residential property
market attracted special attention. Observers worried about a repeat of
Japan's experience with the collapse of its property market.

With structural change in the real economy, the flow of funds in the financial sector underwent a corresponding change. By the end of September
1997, 21% of the total loans and advances of the banking sector was extended to building construction, property development and investment,
and another 26% to individuals for the purchase of residential properties.
Thus 47% of total bank lending was related to the property market; of
course, some banks would have had an even higher ratio. Since 1996 the
banks had been competing vigorously for customers in the mortgage market. The typical lending rate decreased from 1.75% over the prime rate to
only 0.75% or less. As a result, some 59% of the net increase in total loans
and advances of the banking system in 1996 was attributable to activity in
the property market.

In the second half of 1997, the over-reliance of the banking sector on the property market and concerns about a property bubble aroused the attention of the HKMA. It asked banks to gradually reduce the proportion of loans for property-related activities to 40%. As early as July 1996 the government had decided to set up the Mortgage Corporation Limited, owned by the government through the Exchange Fund. Its establishment provided an avenue for banks to offload mortgages when needed. Mortgage-backed securities encouraged fixed rate mortgages, helping to insulate borrowers from interest rate shocks. Using HK$1 billion capital from the Exchange Fund, the Mortgage Corporation was to begin operations in the fourth quarter of 1997. The strategy was to issue unsecured debt securities in the first phase to raise funds for the purchase of residential mortgage loans.

The banking sector faces a difficult year in 1998, as interest rate margins have been narrowing. Although the level of defaults is expected to increase, the banking system remains robust. At the end of September 1997 non-performing loans were only 2.3% of the total. The HKMA plans to review the banking sector in August 1998 to refine its supervision of the system and enhance its capacity to respond to rapid financial product innovation in an era of global financing.

FISCAL POLICY

Singapore

Recurring high budget surpluses in Singapore have been controversial. Some argue that the government is siphoning liquidity from the economy and depriving business of much-needed capital. The government counters that these surpluses help augment Singapore's foreign reserves, which provide an important buffer in hard times, given the country's small and highly open nature and its lack of natural resources, because a healthy reserves position instils confidence among foreign investors. The government also wants to generate a higher stream of investment income to meet the longer-term financing needs of a slower-growing economy with an ageing population, so that it does not have to raise taxes or borrow abroad.

In the budget for fiscal year 1998 released in February – while continuing to spend heavily on defence and on a number of costly long-term projects in the priority areas of education, transport and other economic infrastructure development – the government revealed its intention to postpone less essential projects. Even the program to upgrade older public housing estates – a vote-winner in the 1997 general elections – is not to be spared. The Main Upgrading Program, which is funded from budget surpluses, will be scaled down by about a third in 1998, but there has been no public outcry. Overall, however, the estimated budget surplus of S$2.7 billion (US$1.8 billion) will be one of the smallest in recent years, with slower growth in revenue.

Business was disappointed that there was no corporate tax cut in the 1998 budget, and particularly concerned over the lack of measures to promote manufacturing.[3] The government will grant industrial land rental concessions, and will expand its Local Enterprise Financing Scheme to cover more small and medium-sized enterprises and give them greater access to working capital loans. But some businesses point out that these measures may benefit landlords more than industry. Many of the tax incentives in the 1998 budget aim to boost the financial sector, logistics and exhibition services. Cyber-trading will also receive tax breaks as Singapore bids to become an electronic commerce hub. The government has held back on pump-priming the economy for the moment, but says it has adequate resources to respond with off-budget measures in the event of any serious deterioration in Singapore's economic conditions.

Hong Kong

Hong Kong has a tradition of conservative fiscal policy. Colonial era governments avoided budget deficits. Influenced by business people, the Chinese government wrote into the Basic Law – the mini-constitution for Hong Kong – that fiscal policy in the Hong Kong Special Administrative Region should follow the principle of limiting spending to the means available. Whether the United Kingdom would return Hong Kong to China with heavy debt burdens was one of the most important concerns of the Chinese government before 1997. As revenues from land sales often constituted over 20% of government income, China and the United Kingdom agreed that half of the revenues accrued before the handover should be kept in the Land Fund and retained for the future Special Administrative Region government. Even with this sharing scheme, Hong Kong has registered a deficit only once since the mid-1980s – in fiscal year 1995. Together with the Land Fund, the Hong Kong government had total fiscal reserves of HK$446 billion (US$58 billion) at the end of March 1998, compared with total public expenditure of HK$248 billion (US$32 billion) during the same period.

In the wake of the economic downturn, there was increasing public pressure for the government to expand spending to stimulate demand – and even the suggestion that a deficit budget be introduced in 1998 – but Financial Secretary Donald Tsang has made it clear that prudential guidelines for government budgeting will not be surrendered. His insistence on a budget surplus for 1998–9 aimed to reassure the international community of Hong Kong's healthy fiscal position, which was seen as particularly important in the context of the East Asian currency crisis.

The Hong Kong government has not issued any debt and it is not willing to do so. It chooses to add to its reserves for contingencies rather than raise funds when difficulties emerge. Tsang has proposed that the reserve for fiscal purposes be set at an amount equivalent to nine months of fiscal expenditure (with a margin of plus or minus three months). He also proposed that there be a three-month reserve for operational purposes.

Furthermore, the reserves support a monetary objective. Most are placed with the Exchange Fund and kept in foreign currency. Hong Kong's total foreign reserves were US$97.6 billion at the end of February 1998. Of this, US$78.6 billion is in the Exchange Fund and US$18.1 billion is in the Land Fund – the latter is also managed by the HKMA, in an independent account. The bulk of the Exchange Fund is accounted for by the fiscal reserves. Foreign reserves due to currency issuance constitute only about US$12 billion and the rest consists mainly of accumulated investment returns.

Even in a classical currency board system, a 100% foreign reserves backup for issued currency may not be enough in practice. If people lose confidence in the currency, they can convert their bank deposits into domestic currency first and then convert this to foreign currency. In the Hong Kong system, the judgment is that more reserves are necessary to build up the credibility of the system. But it is impossible to say what quantity of reserves is needed. Some argued that the fiscal reserve should be reduced, prompting Tsang to attempt to justify the current level of reserves in his budget speech. But even he proposed a relatively wide range – suggesting that the optimal range of reserves, held for all three purposes, was from HK$300 billion to HK$500 billion.

EXCHANGE RATE POLICY

Singapore

The exchange rate regime in Singapore is supported by a set of rules on capital transactions. For example, non-residents (such as foreigners who might want to speculate that the value of the Singapore dollar will fall) cannot borrow in Singapore dollars. There is also a regulation in place requiring banks which lend Singapore dollars to residents for use outside Singapore to consult the MAS. But the deputy prime minister said in Parliament on 20 April 1998 that banks were not required to do so, in fact, and that the MAS would be changing this regulation (Lee 20 April 1998). This raises questions about the impact of such rules, and whether common practice is actually more liberal than the regulations suggest.

Examination of these rules forms part of a wider study of the regulatory structure in this area by the MAS, which is challenged by the prospect of developing the regional role of the financial sector in Singapore. The deputy prime minister said, on 19 February, 'we need to weigh the incremental risks to monetary and exchange rate management against the potential benefits of further liberalisation' (Lee 19 February 1998). The tension between the development ambitions of the Singapore leadership and its interest in maintaining tools for macroeconomic control has been highlighted by the crisis.[4]

Work by the IMF highlighted some possible responses to the dilemma (Chan and Ngiam 1996). This work is relevant to the wider debate about the role of speculators and their impact on currency values. The IMF authors argued that the current policy was equivalent to a prohibitive tax, which was sub-optimal. They suggested, for circumstances in which MAS could not distinguish between speculators and others, a loan quota that would become binding in times of currency crisis. They also suggested that such loan quotas could be managed by the banks on the basis of their experience with particular customers.

Hong Kong

The debate about Hong Kong's fiscal reserves has been noted. So has the fact that Hong Kong's asset prices and interest rates have been subjected to much more of a roller-coaster ride than those in Singapore. The issue in this section is the impact of Hong Kong's exchange rate regime on interest rates. Roubini (1998) has argued that

> [s]ince a currency board does not mean that a devaluation will not occur (it is just a more strict form of fixed exchange rates), the possibility of a devaluation implies that when an attack occurs, the domestic authorities have to push up interest rates to credibly show that they are committed to the peg parity. These high interest rates can bankrupt domestic banks and domestic firms and lead to a big recession. It happened in Argentina in 1995 and it will happen in HK this year: high interest rates are already destroying growth in HK in 1998. Compare instead the behaviour of HK with that of Taiwan and Singapore ... their currencies devalued somewhat but they avoided a bigger crisis. Growth in Taiwan and Singapore will be better than in HK this year as they did not have to increase interest rates as much and their real exchange rate was allowed to depreciate.

Financial Secretary Tsang noted, in his budget speech of February 1998, that the IMF had observed that an essential part of the currency board mechanism was that interest rates must be allowed to rise in response to foreign exchange market pressures (Tsang 1998). He also observed that there had been proposals to set up arrangements in which both exchange rates and interest rates would be stable. In other words, some people wanted to have it both ways.

One controversial proposal was that the government should introduce an option-like mechanism to defend the Hong Kong dollar, in which the HKMA would allow the banks to borrow US dollars from it and repay in either US dollars or an equivalent of Hong Kong dollars, calculated at the rate of HK$7.80 per US dollar. Similarly, Nobel Laureate Merton Miller suggested (orally to the media) that the HKMA should issue insurance securities so that investors could obtain compensation if the Hong Kong dollar were devalued (APEG 1998: 148). The idea was to force the HKMA to make a strong commitment to the ongoing rate, such that if the HKMA devalued the Hong Kong dollar the HKMA would suffer a loss. The point of departure was to look for some mechanism under which the interest rate would not rise much if there were speculative attacks on the currency. The supporters of these ideas believe that if the HKMA's commitment to the ongoing rate is strong enough, there will be no need for interest rates to rise to attract capital inflow when the Hong Kong dollar is under attack.[5]

Both suggestions shift the exchange rate risk to the HKMA rather than eliminating the risk. Given the limited (though large as compared with other countries') reserves of the HKMA, the issuance of options or insurance securities could provide only partial cover. The price of the securities might fluctuate if devaluation expectations emerged and, in that case, people would still sell Hong Kong dollars. The commitment might be too costly, making it impossible to commit absolutely to the fixed rate. Also, if there were a reduction in, or stoppage of the issuance of, such securities, it would trigger speculation. The HKMA therefore prefers to see an increase in the interest rate to attract capital inflow in order to maintain the exchange rate, and academics and specialists in the financial sector generally do not favour the other proposals. Tsang adopts a similar position in his report, and goes on to note the implication of his approach. It is important, he says, that banks in Hong Kong pay special attention to the quality of their assets and the degree to which they are exposed to interest rate variability.

An even more immediate issue in Hong Kong is the flexibility of its factor markets – particularly the labour market. Property markets show a high degree of price flexibility, and wages have been showing signs of coming down. Yet this flexibility might go only so far. Further decreases in property prices could pose problems for the banking system, because of the reduction in the value of the collateral securing their loans, while further reductions in wages (or increasing unemployment if the wage adjustment is slow) could create social unrest. Deterioration of the situation in other East Asian economies would make further adjustment more difficult. If factor markets do not work well enough, the long-run consequence will be idle resources as well as strong pressure against the peg – even though the governments of mainland China and Hong Kong are strongly committed to maintaining it.

CONCLUSION

Policy coherence matters. In the present context, what is important is the consistency of the bundle of macroeconomic and financial sector policies.

In this respect, both Singapore and Hong Kong have performed better than other countries affected by the contagion in the region. Hong Kong achieved this result even with its 'dirty' currency board system. It was able to stick to a fixed rate against the US dollar, although some would argue that a more credible currency board system would have avoided the extreme interest rate movements that Hong Kong experienced. Singapore also weathered the storm well, relying on a 'dirty' float. It let the nominal rate depreciate while at the same time absorbing a much smaller degree of interest rate volatility. Both economies had very large reserves with which they could defend their currency regimes.

A key in both economies was the strength of financial institutions. In Singapore there were some lucky interventions to support the regime. Also present in Singapore – but absent from Hong Kong – were residual restrictions on capital transactions. Singapore had pursued a very conservative fiscal policy; this was a feature of Hong Kong's policy, too.

The two economies have chosen different points in the trade-off between control and financial sector deepening and widening. The implications of Hong Kong's current policy mix include a high degree of interest rate variation and the costs associated with that. But there are few constraints on financial sector development or on the openness of the financial sector.[6] Tightening up the credibility of the currency board is a possibility, but a costly one. Hong Kong is likely instead to concentrate on financial sector regulation and prudential control; on designing systems that take account of the interest rate variability which the banks will face; and on exercises in increasing transparency. All of these responses will strengthen the international competitiveness of Hong Kong's financial institutions.

Singapore has exercised more discretion in the ways in which a currency shock affects a series of variables in the economy. However, as Duncan et al. (1998) argue, 'the adoption of the regime (of a real target rate) does not by itself bring about sensible monetary and fiscal policies'. They go on to observe that if such policies were adopted in the first place, much of the reason for the adoption of such a regime would be lost. Such a condition is one which Singapore could be expected to meet.

In Singapore, an additional cost of the current policy mix is the inhibition of development of the financial sector. Singapore's ambitions to be a regional service centre will be impeded by its choice of macroeconomic management instruments. Some reforms have already occurred and commitments have been made to others. Given its development goals and other assets, Singapore is likely to move closer to the 'hands off' position of Hong Kong in the management of its capital account transactions. Singapore's experience of terms of trade shocks (in electronic product markets, for example) and its capacity to commit to sensible monetary policy suggest that its wisest long-term choice of exchange rate regime would be a genuinely floating rate. Singapore will also have learned from the experience of those

around it that any sort of targeted but flexible system is subject to speculation against the currency, a point also stressed by Duncan et al. (1998).

In terms of lessons for other East Asian economies, the experiences of
these two economies highlight some points about exchange rate regimes
and, in particular, situations wherein an arrangement such as a currency
board might be appropriate.[7]

One is that a currency board system is more likely to be sustainable in
economies where there is internal price flexibility, or where that flexibility
can be attained through the management of migration policy. Second, a robust banking system is required to sustain a currency board system when it
is associated with substantial interest rate changes. Third, an economy
adopting a currency board system has to be prepared to give up monetary
autonomy, to gain the advantage of having monetary policy automatically
preserve the fixed rate. Finally, currency board systems are less likely to be
appropriate for economies that face large terms of trade shocks (resource exporters, for example) that require significant internal price changes to maintain external balance. The export mix of Hong Kong is less likely to have
this feature; that of Singapore may be more vulnerable.

NOTES

1 The IMF report went on:

> [The directors endorsed] the authorities' intention to maintain an easier
> monetary policy stance as long as the inflationary outlook remains subdued,
> but to review the stance at frequent intervals to ensure that inflation remains
> low. They supported the recent increase in the flexibility of exchange rate
> policy, given the volatility of regional currencies, although a renewed trend
> appreciation of the Singapore dollar would be appropriate once the regional
> situation stabilizes and output returns to its potential level. They considered
> that market-driven hikes in interest rates should not be resisted during peri-
> ods of currency turmoil.
>
> (IMF 1998a)

2 Tsang (1997) argues that this is the case, and goes on to observe that the lack
of arbitrage is associated with lack of direct access to the Exchange Fund by depositors or by financial institutions other than the note-issuing banks, which
would regard large-scale arbitrage activities as equivalent to a bank run. Tsang
suggests a way of making the arbitrage process more efficient which bypasses
the requirement to move cash around. Also see his papers at his web site
<http://www.hkbu.edu.hk/~econ/tsang.html>.

3 So was the IMF. As the IMF directors observed,

> there are still downside risks associated with the regional economic slow-
> down, and that, even in the absence of further unexpected regional spill-
> overs, growth in Singapore will slow down sharply this year ... In these
> circumstances, and given the strength of the external and fiscal positions,

Directors saw the small reduction in the primary operating surplus envisaged for FY 1997/98 as appropriate. They suggested that, in moving toward the medium-term objective of a lower primary operating surplus, corporate and personal income tax rates should be reduced in next year's budget alongside the intended increases in development expenditure.

(IMF 1998a)

4   The IMF noted that

[s]everal Directors felt that further steps to ease restrictions on the internationalization of the Singapore dollar would be appropriate and in the long-term interest of Singapore as a regional financial center. They stressed that Singapore's strong fundamentals and healthy reserve position would tend to mitigate any costs associated with possibly greater volatility of capital flows. However, some Directors, noting that the existing restrictions, backed by strong fundamentals, had helped to mitigate the impact of regional speculative pressures on Singapore, suggested that a cautious approach in eliminating the restrictions would be warranted in present circumstances. Directors welcomed the recent recommendations made by the Subcommittee on Finance and Banking of the Committee on Competitiveness aimed at securing Singapore's position as a regional financial center.

(IMF 1998a)

5   For this and other reform proposals on Hong Kong's exchange rate arrangements and the response of the HKMA, see *Report on Financial Market Review*, published by Financial Services Bureau, Government of the Hong Kong Special Administrative Region, April 1998, downloadable at <http://www.info.gov.hk/fsb/finance>.

6   A World Bank study has assessed the degree of openness of Hong Kong's markets compared with that in other East Asian economies. Hong Kong ranks highly, and the indicators – based on commitments expressed in schedules of the General Agreement on Trade in Services – identify Hong Kong as a much more open market for banking and securities services than Singapore. The two economies score about the same for insurance services (see Claessens and Glaessner 1998).

7   For further reading on currency boards, visit, for example, the web site of Kurt Schuler at <http://www.erols.com/kurrency>, or the Roubini site listed in the references.

11 Taiwan

Shirley W.Y. Kuo and
Christina Y. Liu

INTRODUCTION

In the midst of the world's eulogising of the emergence of the dynamic Asian century, a financial crisis broke out in Thailand in July 1997 and swiftly spread throughout the emerging market economies of Asia. The value of their currencies plunged and their stock markets collapsed. Within the six-month period to the end of 1997, the combined rates of currency depreciation against the US dollar and stock price decline together reached 97% in Indonesia and Korea, 80% in Malaysia, 75% in Thailand, 68% in the Philippines, 38% in Singapore and Japan, 29% in Hong Kong and 24% in Taiwan (see Figure 1.1).

By this measure, the damage suffered by Taiwan was the least suffered among these economies. Even when we observe the changes in exchange rates and stock prices up to the end of March 1998, when the troubled countries registered a considerable improvement, we find the Taiwan economy recording by far the smallest decline.

The real sectors of the troubled countries were also significantly damaged, and their growth rates plunged dramatically. Some countries even experienced negative growth. Amidst this environment, the performance of the Taiwan economy in 1997 was relatively satisfactory. Its real gross national product (GNP) growth rate was 6.8% and private fixed investment increased by 15.6%. The consumer price index (CPI) inflation rate was 0.9% and the wholesale price index (WPI) rate –0.5%. The unemployment rate was 2.75%.

This chapter examines the characteristics of Taiwan's economy in the context of the Asian financial crisis. Why was Taiwan able to avoid heavy damage, at least up to March 1998? We discuss this issue in comparison with the experiences of some of the troubled economies. The topics covered are: the saving–investment imbalance; trade deficits and surpluses; exchange rate policies; the soundness of the financial sector; the order of financial liberalisation; and financial policies. A comparison based on those factors seems to show that conditions in Taiwan were significantly different to those in the troubled countries.

CHARACTERISTICS OF THE ECONOMY

To get some idea of what factors have enabled Taiwan to avoid heavy damage, we identify some basic features of the crisis for the purpose of comparison. The following features come from observation of five countries: Thailand, Korea, Indonesia, Malaysia, and the Philippines.

First, except in Indonesia, investment has been far greater than saving since 1990, leading to current account deficits in every year of the 1990s. Second, accordingly, these economies have had to take on huge amounts of foreign debt. Third, their weak financial sectors have led to the following problems: a large amount of foreign debt was misallocated to the overvalued property and stock markets; government-directed lending practices led to excessive lending to the private sector; corporate financial structures became very weak; and banks incurred large amounts of bad loans. Finally, the increased difficulty of rolling over foreign debt – predominantly short-term debt – was a direct cause of the financial crisis.

In comparison, conditions in Taiwan were significantly different.

Current account surplus and excess saving

In contrast to the current account deficits in the abovementioned five countries, the current account in Taiwan has recorded a surplus in every year of the last two decades. The current account surplus (the excess of saving over investment) as a percentage of GNP averaged 3.9% in the period 1990–7. Therefore, there was no build-up of net foreign debt.

Current account surplus: a lesson of the mid-1980s

When most countries talk about problems generated by 'serious trade deficits', it sounds a little peculiar to talk about the problems incurred by 'serious trade surpluses' in Taiwan, but this was indeed the story of the mid-1980s. A huge trade surplus was a continuing highlight of the economy at that time, which created serious financial problems in the second half of that decade. The surplus was as large as 14.8% of GNP in 1985, increasing to 21.4% and 18.3% in 1986 and 1987 respectively. Notwithstanding the central bank's sterilisation efforts, this huge trade surplus, together with the massive net inflow of foreign private capital, created rapid money supply growth, asset inflation (including skyrocketing stock prices) and heavy pressure for New Taiwan (NT) dollar appreciation. For example, during 1986 and 1987 the money supply grew by 51.4% and 37.7% respectively. Stock prices rose by 125% in 1987, from a year earlier, and by 119% in 1988.

Although the growth rates in these two years (1986–7) were at record-breaking levels, registering 11.6% and 12.7% respectively, and the CPI inflation rate had not yet been affected, there was appreciable stock price inflation. In order to prevent a serious financial crisis, the government de-

Table 11.1 Taiwan: tariff reductions for selected years (%)

	Number of revised items			Average rate of reduction	Average nominal tariff
	Reduction	Exemption	Total		
1982	106	5	111	0.4	31.0
1984	281	2	283	0.7	30.8
1985	1,058	35	1,093	14.1	26.5
1986	777	28	805	13.7	22.8
1987	1,699	15	1,714	9.8	20.6
1988	3,313	154	3,467	41.3	12.1
1989	4,545	155	4,700	20.2	9.7
1992	1,492	279	1,771	8.0	8.9
1995	758	0	758	2.8	8.6

Source: Directorate-General of Budget, Accounting and Statistics (1998) *Statistical Abstract of National Income in Taiwan Area, Republic of China, 1951–1998, March.*

signed a series of economic and financial measures that have been implemented over the last decade. In retrospect, even though the policies designed at the time were largely problem oriented, they seem to form a systematic restructuring and liberalisation package. Let us refer to this as the 'lesson package'.

Since the main causes of the abovementioned problems were believed to be the excessively large trade surplus and the excessively rigid foreign exchange operations of the central bank, these two fields received high priority in the policy reforms. The new policies included in the 'lesson package' were: the reduction of tariffs, the relaxation of non-tariff barriers, and improvements in the structure of production. In the financial sector, new policies emphasised the liberalisation of interest rates, exchange rates and capital movements. The implementation of these policies in the last decade not only cured the serious external imbalance of the mid-1980s, but also built sound fundamentals for the economy of today.

As one element of the 'lesson package', the largest ever tariff reduction was carried out in 1988 (Table 11.1). The adjustment package covered 3,467 items, or 45% of the total, with an average rate reduction of 41.3%. This was followed up in 1989 with an adjustment covering 4,700 items, which lowered rates on average by 20.2%. As a result, the average nominal rate declined from 30.8% in 1984 to 9.7% in 1989. (It was further reduced to 8.6% in 1995.) In the same period, non-tariff import controls were largely removed.

A basic perception since the early 1990s has been that development should proceed rapidly in the direction of liberalisation and internationalisation on the one hand, while raising the competitive ability of industries in the international market on the other. Many measures were designed to upgrade industries in the 1990s.

Table 11.2   Taiwan: structural change in the manufacturing sector (% shares)

	Technology-intensive industry	Traditional industry	Basic industry
1981	20.2	42.9	36.9
1986	24.0	40.4	35.6
1991	31.2	33.7	35.1
1995	35.5	26.8	37.7
1996	37.5	26.6	35.9

Note: Definitions: 'Technology-intensive industry' consists of electrical and electronic equipment; precision machinery; machinery; and vehicles industries. 'Traditional industry' consists of food, tobacco and beverages; textiles, clothing and accessories; skins, furs and their products; wood and bamboo products; furniture and decorations; paper pulp, paper and paper products; printing and related industries; products from non-metal minerals; and miscellaneous industries. 'Basic industry' consists of chemical materials; chemical products; oil and coal products; rubber products; plastic products; basic metals; and metal product industries.
Source: Ministry of Economic Affairs.

The Hsinchu Science-based Industrial Park, established in 1980, became a powerful driving force for advancement and growth in the manufacturing sector. Taiwan became the world's third-largest producer of information technology products in 1995. Some such products, which came mostly from the Park, accounted for the largest share of the world market – notably scanners (with a world share of 64% in 1995), monitors (59%) and network interface cards (38%).

The upgrading of the manufacturing sector in the 1990s has been significant. In addition, Taiwan's economic structure is largely dominated by small and medium-scale enterprises that can adjust promptly to the changing environment. Thus the share of traditional industries in manufacturing output decreased from 42.9% of the total to 26.6% between 1981 and 1996, while that of technology-intensive industries increased from 20.2% to 37.5% (Table 11.2).

Structural change in industries can best be seen in changes in the composition of exports. During the period 1989 to 1996, the share of technology-intensive exports in total exports increased from 24.3% to 38.0%. The upgrading of exports also can be seen from the fact that the share of high-technology products increased from 33.9% to 47.3% of the total.

In short, the implementation of the 'lesson package' has largely removed government protection, while at the same time enabling the economy to maintain its competitiveness in the world market in the 1990s.

Saving–investment gap

One policy directed towards the reduction of Taiwan's huge excess saving was expansion of domestic demand through an increase in public investment. During the period 1984–7, when the saving–investment gap grew to a record high, public investment constituted a record low share of GNP. This conservative public investment policy resulted in a lack of infrastructure. In view of this deficiency, an emphasis on infrastructure construction and environmental improvement was adopted as the main theme of the Ninth Four-year Plan (1986–9) and the Tenth Four-year Plan (1991–3). The result of this emphasis was the rapid growth of government investment during the 1988–90 period, at an annual rate of 22.4%. The Six-year National Development Plan (1990–6) continued to emphasise infrastructure construction. Public investment has increased to about 11% of GNP, and private investment to around 13% of GNP, in the 1990s. Thus, total investment has risen to 23–4% of GNP.

On the other hand, the saving rate declined due to a decrease in both government and private savings. The reduction in government saving was due partly to a decline in tax revenue, and partly to an expansion in government current expenditure, such as welfare spending. One possible contributing factor to the reduction in private saving was an improvement in the social security system, including the implementation of national medical care. In short, changes in both investment and saving contributed to the desired reduction of the saving–investment gap by the mid-1990s.

Exchange rate policies

The exchange rate system was converted from the original fixed rate system to a flexible rate system in February 1979. The functioning of the exchange rate system in force for the past 20 years can be divided into two stages, with 1988 as the demarcation year.

At first, the central bank took a very cautious stance regarding the exchange rate. Changes were very mild, and the frequency of change was low – for example, change occurred six times in 1979 and seventeen times in 1980. In practice, the central bank held to a kind of fixed rate system, though with slightly greater flexibility than previously. Finally, on 12 August 1981, the central bank allowed the NT dollar to decline by 4.6% against the US dollar in a single day, as might have been done in a system of adjustable fixed rates.

In 1986 and 1987, when the current account surplus was increasing dramatically, the central bank intervened heavily. The philosophy held generally in the community and in most of the government sector during this period was that any drastic appreciation of the local currency would incur high adjustment costs in both the export- and import-competing sectors. The central bank thus adopted a 'gradual appreciation policy', under which the appreciation of the NT dollar was limited to one cent per day.

Through heavy central bank intervention, foreign exchange reserves increased by US$51.4 billion during these two years. This brought reserves to US$75.9 billion at the end of 1987, up from just US$24.5 billion previously. Despite this intervention, the NT dollar appreciated by 37.8%

Figure 11.1 Taiwan: exchange rate and foreign reserves

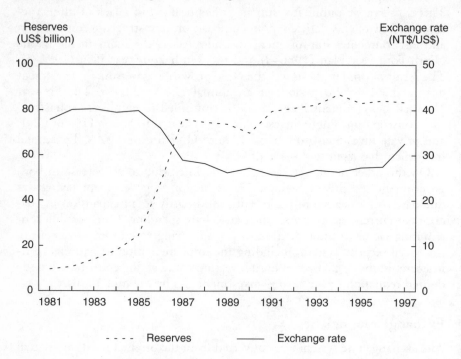

against the US dollar (Figure 11.1). The real effect of the intervention, therefore, was only to delay appreciation – at the cost of a significant capital loss for the central bank because the value of its international reserves decreased in terms of NT dollars.

It was also felt that an undervalued domestic currency was contributing to the serious trade surplus, so the exchange rate system was liberalised. The central bank dropped its intervention in early 1988, allowing the exchange rate to be determined by the market. This marked the end of the first-stage exchange rate system. In a way, it also marked the beginning of a floating rate system in Taiwan. After 1988, the central bank seldom intervened in the foreign exchange market, except during 1991 and 1994 when political tensions forced it to act.

Response to the crisis

At the beginning of the Asian financial crisis, the central bank saw it as a temporary phenomenon and tried to maintain a stable exchange rate of NT$28.6 per US dollar. But, as the crisis had gained momentum by October, the central bank ceased its intervention on the seventeenth of that month and allowed the value of the NT dollar to be determined by the market. By the end of 1997, the NT dollar had devalued by 14.8% against the

Figure 11.2 Taiwan: exchange rate and stock prices during crisis

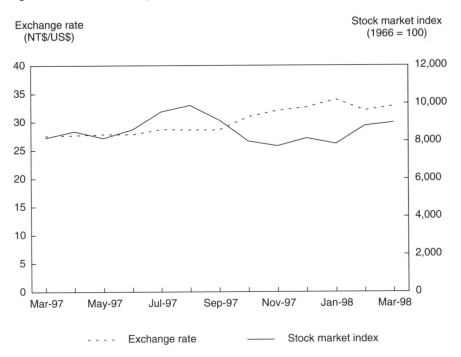

US dollar, and by March 1998, 14.9% (Figure 11.2). Note that stock prices were actually 4% higher by March 1998 than in June 1997, prior to the crisis. It is interesting to note also that the crisis had only a modest impact on interest rates (Figure 11.3). Certainly there was no need for any severe tightening of monetary conditions in order to prevent a large decline in the currency.

Liberalisation of capital movements

In response to the huge trade surplus and foreign capital inflow of the mid-1980s, a significant step towards liberalisation of capital outflow was taken in July 1987. Foreign exchange controls were greatly relaxed to allow direct capital outflow by the non-bank private sector: the ceiling on purchases of foreign exchange for outward remittances was raised dramatically from US$5,000 to US$5 million per adult per year on 16 July 1987, while the maximum amount of inward remittances was restricted to just US$50,000 per adult per year. However, net capital outflow did not respond immediately to this relaxation, because of the expectation of appreciation of the currency. (Following a series of further adjustments, the regulations now allow each adult to remit up to US$5 million in or out of the country annually.)

Besides these changes, the inflow of capital to the securities market was

Figure 11.3 Taiwan: money market rates during crisis (% p.a)

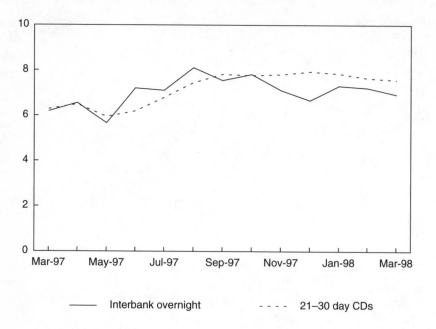

——— Interbank overnight   - - - - 21–30 day CDs

opened up in three phases. Phase one permitted foreigners to buy and sell four funds issues abroad. Phase two allowed foreign institutional investors, but not individuals, to invest in the Taipai stock market. Finally, in 1996, phase three allowed foreign individuals also to invest in the market. There is still a limit on foreign investment in each individual company, however, although the maximum permitted amount has been gradually raised, from 15% of total issued shares in 1996 to 30% in January 1998. The liberalisation of foreign capital inflow to the securities market is therefore still in process.

The financial sector

Financial liberalisation has been in progress in Taiwan for fifteen years, based on an appropriate sequencing. After inflation was brought under control, the government proceeded with the reduction of tariffs. Interest rates, the exchange rate, and capital account liberalisation then followed in succession.

At the end of 1997, foreign exchange reserves stood at US$83.5 billion, while public foreign debt was only US$0.1 billion. Foreign debt of the private sector was US$30.0 billion at the end of June 1997, while its foreign assets were US$35.5 billion, leaving private sector net foreign assets of US$5.5 billion.

Improvement of the financial system

The financial system has been relatively sound in recent years. Financial institutions have been prudent in their provision of loans secured by stocks, in that for this purpose the valuation of stocks has been set at 60% of their market price. Moreover, at the end of 1997, loans secured by stocks accounted for only 3.7% of total loans of financial institutions. Table 11.3 shows the ratio of bank borrowings to net worth for bills finance companies, securities finance companies and securities firms. For bills finance companies and securities finance firms, the ceiling on borrowings from banks is set by regulation at 600% of the net worth of each company. During 1996 and 1997, the actual borrowings of such companies were all far less than the ceiling. For securities firms, for which the ceiling is set at 150% of net worth, borrowings were in fact less than 30%. In short, it may be argued that there is no excess borrowing by private financial institutions. At the same time, the financial structure of non-financial companies is also sound. For example, the ratio of liabilities to net worth for all listed non-finance companies was only 78% on average in September 1997; if financial institutions are included, the ratio was 145%.

Table 11.3 Taiwan: ratios of bank borrowing to net worth (%)[a]

Quarter	Bills finance companies[b]	Securities finance companies[c]	Securities firms[d]
Ceiling	600	600	150
1996			
Q1	75	15	20
Q2	79	33	23
Q3	91	16	23
Q4	79	43	28
1997			
Q1	79	34	26
Q2	52	71	28
Q3	50	39	17
Q4	43	58	21

Notes:
a The ceilings on the ratio of bank borrowings to net worth of these financial institutions are set jointly by the Central Bank of China and the MOF. The ceilings are determined according to their business content, funding sources, risks and the future growth of the industry.
b Bills finance companies are special intermediaries in the money market, buying and selling short-term funds such as Treasury bills, bankers' acceptances, negotiable certificates of deposit issued by banks, and commercial paper and bonds with a maturity of less than one year.
c The scope of business of securities finance companies includes loans for margin trading, and refinancing for securities firms.
d With the approval of the MOF, securities firms can also undertake margin loan and stock loan business.
Source: Central Bank of China.

Table 11.4   Taiwan: capital adequacy ratio for domestic long-established and new banks (%)

Year	Long-established	New
1993	10.3	32.5
1994	10.2	20.6
1995	9.6	17.1
1996	11.1	15.0
1997	11.3	12.3

Notes:
'Capital adequacy ratio' refers to the ratio of capital to risk assets, as required by the BIS. 'Long-established' banks are banks existing more than 50 years; 'new' banks are banks established in 1992. There are sixteen long-established banks and sixteen new banks; their shares of assets were 83% and 17%, respectively, in 1997. There are also some 46 foreign banks with 73 branches in Taiwan. In aggregate they account for about 5–6% of total bank sector assets.
Source: Central Bank of China.

For all domestic banks, the proportion of non-performing loans was 3.8% on average from the first quarter of 1996 to the end of 1997. The Bank for International Settlements (BIS) capital adequacy ratio requirement of 8% has been included in the Banking Law as amended in 1989, as a result of which banks embarked upon recapitalisation in the early 1990s. By the end of 1997, the capital adequacy ratios of domestic long-established banks and new banks were 11.3% and 12.3% respectively (Table 11.4). Furthermore, one of the requirements for the establishment of new banks set in 1989 was a high self-owned capital equivalent to US$400 million; this requirement has also contributed to the soundness of the banking system.

CONCLUSION

Given the above observations, we may argue that in many ways the economic structure of Taiwan is relatively sound in comparison with those of the troubled economies. The distinctive features of economic policies implemented in Taiwan in the past decade were: reduction of tariffs; relaxation of import controls; financial liberalisation; and upgrading of industries. These policies resulted in the advancement of productivity and the expansion of exports of technology-intensive industries, as well as improvements in the financial system.

The upgrading of industries and the advancement of competitive ability in the international market certainly provided an important foundation for weathering the crisis. The series of liberalising and restructuring measures designed and implemented during the past ten years played a vital role in establishing an economic – and, in particular, financial – system that could withstand the shock of the East Asian crisis.

12 Japan

Akiyoshi Horiuchi

INTRODUCTION

The 1980s and the early 1990s saw bank crises in many countries. Many industrialised countries, most developing countries and economies moving from central planning to market-oriented systems experienced some degree of bank crisis. Of the 181 such countries reviewed by Lindgren and others in 1996, 133 had experienced significant banking sector problems at some stage during the past fifteen years (Lindgren et al. 1996: 20).

However, the Japanese bank crisis seems to have been unique in its long duration and in the seriousness of its influence on economic performance. Japan has taken half a decade to deal with the bad loan problem in its banking sector, without remarkable success – the problem had grown serious enough to endanger the viability of the financial system by late 1997.

This chapter tries to explain the Japanese bank crisis from the perspective of corporate governance. Any bank is a corporation of managers who must be monitored and disciplined by some means. However, in Japan, bank management has not been effectively controlled, and that deficiency led to the current bank crisis.

This chapter first describes the current banking crisis in Japan, and argues that there is still a danger of undermining the capital base of the banks. It examines the governance structure of Japanese banks, and explains how the comprehensive safety net implemented by the government undermined the capital market mechanism of monitoring bank management. It argues that the Japanese government rigidly controlled financial markets to the extent that market competition was unable to exert a disciplinary influence on bank management. It examines the regulatory authority's monitoring of bank management, and argues that the pervasive relationship between the regulatory authority and private banks (*amakudari*) increased the fragility of the banking industry. A key problem is that the management of the Japanese banks is 'entrenched', in the sense that managers are immune from external disciplinary influences. Entrenched management delayed necessary structural readjustments in the banking industry. The chapter concludes by drawing out policy implications.

DETERIORATION OF BANK BALANCE SHEETS

Table 12.1 summarises the official semi-annual figures on non-performing loans from March 1996 to September 1997 in the Japanese banking sector. The average ratio of non-performing to total loans was around 4% as of September 1997. This is more than 0.8% lower than the figure for March 1996. More than half of the non-performing loans were covered by provisions for loan losses (the provision ratio was 2.4% at September 1997). Table 12.1 appears to show that the problem of non-performing loans has already been reduced to a minor policy problem in Japan.

A series of financial upheavals late in autumn 1997 made it clear that the banking problem was still considerable. Figure 12.1 shows recent changes in the Bank for International Settlements (BIS) capital ratios for the major banks, revealing that most major banks had been able gradually to increase their capital ratios until March 1997. The turmoil of 1997 retarded this improvement, precipitating a government injection of public funds into their capital bases in March 1998.[1] There is still a rather serious problem of capital inadequacy in the Japanese banking industry.

The cooperative credit banks have not recovered from their serious difficulties with non-performing loans (Table 12.1). Their non-performing loan ratio has stayed higher than 10%, with no signs of significant reduction. The provision for losses is still very small. Thus, the cooperative credit banks are a weak point in the Japanese banking sector. As for *shinkin* banks – which are non-profit financial institutions – it was reported that, if they were to subtract non-performing loans from their equity capital, almost 90% of these banks would be unable to satisfy the domestic standard of capital adequacy requirement (4%) imposed on commercial banks in Japan (*Nihon Keizai Shimbun* 16 May 1996). The same newspaper report suggested that non-performing loans represent a serious problem for the cooperative banks.

Some people suspect the published figures underestimate the actual situation facing Japanese banks. This suspicion was reinforced by a tentative report about the amount of problematic loans in the banking sector published by the Ministry of Finance (MOF) in January 1998. The report made a survey of the loans that banks themselves recognised as 'problematic' during the period from March to September 1997, following the supervision criteria adopted by the MOF. According to this report, the total loans which were either impossible or very difficult to collect amounted to ¥11.4 trillion for the major and the regional banks (i.e. just 1.8% of the total loans of these banks). However, in addition to this they held ¥65.3 trillion in loans which were likely to be more or less difficult to collect. In total, the proportion of problematic loans was higher than 12% of the total outstanding loans for these banks. This figure is substantially higher than the non-performing loans ratio estimated in the published figures (i.e. around

Table 12.1 Japan: non-performing loans in the banking sector (¥100 billion)

	March 96	September 96	March 97	September 97
Major banks				
a Total loans	3,918.5	3,868.0	3,953.1	3,804.0
b Non-performing loans	218.7	174.1	164.4	161.3
b/a: %	(5.58)	(4.50)	(4.16)	(4.24)
c Provision for losses	103.5	82.4	93.9	103.3
c/a: %	(2.64)	(2.13)	(2.38)	(2.72)
Regional banks				
a Total loans	1,896.8	1,876.5	1,902.9	1,900.0
b Non-performing loans	66.4	55.8	53.5	56.0
b/a: %	(3.50)	(2.97)	(2.81)	(2.95)
c Provision for losses	29.5	24.7	29.5	33.6
c/a: %	(1.56)	(1.32)	(1.55)	(1.77)
Total cooperatives				
a Total loans	1,312.1	1,299.3	1,285.4	1,270.7
b Non-performing loans	63.0	62.3	61.1	63.5
b/a: %	(4.80)	(4.79)	(4.75)	(5.00)
c Provision for losses	17.6	18.6	26.6	28.1
c/a: %	(1.34)	(1.43)	(2.07)	(2.21)
***Shinkin* banks**				
a Total loans	696.0	696.7	702.0	701.3
b Non-performing loans	32.0	33.7	32.4	33.8
b/a: %	(4.60)	(4.84)	(4.62)	(4.82)
c Provision for losses	10.3	11.3	16.2	16.7
c/a: %	(1.48)	(1.62)	(2.31)	(2.38)
Credit cooperatives				
a Total loans	173.7	172.8	172.1	165.1
b Non-performing loans	20.5	21.3	21.2	20.0
b/a: %	(11.80)	(12.33)	(12.32)	(12.11)
c Provision for losses	1.8	1.8	3.0	2.6
c/a: %	(1.04)	(1.04)	(1.74)	(1.57)
Total				
a Total loans	7,127.4	7043.8	7,141.4	6,974.7
b Non-performing loans	348.0	292.3	279.0	280.8
b/a: %	(4.88)	(4.15)	(3.91)	(4.03)
c Provision for losses	150.5	125.7	149.9	165.0
c/a: %	(2.11)	(1.78)	(2.10)	(2.37)

Note: Those banks which collapsed during the sample period are excluded from the table.
Source: Federation of Bankers Associations of Japan, *Analysis of Financial Statements of All Banks*.

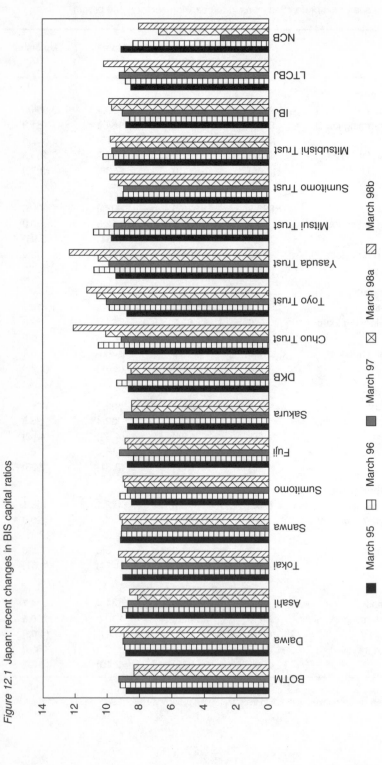

Figure 12.1 Japan: recent changes in BIS capital ratios

Legend: March 95 ■ March 96 ▨ March 97 ▨ March 98a ▨ March 98b ▨

Notes: Figures for March 98a are the ratios expected if no public funds were injected. Figures for March 98b are the ratios attained with the help of capital injection.
Source: Deposit Insurance Corporation.

3.8%). The MOF's tentative figures are based on different criteria to those utilised to calculate the official figures presented in Table 12.1.[2]

Danger of a vicious circle

After the 'bubble' burst in 1990, the Japanese banks faced 'the Japan premium' (defined as the difference between the yen London interbank offered rate on Japanese banks and the average on US and UK banks) for the first time since the first oil crisis of 1974. This was apparent in the international money market immediately after mid-summer 1995, when some Japanese financial institutions failed. After rapidly rising to higher than 30 basis points, the Japan premium remained at around 10 basis points until the beginning of November 1997. In late November, the Japan premium jumped to 90 basis points, reflecting the turmoil in the domestic money market.[3]

The development of the Japan premium suggests that the international money market was already starting to send an alarm signal about the Japanese banking system in the summer of 1995. The Japanese government belatedly started to force bank recapitalisation by announcing that new rules would be introduced in April 1998. This announcement, and the prolonged sluggishness of stock prices, led to a 'credit crunch' in 1997.

The requirement for more comprehensive disclosure of non-performing loans seems to have intensified the credit crunch. Combined with the impact of the tax increases which occurred in the first half of 1997, the credit crunch has contributed to increased non-performing loans in the banking sector. Obviously, this represents a vicious circle between the deficiency of bank capital and the macroeconomic slowdown.

GOVERNANCE STRUCTURE IN THE BANKING SECTOR

The bank crisis in Japan arose from failings in governance. A disciplinary influence could be exerted on bank management through three channels: capital market forces, whereby either investors including depositors monitor bank performance or the threat of hostile takeovers disciplines bank managers; competition in the banking industry, which weeds out inefficient banks; and supervision by the regulatory authorities, which should prevent banks from taking excessive risks and force managers to restructure their businesses in the case of crisis. These disciplinary mechanisms have not worked effectively in the Japanese banking industry, for reasons that are now explained.

Government safety net

The most important reason why the capital market has not effectively monitored and disciplined Japanese bank management is that the government has kept in place a comprehensive safety net – a social system for dealing with distressed banks and distributing any social costs associated with financial institution failures among related parties. Such a safety net has important implications for risk sharing. By taking control of the distribution of costs associated with bank failures, the safety net decreases the monitoring incentives of depositors and other investors in bank debt, who are either explicitly or implicitly protected from bank failure losses.[4]

The MOF has programs to rescue distressed financial institutions, in collaboration with both the Bank of Japan (BOJ) and private financial institutions, particularly major banks. Before 1990 there were some bank failures, though the number was quite small, and in all cases the MOF pressured private banks to rescue their distressed peers.[5]

In addition, the MOF often placed its officers on the board of the distressed bank, with a view to reorganising management. Dispatching MOF officials to a distressed bank may be an effective signal that the government has made a commitment to rescue the bank at any cost, which helps to persuade other banks to collaborate with the bailing out program. However, this signalling is not always successful.[6]

Since the actions taken by the authorities in rescuing troubled banks have been covert, it is difficult to estimate the social costs of the safety net and the exact distribution of the burden among various agents. Not only depositors but also almost all other debt holders (except a few major banks) have been exempted from the burdens of bailing out distressed banks. Even the shareholders of failed banks seem to have been rescued from bank failures. For example, in the case of credit cooperative banks, their failures did not require equity holders to share the costs of failures. Until the early 1990s, the financial authorities rarely paid the costs of the bailout procedure themselves, confining their role to coordinating the rescue programs. Thus the costs of preserving financial stability have fallen disproportionately on sound private banks, particularly major banks.

In some cases, the BOJ may have extended loans to distressed banks at the official discount rate, which was substantially lower than money market interest rates, but it is impossible to obtain any information about these unofficial rescue programs. The BOJ utilised emergency loans (authorised by Article 25 of the BOJ Act) for the first time since 1965 to support the Tokyo Kyodo Bank, newly established in 1995, to take over two failed credit cooperatives in the Tokyo prefecture. The BOJ's emergency loans increased sharply during 1995, due to managerial crises in several small and medium-scale banks (including Hyogo Bank), reportedly to a little more than ¥1.0 trillion.

Deposit insurance in Japan

Deposit insurance has not been an element of the Japanese financial safety net. A system of deposit insurance was introduced in 1971, but it was not actually utilised in Japan until 1992. The MOF continued to implement the traditional safety net to avoid the bankruptcy of deposit-taking institutions. It gave priority to the protection of weak (and therefore inefficient) banks over the promotion of competition in the financial industry, even after the introduction of deposit insurance. The Deposit Insurance Corporation (DIC) remained nominal for a long time, and its functions were limited to paying out insured deposits in cases of bank failure (although the DIC never did any paying out). In 1986, the Law of Deposit Insurance was amended to extend the DIC's powers. The amended law allows the DIC to support the rescue or disposal of distressed banks by subsidising private agents. In April 1992, the DIC supplied ¥8.0 billion to help a medium-sized regional bank absorb another small bank in distress.

In December 1997 the government made a commitment to protect all deposits and other debts, such as bank debentures, issued by banks and financial institutions participating in the deposit insurance system, in order to calm people's anxiety about bank failures following the bankruptcy of the Hokkaido-Takushoku Bank and the failures of a few major securities companies, including Yamaichi.

The government's commitment is likely to increase moral hazard by weakening the incentives for depositors and investors to monitor bank management. However, the long-standing implementation of the comprehensive safety net has produced among depositors and other investors a perception that they will never be required to share the burden if their banks go bankrupt. Because of this widespread perception, the government's paying off insured deposits without rescuing investors in bank debts other than insured deposits would result in an unexpected shock to the financial system. Thus, at the end of 1997, the Japanese government felt that it had to support the widespread perception about the safety net.

The comprehensive safety deprived investors of incentives to monitor the performance of individual banks and hindered the development of capital market mechanisms to discipline bank management. The lack of market mechanisms, in turn, has made it quite difficult for the government to abandon the traditional safety net.

Disciplinary influence of market competition

What about the disciplinary influence of market competition on bank management? Nickell et al. (1997) show with regard to manufacturing industries that full-scale market competition exerts a strong disciplinary influence on corporate management by weeding out inefficiently managed firms. Regardless of a corporation's specific ownership or governance structure, corporate managers are disciplined by fierce market competition. Firms disappear if they have inefficient management.

Japanese manufacturing firms have performed excellently because they have long faced fierce competition in the global market. In contrast, the

Japanese financial services industries have been protected from full-scale competition by regulation. Thus, market competition has not worked to discipline management in the banking and other financial services industries in Japan.

Role of regulation in restricting competition

Various restrictive regulations – such as controls on interest rates, new entries into banking and other financial services, and new branches – conferred handsome rents on existing banks and other financial institutions during the high-growth era of the 1960s and 1970s. The primary purpose of the MOF's administrative guidance was to suppress full-scale competition in each of the compartmentalised financial businesses, thereby protecting the less competitive small-scale banks such as *sogo* banks, *shinkin* banks and credit cooperatives. The MOF's policy stance was often called the 'convoy administration'.

Economic theory shows that the existence of rents can provide private banks with incentives to refrain from excessive risk-taking without effective prudential regulations, in order to continue enjoying handsome rents (Hellman et al. 1997).[7] In addition, the regulatory authority was able to utilise the rents accumulated in the banking sector as a means of dealing with banks in financial distress. Specifically, the regulator relied on private banks' collaboration in implementing the safety net, and major banks faithfully bore a disproportionate share of the costs involved. This mechanism would not have worked had the major banks not enjoyed the rents stemming from the restrictive regulations. The MOF also utilised the restrictive regulations to give private banks an incentive to accept its initiatives in the process of dealing with bank failures. The MOF manipulated the regulatory framework to favour banks which toed the line and to penalise banks which failed to heed their guidance.[8]

Delayed deregulation of the financial markets

Since the mid-1970s the competition-restricting regulations have gradually weakened the ability of Japanese banks and other financial institutions to adapt to environmental changes. The Japanese government adopted a policy of gradual deregulation for the purpose of preventing 'undue destabilisation'. In reality, this gradualism was synonymous with the policy of protecting established vested interests in the financial industries, thereby suppressing the disciplinary effects the financial deregulation was expected to exert.

Japanese financial deregulation was prompted by pressures from abroad, particularly from the United States, rather than Japanese government initiative. For example, the yen/dollar agreement between Japan and the United States in 1984 compelled the Japanese government to provide an explicit timetable for liberalising financial markets (Frankel 1984; Takeda and Turner 1992). Compared to the international capital market generally, the Japanese financial markets have been belatedly deregulated. The 'big bang' proposed by Prime Minister Ryutaro Hashimoto in November 1996 was the government's commitment to abandoning the policy of gradualism. This is a sort of shock therapy to make up for lost time.

We should not totally deny the impact of financial deregulation on domestic financial markets during the 1980s. In particular, major companies reduced their dependence on bank borrowing by issuing a large amount of corporate bonds in international markets. This 'internationalisation' of corporate finance has induced deregulation in domestic corporate bond markets since the mid-1980s (Horiuchi 1996). However, generally speaking, the Japanese banks and other financial institutions have been able to base their business on the huge amount of wealth accumulated by households.

The role of government in bank managerial governance

The fact that official regulation led to neither the capital market nor market competition disciplining bank management in Japan is to some extent a natural outcome of the assignment of responsibility for monitoring bank management to the MOF and the BOJ. The Banking Law authorises the MOF to intervene in the management of banks for purposes of prudential regulation. The BOJ is also in charge of monitoring bank management, particularly from the viewpoint of money market adjustment. In the following section, we first examine how the Japanese government has implemented prudential regulations, then show how the weakness of regulatory monitoring contributed to the fragility of the banking industry, by examining the '*amakudari*' relationships between the regulator and the private banks.

Capital adequacy regulations

During the period of economic reconstruction immediately after World War II, the MOF was seriously concerned about the prudence of bank management, because banks' equity capital per deposit had fallen sharply from 29.9% in 1930 to only 5.6 % by 1953. With a view to strengthening banks' capital bases, in 1953 the MOF started instructing banks to reduce current expenses to 78% or less of current revenues. This administrative guidance continued until 1973.

In 1954, the MOF introduced capital adequacy regulation, which required banks to increase 'broadly defined capital' to more than 10% of total deposits.[9] However, some depository financial institutions were not covered by this capital adequacy regulation – for example, the *sogo* banks. When the *sogo* banks converted to regional banks in February 1989, the MOF imposed the same minimum capital adequacy ratio on them as on city banks and other regional banks. *Shinkin* banks were free of the capital

Figure 12.2 Japan: capital:deposits ratios of commercial banks (%)

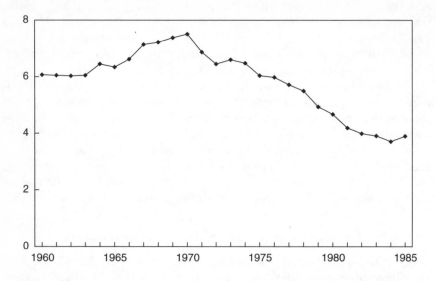

Source: Federation of Bankers Associations of Japan, *Analysis of Financial Statements of All Banks.*

adequacy regulation until May 1986, when the MOF introduced administrative guidance in the form of a minimum capital adequacy ratio.

Thus, until the late 1980s, the capital adequacy regulation did not cover
the whole range of deposit-taking institutions. Moreover, the regulation
seemed to be ineffective. Figure 12.2 shows that, from 1960 to the mid-
1970s, the average capital adequacy ratio for the banking sector (city banks
and regional banks) remained almost constant at 6%, far below the MOF's
requirement of 10%. Furthermore, the average capital:deposits ratio
dropped abruptly, to below 4%, during the 1980s.[10]

Bank capital and *amakudari*

If the prudential regulation implemented by the MOF was ineffective in
making bank's management sound, it was not the only tool at the MOF's
disposal. Aoki et al. (1994) argue that the financial authority effectively
monitors bank management through the *amakudari* system – the system
prevailing among private banks (and other firms) whereby state officials are
granted positions on corporate managerial boards after retirement. According to this argument, this system has given regulatory officers ample incentives to rigorously monitor bank management because, if they fail as
regulators, they will lose chances to obtain good jobs in private banks on retirement. Therefore bank performance will be positively influenced by, or at
worst be independent from, *amakudari*.

However, this *amakudari* system is accompanied by an agency problem,

Table 12.2 Japan: *amakudari* and performance of regional banks

	MOF & BOJ	MOF	BOJ	NON
Panel A: Period 1980–4				
	(42)	(48)	(19)	(16)
EQT	2.648***	2.739***	3.484	3.575
BRN	3.388	3.325	3.047	3.006
GAS	8.736	7.908	7.953	7.984
PRO	8.001	8.096	8.456	7.604
Panel B: Period 1985–9				
	(41)	(43)	(21)	(20)
EQT	2.849***	3.008***	3.390	3.411
BRN	2.513	2.430	2.777	2.206
GAS	10.945	9.927	10.526	9.815
PRO	8.913	9.087	8.641	8.610
BAD	4.145***	4.145***	2.205	2.200
Panel C: Period 1990–4				
	(40)	(43)	(20)	(22)
EQT	3.427***	3.698**	3.696*	4.046
BRN	1.877	1.853	1.795	1.698
GAS	1.985	2.570	2.359	2.405
PRO	4.054	4.148	4.809	4.950
BAD	4.225***	3.843**	2.761	2.159

Note: The symbols *** , **, and * indicate the figures are different from those of 'NON' significantly at 1%, 2.5%, and 5% levels respectively. Panels A and B exclude Daiko Bank because of its abnormal performances during the 1980s, and Panel C deletes Kumamoto Family Bank because of merger with regional financial institutions at the beginning of the 1990s. The figures in parentheses are the numbers of banks belonging to the respective categories.

because the bureaucrats assigned the role of monitoring banks' management expect to be employed by the same banks. If the financial authorities and private banks were to bargain with each other, the *amakudari* system might undermine the effectiveness of the regulators and allow banks to engage in unsound management (Horiuchi and Shimizu 1998). This hypothesis predicts that the banks accepting *amakudari* officials from the financial authority will show poor performance in terms of soundness.

These hypotheses can be tentatively tested using Table 12.2, taking the 125 regional banks operating in March 1996 as a sample. The 125 regional banks are categorised according to which *amakudari* officers, if any, they accept. Category 'MOF & BOJ' contains the banks which accept *amakudari* officers from both the MOF and the BOJ. Category 'MOF' consists of the banks which accept officers only from the MOF, and category 'BOJ' consists of the banks which accept them only from the BOJ. Finally, category 'NON' consists of the banks that do not accept *amakudari* officers at all.

Each panel of Table 12.2 shows performance averages over a five-year period. In all three of the panels, the capital:asset ratio (EQT) is significantly lower for both categories MOF & BOJ and MOF than for category NON.

For example, during the first half of the 1980s, the capital:asset ratio (EQT) for category MOF & BOJ banks was on average 0.927% lower than that of category NON banks. The differences are statistically significant at the 1% level. As Keeley (1990) argues, the lower capital:asset ratio implies a higher level of risk. As for asset growth (GAS) and profitability (PRO), we find no significant difference between the banks belonging to either category MOF & BOJ or MOF, and the banks of category NON. Thus, Table 12.2 suggests that the banks accepting *amakudari* officials from the MOF tend to embrace higher levels of risk.

The bad loan ratio (the amount of non-performing loans per total loan) is another useful measure of bank risk. In March 1996, Japanese banks started to comprehensively disclose the amount of non-performing loans they held for the first time.

The rows of BAD in Panels B and C of Table 12.2 present the bad loan ratios for each category of bank. Panel B shows that the two groups of banks accepting *amakudari* officials from the MOF had almost double the bad loan ratios (4.145 as of 1985) of the banks totally independent from the *amakudari* relationship.These differences are statistically significant at the 1% level. In contrast, the average level of bad loan ratios for the banks accepting *amakudari* from the BOJ is not significantly different from that of the NON. The same is true in Panel C, which classifies sample banks according to their *amakudari* status as of 1990. Thus, if we measure (ex post) risk by the bad loan ratio, the results are consistent with the hypothesis that the *amakudari* relationship undermines monitoring by the MOF.

Our examination of the influence of the *amakudari* relationship suggests that, rather than closely monitoring bank management, the financial authorities tend to help incumbent bank managers to continue their operations. Thus, we conclude that a lack of effective monitoring by the regulators is a conspicuous feature of the governance of Japanese bank management.[11]

It would be an exaggeration to say that the MOF has totally neglected prudential regulation. Table 12.3 provides a list of prudential regulations for commercial banks – the city banks and the regional banks – as of 1974. The MOF has kept almost all of the prudential guidance listed in this table intact. However, on the whole, bankers did not consider that these official guidelines were to be met at any cost, and the MOF generously permitted some divergence between the required and the actual figures for individual banks.

VACUUM OF GOVERNANCE

This chapter has stressed that the Japanese bank management has enjoyed independence from outsiders' disciplinary influence. This is the 'entrenched

Table 12.3 Japan: prudential regulations as of 1974

1	Loans/deposits ratio is to be no higher than 80%.
2	(a) Liquid assets/deposits ratio is to be higher than 30%.
	(b) For banks that do not satisfy (a), increment of liquid asset/increment of total deposits ratio is to be higher than 30%.
3	Ratio of current expenses (excluding tax) to current revenue is to be constantly decreased. (Until 1973, the MOF indicated a maximum level of 78% for this ratio.)
4	Annual dividend per share is to be less than 12.5% of the face value of the share.
5	Broadly defined capital/deposits ratio should be higher than 10%.
6	The amount of loan to a single borrower is to be less than
	(a) 20% of the bank's equity capital for city banks and regional banks;
	(b) 30% of the bank's equity capital for long-term credit banks and the trust banks;
	(c) 40% of the bank's equity capital for foreign exchange banks.

Note: The MOF designated the above items as the desirable standards under administrative guidance. It has since altered the regulations to some extent. For example, ceilings on credit to individual borrowers were introduced in the revised Banking Law in 1982; the total amount of credit to any individual borrower should not exceed 20% of the bank's equity capital.
Source: The Banking Bureau of the MOF.

management' phenomenon. Entrenched bank managers tended to take excessive risks under the comprehensive safety net during the latter half of 1980s. At the same time, entrenched managers tended to delay structural changes after recognising their failure in risk-taking (Boot 1992). This is particularly significant to the extent that the Japanese bank crisis was exacerbated by delayed responses on the part of bank management, rather than the absolute amount of non-performing loans. The Japanese banks hesitated to undertake the necessary drastic restructuring, and the MOF's forbearance policy supported the reluctance of banks to restructure, making the situation worse.

Delayed restructuring in Japanese banking

As Lindgren et al. (1996) show, the bank crisis is not peculiar to Japan. However, Japan has taken too long to deal with this problem, without any remarkable success. Figure 12.3 presents an international comparison of banking restructuring during the first half of the 1990s, based on the BIS *Annual Report* (1996). This figure shows that, except in the United States, the profitability of commercial banks decreased in the first half of the 1990s, compared with the latter half of the 1980s, in all of the major industrial countries including Japan. In terms of the growth rate in the number of bank branches, the growth rate in the total number of employees, and the changes in wage index, Japan was unique in the sense that none of these

Figure 12.3 Japan: restructuring in the banking industry: international comparisons

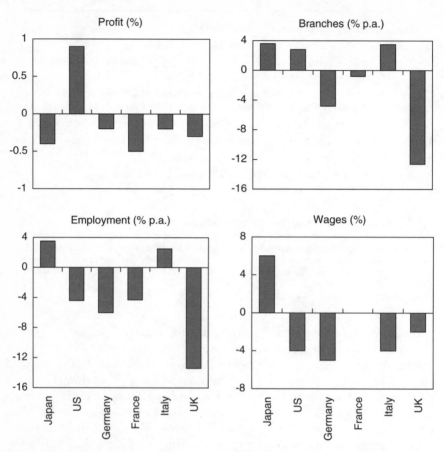

Notes: Profit (return on assets) is the difference between the average for 1986–8 and 1992–4; branches is the growth rate in the total number of branches from 1990 to 1995; employment is the growth rate in total employees from 1990 to 1994; wages (ratio of wage payments to total revenue) is the difference between the average for 1986–8 and 1992–4.
Source: BIS 1996.

measures decreased during the 1990s compared with the latter half of the 1980s. In other words, the commercial banks in all the other major industrialised countries downsized or reduced their scale of business after recognising a fall in profitability during the 1990s. Thus, Figure 12.3 confirms that the Japanese banks were hesitant to restructure their business in spite of decreasing profitability after 1990.

Limitation of the traditional rescue method

Since the 'bubble' burst at the beginning of the 1990s, it has become increasingly difficult for the MOF to maintain its traditional procedure of bailing out bank failures. In fact, the MOF has utilised the deposit insurance system extensively to deal with banks in distress. The scale of the DIC is still limited, but its increasing use marks a significant change in the operation of the Japanese safety net. Between April 1992 – when the DIC played a role in bailing out a distressed bank for the first time – and January 1998, the DIC has intervened in 22 cases of bailing out troubled banks, to the extent of more than ¥2.4 trillion.

One of the reasons for this shift is that structural changes in financial markets have decreased the rent accruing to major banks, so that the MOF has been unable to totally depend on the collaboration of those banks in implementing the safety net. Financial deregulation has made it difficult for the MOF to compensate major banks for their participation in rescue programs. The traditional methods of dealing with bank failures have not yet disappeared, and many private banks are still playing an important role through collaboration with the regulators. However, it is likely that the deposit insurance system will be utilised substantially in the future.

Use of the deposit insurance system to facilitate reorganisation does not, however, imply that banks will undergo formal bankruptcy procedures. The MOF has continued to avoid explicit bank failures, by using the deposit insurance system to provide sound banks with incentives to merge with insolvent ones or to collaborate with the authorities in restructuring troubled banks. This implies a slow reorganisation of the financial system and a marked increase in the burden borne by the DIC.

This policy stance adopted by the MOF reached a dead end when the principle of 'too big to fail' was abandoned and the Hokkaido-Takushoku Bank was allowed to go bankrupt in November 1997. Both domestic and international financial markets recognised that the Japanese traditional safety net was no longer sustainable. This market perception caused turmoil in Japanese money markets, as well as a sharp jump in the Japan premium in the international money market, at the end of 1997.

CONCLUSION

Bank management has been largely independent of outside control. More specifically, the comprehensive safety net has prevented the capital market from exercising discipline over bank management, and there have been no significant disciplinary pressures from market competition because of the deliberately controlled deregulation of financial services industries. In such circumstances, the regulatory authority should have actively monitored bank management in order to keep soundness in the banking sector. However, the regulatory authority (the MOF) was more concerned with preserving the viability of existing banks and other financial institutions than with effective monitoring from the viewpoint of managerial soundness. In addition, the traditional human ties between the MOF and private banks seem to have undermined the effectiveness of regulatory monitoring, thereby making the banking industry more fragile. Obviously, we have not resolved the issue of 'who monitors the monitor' in the Japanese financial system.

The vacuum of governance in the banking sector was responsible for the delayed restructuring of the banking industry, which has been suffering from the bad loan problem since the beginning of the 1990s. As recently as April 1998, the Japanese government adopted a policy of introducing the prompt corrective action rule. Also, in March 1998, the government ordered banks to submit explicit time schedules for managerial restructuring, as a condition for government injection of public funds into banks' capital. These policy measures seem to have at last induced hesitant banks to start restructuring their businesses. This fact in itself tells us that Japanese banks have no strong intention to drastically reform their businesses on their own initiative.

The recent government policy of strengthening both bank supervision and prudential regulations make sense from the long-term perspective of building a stable financial system. However, we need to note two issues related to strengthening bank supervision.

First, the supervision of bank management by the government has its own agency costs, as the examination of *amakudari* in this chapter suggests. Market competition and the capital market must also play a role in disciplining bank management. The Japanese 'big bang' advocated by the government is expected to enhance the capability of such market mechanisms.

Second, strengthening prudential regulation during the crisis situation has at least temporarily weakened the banks' intermediary capability even more. The strengthening of prudential regulations has led to a 'credit crunch' since 1997, exacerbating the slowdown of the Japanese economy. This side effect of strengthening prudential regulations might hinder the full-scale strengthening of government supervision. Thus, we need to prepare supplementary measures to mitigate the side effects of strengthening prudential regulations. What are those supplementary measures? They should be purely temporary ones which would not hinder the implementation of prudential regulation based on long-term perspectives. The government could help bank restructuring by injecting public funds. However, this policy should not allow the survival of moribund banks, but promote the necessary downsizing of the banking industry. At the beginning of this year, the Japanese government decided to inject capital into all existing banks, regardless of their performance, to overcome the current bank crisis. We doubt whether this policy is compatible with the long-term objective of strengthening the soundness of banks and, therefore, the banking system's contribution to Japan's economic growth.

NOTES

1 In March 1998, the government injected a little more than ¥1.8 trillion into 21 major banks (nine city banks, three long-term credit banks, six trust banks, and three big regional banks) by buying either preferred stocks or perpetual subordinated debt. This injection is estimated to have increased the equity capital of those banks by 5.1%.

2 The definition of non-performing loans in Table 12.1 consists of: 'non-accrual loans'; loans over 180 days overdue; and some 'restructured loans'. This is a much narrower definition than that adopted by the Securities Exchange Commission (SEC) in the United States, which includes loans over 90 days overdue and more comprehensive 'restructured loans'. In addition to the non-performing loans defined above, the Japanese banks have disclosed loans for the purpose of rescuing borrowers since March 1997. These 'rescue loans' are also contained in the SEC's 'restructured loans'. (The total amount of rescue loans held by the major and regional banks amounted to ¥3.4 trillion and ¥3.1 trillion in March and September 1997 respectively.) On the advice of the MOF, the Federation of Bankers Associations of Japan decided to bring its definition of non-performing loans into line with the SEC definition in March 1998. The amount of 'non-performing loans' defined by the SEC criteria is close to the amount of 'problematic loans' reported by the MOF.

3 See 'The Japan Premium: Work in Progress', a paper submitted by Joe Peek and Eric S. Rosengren to the NBER–Japan Project on 17–18 April 1998.

4 Since most depositors are small-size wealth-holders enjoying no economies of scale in collecting and analysing information about bank management, and since there is a 'free-rider' problem to hinder efficient information production, it would be unrealistic to depend totally on market discipline to maintain the stability of the banking system. As Dewatripont and Tirole (1994) argue, we need to have financial safety net in order to protect small investors in the banking sector.

5 Until the end of the 1980s, the number of banks that had come close to failing was small, with the largest rescue program involving not a bank but Yamaichi Securities Company in 1965. In this rescue, coordinated by the MOF, the BOJ provided emergency loans of ¥28.2 billion to Fuji Bank and two other banks which functioned as conduits supplying financial support to Yamaichi. Probably, the most important rescue program implemented by the MOF before 1990 was the merger of Heiwa–Sogo Bank into Sumitomo Bank in October 1986. Heiwa–Sogo got into managerial difficulty during the first half of the 1980s. Despite de facto bankruptcy, the closure of Heiwa–Sogo did not cause damage to depositors and other holders of debt issued by this bank. Sumitomo bore the costs of dealing with the distressed bank, and was able to expand its branch network at once by absorbing Heiwa–Sogo's branches.

6 One of the most recent cases was Hyogo Bank, to which the late chief of the Banking Bureau was sent to reorganise its management. Despite this intervention, Hyogo finally went bankrupt in October 1995.

7 Aoki (1994) argues, by assuming asymmetric information about banks' monitoring activities, that the rent was necessary to motivate private banks to faithfully and efficiently monitor their borrowers. He suggests that the long-term

relationship between major banks and borrower firms – called the 'main bank relationship' – in Japan was crucially dependent on the competition-restricting regulations. However, restricting full-scale competition is not always necessary to motivate banks to supply a 'high quality' level of monitoring. A competitive market would be able to motivate banks to conduct good monitoring. See Klein and Leffler (1981).

8   In 1994, for example, Mitsubishi Bank obtained preferential treatment from the MOF in exchange for rescuing Nippon Trust Bank, which had been seriously damaged by the accumulation of a huge amount of bad loans since the early 1990s. Mitsubishi Bank was 'rewarded' by being allowed to pursue a full complement of trust banking business through Nippon Trust, which is now its subsidiary. Other banks are prohibited by the MOF from engaging in full-line trust banking business through their trust bank subsidiaries. The same story applied when Daiwa Bank financially supported Cosmo Securities Company, which was seriously damaged by the depression in the securities market after the 'bubble' burst at the beginning of the 1990s. Cosmo became a subsidiary of Daiwa Bank yet retained its stock brokerage business, which the securities subsidiaries of other banks are not yet permitted to do.

9   Equity capital (net assets) and some reserve items.

10 The MOF amended the capital adequacy regulation in 1986, to at least 4% of total assets – hardly a stringent requirement. Since 1987, banks with branches or offices in foreign countries have been subject to the BIS capital adequacy rule, but other banks continue to face only this domestic capital adequacy requirement of 4%.

11 Unfortunately, we have observed a number of cases which suggest a weakness of regulatory authority during the early 1990s. The failure of Musashino Shinkin Bank in 1996 gives an example. Musashino Shinkin had been in trouble since 1993 and the MOF was in charge of examining the bank's account statements before publication. The MOF reportedly allowed the bank to engage in window dressing to record positive profits even as of March 1996, when the estimated amount of problem loans was nearly 70% of total loans. In September 1996, the MOF decided to introduce an explicit system of ordering banks in trouble to improve their management based upon officially announced criteria (*Nihon Keizai Shimbun* 11 October 1996). According to the National Federation of Credit Cooperatives, nearly 40% of credit cooperatives had violated the regulation limiting loans to a single party (to 20% of capital in the broad sense) as of September 1994.

13 Australia

David Gruen,
Brian Gray and
Glenn Stevens

INTRODUCTION

Two important episodes that took place in Australia, in the space of less than a decade, form the basis of this case study.

The first was a balance of payments and currency crisis in the mid-1980s. After the Australian dollar was floated in December 1983, its initial tendency was towards appreciation, followed within a few months by gentle depreciation. As of 1 January 1985, it was still at about the same level as it had been at the end of the fixed exchange rate era. Eighteen months later, in July 1986, the currency had fallen by almost 40% in trade-weighted terms. If a 'currency crisis' is a large fall in a previously reasonably stable exchange rate, this event certainly qualifies.

The second episode was a serious weakening in the banking system in the late 1980s and early 1990s. The substantial financial liberalisation process that had occurred through the 1980s had led to the emergence of a more competitive banking system. It was understood by some observers that this meant that the banks would be inherently less risk averse. This proved to be the case. A greater preparedness to chase business combined with, and contributed to, a generally expansionary macroeconomic climate, to produce a very substantial increase in credit growth, associated with increased corporate leverage and rising asset prices. By around 1990, this process had gone too far and the cycle was going into reverse. This problem, combined with corporate over-indebtedness, helped to make the 1990–1 recession more severe than it would otherwise have been, and the recovery more protracted.

This chapter catalogues the essential features of these two episodes. The first part examines the exchange rate movements of the mid-1980s and the associated policy responses. The second part looks at the behaviour of financial intermediaries in the late 1980s and early 1990s, and their asset quality problems. These two events were related, in the sense that they were both manifestations of a newly liberalised financial system learning (as were the policy authorities) about how the new world worked. They occurred sequentially – fortunately so – and are dealt with that way here. The final section offers some observations that may be relevant to thinking about the East Asian crisis and the prospects for recovery in the coming years.

THE CURRENCY CRISIS OF THE MID-1980s

Between February 1985 and July 1986, the Australian dollar fell by 39% in trade-weighted terms. This was the largest decline in a period of that length in the history of the Australian currency.[1] Several factors were at work.

The government's overall economic strategy since 1983 had been to pursue strong growth in output so as to generate employment, and to keep inflation contained by use of an effective incomes policy. In 1985 and 1986, however, prices for Australia's commodity exports fell as part of a mild world business cycle slowdown. This, plus strong growth in domestic demand, saw a large widening of the current account deficit and a rapid rise in the stock of foreign debt.[2] As financial markets absorbed this change in Australia's circumstances, the Australian dollar came under downward pressure.

Table 13.1 provides macroeconomic data for five consecutive two-year periods, chosen to span the two crises we are considering. The first two-year period predates the currency crisis; the second is during and immediately after it; the third period is the boom of the late 1980s; the fourth is the early 1990s recession; and the final period is the recovery after the recession.

'Fundamentals' versus other factors

It can hardly be argued that the exchange rate should not have fallen, based on trade and other macroeconomic fundamentals. But with the benefit of more than a decade of hindsight, it seems that the 32% real depreciation of the Australian dollar over the seven quarters from 1984Q4 to 1986Q3 was a substantial overreaction to the admittedly sharp worsening in Australia's external circumstances. In Gruen et al. (1998), we present a simple econometric exercise in support of this conclusion. In brief, an equation for Australia's real exchange rate is estimated using 'fundamental' variables over the post-float period, but excluding 1985–7 from the estimation. When the model is dynamically simulated through the 1985–7 period we have an estimate of how the exchange rate would have behaved over this three-year period had its response to the deteriorating economic fundamentals been the same as its average response over the rest of the post-float period. For two years of this three-year period, from 1985Q2 to 1987Q1, the observed real exchange rate averaged about 7% below its predicted level, with a maximal difference of about 15% in the September quarter 1986. The observed fall in the real exchange rate in the seven quarters to September 1986 was nearly twice what would now be expected in response to a comparable

Table 13.1 Australia: the Australian macroeconomy (period averages, unless otherwise stated)

	1983/4– 1984/5	1985/6– 1986/7	1987/8– 1988/9	1989/90– 1990/91	1991/2– 1992/3
GDP growth (% p.a.)	7.0	2.8	4.6	0.2	3.3
Underlying inflation (% p.a.)[a]	6.2	9.4	6.5	5.2	2.3
Unemployment rate (%)	9.1	8.1	7.2	7.3	10.7
Wages (AWOTE) growth[b] (% p.a.)	7.5	6.8	7.2	5.8	3.3
Balance on goods and services (% of GDP)	−2.0	−2.6	−1.4	−1.1	−0.2
Current account balance (% of GDP)	−4.7	−5.6	−4.8	−5.4	−3.6
Net foreign debt (% of GDP, end period)	23.4	31.6	33.2	38.2	41.4
Terms of trade (index 1989/90 = 100)	95.2	84.2	93.6	97.4	90.1
Exchange rate (trade-weighted index, June 1970 = 100)	76.1	55.6	55.2	56.4	52.5
Official cash rate (% p.a.)	10.9	15.7	13.0	14.4	6.7
Credit growth (% p.a.)	18.2	19.6	22.3	6.5	0.3
Budget balance (underlying % of GDP)	−3.1	−1.4	1.1	1.0	−3.6

Note: Averages of year-end values for the two financial years shown in each column are used for GDP growth, underlying inflation, wages, and credit growth.

a Underlying inflation excludes volatile and interest-sensitive items from consumer price index.

b AWOTE is average weekly ordinary time earnings.

deterioration in external fundamentals – which seems like a substantial over-reaction.

Why did this happen? The process of learning about the functioning of a floating exchange rate system may have contributed. The sharp deterioration in Australia's external fundamentals occurred when there had been only limited experience of the float. Markets took some time (measured in years) to 'learn' the appropriate reaction to a serious adverse external shock. This may well be a general phenomenon; foreign exchange markets may be particularly susceptible to overreaction when they have only limited experience in a floating regime.

The authorities were also learning about the new system, and there was a period of heightened uncertainty about the nature of the goals of monetary policy. In early 1985, the previous practice of the government announcing a target for growth in the monetary aggregate, M3, was discontinued. This decision was well founded, given that the relationship between M3 and the economy was shifting dramatically in response to financial liberalisation and innovation. But changing monetary policy regimes is never easy.

Despite the best efforts of the Reserve Bank and the government to articulate a new framework, there was an inevitable period in which observers probably had a very imprecise idea of what monetary policy was seeking to achieve. The susceptibility of markets to overreaction is almost certainly heightened under such circumstances.

There was also a considerable range of views about what the 'fundamentals' actually implied for the exchange rate, even among trained economists. Some thought the exchange rate would reverse some of its fall; others thought the fall would continue.[3] So the very large real depreciation that had occurred did not quickly generate a consensus among informed observers that the exchange rate had overreacted to changes in the fundamentals, even though this seems clear in hindsight. There seem to be three main reasons why such a consensus failed to emerge.

First, there is disagreement among economists about what the crucial economic determinants of short- to medium-term exchange rate movements are. Second, especially when economic fundamentals have changed sharply, there is usually a range of plausible alternative views about the future, which have materially different implications for the current exchange rate, since the market is forward-looking. Third, witnessing a very large movement in the exchange rate leads many observers to revise their views about what, in fact, the appropriate market response to changes in economic fundamentals is. After all, the observed exchange rate response represents a summary measure of the views of market participants. As such, it is not easily dismissed, especially by economists whose training makes them particularly respectful of market outcomes.

This is a feature of markets which are highly developed – such as the US share market, to take one topical example – but the problem may be more acute when large shocks occur early in the life of a new regime, as in Australia in the mid-1980s. Moreover, in a period of additional uncertainty about the objectives of monetary policy, the problems are compounded.

Policy responses: monetary policy and foreign exchange intervention

Policies responded to exchange rate developments on several fronts. The most important immediate response was tighter monetary policy. Budgetary policy was also tightened, but this takes longer to have an impact, so monetary policy responses were critical in stabilising market conditions so as to buy time for other changes to be put in place.

Figure 13.1 shows the exchange rate and the chief operational instrument of monetary policy, the overnight 'cash' interest rate. Short-term interest rates rose from around 10% prior to the exchange rate crisis to about 15–16% by mid-1985, and to 18% by the end of that year. As the exchange rate stabilised they declined again, only to be increased once more in mid-1986 in response to further exchange rate weakness. There was another brief

Figure 13.1 Australia: exchange rate and official cash rate

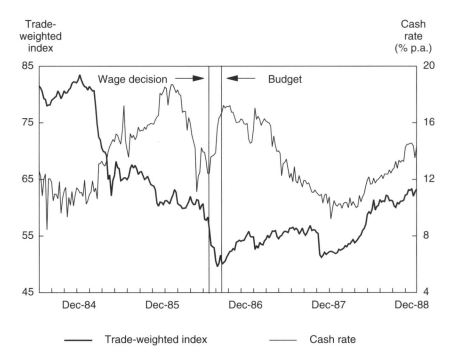

Trade-
weighted
index

Cash
rate
(% p.a.)

Wage decision ➔   ◀ Budget

——— Trade-weighted index   ——— Cash rate

period when interest rates were increased in response to exchange rate pressures in early 1987. On these occasions, domestic policy objectives gave way to the immediate importance of restoring foreign exchange market stability. The Reserve Bank also undertook quite substantial intervention in support of the Australian dollar at various times during this period.

Some elements of this episode, and subsequent experience in operating with a floating exchange rate, are worth emphasising. While a floating exchange rate can move at a speed which alarms observers and policymakers (especially those accustomed to pegged rates), it also confers an advantage. With a pegged or quasi-pegged exchange rate, intervention is automatic and occurs essentially at the market's discretion, and domestic monetary policy responses are virtually automatic as well, regardless of domestic circumstances. The authorities are bound to the defend the peg, perhaps without knowing – at least to begin with – the nature of the shock affecting the economy. The peg may not ultimately be defensible, but it is hard to tell that to begin with.

A floating exchange rate, on the other hand, offers the possibility of tactical retreat: the authorities can allow the exchange rate to move while they decide what sort of shock is in operation and what might be the appropriate response. Intervention is at the authorities' discretion, which at least in principle increases its chance of success. Our view is that foreign exchange market intervention, while certainly not always successful, can make an important difference – and on certain important occasions has done so. Because the exchange rate has flexibility, moreover, it is easier to re-establish a sense of two-way price risk for market participants than it is when defending a pegged or fixed rate. The possibility of an unstable situation, where extreme exchange rate pressures force domestic interest rates to absurd and obviously unsustainable levels – even 100% or more, as in some of the failed European ERM (exchange rate mechanism) defences – is greatly lessened.

Fiscal policy, the 1986 National Wage Case and market perceptions

Other policies also responded to the exchange rate decline. Fiscal policies were tightened, and real wages were reduced through the centralised wage fixing system that operated in Australia at the time.[4] In this section we examine the reactions of markets and commentators to two policy announcements made around the time the currency reached its lows in mid-1986.

We focus on the Arbitration Commission's National Wage Case decision announced on 26 June,[5] and the federal government's 1986 budget brought down two months later, on 19 August. (The timing of these events is also shown in Figure 13.1.) The National Wage Case decision aimed to contain the inflationary pressures arising from the exchange rate depreciation by awarding a centralised wage increase two percentage points lower than the increase in the consumer price index (CPI) over the second half of 1985, and making no wage adjustment to compensate for increases in labour productivity. The 1986 budget continued the process, begun two years earlier, of tightening fiscal policy to reduce the public sector's demands on national savings and thereby to reduce the current account deficit. The budget deficit for 1986–7 was forecast to be A\$3.5 billion, or 1.3% of gross domestic product (GDP), down from A\$5.7 billion (2.4% of GDP) in 1985–6.

Standard macroeconomic analysis would suggest that these measures were appropriate responses to the very large currency depreciation and the significant widening in the current account deficit that had occurred by mid-1986. One might argue that the announced measures did not go far enough, and that more substantial policy adjustments were desirable. Nevertheless, both measures seem to have been significant policy adjustments in the desired direction. As such, the announcements might have been expected to improve financial market confidence in the authorities' determination to deal effectively with the crisis.

As events were unfolding, however, this confidence seemed hard to come by. Macroeconomic policy measures, by their nature, take a considerable time to have any discernible effect on the real economy. In the time before these effects become apparent, judgments as to the appropriateness of the measures tend to be based not only on assessments of their intrinsic worth, but also on how the markets have reacted to them.

In the hours immediately after both the National Wage Case announcement and the presentation of the budget, the foreign exchange market reacted favourably and the currency rose modestly. The initial commentary (at least judged by reports in the *Australian Financial Review* (*AFR*) on the day after the decisions) was also generally favourable.[6]

Within a few days of both announcements, however, positive sentiment in the foreign exchange market had evaporated and the currency had fallen quite sharply. The commentary in the *AFR* at the time is quite revealing. It brings into focus how difficult it is to judge the appropriateness of policies at a time of crisis. As is the rule with macroeconomic policy decisions, the initiatives were sufficiently detailed and complex that they were not easy to assess in the immediate aftermath of their announcement. The sharp falls in the currency in the days following the announcements were taken as evidence, at least by some commentators, that the announcements represented insufficient policy responses to the crisis. Doubts were expressed about whether the policies would have their intended consequences, and about the assumptions underpinning them.[7]

It would be wrong to conclude from these episodes that the reactions of financial markets are irrelevant to an assessment of the appropriateness of economic policies. These reactions always provide feedback on how policies are being received. Furthermore, maintaining (or regaining) financial market confidence is an important aspect of policy – never more so than at times of crisis. But it is also true that policy measures that would be greeted as responsible in quiet times can be quickly dismissed as insufficient in times of crisis. As one private sector analyst said when asked how small the 1986 budget deficit would need to be to generate a favourable market reaction, '[in the current environment] no number can satisfy the market' (*AFR* 18 August 1986: 36).

This is not to argue that macroeconomic policy responses to the crisis were futile. The policy responses gradually had the desired effects on the economy. These responses, combined with a turnaround in Australia's external fundamentals, saw confidence return slowly to financial markets. As the sense of crisis abated, the currency gradually appreciated.

THE OVER-BORROWING CRISIS OF THE LATE 1980s AND EARLY 1990s

At the end of the 1980s and into the 1990s, Australia experienced its first post-deregulation banking 'crisis'. Over this period, loan losses reached their highest levels in at least a century. In 1992 alone, banks' charges to profit and loss for bad debts came to A\$7.4 billion (equivalent to 1.4% of the assets on banks' global balance sheets). Over the five years to 1993, overall loan losses in the banking system totalled around A$25 billion.

All segments of the banking sector were affected during this period, albeit to differing degrees. Foreign banks were the earliest casualties, making heavy write-offs against profits from around 1989. As a group, the foreign banks (which had gained entry into the system in the mid-1980s) had incurred losses roughly equivalent to their initial start-up capital by the end of the decade. Most of these banks were subsequently recapitalised by their foreign parents, while a few withdrew permanently from the Australian market. State banks (specifically the State Bank of Victoria and the then State Bank of South Australia) incurred very heavy losses and required substantial support from their state government shareholders, who unconditionally guaranteed the banks' liabilities.[8] The major banks recorded large loan losses which, in the cases of Westpac Banking Corporation and the Australia and New Zealand banking group ANZ, translated into overall group losses – the first ever recorded by either institution. The remaining banks in the system, though much less affected than the other main groups described above, nonetheless experienced charges against profit and loss around three times the average level of the previous decade (Figure 13.2).

Beyond the banking sector, losses and institutional failures were experienced in the merchant banking sector and amongst some other non-bank financial institutions (the most notable being the collapses of the Farrow Group and Estate Mortgage).[9]

In important respects, the financial crisis was contained. No bank depositors lost funds or even came close to doing so (though investors in some non-bank institutions experienced losses). Despite some large losses, there were virtually no runs on individual banks or financial institutions more generally. The very isolated instances where minor runs did occur could be traced to groundless rumours that were quickly dispelled. There was little evidence of contagion from one institution to another.

The experience of this period, nonetheless, proved to be a defining event in the history of the Australian financial sector. It marked the end of the first and volatile phase of the financial deregulation era, and signalled the start of a period of dramatic structural change within the system. It also began a period of reassessment by financial institutions and financial supervisors of a range of issues including: the long-term forces (including competitive forces) operating in the deregulated financial system; the implications of these forces for risk-management systems within financial institutions; and the tools and techniques needed by supervisors and regulators to be effective in the new environment.

Causes of the credit cycle

In considering the events in the banking sector around the turn of the decade, it is worth reflecting briefly on the history of the Australian bank-

Figure 13.2 Australia: banks' total write-offs (% of bank assets)

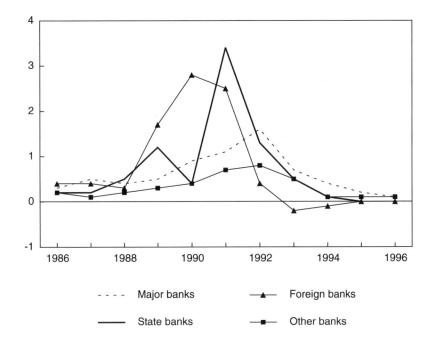

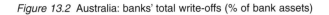

Source: Banks' published annual accounts.

ing and financial sector in the years leading up to the era of financial dereg-ulation (which for present purposes can be dated from around the late 1970s). For many years up to that time banking, though traditionally thought of as involving the acquisition and pooling of risk, could in fact be viewed as a very low-risk activity. For virtually all of the period since World War II, bank balance sheets were heavily constrained by regulations restricting interest rates and asset composition. Bank credit was effectively rationed, with banks dealing almost exclusively in low-risk residential mort-gages and high-quality corporate and government lending and government debt. Higher-risk lending propositions were either left unsatisfied or given over to the unregulated non-bank sector – which had begun to grow rapidly, especially from the 1960s.

Over the five years to the mid-1980s, deregulation led to a transforma-tion of the financial system. As well as the exchange rate being floated, in-terest rates were largely freed from controls, most restrictions on bank balance-sheet composition were removed or relaxed, and entry into the banking system was liberalised. The stage had been set for a significant boost in competitive pressures in the system and a reversal in the long-term stagnation of the ratio of intermediated financial assets to GDP, as described by Grenville (1991).

One of the most obvious manifestations of this financial revolution was a very rapid expansion in credit availability. As illustrated in Table 13.1, credit growth averaged around 20% annually from 1983–4 to 1988–9. Over the same period, banks' balance sheets expanded almost fourfold. Asset prices rose sharply, particularly for commercial property, which served to underpin (as collateral) many of the largest exposures acquired by banks over this period (Figure 13.3).

The events that followed have been well documented: a sharp contraction in economic activity and a collapse in asset prices, leading to a severe deterioration in credit quality in the banking and finance sectors, heavy provisioning and large losses by banks, and a subsequent sharp slowing in credit expansion as the corporate sector sought to reduce ratios of debt to equity in their balance sheets.

In a general sense, an experience like that of the late 1980s and early 1990s was not entirely unexpected; the potential for losses in a deregulated financial system had been recognised. The report of the Campbell Committee in 1981, for example, noted the possibility of 'competition of a kind

Figure 13.3 Australia: commercial property price indices: Australia and Sydney central business district (1989–90 = 100)

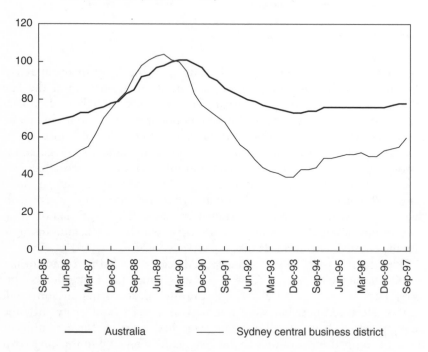

———— Australia   ———— Sydney central business district

Sources: Data for Australia are from the Australian Bureau of Statistics; for Sydney CBD, they are from Jones Lang Wootton Research.

that might be destabilising, i.e. which could lead to the adoption of higher risk portfolios and possible failures' (Campbell 1981).[10]

In other words, it was known that the transition from a protected banking system to a much more competitive and open system carried the potential for credit-related problems. Nevertheless, it would be fair to say that this possibility was underestimated, especially given the general view at the time (and subsequently) that there were substantial net benefits to be gained from financial deregulation. Furthermore, there was little basis on which to assess in advance the nature of potential problems in the transition to a deregulated environment.

At the same time, there was a debate about the dynamics of the shift from a regulated to a deregulated banking system. It was understood that banks' increasing competitiveness would lead to intermediated forms of financing replacing direct forms, and that this re-intermediation could, at least to some extent, explain the faster credit growth being seen at the time. This benign explanation for the faster credit growth may well have dulled people's sense of the dangers inherent in a sustained period of high credit growth.

With hindsight, what was also not well appreciated by commentators and policymakers was the inability of existing systems and controls within financial institutions to either measure or manage their rapidly expanding credit risk. The goal for the bulk of these institutions was the maintenance or growth of market share in the more competitive system. One of the crucial consequences of the imbalance between pressures for rapid acquisition of credit and systems to manage risk has been well described by a former chief executive of the Westpac Banking Corporation:

> The problem was that the bank [Westpac], and banks in general, lacked the capability to aggregate exposures to individual borrowers across the various subsidiaries within their banking groups. This was obviously a serious risk-management flaw. Without proper consultation with the lead bank, the subsidiaries continued to lend to CBD developers as well as to developers of second and third tier properties. We now know how heavily those associated companies drew on the lead bank's capital.
>
> (Conroy 1997: 22)

This experience was not unique to Westpac. It was a classic case of growth without appropriate controls, and was symptomatic of problems being experienced within banks in general, domestically and abroad.

Could bank supervisors have done more?

The second half of the 1980s was a period of rapid policy development for bank supervisors, both domestically and internationally. Supervisors in Australia were busy developing the new prudential regulation framework for banks that had come into existence only a few years earlier. Prior to financial deregulation, and given the restrictive bank entry arrangements and the array of controls in place, there was no obvious need for an explicit system of bank supervision. The regulated financial system was itself an effective mechanism for ensuring bank soundness. That would not be true in a deregulated system, so a small bank supervision function was created in the Reserve Bank in 1984. Emphasis placed on bank supervision grew in the second half of the 1980s, and it is ironic that, as some of the worst of the credit exposures were being incurred by banks late in the 1980s, supervisors in Australia and elsewhere were putting the finishing touches on new risk-based capital adequacy arrangements (the 1988 Capital Accord),[11] which were designed to ensure higher levels of capital in banking systems, and to guard specifically against credit risk.

Were there policy failings over this period? In addressing this issue it must be recognised that, against the weight of an international credit cycle of the magnitude seen in the late 1980s and early 1990s, no system of supervision would have been capable of totally insulating the banks. That said, if there was a policy failing by supervisors over this period it was the tendency to accept, without serious challenge, assurances given by bankers as to the health of their balance sheets. For much of this time, supervisors did not have access to (nor had they developed) the early warning tools or techniques to detect problems in banks or to challenge bankers' assertions that their balance sheets were sound. This problem appears to have been widespread, and has had a very significant effect over recent years in the development of supervisory policy and practice.

How has risk management in financial institutions changed?

The experience of the late 1980s also had a dramatic effect on banks and their attitudes to the acquisition and management of risk.

In its immediate aftermath, while banks did not turn away from acquiring risk, their interest in property-related exposures fell to very low levels for a time. More important for the longer term was the changed attitude of banks' management to the measurement and management of risk. The past four or five years in particular have witnessed significant upgradings in the risk management systems in place in virtually all Australian banks, and the emergence of a more focused credit 'culture'. Symbolic of that change has been the development of centralised credit bureaus in banks, designed to separate credit management from the credit origination function and then take responsibility for credit risk management at the group level. An even more recent trend has been the emergence of centralised and independent risk management groups to assess, in an integrated fashion, all the risks faced by the banking group.

The upgrading of risk management practices in banks was the key finding of a program of credit risk visits to banks initiated by the Reserve Bank in 1992. The program has found that, compared with the position in the

1980s, credit processes now appear to be much better documented and understood within institutions. Asset and security valuation arrangements are much tighter than in the past, and place much greater emphasis on the use of external valuation resources and specialised property units, especially within the major banks. There is a new focus on the accuracy and timeliness of information on counterparties, such as up-to-date cash flow analysis for the business in question. Credit approval and monitoring systems are being automated, increasing accuracy and internal efficiency. There is now widespread use within banks of packages designed to enhance financial analysis for corporate and commercial exposures, as well as application of formal credit risk grading systems. Credit scoring techniques for consumer exposures such as credit cards and housing loans are widely used. Also, greater emphasis is being given to portfolio-level information including identification of risk concentrations and the quantification of 'risk/reward trade-offs'.

The development of improved credit risk measurement practices in banks over recent years has been greatly influenced by banks' introduction of innovations in the measurement of market risk. The critical insight has been the realisation that all exposures have some probability of loss and that this probability can in theory be quantified and built into risk acquisition, capital allocation, pricing and – importantly – managers' remuneration arrangements.

How has bank supervision changed?

The 1990s have also seen a rapid evolution in supervisory practice. At the broadest level, the most dramatic of all will be the forthcoming reorganisation of the regulatory system, based on the recommendations of the Wallis Inquiry.[12] Setting aside structural changes to the regulatory system, however, there has also been a significant change in approach at the micro level. This can be characterised as the replacement of an informal and somewhat mechanistic approach to supervision (focusing on banks' reporting of prudential indicators, annual consultations with banks' senior management, and informal agreements relating to capital adequacy, large exposures and the like) with a higher level, more analytical style of supervision, in which on-site reviews and regular and ongoing discussions with senior bank staff are the centrepieces.

The development of the on-site review program is especially noteworthy. It grew directly out of the banking problems of the late 1980s and the recognition that existing information sources had not provided sufficient early warning of problems. As noted above, the realisation that credit risk measurement and management practices within banks in the late 1980s were inadequate suggested the need to go well beyond what had previously been done in the supervisory sphere. The approach has been to reach increasingly into the information in banks which managers themselves use to assess risk and performance, and to make use of this available information in the supervisory process more extensively than in the past. An emerging development has been an increased interest in the use of banks' own internal risk measurement models as a means of establishing minimum (regulatory) capital requirements. This approach has already been adopted in relation to market risk capital charges, and work is underway towards applying a comparable approach to other forms of banking risk, including credit risk.

CONCLUSION

Several lessons emerge from these episodes, which are of interest in assessing the financial crises in East Asia. One important lesson is that crises are easier to handle separately than together. In the mid-1980s, a monetary policy strategy of being prepared to implement quite high interest rates at times to stabilise the exchange market was feasible because the domestic economy, and particularly the financial sector, was reasonably robust. There were some unhedged foreign borrowings, but these were mainly small (such as the notorious Swiss franc loans to farmers)[13] or incurred by government enterprises such as electricity authorities. As a consequence, the lower exchange rate had the usual stimulatory effect on the economy, and no financial intermediaries were put under significant pressure by the exchange rate fall or higher interest rates.

A second lesson is that a great deal of learning and institutional development is necessary to make a deregulated financial system work effectively. This takes time, and during this time an economy has heightened vulnerability to both currency and banking crises.

A corollary to this second lesson is that there are unavoidable risks in liberalisation that can be seen as an investment that is necessary to generate improved long-term economic performance. Australian financial institutions learned much about the management of an open, competitive system in the currency and banking crises, that placed them well to withstand the shocks from the East Asian financial crisis. The current experience in East Asia may reduce the risk of future crises, provided that open regulatory reforms are implemented.

A third lesson is that it is very hard to make 'real time' judgments about the appropriate value of the exchange rate, especially when fundamentals have changed sharply. The mid-1980s depreciation of the Australian dollar now seems like a substantial overreaction. That was far from clear at the time, however. Related to this is the point that a floating rate regime confers some important advantages over a fixed rate regime. Among other things, in the event of worsening external fundamentals, the authorities can choose whether, and/or when, to intervene in the foreign exchange market, and to what extent to subordinate domestic monetary policy objectives to exchange rate ones, rather than being caught defending the indefensible.

With exchange rate flexibility, of course, comes a greatly heightened need for monetary policy to have a clear domestic anchor, which is why a number of countries with flexible exchange rates have moved to formal inflation targets during the 1990s. These medium-term issues are likely to come to the fore in some of the Asian countries that now have flexible exchange rates once the immediate financial crisis has been overcome.

A fourth lesson of the Australian experience is that assessment of policy measures by many or even most observers in the midst of crises is difficult, with judgments being clouded by the prevailing mood of markets, which may be only loosely tied to 'fundamentals' in the short run. Policy measures that in normal circumstances might be greeted with resounding applause, and which prove subsequently to be quite effective, can under conditions of crisis be dismissed as insufficient.

A fifth lesson is that inherent flaws in institutional design (such as an inability to assess a banking group's aggregate exposure to individual borrowers) may not become apparent until a crisis occurs. Severe problems can create an opportunity to implement changes that strengthen the system's capacity to cope with future difficulties, however. The very significant, and continuing, changes in the approach to the assessment of risk by both financial institutions and the regulatory authorities in the aftermath of the over-borrowing of the late 1980s are surely examples of this.

A final lesson is that there are substantial advantages in dealing quickly with outstanding non-performing loans in the financial system. As the example of Japan in the 1990s shows, it is hard for the economy to resume sustained growth when the financial sector cannot function effectively because of a large overhang of non-performing loans.

NOTES

The opinions expressed in this chapter are those of the authors and should not be attributed to their employer.

1   The previous largest depreciation was a devaluation of 20% in 1931.
2   The terms of trade fell by 11% over the six quarters to the June quarter 1986; the current account deficit widened to 6.5% of GDP in 1985–6, having averaged 2.9% over the previous 25 years; and net foreign debt rose from 11% to 32% of GDP over the four years to mid-1986.
3   For example, O'Mara (1987) argued that at the end of 1986Q3 the exchange rate was at least 15% below the level consistent with fundamentals, and that it would appreciate substantially over the medium term. By contrast, Dixon and Parmenter (1987) expressed the view that the 30% real depreciation during 1985 and 1986 was not an overreaction. They forecast a further depreciation of the real exchange rate of about 30% by the end of 1990, based on an

expectation of further modest falls in the terms of trade. In the event, both forecasts were wide of the mark: both the terms of trade and the real exchange rate rose strongly from 1987.

4   There was also a longer-term commitment to raise national savings by gradually increasing the amount of privately funded pension arrangements.

5   The Arbiration Commission, an institution whose role is to settle industrial disputes through conciliation and arbitration, had authority over national wage cases.

6   The lead story in the *AFR* the day after the National Wage Case spoke of 'a deftly crafted decision which will go a long way to preserve the prices and incomes accord [the incomes policy negotiated between the Federal Labor government and the peak trade union organisation] as the centrepiece of Australia's economic policy' (*AFR* 27 June 1986: 1). The editorial was less complimentary: 'The Arbitration Commission has come up with a masterly political compromise. We can only hope that our economy can carry the increased economic burden it imposes' (*AFR* 27 June 1986: 14). The day after the budget, the opening paragraphs of the *AFR* editorial argued that 'the Treasurer, Mr Keating, has produced a remarkable Budget. He has met the most optimistic of market expectations ... [The Budget] is also economically responsible and politically honest' (*AFR* 20 August 1986: 1).

7   A couple of examples from the *AFR* in the days after the 1986 budget give the flavour of these reactions. First, a front-page article on 21 August, under the headline *Market's qualms may force even tougher decisions*, argued:

> The Budget has come under immediate pressure as a result of a negative response from the financial markets, threatening the Government's strategy to lower interest rates to stop the economy falling into a sustained slump. The financial markets yesterday began to pick holes in the Budget's fine print, suggesting that they will not be swayed by the Government's 'trust us' arguments that they have laid down the fundamental economic adjustments to eventually correct the balance of payments blowout.

Second, a private-sector economist quoted on 20 August argued: 'The unfortunate reality for the Government is that [it] won't be able to achieve the $3.5 billion deficit [forecast for the 1986–7 Budget] because [its] growth assumptions [year-on-year GDP growth of 2.25%] are quite unrealistic' (*AFR* 20 August 1986: 4). In the event, year-on-year growth in 1986–7 came in very close to forecast, at 2.1%, and the budget deficit came in a little below forecast at A$2.6 billion.

8   This led to a reassessment of the benefits and costs of government ownership of banks, following which the unimpaired businesses were transferred into private hands.

9   The Farrow Group and Estate Mortgage were both non-bank financial intermediaries which experienced runs on their deposits in 1990 and were closed down.

10   The Campbell Committee was set up by the federal government in 1979 to inquire into Australia's financial system (Campbell 1981).

11   The Capital Accord was based on the recommendations of the Basle committee on bank supervision and marked an international move towards a greater focus on risk in the assessment of capital adequacy (BIS 1988).

12 The Wallis Inquiry was set up in 1996 to report on the results of financial deregulation in Australia since the early 1980s, assess the sources of future change, and make recommendations regarding the regulatory environment (Wallis 1997).

13 These were unhedged loans from banks, at low (Swiss) rates of interest. Since they were unhedged, these loans became very expensive after the Australian dollar depreciated.

Part V

Global perspectives

14 Internationally mobile capital and the global economy

Warwick J. McKibbin

INTRODUCTION

The financial and economic crisis in Asia that erupted in July 1997 has sparked a vigorous debate on its causes and on the role of domestic and international policy responses during its evolution. An excellent overview of this debate and analysis of the economies concerned can be found in Corsetti et al. (1998). Some authors have argued that the shock was purely the result of a shift in investor confidence (Radelet and Sachs 1998a), while others argue that a build-up of pressure from country-specific problems and evolving global macroeconomic conditions eventually led to the crisis (Corsetti et al. 1998; Krugman 1998a).[1] All that was needed to set it off was a trigger. McKibbin (1998) argues that the crisis was triggered by a rise in US interest rates and falls in US equity markets in March and August 1997, causing the collapse of the pegged exchange rate regimes in some economies. The response of each economy in the aftermath of this shock then reflected varying degrees of financial weakness and shortcomings in institutional and political structures.

This chapter will focus on one important (perhaps the most important) aspect of the crisis: namely, the impact of a jump in the perceived risk of investing in the Asian economies.[2] The Bank for International Settlements (1998) estimates that the jump in the risk premium for ten-year eurobonds in the Asian economies was significant. Whether this caused the crisis or was a response to it, it is worth examining the impact of such a risk re-evaluation in some detail.

In order to understand the full extent of the process of adjustment to a change in risk, a general equilibrium framework is essential because there are many complicated processes at work. Many analysts have examined the impact of the crisis on non-Asian economies simply by looking at the composition of international trade and mapping the projected fall in domestic demand in the Asian economies to a fall in exports from the industrial economies. The fall in exports is then equated to a fall in gross domestic product (GDP). The analysis described here, however, shows that not only is this misleading, but that it can in fact suggest erroneous outcomes. The crucial missing ingredient is that the capital that flowed out of Asia did not evaporate but was reallocated to non-Asian economies. To ignore this fact is to miss a key part of the global adjustment story.

In order to bring this and other general equilibrium factors into the analysis, this chapter uses the G-Cubed (Asia Pacific) model which is out-lined in the next section. It is derived from the G-Cubed model developed by McKibbin and Wilcoxen (1995), but with a specific focus on the Asian economies. As with G-Cubed, this model captures simultaneously the macroeconomic and sectoral linkages in a global model with partially for-ward-looking asset market and spending decisions, in which evaluations of risk are integral to the functioning of domestic economies and the global economy.

The G-Cubed (Asia Pacific) model has country or regional disaggrega-tion for Korea, Japan, Thailand, Indonesia, China, Malaysia, Singapore, Taiwan, Hong Kong, the Philippines, Australia, New Zealand, the United States, India, the rest of the OECD, the oil-exporting developing countries, Eastern Europe and the former Soviet Union, and all other developing countries. Each country or region has an explicit internal macroeconomic and sectoral structure, with sectoral disaggregation in production and trade into six sectors.

This is a model in the class of dynamic intertemporal general equilibrium models (DIGEM) that incorporate both financial and real economic activ-ity in a global framework. This new class of models, designed specifically for the highly integrated world economy of the late twentieth century, inte-grates the desirable features of both macroeconometric models and com-putable general equilibrium models. They have proven useful for understanding other recent global shocks, such as US fiscal policy in the 1980s, the establishment of the North American Free Trade Agreement (NAFTA), and German reunification (Gagnon et al. 1996; McKibbin 1994). A key feature of these models is the role of international capital mo-bility in economic adjustment, and the role of financial markets in real eco-nomic activity.

The third section presents a framework for thinking about how to intro-duce changes in risk perceptions into a model such as G-Cubed. The sce-nario is a sharp but temporary rise in the risk premium on assets denominated in the currencies of Thailand, Malaysia, Indonesia and Korea. (Smaller risk premiums are used for other economies in the region, as dis-cussed later.) The risk premium jumps in the first year, and then dies away over the next three years. The shock is benchmarked to yield the actual fall in the nominal exchange rate observed in each economy by the beginning of 1998. The intention in this chapter is not to predict what will happen in Asia as result of the overall crisis, but to draw crucial lessons from the im-pact of changes in risk perceptions on general equilibrium.

The results of the analysis are presented in the subsequent section. It is clear that a revision of risk can cause significant declines in real economic activity, although many of the costs are buffered by changes in real exchange rates. Once risk perceptions are reversed, the shock dissipates, although there are persistent consequences. The key reason the financial shock has real implications is the role of adjustment costs in physical capital formation. In the G-Cubed model, arbitrage between financial assets and physical capital takes into account the fact that physical capital is sector- and country-specific for significant periods of time, whereas financial capital can move extremely quickly across sectors and economies.[3]

The impact on the rest of the world is quite different from that portrayed by many commentators. The modelling shows that the collapse in economic activity in Asia reduces the exports of non-Asian economies, but it also reduces global real interest rates, stimulating domestic economic activity in interest-sensitive sectors. This stimulus to domestic demand can more than offset the negative impacts of the decline in exports, depending on the relative dependence of each economy on domestic demand versus trade with Asia. Indeed, while the export sectors in countries and regions like the United States and Europe are suffering from the crisis, the relocation of financial capital would be expected to stimulate an investment boom in non-traded production, in all economies outside Asia.

The impacts within each economy are sustainable, but will be associated with significant shifts in their current account balances. Those countries receiving capital from Asia would be expected to experience an increase (decrease) in their current account deficits (surpluses), reflecting new capital inflow. Resisting this adjustment would be costly, both for the Asian economies that need the temporary export surge to dampen the negative economic shock, and for the other economies that need additional investment demand to offset the fall in foreign demand.

A GENERAL EQUILIBRIUM MULTI-COUNTRY FRAMEWORK

In order to put the Asian crisis into a global perspective, a multi-country general equilibrium model is required. The G-Cubed (Asia Pacific) multi-country model combines the intertemporal macroeconomic approach taken in the MSG2 model of McKibbin and Sachs (1991) with the disaggregated, econometrically estimated, intertemporal general equilibrium model of the US economy by Jorgenson and Wilcoxen (1990).

The G-Cubed model has many features that make it useful for analysing a range of issues in environmental regulation, and in microeconomic, macroeconomic and trade policy areas. Countries and regions are linked in the model both temporally and intertemporally through trade and financial markets. The explicit treatment of financial flows has been shown to be important for analysing the response to trade liberalisation (McKibbin 1996), but it is absolutely crucial for analysing the consequences of financial shocks such as the re-evaluation of risk. G-Cubed provides a strong foundation for analysis of both short-run macroeconomic policy as well as the long-run growth implications of alternative macroeconomic policies.

Intertemporal budget constraints on households, governments and nations are imposed. To accommodate these constraints, forward-looking behaviour is incorporated in consumption and investment decisions. The response of the monetary and fiscal authorities in different countries can have important effects in the short to medium run which, given the long lags in physical capital and other asset accumulation, can be a substantial period of time. Overall, the model is designed to provide a bridge between computable general equilibrium models and macroeconomic models by integrating the more desirable features of both. The G-Cubed (Asia Pacific) model differs from the G-Cubed model because of the focus on the Asia Pacific region and because it has only six sectors, compared with twelve for G-Cubed. The theoretical structure is essentially the same.

The country and sectoral breakdowns are summarised in Table 14.1. The model consists of eighteen economic regions, with six sectors in each region. There are also two additional sectors in each region (not shown in the table) that produce capital goods for firms and households, respectively. The regions can be divided into two groups: fifteen core countries or regions and three others (oil-exporting developing countries; Eastern Europe and the former Soviet Union; and other developing countries). For the core regions, the internal macroeconomic structure as well as the external trade and financial linkages are completely specified in the model. Each core economy or region consists of three economic agents: households, the government and firms, together with the six production sectors listed in the table. These economic agents interact in a variety of markets, both domestic and foreign.

The eighteen regions in the model are linked by flows of goods and assets. Flows of goods are determined by import demands for final consumption and for intermediate inputs. Trade imbalances are financed by flows of financial assets between countries. It is assumed (based on calibrating the model to 1996 as the base year) that existing wedges between rates of return in different economies are generated by various restrictions that generate a risk premium on country currency-denominated assets. These wedges are calculated using a technique outlined below and are assumed to be exogenous during simulation. Thus, when the model is simulated, in general the induced changes in expected rates of return in different countries generate flows of financial capital reacting to marginal return differentials. This chapter also examines the impact of changes in these wedges in some countries, primarily as a result of risk re-evaluation. These can also be used to explore the consequences of financial liberalisation (McKibbin 1997).

International capital flows are assumed to be composed of portfolio

Table 14.1 Overview of the G-Cubed (Asia Pacific) model

Regions	Sectors
United States	Energy
Japan	Mining
Australia	Agriculture
New Zealand	Non-durable manufacturing
Rest of OECD	Durable manufacturing
India	Services
Korea	
Thailand	
Indonesia	
China	
Malaysia	
Singapore	
Taiwan	
Hong Kong	
Philippines	
Oil-exporting developing countries	
Eastern Europe and the former Soviet Union	
Other developing countries	

Agents	Markets
Households	Final goods
Firms	Services
Government	Factors of production
	Money
	Bonds
	Equities
	Foreign exchange

investment, direct investment and other flows. These alternative forms of capital flows are perfectly substitutable ex ante, adjusting to the expected rates of return across economies and across sectors. Within an economy, the expected return to each type of asset (i.e. bonds of all maturities, equity for each sector, and so on) are arbitraged, taking into account the costs of adjusting stocks of physical capital and allowing for exogenous risk premia. Because physical capital is costly to adjust, any inflow of financial capital that is invested in physical capital (i.e. direct investment) will also be costly to shift once it is in place. The decision to invest in physical assets is based on expected rates of return. However, if there is an unanticipated shock, then ex post returns can vary significantly. Total net capital flows for each economy in which there are open capital markets are equal to the current account position of that country. The global net flows of private capital are constrained to zero.

MODELLING A SHIFT IN RISK PERCEPTIONS

This section discusses how the re-evaluation of risk of investing in Asian economies is modelled. First, however, it is useful to describe how the baseline of the model, without the shocks to risk, is generated. The model is first solved from 1996 to 2070 to generate a model baseline based on a range of assumptions. These include assumptions about population growth by country (based on World Bank projections) and sectoral productivity growth by country and by sector (based on a technology catch-up model), and about tariffs, tax rates, and a range of other fiscal and monetary policy settings. Monetary policy is assumed to target a stock of nominal money balances in each economy, such that money growth equals the inflation rate from the previous period. Fiscal policy is defined as a set of fixed tax rates (apart from a lump sum tax on households that varies to satisfy the intertemporal budget constraint facing the government) and government spending constant relative to simulated GDP. The issue of projecting the future using a dynamic intertemporal general equilibrium model such as G-Cubed is discussed in detail in Bagnoli et al. (1996). This initial projection step is important for simulations because it builds in underlying structural change in the global economy that is endogenous to the assumptions about differential productivity growth.

Given all of the exogenous assumptions and initial conditions, the full rational expectations solution of the model is found using a numerical technique outlined in McKibbin and Sachs (1991: appendix C). Without additional intervention, this initial model solution will not generate the actual outcomes for the first year of simulation (in the current example, 1996) because a range of forward-looking variables, such as human wealth, exchange rates, stock markets and so on, will be dependent on the future path of the world economy, and there is no reason why these should be equal to the observed values for the initial year. The next step of baseline generation is then to calculate a vector of constants for all equations in the model, including arbitrage equations, such that the solution of the model in the base year (1996) is exactly equal to the observed data in that year. It is important to stress that no assumption is made that 1996 is a steady state solution of the model. It clearly cannot be. What is imposed is that the 1996 database is on the stable manifold of the model, in which all variables are moving on a stable path towards a steady state in the far distant future.

To see more precisely what the technique does and how a re-evaluation of risk is modelled, consider the uncovered real interest parity assumption used in the model that relates the returns to government debt in each country. This is shown in equation (1).

$$r_t^i = r_t^U +_t e_{t+1} - e_t + \xi_t^i \tag{1}$$

Here the real interest rate (r) on one-year government bonds in country

i in period t is equal to the interest rate in the United States (r^U) in period t, plus the expected rate of depreciation in the bilateral real exchange rate (expressed as local currency per US dollar) between country i and the United States ($_te_{t+1} - e_t$), where e_t is the log of the real exchange rate in period t and $_te_{t+1}$ is the expectation, formed in period t, about the exchange rate to prevail in period $t+1$. In addition, it is assumed that there is a risk premium ξ_t^i which, if positive, means that country i interest rates on government debt (in real terms) are above the interest rates on comparable US government debt expressed in the same currency. In principle, this risk premium varies over time.

The wedge term ξ_t^i captures a range of issues, including sovereign risk, impediments to financial flows, the degree of departure from rational expectations in actual data, as well as various other factors.

Equation (1) can also be interpreted differently. Solving for e_t, it can be shown that:

$$e_t = \int_t^T (r_s^U - r_s^i + \xi_s^i)ds +_t e_T \tag{2}$$

The real exchange rate in any period t is the sum of future expected interest rate differentials and the expected future risk premia on bonds denominated in the home currency, plus the equilibrium (period T) value of the real exchange rate.

In the baseline we calculate a constant value for ξ_t^i such that the exchange rate (e) converted into nominal terms using the appropriate price deflator in 1996 is equal to the observed nominal exchange rate. We also calculate a wedge for each asset class in each economy. The model is used here to calculate the expected change in the real exchange rate. It is important to stress that, although the arbitrage relation outlined above focuses on the bond rate differential, all financial assets (bonds, money, equity) within each economy are being arbitraged, so similar wedges exist for all assets. Thus there are country-specific wedges as well as asset-specific wedges. In addition, changing the wedge between bond rates will also affect the relative returns on a range of domestic and foreign assets that are being arbitraged to the yield on government bonds.

In the simulations that follow, a path is selected for the expected future risk premium. This is completely arbitrary, but illustrative. The values of the risk shock are selected such that changes in the nominal exchange rates generated by the model are equal to the observed changes as of December 1997. The degree of permanency of the actual risk shock that is being reflected in current exchange rates is difficult to determine at this stage.

It is also clear from equation (2) that we can choose any path for ξ^i and get the same exchange rate for the first year of the simulation for given paths of interest rates. However, over time, different paths for the risk premium will have different impacts on the path for the real exchange rate.

SIMULATION RESULTS FOR THE SHIFT IN RISK PERCEPTIONS

The simulation is a temporary shock to the risk premium, as outlined above. The exact shock is set out in Table 14.2. Note that these differ from the temporary shock shown in McKibbin (1998), because in that paper there was both a risk shock and a collapse of the domestic financial systems in some economies (modelled as a fall in productivity), whereas in this chapter only a risk shock is considered. In order to benchmark the change in the nominal exchange rate to replicate the actual data at the end of 1997, a larger shock to risk is required in the absence of any productivity shock.

There is also a problem with the timing of the shock in an annual model, because the actual shock began in mid-1997. In these simulations the shock is assumed to have occurred at the end of 1997, and therefore 1998 is the first year to show its impact. This will cause problems lining up model-generated data with actual data, but the goal of the simulations is not to predict future outcomes but to provide insights into key adjustment processes in an empirical framework.

The results of a temporary increase in risk are contained in Figures 14.1 to 14.11. All results are expressed as percentage deviations from the baseline, except where noted.

Figure 14.1 shows results for nominal exchange rates in a number of crisis-affected economies. The rise in perceived risk leads to a large outflow of financial capital. This outflow depreciates the nominal and real exchange rates by between 15% and 60% through 1998. The exchange rates recover over time, reflecting the restoration of confidence in each economy. The outflow of capital also leads to a sharp rise in real interest rates in each economy and to a general deflation of asset prices. The rise in real interest rates, the decline in wealth and the sharp reduction in expected future incomes lead to a sharp fall in domestic demand, illustrated in Figure 14.2 for consumption and Figure 14.3 for investment. According to the model, consumption falls by 50% in Indonesia through 1998. Investment falls by over 40% during 1998 in Indonesia and by 60% in Malaysia. This apparently

Table 14.2 Time profiles for the risk shock (% change relative to base)

Country	1998	1999	2000	2001 and beyond
Indonesia	40	30	10	0
Malaysia	40	30	10	0
Thailand	35	20	10	0
Korea	35	25	15	0
Japan	6	4	2	0
Philippines	30	20	10	0
Singapore	16	8	0	0

Figure 14.1   Change in nominal exchange rates (local currency per US$, % deviation from baseline)

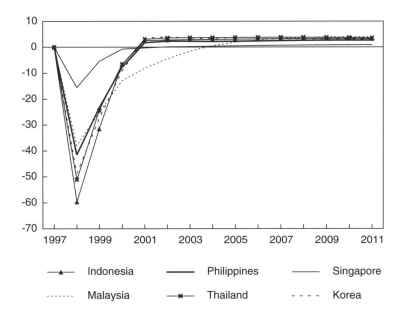

Figure 14.2   Change in private consumption (% deviation from baseline)

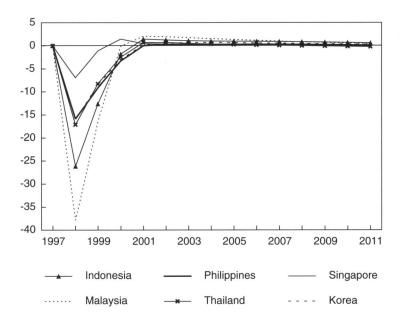

Figure 14.3   Change in private investment (% deviation from baseline)

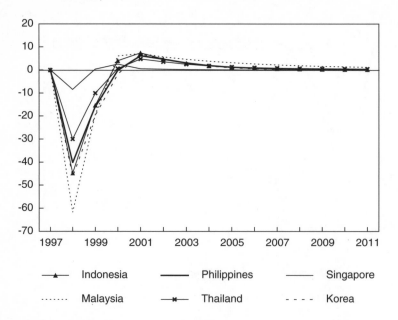

reflects the reliance of Malaysia on imported inputs into production of manufactured goods for export, which become very expensive as the currency depreciates. This sharp contraction in economic activity reflects the large capital losses experienced by residents of these economies. In particular, the fixity of physical capital implies a significant reduction in return to capital at the same time that there is a large increase in the cost of financial capital. For example, Figure 14.4 illustrates the change in the stock market value of industries in the non-durable manufacturing sector in each economy.

Despite the large contraction in domestic demand, GDP is quite surprisingly not so badly affected (Figure 14.5). The economies hit by the shock are able to maintain production in the face of a sharp fall in domestic demand because of an adjustment in exports (Figure 14.6). The sharp depreciation in the nominal and real exchange rates increases the demand in non-Asian economies for products from the Asian economies.

The model distinguishes between nominal and real exchange rates, since the overall price level is endogenous. In the simulation, there is a sharp jump in inflation in the shocked economies, although monetary policy is assumed eventually to return the price level to its starting point. In practice, there is likely to be some monetary accommodation (as we have seen in Indonesia, in particular), which implies a bigger difference between the changes in real and nominal exchanges rates shown in this experiment. The larger the inflationary shock, the less the nominal exchange rate change will

Figure 14.4 Change in stock market value of manufacturing firms (% deviation from baseline)

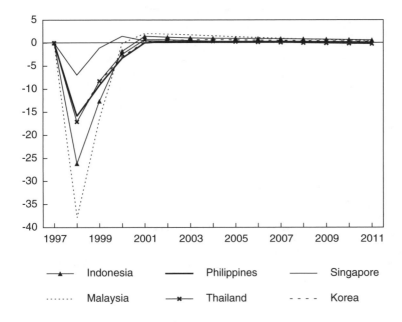

Figure 14.5 Change in real GDP (% deviation from baseline)

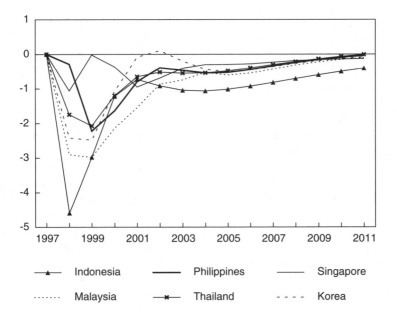

Figure 14.6 Change in real exports (% deviation from baseline)

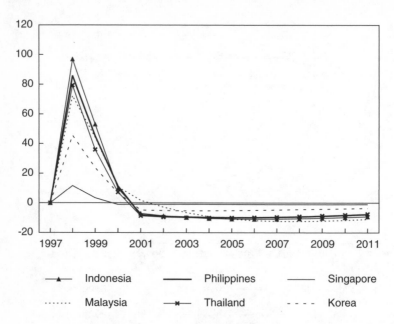

| ——▲—— Indonesia | ——— Philippines | ——— Singapore |
| ········ Malaysia | ——✕—— Thailand | - - - - Korea |

translate into a real exchange rate change, and the smaller the expected export surge. The sharp export surge shown in Figure 14.6 is consistent with
the change in the balance of payments, reflecting a capital outflow, which
must generate a current account surplus. This can be achieved either by a
rise in exports or a fall in imports (or both). This adjustment occurs in the
model by way of a large rise in exports and a small fall in imports. In early
1998 it appeared, in fact, that the actual adjustment was the reverse of this,
with little change in exports but a rather sharp fall in imports. This largely
reflected the collapse of the domestic and international financing of international trade. Given a recovery in each economy, apart from Indonesia, it
is expected that the model projections should come closer to being realised
through 1998.

The effects on domestic demand in Asia are large. What are the effects
on the rest of the world? Many analysts try to answer this question using a
back-of-the-envelope calculation that relies entirely on the pattern of trade
flows between economies before the crisis. The fall in domestic demand signals a fall in demand for imports from non-Asian economies, and therefore
a decline in growth in these economies in rough proportion to the decline
in Asian domestic demand. The first indication that such projections may
be less than accurate has already been suggested by the above results: the fall
in domestic demand does not translate into a similar fall in output, given
the export response. Thus, if a country is exporting goods to Asia, not
to satisfy domestic demand but as inputs into products that are largely

exported, the change in the demand for that country's goods is not likely to reflect the fall in domestic demand in Asia. More important is the fact that partial analyses such as these ignore completely the general equilibrium effects of the large shifts in international capital flows that are a crucial part of the Asian crisis. The model in this chapter captures these effects.

Figure 14.7 shows the results for changes in the Australian and US current account balances (expressed as a percentage of GDP). The reduction in the current account balances of both countries reflects the capital that flows into these economies from Asia. As capital flows into the United States and Australia, the real exchange rate of each economy tends to appreciate, reducing exports and increasing imports. Indeed, the rise in Asian exports is accommodated by this increase in imports by non-Asian economies. The Australian dollar strengthens relative to the Asian currencies, but depreciates relative to the US dollar, by around 1.7% in the short term (Figure 14.8). This is not as large as was actually experienced in the early stages of the crisis. The Australian dollar depreciates relative to the US dollar because Australia is relatively more exposed to the crisis through trade with Asia than is the United States. The importance of capital inflow to non-Asian countries is illustrated in Figure 14.9, which shows both Australian and US exports and investment. As expected, the fall in demand in Asia is reflected in a fall in exports – by 10% in the United States and 18% in Australia. Investment, on the other hand, rises by close to 5% in each economy. The fallout from the Asia crisis includes a fall in non-Asian long-term interest rates. This stimulates domestic economic activity outside the export industries in

Figure 14.7   Change in Australian and US current accounts (% GDP deviation from baseline)

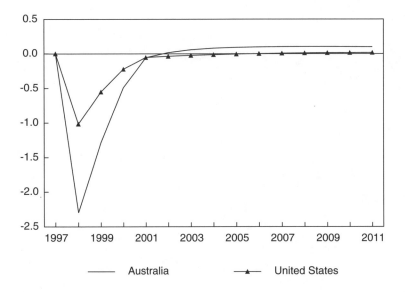

Figure 14.8   Change in Australian dollar (% deviation from baseline)

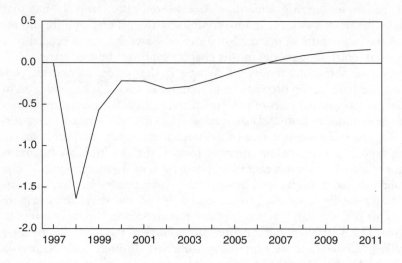

Figure 14.9   Change in Australian and US exports and investment (% deviation from baseline)

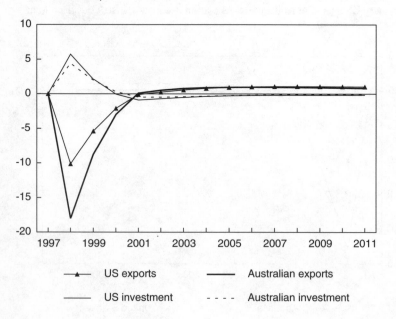

non-Asian economies. Whether GDP will rise or fall in countries such as the United States and Australia depends on whether the negative demand shock from lower exports is more or less important than the positive demand shock from higher investment spending that results from lower long-term real interest rates. Figure 14.10 shows that, in the case of the temporary shock, the effect in the very short term is negative on balance, but more so for Australia (where GDP is lower by 0.25%).

The results for GDP shown in Figure 14.10 reflect the reallocation of production in the global economy, since GDP is a measure of value added, according to location of production. A better measure of welfare is reflected in income changes. Gross national product (GNP) is the income earned from all factors of production owned by domestic residents, whether located domestically or overseas. The results for GNP for Australia and the United States are shown in Figure 14.11. GNP falls in the short term, but then rises for several years before settling at a permanently lower level. The altered pattern of physical capital accumulation increases production in the United States, but capital owned by US residents now earns a lower rate of return than it would have earned in the previously high-return Asian economies. Thus, although GDP rises over time, GNP is permanently reduced for non-Asian economies. The perceived increase in risk thus reduces world income, even though it raises production in some countries while lowering it in others. The fact that physical capital is difficult to move in the short run means that there are permanent capital losses. In other words,

Figure 14.10 Change in Australian and US GDP (% deviation from baseline)

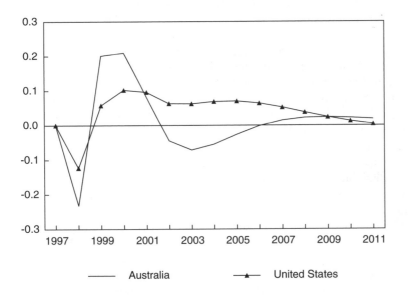

Figure 14.11   Change in Australian and US GNP (% deviation from baseline)

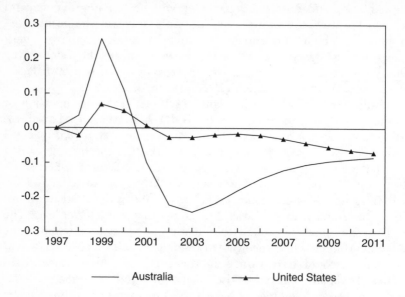

the Asian crisis is not good for the world economy as a whole, despite what it may do for the level of production in various countries.

CONCLUSION

This chapter has explored the global implications for trade and capital flows of a change in the perceived risk of investing in Asia. An important lesson is that a financial shock can quickly become a real shock because of the interdependence of the real and financial economies. Too often policymakers and modellers ignore this interdependence. The reaction of policymakers directly, and the implications for risk of their responses, are crucial to the evolution of the crisis. We know far too little about the determinants of risk perceptions, but their impacts, as suggested here, appear to be large. The second lesson is that, if the model is realistic, the impact of the apparently large contractions in domestic demand is largely offset through a rise in exports, so that the consequences of the temporary rise in risk perceptions are quickly dissipated. This is not the case for a more permanent shift in risk (McKibbin 1998). The fact that the real effects of the shocks on production actually being experienced in the affected economies appear to be larger than the model simulations predict suggests that other policy mistakes or market failures are inhibiting adjustment. This is evident in the lack of a strong export response. The current lack of export growth reflects the initial collapse of domestic and international export financing arrangements, which should be a key focus of policies to ameliorate the crisis.

One implication of the approach taken here is that the re-evaluation of risk and subsequent capital outflows can lead to severe economic disruption. Is the policy implication that countries should act to hinder the movement of international financial capital? The framework used here for thinking about exchange rate determination suggests that this could be a very expensive strategy to follow. The impact of restrictions, or a 'Tobin tax', on capital flows in the model is exactly the same as a rise in ξ (reflecting an increase in the risk premium on investment in a country), unless all countries impose the same tax. In a forward-looking view of exchange rate determination in which the expected rates of return on alternative assets determine the exchange rate, a Tobin tax or any other capital flow impediment (actual or expected) has exactly the same implications as the experiments that form the basis of this chapter. Unless all countries impose the same tax, a large real exchange rate depreciation could be expected in those countries that do impose it relative to those that do not, as markets adjust for the changes in expected rates of return differentials in response to the tax.

The better policy would be to allow free mobility of financial capital, but to improve the way in which domestic financial systems allocate capital within the economy. This includes improving systems of accountability, increasing transparency in accounting systems, and monitoring financial systems more effectively so that more accurate evaluations of risk can be formulated. For every country that experienced an economic crisis after the exchange rate crisis, there are other countries – such as Taiwan, Singapore, Australia and New Zealand – that were able to survive the turbulence because of relatively recent improvements in their domestic financial systems. In particular, the crisis in Asia has illustrated the important lesson that having governments act as insurers (either ex ante or ex post) for a wide range of economic activities, and especially in relation to exchange rate risk, is a hazardous exercise.

Finally, it has been shown that the current account effects of the capital flows are relatively large, with the US current account projected to fall by about 1% of GDP over 1998 and the Australian current account projected to fall by over 2% of GDP. Falls of similar magnitudes would be expected for other non-Asian economies. Attempts to prevent this adjustment would be counterproductive for the Asian economies, since the export adjustment is crucial for offsetting the collapse in domestic demand. It would also be counterproductive for the non-Asian economies, since the reason the spillover effects from the Asian crisis are small in the model results is precisely that the capital inflow (which matches the current account deficit) reduces long-term real interest rates in these economies and sustains continued strong economic activity. Trying to prevent the current account deficit from increasing would worsen the economic outcome in Asia as well as reduce the domestic investment stimulus in economies outside Asia.

In a world of increasing economic integration and high capital mobility, understanding the response of capital markets to shocks in the global economy is a fundamental priority for policymakers. Understanding the determinants of risk perceptions is also a crucial area for future research. This chapter demonstrates that a change in the perception of risk in investing in an economy can have a large impact on real economic activity. How policy responds to shocks, and how this response affects risk perceptions, are clearly of fundamental importance. A great deal of research is needed in these areas.

NOTES

This chapter has benefited from helpful comments by Ross McLeod, Will Martin and Graeme Wells.

1   Emerging problems were alluded to in country-specific studies in APEG (1996, 1997).
2   The permanent and temporary changes in risk perceptions, combined with a domestic financial collapse, are examined in McKibbin (1998).
3   See McKibbin and Wilcoxen (1997) for a detailed analysis of the role of adjustment costs in physical capital formation and the implications of this for macroeconomic volatility.

15 The role of the International Monetary Fund

David C.L. Nellor

This chapter discusses the approach adopted by the International Monetary Fund (IMF) to address the economic crises experienced by countries in East Asia since mid-1997. It focuses on Thailand, Indonesia and Korea, although, through surveillance, technical assistance, and programs, the IMF is working closely with all member countries in the region.[1]

The first section describes the *raison d'être* of the IMF and its activities in the region. The second discusses the premises underlying the IMF-supported reform programs. The third looks at three key policy areas: monetary and exchange rate policy, fiscal policy, and financial sector restructuring. The fourth section reflects on alternative views about reform, and outlines two challenges for the international financial system highlighted by the crisis.

THE *RAISON D'ÊTRE* OF IMF-SUPPORTED REFORM PROGRAMS

In supporting the Thai, Indonesian and Korean reform programs, the IMF is discharging the responsibilities prescribed in its Articles of Agreement. The IMF was established recognising that globalisation required an institutional mechanism to help shape, in a cooperative framework, individual country economic policy. An earlier economic crisis provided the impetus for establishing the IMF. The experience of competitive devaluations, trade restrictions and other destructive policies that contributed to the Great Depression taught the world a costly lesson. This lesson is that the outcome can be worse for all when countries pursue their own, narrowly defined, self-interest. Or, more positively, all countries can be better off by recognising their mutual interests when setting policy.[2] The IMF is the institutional mechanism to help achieve this mutual benefit.[3] International financial market integration makes these tasks more important today than ever.

Countries will inevitably fail to foresee some economic problems or, even when anticipated, fail to prevent their occurrence. In these circumstances, it is in the mutual interest of the IMF membership to help those countries to rectify the situation as quickly as possible, sustainably, and consistently with international financial stability. The IMF's Articles of Agreement call for the IMF

> to give confidence to members by making the general resources of the Fund temporarily available to them under adequate safeguards, thus providing them with an opportunity to correct maladjustment in their balance of payments without resorting to measures destructive of national or international prosperity.

For countries seeking IMF assistance, adoption of a reform program that restores macroeconomic stability and lays the foundation for sustainable growth is an indispensable element of the cooperative character of the IMF. The IMF executive board decides whether to support the country, and the scale of support, based on the balance of payments and the strength of the country's reform program. IMF resources are made available in instalments, each conditional on the country's meeting the conditions to which it has agreed.

The IMF is a cooperative organisation in which a country chooses its own policy direction. Thus, the ownership of a reform program always rests with the country itself. A country lays out its program of economic reform and policy intentions in a Letter of Intent. The international community can support that reform program, but it can only be effective with the commitment of the country to its implementation. It is the country itself that carries out the reform measures and must provide the domestic support and stability in which economic reforms can convey the signals that restore macroeconomic stability and growth. The IMF helps in this task by providing technical expertise and endorsement, but cannot go beyond that.

Of course, support of a country's reform effort depends on the IMF's assessment of the strength of the program, and disbursements of financial support depend on its implementation. Other member countries must be confident that the reform program will correct the economic problem being experienced, and that the country can repay the resources provided by the international community. In developing such a program, the IMF is likely to seek policy measures that the country may not have otherwise considered. However, it would be wrong to conclude that every measure contained in a Letter of Intent is required by the IMF. It is the country's Letter of Intent, and the country's authorities often include specific reform measures that the IMF may see as desirable, even if not pivotal to the success of the reform program.

IMF-SUPPORTED REFORM PROGRAMS IN EAST ASIA

In response to mounting market pressures, reflected in a dramatic reversal

Table 15.1 Summary of IMF-supported reform programs in Thailand, Indonesia and Korea

	Program	Date approved	Amount (US$ billion)[a]	Quota (US$ billion)[a]
Thailand	Stand-by 34 months	20 August 1997	4.0	0.78
Indonesia	Stand-by 36 months	5 November 1997	10.0	2.04
Korea	Stand-by[b] 36 months	4 December 1997	21.1	1.09

Notes:
a Converted from SDR at an exchange rate of SDR 1 = US$1.3628.
b At the first review of the arrangement, a drawing of US$3.5 billion was made under the terms of the Supplemental Reserve Facility established in December 1997.

of capital flows and collapsing exchange rates, Thailand, Indonesia and Korea each requested the support of the IMF during the latter half of 1997. In Thailand and Korea, in particular, international reserves had declined sharply and to perilous levels. Currency market turmoil followed the float of the Thai baht on 2 July and, after the baht had depreciated considerably and failed to stabilise, the Thai authorities requested the assistance of the IMF on 5 August. Indonesia asked for IMF support on 8 October, following the 14 August announcement that the trading band for the rupiah was being abandoned. The Bank of Korea announced its decision to stop defending the won at the exchange rate of W1,000 per US dollar on 17 November. The authorities requested IMF support on 21 November.[4]

In each case, program discussions took place in the difficult circumstances posed by currency market turmoil and growing economic dislocation. Yet the need for a policy package that would restore confidence in these economies was immediate. The potential costs of failing to restore confidence swiftly, both for the countries themselves and from a global perspective, were rightly judged to be consequential.[5] All of these countries therefore employed the emergency financing procedures introduced following the Mexican crisis of late 1994 to gain extraordinary access to IMF resources and to expedite the approval of their reform programs (Table 15.1).[6]

Characterising the reform programs

The Thai, Indonesian and Korean reform programs are based on the presumption that the economic difficulties of these countries stem largely from structural distortions. Reform programs will not be effective in restoring macroeconomic stability and laying the conditions for sustainable growth unless these distortions are addressed meaningfully.

Thailand, the first country to experience difficulties, exhibited macro-economic imbalances, along with structural distortions, far more clearly than the other countries. Thailand's exchange rate arrangement, effectively pegging the baht to the US dollar, resulted in a 'one-way bet' or non-equi-librating arbitrage opportunity for short-term capital flows. The rapid rise in these short-term flows was reflected in a widening of the current account deficit to about 8% of gross domestic product (GDP) in 1995 and 1996. This large external financing requirement, combined with the possibility that investors may at some point question the continuity of the exchange rate peg, left Thailand vulnerable to a reversal of capital flows. In addition, Thailand also suffered from structural problems reflected in the failure to intermediate large capital flows effectively.

In all three countries, the resolution of their problems rested with restor-ing macroeconomic stability and addressing financial sector and other structural distortions: weak financial institutions, inadequate bank regula-tion and supervision, and complicated and non-transparent relations among governments, banks and corporations. Without these issues being addressed, the ability of these economies to return to sustainable growth was placed in question by distortions that prevented resource flows and in-vestment from responding appropriately to changes in market prices.

Reflecting this assessment, the reform programs are intended to make markets work better. This is being done in at least three ways: first, by re-moving the distorting links between the state, financial, and non-financial enterprises; second, by defining a new role for government – to provide the infrastructure in which markets can operate; and third, by providing better information – economic statistics by government, and transparent accounts by market participants.

A comprehensive effort addressing both macroeconomic imbalances and structural distortions is thus central to reform in all three countries. Such an effort is necessary to regain policy credibility with markets and also to give the international community confidence that the causes of the eco-nomic difficulties are being corrected. A compelling asymmetrical cost–benefit ratio favours a comprehensive reform plan. Consider the cir-cumstances at the time that each of the arrangements was adopted. Any lin-gering confidence in the local currency was withering, and broader macroeconomic stability was threatened. In that context, the cost to policy credibility of doing too little is much greater than the cost of undertaking reform that some may judge as unnecessary or excessive to resolving the cri-sis, even if appropriate on its own merits. The cost of failure of a reform package is high. Failure means not only continued instability for the coun-try to endure, but also that the next policy package has to be even more dra-matic to surmount the credibility hurdle created by the first policy failure. And we know well that mustering the political will for undertaking a major reform is difficult. Anything other than comprehensive reform raises the risk of failure.[7]

Comparison with other IMF-supported reform programs

The framework and objectives of the Thai, Indonesian and Korean reform programs are necessarily the same as other IMF-supported programs. Nevertheless, reflecting the nature of the imbalances in these economies, the programs have important differences from those adopted in other countries.

Like all IMF-supported reform programs, those in the three Asian countries are designed to correct balance of payments problems and to restore sustainable economic growth. In agreeing to support a country's reform efforts, the IMF is charged with ensuring equal or uniform treatment of all IMF members. In this regard, the IMF does not make a program any more onerous for one country than another.

The IMF's mandate also requires it to take account of the implications of the reform program for other countries and the global financial system. The Fund must be cognisant of the implications for competitiveness and stability in third countries when assessing the scale of currency depreciations and the design of monetary policy. Likewise, the IMF considers carefully the consequences for third countries and the international financial system when looking at external debt. For example, a hasty intervention to restructure private sector debt in Indonesia or Korea could have precipitated other crises by reversing capital flows to third countries. Finally, the IMF recognises policy interaction between countries in its surveillance activities. Thus, for example, exchange rate policy discussions with China and reforms in Japan are both shaped by regional considerations.

Against this backdrop, the Thai, Indonesian and Korean reform programs differ considerably from earlier IMF programs in at least two respects. The first is in the extent of emphasis on structural reform measures versus reliance on more narrowly defined macroeconomic policy measures. The second is in the nature of the structural reforms, two features of which stand out: extensive financial sector reform, and measures to improve governance in the corporate sector and government-corporate relations.

These three programs are not 'conventional IMF austerity programs'. If one wishes to draw similarities with other IMF-supported reform programs, these are closer to reform programs in the transition economies. With the collapse of central planning, the transition economies faced a macroeconomic shock, and lacked the market and policy institutions for economic management and resource allocation. The Asian crisis economies also have deficient policy and institutional structures. In some instances, like the transition economies, government direction of resources is an issue. However, the key transition for the Asian economies is the shift from financial autarky to financial market integration. Institutional and policy development did not match the massive growth of capital flows, the process of globalisation or the scale of domestic savings. The Thai, Indonesian and Korean reforms seek to build the necessary institutional and policy structures consistent with their integration into global financial markets.

POLICIES IN SUPPORT OF MACROECONOMIC STABILISATION AND SUSTAINABLE GROWTH

This section discusses three key policy areas; monetary and exchange rate policy, fiscal policy, and financial sector restructuring. The task is to explain the rationale for the IMF's policy stance and to provide a general characterisation of the policies in the three countries.[8]

Monetary and exchange rate policy

Foreign exchange market stabilisation is the first task of monetary policy in the reform programs. In this regard, interest rates are set so as to restore confidence in holding the local currency. Consideration is given to both the net domestic assets of the banking system and the net foreign assets components of the monetary aggregates, the latter being captured in the program by setting a floor on net international reserves. Nevertheless, there is less focus in the initial phase of the crisis on growth of the monetary aggregates, owing to uncertainty about the money-demand function. The exchange rate is allowed to float freely, apart from short-term smoothing operations. In Indonesia, where the starting point for international reserves was different from the other countries, some initial foreign exchange market intervention was envisaged as possible if undertaken as part of a comprehensive reform effort.

The use of high interest rates on a temporary basis to reduce currency market instability is essential. In all three countries, the value of the local currency was depreciating rapidly and, in Thailand and Korea, international reserves were low. In Korea, some market participants were speculating on the possibility of international default. The reversal of capital flows itself pushes up interest rates and this must be endorsed by raising official rates. The first task is to make it more attractive to hold the local currency; once confidence is restored, interest rates can return to normal levels.

Even though the use of high interest rates has provoked concern because of its implications for weak banking and corporate sectors, an accommodative monetary policy would be worse. It would provide local currency to fuel the exchange rate weakness and would result in an inequitable inflationary tax. Sustained foreign exchange market instability and inflation can wreak long-term damage on the payments system and cause a breakdown in external trading arrangements. Clearly, each of these countries had, in various ways, a simultaneous currency and banking sector crisis. It is this simultaneity of crises that raises concerns about using interest rates to address the currency crisis side of the equation, but the answers to this question are clear. First, this is a 'policy instruments and targets' issue. Interest rates should be targeted to the price of currency, and other policies targeted to correct the banking system problem; one policy without the other, rather than the level of interest rates, is the source of any problem. Second, the currency crisis must be addressed promptly because, if it is not, the banking system will be badly damaged, irrespective of the level of interest rates.

Reluctance to increase interest rates in a determined way at the beginning of the exchange rate turmoil has perhaps been one factor perpetuating the crisis. When interest rate action is delayed, confidence continues to erode. Thus, the eventual increase in interest rates needed to stabilise the situation is likely to be far larger than if decisive action had been taken at the outset.[9] Thailand floated the baht on 2 July 1997 and, at that time, increased the bank interest rate from 10.5% to 12.5% per annum. The authorities adopted further measures, after requesting IMF support, more than one month later. Likewise, the Korean authorities had difficulty demonstrating commitment to effective reform when they embarked on reforms in December 1997. Candidates in the 18 December elections wavered in their support for reform efforts.

The possibility of operating with lower interest rates and a larger devaluation is not a useful option. A case can be made that an easier monetary policy and a weaker exchange rate are justified because the terms of trade are continuing to move adversely for the three crisis countries. From a broader perspective, however, the devaluation of currencies in the crisis countries is excessive. At the country level, companies with substantial foreign currency debts stand to suffer far more from a steep slide in the value of their domestic currency than from a temporary rise in interest rates. From the viewpoint of the international system, the devaluations in Asia will lead to large current account surpluses in those countries, damaging the competitive positions of other countries and requiring them to run current account deficits. The IMF anticipates a sizeable swing in the current account balances of the crisis countries. In part, of course, the stronger current account reflects import compression from slowing domestic demand, but over time it will also reflect growing exports. By 1998, the three crisis countries are expected to have recorded surpluses amounting in aggregate to a swing of about US$60 billion from the deficit in 1996 (or about 8 percentage points of aggregate GDP). Recent revisions expect this surplus to be considerably larger than shown in Table 15.2.

Table 15.2 External current account balances

	% of GDP			Change 1996–8 (US$ billion)
	1996	1997	1998	
Thailand	−7.9	−2.2	3.9	18.4
Indonesia	−3.3	−2.6	1.9	10.0
Korea	−4.9	−2.0	5.5	31.7
Total	−4.8	−2.4	3.2	60.1

Source: IMF 1998b.

Table 15.3   Exchange rate changes (%), June 1997 through March 1998

	Bilateral exchange rate		Nominal effective exchange rate		Real effective exchange rate	
	Versus US dollar	Versus yen	INS[a] weights	DOT[b] weights	INS[a] weights	DOT[b] weights
Thailand	−37.5	−29.4	−31.8	−29.8	−27.1	−25.3
Indonesia	−73.9	−70.6	−71.4	−70.3	−63.2	−61.9
Korea	−39.0	−31.0	−35.3	−30.6	−30.3	−26.4

Notes:
a IMF Information Notice System (INS) captures bilateral and third country effects based on 1988–90 data.
b IMF Direction of Trade (DOT) Statistics capture only bilateral trade based on 1994–6 data.
Source: IMF 1998b.

Although not intended by the authorities in the crisis countries, the exchange rate changes shown in Table 15.3 are excessive competitive devaluations that pose a risk to financial market stability – precisely the type of devaluation the IMF has the obligation to seek to prevent. This is one reason why the IMF has stressed the need first to stabilise and then to strengthen exchange rates in the Asian crisis countries – and for this purpose, not to cut interest rates until the currencies stabilise and begin to appreciate.

Later, following stabilisation of the foreign exchange market, monetary policy will be set by specifying a path for the monetary aggregates defined by growth and price objectives. At that stage, monetary policy is likely to be relatively accommodative, as the economies will be operating considerably below potential. Developments in the foreign exchange market must guide the precise timing of interest rate easing. A sustained appreciation of the nominal exchange rate, the ability of central banks to reconstitute their much-depleted reserves, and signs of an easing of market-related interest rates signifying a decline in risk premia are all useful indicators. But, of course, much also depends on judgments regarding a reasonable range for the nominal exchange rate.

Some related issues

Weaknesses in the banking systems have hampered monetary policy. In Indonesia, private banks suffered from a flight to quality. To finance the declining deposit base, banks went to the interbank market but, despite paying high interest rates, were unable to get sufficient funds to meet their obligations. Consequently, these banks went to Bank Indonesia for support, which amounted to about 5% of GDP in the last two months of 1997, and to some 8% of GDP (200% of base money) by March 1998, and clearly pushed monetary policy off track. Monetary policy could have stayed on a more appropriate path if Bank Indonesia had been able to increase interest rates on its certificates of deposit (SBIs) so that it could intermediate funds from high deposit banks to illiquid banks. This intermediation problem was partially resolved in late 1997. In Thailand, the broader interest rate structure proved somewhat rigid to the increase in policy interest rates by the Bank of Thailand. Large banks had little incentive to raise deposit rates because they were beneficiaries of the flight to quality, while smaller banks were constrained by a cap on interest rates anchored to the deposit rates of the four largest banks. On the lending side, banks responded to the crisis by focusing on the quality of their lenders rather than on interest rates.

While recognising the importance of adjustment and reduction of leverage, countries are concerned that banks have indiscriminately reduced *credit availability*. In other words, a credit crunch is being applied to all sectors, including exporters with reliable flows of foreign currency receipts. The reaction of the banking system to the currency and financial crisis is, of course, quite predictable. The anticipation of rising non-performing loans and the need to boost capital adequacy has led them to constrain their lending activities. Some of these developments are policy-related. For example, many banks in Korea appeared to be under a misperception that they were required to raise their capital adequacy ratios to 8% by mid-1998, when in fact that was the time when their plans to achieve that level had to be supplied. Countries have each introduced measures to try to alleviate this pressure on credit, particularly to the export sector. Indonesia has a temporary program to extend credit to small-scale enterprises through the state banks at subsidised interest rates and an export finance facility. The cost is borne in the central government budget. In Korea, a guarantee ceiling for exports and domestic operations for small and medium-sized enterprises was raised from W21 trillion to W57 trillion through Asian Development Bank (ADB) capital and an easing of the export credit agency's capitalisation requirements. The Bank of Korea rediscount facility for small and medium-sized enterprises was raised by W1 trillion. In Thailand, EXIM Bank of Thailand and the Industrial Finance Corporation have negotiated trade finance facilities with the Japanese Export Import Bank and the ADB, supported by refinancing (up to 60%) by the Bank of Thailand at concessional interest rates.

Strengthening the *central bank* in the conduct of monetary policy is an important reform in Korea and Indonesia. Central banks in these countries had been very much directed by their respective finance ministries. The reform programs sought to provide an independence and focus to monetary policy that had been lacking heretofore.

Fiscal stance

Fiscal policy was not the cause of the crisis, yet its design is critical: it must balance the need to support adjustment, while recognising a possible adverse impact on aggregate demand. This assessment was the basis for fiscal adjustment in Thailand, Indonesia and Korea. Fiscal policy in Indonesia and Korea did not impose any contractionary adjustment beyond financing the cost of financial sector restructuring. In Thailand, the initial program used fiscal policy to ease the adjustment in the external current account deficit. The amount of initial fiscal adjustment in Indonesia was 1% of GDP; in Korea it was 1.5%; and in Thailand, 3%. These measures were revised to reflect developments in later phases of the crisis. Several factors entered the definition of the fiscal balance and the implied scale of fiscal adjustment: external adjustment, financial sector restructuring costs, social outlays, financing and market credibility, and the weakening growth outlook.

The scale of fiscal adjustment depends, in part, on how much *adjustment in the external current account deficit* is necessary. The Thai current account deficit was about 8% in both 1995 and 1996, and was envisaged in August 1997 to decline to 5% in 1997 and 3% in 1998. The large programmed reduction in the current account deficit raised the question of whether this decline in the contribution to activity of foreign savings was going to be borne by reduced financing of public or private sector activity. The larger the public sector fiscal adjustment, the lower is the required reduction in private sector activity; simply put, austerity in the budget means scope for private sector activity. The Thai external current account balance has, in the event, narrowed rapidly, and has been in surplus over the last several months. By contrast, the Korean external current account balance had narrowed from the outset, and the fiscal program saw no need for adjustment on this score.

The budgets include the expected interest costs of *financial sector restructuring* in calculating the amount of fiscal tightening needed. Indonesia will issue an estimated Rp155 trillion Indonesian Bank Restructuring Agency (IBRA) securities in 1998–9 to finance its restructuring efforts. The estimated interest cost of this is equivalent to about 1.5% of GDP; fiscal measures were adopted to help cover these costs. A similar practice was applied in the other two program countries. This is an attempt to spread the costs of the adjustment over time, rather than concentrate them at the time of the crisis.

An increasingly important element of budgetary outlays is *social spending*. These outlays are reflected partly through a reorientation of expenditures, and partly through a higher fiscal deficit. In Korea, for example, the unemployment rate is expected to rise sharply, and there is a very limited social safety net. Consequently, in designing the program, a concern was to extend protection for those who became unemployed. Thus, fiscal targets have been set flexibly to allow for additional social spending to ameliorate the effects of the expected increase in unemployment. Social safety net spending has increased fivefold to W5 trillion, or 1.1% of GDP, and is likely to be increased further.

The ability to source *fiscal deficit financing* consistent with monetary policy is a macroeconomic dimension of assessing the fiscal balance. Countries cannot remain indifferent to the level of the fiscal deficit, particularly since a country in crisis typically has only limited access to borrowing and since the alternative of printing money would be potentially disastrous in these circumstances. Thus, in the revised Indonesian program, the fiscal deficit increased, reflecting the depressed level of economic activity, and will be financed entirely with external funds.

Beyond these considerations, the IMF has seen it as appropriate to let *automatic stabilisers* work and the deficit to widen should the outlook for economic growth weaken. It is not the intention to use fiscal policy to restrain domestic demand, except in the circumstances of a large external deficit. Thus, statements that the IMF is requiring austere fiscal policies lack any basis in fact.

The budgetary positions of the three countries must be assessed cautiously. First, the headline budget balance numbers were often not a fair reflection of the overall budgetary position. Thus, in Indonesia, the reform program calls for two of the more important off-budget accounts – the reafforestation fund and the investment fund – to be reported as part of the government budget. Second, the simple existence of a budget balance or surplus does not make fiscal policy appropriate from a macroeconomic perspective. A prevalent view in Asia is that budget policy was strong and appropriate, so that large current account deficits were acceptable because they were private sector driven. In fact, the policy prescription for Thailand in 1995–6 called for an even larger fiscal surplus, along with other reform measures. Third, the underlying or structural budget balance is not as strong as the headline budget position. The budget balance has benefited enormously from sustained high growth that boosted revenues sharply. Maintenance of a strong headline fiscal balance has been consistent with buoyant expenditure growth because revenues have grown much more rapidly than GDP (Table 15.4).

Table 15.4 Government revenue (% of GDP)

	1987	1996	Implicit elasticity[a]
Thailand	15.2	18.9	1.24
Indonesia[b]	8.3	10.7	1.29
Korea	16.6	21.6	1.30

Notes:
a Ratio of preceding two columns.
b Non-oil and gas revenues.
Source: Data provided by the country authorities.

Whatever one thinks potential growth might be, slower growth would have meant a sharply wider fiscal inbalance in the absence of action on the spending side of the budget. The dramatic turnaround in Thai budget revenues, prompted by slowing economic growth – now happening to various degrees in other countries – shows the importance of this (Table 15.5). The absolute level of revenue fell in 1997, even though growth remained positive.

Fourth, quasi fiscal costs may be considerable. For example, the bank restructuring in Indonesia that commenced in 1994 incurred a fiscal cost of 2% of GDP (Dziobek and Pazarbasioglu 1997). Moreover, the implicit subsidies of directed lending are quite likely to be considerable.[10] The unwritten public balance sheets clearly contain extensive contingent liabilities in the form of guarantees for various financial obligations. Fifth, recent developments have changed the structural fiscal picture. In Thailand, for example, large capital inflows, the focus on property sector activity, and the previous high levels of investment are all unlikely to generate income in the near term, and this may well change the tax base. On the expenditure side of the budget, outlays not previously part of the budget will become more important. These outlays include public debt interest related to financial sector restructuring and social spending.

Financial sector

Restructuring of the financial sector is at the centre of reform efforts. The following steps were taken in designing these reforms:

1   Assess the true state of the various financial institutions: which are solvent but suffering liquidity problems and which are insolvent? This assessment guides decisions about suspending or curtailing the operations of particular institutions.
2   Develop rehabilitation plans for solvent institutions, recognising that public funding may be required. Public funding should be forthcoming only when two criteria are met: owners have their equity reduced, per-

Table 15.5   Thailand: government revenue (billion baht)

	Q1	Q2	Q3	Q4
1993	113.2	148.9	141.9	117.9
1994	126.2	176.2	175.3	141.7
1995	151.9	202.1	202.3	154.8
1996	173.5	230.2	221.1	161.4
1997	172.9	222.2	206.9	160.1

Source: Data provided by the authorities.

haps to zero, and management is changed. Institutions must provide plans for building up capital to acceptable levels.

3 Build a more effective financial sector infrastructure. This means improving supervision and prudential standards; ensuring banks meet capital requirements; ensuring adequate provisions for bad loans; limiting related party lending; publishing comprehensive and timely financial information; and ensuring that insolvent institutions are dealt with promptly.

Thailand has made considerable progress in addressing financial sector reform. First, with respect to resolving the status of non-viable finance companies: the closure of 56 finance companies in early December 1997 and the establishment of institutions to sell the assets of these companies was the first step. The Thai authorities are seeking to maintain a careful balance between maximising sales of the assets and maintaining asset prices at levels consistent with the value of future income streams.

Second, the government has injected significant amounts of capital into selected banks in conjunction with restructuring and recapitalisation. The Bank of Thailand replaced bank managements and wrote down the capital of the existing shareholders almost to zero. The availability of new private capital constrains the speed of recapitalisation.

Third, ensuring a sound institutional framework: to strengthen the banking system, the authorities will phase in tighter rules for loan classification and provisioning, and will require banks to raise additional capital.

In Korea, considerable progress has also been made. First, in relation to recapitalisation of weak but viable institutions, the government through its asset management company has purchased about half of the impaired loans at a discount to face value. It has also subscribed to subordinated debt issued by commercial banks (sufficient to raise the capital adequacy ratio by 1–2 percentage points).

Second, progress has been made towards clear and firm exit policy. All merchant banks submitted rehabilitation plans and, on the basis of preliminary versions of these plans, the authorities ordered the closure of ten of the fourteen merchant banks whose operations were suspended in mid-December. A 'bridge' merchant bank was established to pay out depositors and to dispose of the assets of the suspended institutions. The government has recapitalised the two distressed banks and assumed effective control, after existing shareholders' equity was substantially written down. It is intended to privatise these two banks, for which bids are expected by mid-November 1998.

A third relates to increased competition. Restrictions on commercial bank ownership have been eased in order to encourage foreign investment in domestic financial institutions.

The fourth concerns the strengthening of market and supervisory discipline. A legal framework has been established to strengthen the regulatory and supervisory system. The National Assembly passed or amended, on 29 December 1997, several laws affecting the financial system. The main initiatives were to specify price stability as the overriding objective of an independent Bank of Korea; to consolidate the supervision of all financial institutions in an autonomous agency; to clarify the conditions under which distressed financial institutions can be resolved through closure, mergers and acquisitions, or injections of government resources; to tighten prudential rules on large exposures of merchant banks; and to consolidate the various deposit insurance schemes in the Korea Deposit Insurance Corporation.

In Indonesia, problems in the banking sector intensified as the crisis unfolded, with some measures taken that, in aggregate, proved to be inadequate. In late January 1998, the authorities provided a two-year guarantee for depositors and creditors of all locally incorporated banks. The IBRA became operational in February, taking responsibility for overseeing a large number of banks and imposing tight prudential restrictions and other limitations on them. In early March, new standards for loan classification and loan loss provisioning were adopted. In early April, the IBRA took control of several of these banks and terminated the operations of some of the smaller ones, according to well-defined and uniformly applied criteria. The government will establish an asset management company to recover something from assets of closed or supervised institutions. By June, the government was to introduce legislation to remove restrictions on the foreign ownership of banks.

REFLECTIONS ON THE REFORM EFFORTS IN EAST ASIA

This section considers some alternative views on reform and two challenges for the international financial system posed by the East Asian crisis.

Some alternative views

Financial panic thesis

One approach calls on the IMF and the international community to make significant financing available without requiring reform measures. This view proposes that the Asian crisis is a financial panic that calls for a 'lender of last resort' response. Adherents of the financial panic thesis argue that Asia had a strong track record of macroeconomic performance and so the Asian crisis is nothing more than a crisis of confidence. The way to restore confidence in these countries is to provide substantial sums that show a credible ability to meet all foreign exchange demands.[11] According to this view, specific reforms are not needed and may even harm the country's prospects.

A couple of observations throw doubt on this explanation. First, structural vulnerabilities in all three program countries were evident before the crisis. Thai finance companies had already experienced difficulties, bankruptcies of several Korean *chaebol* had taken place, and Indonesian banking reform had been moving very slowly. Second, the idea that simply providing finance could have averted the crisis seems at odds with market responses to the failure to carry out reform. In Indonesia, for example, the market reaction to the initial program was that the funding package was larger than needed. None of this means that the financial panic argument has no merit, but simply that it cannot be used as a basis for avoiding macroeconomic and structural reforms.

Was the program too comprehensive?

A related suggestion is that the reform programs are 'too comprehensive'. The reasons a comprehensive reform effort was adopted have already been discussed. Markets have remained sceptical when reform efforts have been perceived to be incomplete or half-hearted, and market confidence has not returned. In Thailand, for example, the initial program focused largely on monetary, fiscal and financial sector policies. Only when a new government took office and started to address broader developments – legal reforms, corporate governance, and social safety net issues – did markets react favourably. The IMF has also been accused of encouraging countries to move too quickly on banking sector restructuring. The suggestion is that regulatory forbearance would be appropriate, leaving the solution of banking sector problems for later. This would only have perpetuated these countries' economic problems and compromised monetary policy, thus further jeopardising macroeconomic stability. For example, the enormous liquidity growth generated by supporting troubled Indonesian banks was the source of the acceleration in Indonesian inflation and the plunge of the rupiah in early 1998. The best course is to recapitalise or close insolvent banks, protect small depositors, require shareholders to take their losses, and take steps to improve banking regulation and supervision. Research suggests that meaningful action to resolve banking sector problems was the turning point to recovery in earlier financial crises (IMF 1998b).

A variant on this argument is that the international community set the 'policy hurdle' too high; reform programs could not be followed. This argument seems to be made mainly in the case of Indonesia. However, this view does not offer a useful explanation of developments in Indonesia in late 1997 and early 1998. The authorities did not move forward with their reforms, and in fact adopted some measures that increased the problems facing the economy. In particular, the massive increase in liquidity growth that took place resulted in increasing inflation and a significant weakening of the rupiah. In this context, asserting that the policy hurdle was set too high is of little relevance because the hurdle was not tested. (Of course, the

IMF has recourse to mechanisms such as waivers when countries have legitimate reasons for being unable to meet their reform commitments.) Finally, two key points noted earlier must be kept in mind. First, the country authorities present a Letter of Intent, outlining their intended policies, to the international community for support – the country's own reform program. Second, the IMF's Articles require it to treat all countries uniformly.

Market-based solutions

Distortions are private sector driven and so should be solved by market adjustment, according to another view. The role of structural distortions in the crisis is recognised, but it is argued that these distortions are the result of poor decisions, such as excessive foreign borrowing or poor investment decisions that should be penalised by allowing the investors concerned to incur losses. It is true that many symptoms of the crisis are related to private sector decisions. Nevertheless, this should not confuse the role of economic policy as amongst the primary causes of destabilising private decisions. These policy failures included inconsistent exchange rate and monetary policies, weaknesses in bank supervision, and regulatory distortions. Reform of macroeconomic and structural policies is thus central to overcoming the problems.

A related argument is that large current account deficits were driven by private decisions and so were not of macroeconomic concern. A large current account deficit is a vulnerability simply because it has to be financed. The terms of financing and even the availability of finance can change quickly. This vulnerability is clearly greater if the current account deficit has widened on account of growing capital account flows stimulated by inconsistent macroeconomic policy. Thus, even if the current account deficit is seen as acceptable because imports consist of capital goods and raw materials that are strengthening the export sector, this does not necessarily signify that there is no need for macroeconomic adjustment.

Moral hazard and IMF support

Others oppose IMF financial support because it encourages excessive private sector lending to emerging markets – an example of moral hazard.[12] The principle that investors should incur the full cost (or enjoy the full benefit) of their decisions is clear. If an IMF-supported reform program results in the compensation of investors who would otherwise make losses, there is a possibility that, in the future, investors may undertake more risky investments. The chance of this excessive financing is clear, but it does not obviate the case for IMF support. The IMF tries strenuously to minimise this risk.

The concern over moral hazard in the Asian crisis is more narrow than the picture often conveyed. First, the concern relates only to creditors with short-term claims on financial institutions and sovereign borrowers. These creditors may have received protection that they would not have received otherwise, but other investors are bearing the full cost of recent developments. Foreign equity investors have lost large amounts in some Asian markets. Many firms and financial institutions in these countries will become bankrupt, and their foreign and domestic lenders will share in the losses. International banks are also sharing in the cost of the crisis. Some lenders may be forced to write down their claims against corporate borrowers. Earnings reports and announcements on bank provisioning suggest that, overall, the Asian crisis has indeed been costly for foreign commercial banks. The International Institute of Finance has estimated that private investors lost somewhere between US$100 billion and $125 billion in the last half of 1997.[13]

Faced with a crisis, allowing it to follow its own course – with the possibility of default and its implications for the country and the global economy – would result in the worst outcome. Rather, the task must be to mitigate the effects of the crisis on the global economy in a way that places part of the burden on borrowers and lenders, albeit possibly with some undesired but limited side effects. In fact, to do the contrary would be to invite precisely those developments that the IMF was established to avoid: namely, the risk of closing of markets and a serious risk of greater trade and payments restrictions, a more significant downturn in world trade, and slower world growth.

Challenges for the international financial system

Dealing with external debt

High levels of short-term unhedged private sector external liabilities are a feature of the recent crisis. The international community must address how it should deal with external debt problems and measure vulnerabilities associated with external liabilities.

The IMF must move judiciously in proposing any restructuring of external debt obligations under present arrangements. A criticism of the IMF in Indonesia, and to a lesser extent Korea, is that it did not actively pursue a restructuring of external obligations at an early stage of the crisis. Contrary to these suggestions, the IMF has always considered the external debt issue as important. At a most basic level, the IMF could not structure a balance of payments projection or determine financing requirements without looking at external debt. Thus, beginning with the Thai program, the IMF has held discussions with banks, both to explain the consistency of the macroeconomic programs of these countries and to assess the debt roll-over issue. In Korea, the IMF worked closely with the Korean authorities, creditor (second line of defence) countries and their banks to promote a resolution of the debt problem. Likewise, the IMF met with the banks and encouraged efforts by the Indonesian authorities to resolve the debt problem.

The IMF can actively propose a restructuring of external debt only when there is clearly no other course of action. If the IMF moves pre-emptively in promoting restructuring, it may have two harmful consequences: it may precipitate crises in other countries by causing a drying up of capital flows (and this was a concern in late 1997); and it may create moral hazard problems. As a result, the IMF must wait until there is unambiguously no other means of resolving the problem except by restructuring the country's external obligations.[14] This way of dealing with debt problems is less than optimal, and so one challenge facing the international community is to find ways to shift more of the financial burden to private sector creditors and debtors, and in a timely way.[15]

More comprehensive and accurate data on external debt are required. In Korea, BIS data suggested that Korean external liabilities were about US$110 billion in late 1997, whereas the joint IMF–Korea estimate prepared in late December, based in part on a different classification, put them at about US$160 billion. Similar variations were discovered for external liabilities in Indonesia. Some have termed the Asian crisis a capital account crisis, to distinguish it from earlier crises emanating from the current account of the balance of payments. Reflecting this shift in focus, the use of international reserves cover of imports has given way to the ratio of short-term external liabilities to international reserves as an indicator of vulnerability. If this indicator is to be useful, measurement of external liabilities must be improved, including recognising the role of derivative transactions in modifying this exposure.

Contagion

A surprising aspect of the Asian crisis is the virulence of the contagion effect. There is no question that contagion was anticipated; this was reflected in IMF policy advice to neighbouring countries before 2 July 1997. Apart from theoretical studies of currency crises, a good deal was known from recent experience. The term 'tequila effect' has been part of the commonly used jargon since the Mexican crisis of December 1994. Extensive study of the 1992 ERM (exchange rate mechanism) crisis by the IMF and others had shown how the currency crisis had spread. But none of this experience led observers to anticipate the scale of the crisis in East Asia in the latter half of 1997. Some argue that this reflects the globalisation of financial markets and the massive increases of capital flows that have occurred in recent years. This argument no doubt holds some truth but is not entirely convincing; the developments mentioned were already well underway by late 1994 and 1995.

A key factor was the failure of Thailand to address its problem at the outset. The baht was floated on 2 July but other policy responses were limited.

The request for IMF support came on 5 August and was approved by the executive board on 20 August. Yet markets remained unconvinced of Thailand's commitment to meaningful reform until the new government was installed. By comparison, Mexico acted more quickly once the crisis hit in December 1994, perhaps forestalling a more severe contagion effect.

Recent IMF studies shed some light on the sources of contagion in the Asian crisis (IMF 1998b; Masson 1998). Crises may stem from a common cause. For example, the large appreciation of the dollar, especially against the yen, between mid-1995 and 1997 contributed to the weakening of the external sector in several Southeast Asian countries. Nevertheless, while external events may contribute to, or precipitate, a crisis, a country's vulnerability depends on domestic economic conditions and policies. A second reason why crises may be clustered is that a crisis in one country may affect the macroeconomic fundamentals in another country, either because of trade or capital market linkages. For example, a devaluation in one country adversely affects the competitiveness of other countries or, because of interdependence in creditors' portfolios, illiquidity in one market forces financial intermediaries to liquidate assets in other markets (Goldfajn and Valdes 1997a). Such spill-overs resulting from interdependence have been cited as contributing in important ways to the spread of the Asian crisis. A third reason is that a crisis in one country may lead creditors to re-evaluate the fundamentals of other countries, even if these have not actually changed, or to reduce the riskiness of their portfolios and 'flee to quality'.

CONCLUSION

The IMF's activities in Asia since mid-1997 amount to nothing more and nothing less than fulfilling its charter. Clearly, preventing the crisis would have been preferable, and the international community must find ways to reduce the likelihood of such occurrences. But inevitably crises will occur, and the IMF is the institutional mechanism that the international community has created to address them. This chapter has set out how the IMF is addressing the current crisis. Focusing on the crisis alone, however, gives a very partial view of the IMF's role in Asia. Thailand, Indonesia and Korea have been IMF members for many years. Over that time, the IMF has worked closely with the authorities in these countries through surveillance, technical assistance, reform programs and the training of officials. The IMF and the country authorities know each other well and the dialogue will continue long after the Asian crisis is a subject for history books rather than the daily news.

With the onset of the Asian crisis, the IMF stood ready to help these countries in whatever way possible. At their request, their reform programs were presented to the IMF executive board for endorsement and financial support. The experience from the Asian crisis so far is that only adoption of a comprehensive reform plan carried out with determination will overcome these difficulties. Unfortunately, the opposite is also true, and perhaps nowhere has the asymmetry between confidence creation and confidence destruction been displayed more clearly than in Indonesia in late 1997 and early 1998. Confidence in policymakers and policy is built painstakingly over time by producing a strong track record. Yet that confidence can be dashed dramatically and rapidly when a resolve to adopt strong and needed policy measures is not exhibited. The experience of the last several months shows that this confidence in economic policy, although intangible, is absolutely critical.

What do we have to look forward to now? We should be under no illusions about how far Asia has to go, but within reach is an even stronger Asian growth story than the one celebrated before July 1997. The new Asia will certainly build on the strengths of the past that resulted in rapid growth of per capita incomes and made major inroads into alleviating poverty. But if reform is pursued, more effective resource utilisation and sustainable economic growth is the pay-off. The IMF-supported reform programs in Asia are not austerity programs. True, they respond to the reversal of capital flows but, at their core, they build on macroeconomic stabilisation by promoting more efficient resource allocation through a new role for governments. This role is to build the market infrastructure in the financial, corporate and social sectors to complement the enormous benefits provided by integration with the global economy.

NOTES

The author thanks Helen Hughes and Christopher Morris for comments, and Michi Tanaka for assistance. The views expressed are those of the author and not necessarily those of the International Monetary Fund.

1   IMF (1997c) reviews the causes of the crisis.
2   This, of course, is the familiar rationale for collective action that is sometimes presented in the form of a Prisoners' Dilemma game.
3   Article 1 of the IMF's charter spells out several tasks for the institution. These include: 'To promote international monetary cooperation …'; 'To facilitate the expansion and balanced growth of international trade, and to contribute thereby to the promotion and maintenance of high levels of employment and real income …'; and 'To promote exchange stability, to maintain orderly exchange arrangements among members, and to avoid competitive exchange depreciation'.
4   Observers reasonably trace the beginning of the East Asian crisis from various points: the devaluation of the Chinese renminbi; the strengthening US dollar and declining G7 interest rates; the growing intervention of the Thai central bank to support the baht; the 2 July floating of the baht; or the October attack on the Hong Kong dollar – to name a few possibilities.

5   In the background, other developments elevated the sense of concern: for example, the October 1997 attack on the Hong Kong dollar following cessation of central bank defence of the New Taiwan dollar; and serious pressures outside the region, such as on the Brazilian real.

6   The emergency financing procedures provide for large front-loaded access to IMF resources, and the normal executive board approval process is accelerated. The Philippines was the first country to make use of these procedures. In its case, the currency was allowed to float freely on 11 July 1997, and the request for the augmentation and drawing under its program was approved by the executive board one week later.

7   The final section considers opposing views.

8   The chapter does not review structural fiscal, corporate governance, trade, capital account, labour market, privatisation, deregulation, or social safety net measures. Details of these measures are in the published memoranda of economic and financial policies of these countries.

9   In the 'tequila crisis', interest rates in Mexico were increased more assertively than in the Asian crisis. The Mexican 28-day cetes rate moved from 15% per annum in mid-December 1994 to double that level by the end of the month, and to a peak of 80% in mid-March 1995.

10   See Mackenzie (1996) for a discussion of the quasi fiscal costs of financial institutions.

11   The basis for such financial assistance would have to be carefully crafted under the IMF's present Articles of Agreement. As noted above, the Articles refer to 'making the general resources of the Fund temporarily available to them under adequate safeguards'. The use of policy conditionality is seen as providing such safeguards. The Supplemental Reserve Facility (SRF) established in December 1997 provides for large front-loaded sums with a penalty interest rate. However, the SRF must be accompanied by another IMF arrangement ensuring that conditionality applies.

12   I am ignoring the possibility of moral hazard concerns influencing policymakers. Countries are not likely to adopt more risky policies because the IMF is 'waiting in the wings'. Revealed preference is that, if anything, countries are too slow to come to the IMF.

13   This total is based on estimates for Thailand, Korea, Indonesia, Malaysia and the Philippines, and is made up of US$80–100 billion on equity markets; $10–15 billion on foreign currency bonds; and at least $10 billion by industrial country banks.

14   In this context, recall that Korea still had access to international capital markets in mid-December. The Korean Development Bank was issuing a bond but withdrew the issue when the spread over US Treasuries was larger than anticipated.

15   The international community is actively examining this question. The G10 has presented a report, and the issue is now being examined by the G22, the Manila Group and the IMF.

16 Will Mexico's recovery from crisis be a model for East Asia?

David D. Hale

The East Asian financial crisis of 1997–8 will go down in the history books as a defining event in the evolution of the post cold war financial order. The crisis produced financial contagion on a scale unprecedented since the collapse of Creditanstalt in 1931. It provoked a great debate about the stability of the world financial system and the appropriate role of multilateral agencies, such as the International Monetary Fund (IMF), in serving as lender of last resort. The US government has also used the powers of the IMF to impose on some East Asian countries far-reaching structural changes in regulatory policies affecting trade and investment. In the case of Indonesia, the crisis set in motion economic shocks so great that President Soeharto was forced to resign and the country is now heading for its most dramatic political transformation since the fall of President Sukarno in the mid-1960s.

There have been many financial crises in developing countries during the last 200 years. The crises typically resulted from either external economic shocks which suspended capital flows to them or domestic problems which led to a loss of investor confidence. The shocks responsible for crises have included large interest rate hikes in capital-exporting countries, falling commodity prices for capital-importing nations which have undermined their debt-servicing capacity, or political quarrels about the role of foreign investment. Before last year's financial turmoil in East Asia, the greatest developing country financial crisis of the modern era had occurred in Latin America during the early 1980s. That crisis had resulted from a large hike in dollar interest rates which depressed global commodity prices after a lending boom to Latin American governments and state enterprises during the high inflation years of the 1970s. It was a bank lending boom which financed fiscal profligacy, not private investment. The financial crisis in East Asia startled investors, credit rating agencies and governments because it resulted from very different factors than the Latin American debt defaults of the 1980s or even the Mexican peso devaluation of 1995. It also came seven years after the end of the cold war and an expansion of capital flows to developing countries from only US$50 billion a year during the late 1980s to nearly US$300 billion dollars during 1997.

The financial crisis in East Asia was the by-product of economic policies which were highly conducive to steady low-inflation economic growth when capital flows to developing countries were modest but which encouraged speculative excesses when large amounts of external liquidity became available during the 1990s. As a result of their high level of commercial and financial integration with the United States, the countries of East Asia have long pursued various forms of exchange rate pegs with the US dollar. Hong Kong has the strongest possible link with its currency board. Other countries have had either exchange pegs or target bands centred on the dollar. Such pegs imposed two constraints on the central banks of countries which had them. First, they had to hold their interest rates at levels compatible with US monetary policy. Second, they had to accept the trade competitiveness risks of letting their currencies fluctuate with the US dollar. In the early 1990s, the Federal Reserve pursued a highly expansionary monetary policy in order to help revive the US banking system. As a result of the exchange rate link, America's expansionary monetary policy helped to encourage rapid credit growth in countries including Thailand, Malaysia, Indonesia and the Philippines. Singapore permitted its exchange rate to appreciate in order to lessen the influence of US monetary policy. The exchange rate peg to the dollar also encouraged many Asian companies to reduce their borrowing costs by seeking dollar loans rather than local currency credit. The credit expansion triggered booms in property values and share prices which were reinforced by significant capital inflows from portfolio investors and commercial banks. As a result of the slump in their domestic market, Japanese banks were especially aggressive lenders to East Asia and now account for over one-third of all foreign bank lending in the region.

The boom in the East Asian economies resulting from easy monetary policy and surplus global liquidity produced large current account deficits in some countries (over 8% of GDP in Malaysia and Thailand), but such deficits were not viewed with alarm because of the high levels of domestic savings and investment in the region. But since the exchange rate pegs had encouraged a large volume of dollar-denominated lending, they lowered the cost of capital to a level which encouraged overenthusiastic property development and other speculative forms of investment.

The stage was thus set for a sharp deterioration in the quality of bank assets, which undermined investor confidence in the ability of East Asian governments to sustain their exchange rate pegs to the US dollar. Thailand was the first country to experience a crisis because of both the magnitude and character of its external borrowing. Between 1990 and 1996, it had expanded its foreign borrowing from less than US$20 billion to US$98 billion. Nearly 86% of the foreign debt went to domestic financial institutions, while 70% of the loans had a maturity of less than one year. The domestic institutions used the Japanese credit to finance a boom in property development and consumer spending. The evolving glut in the

Thai property market will probably cause at least 15–20% of the loans to become non-performing by 1998.

In the months after the Thai devaluation, most academic and financial commentators suggested that the great flaw in Thailand's economic policy was its fixed exchange rate vis-à-vis the dollar. As the Thai crisis came only two years after Mexico's shock devaluation of the peso, they also suggested that all developing countries should move towards floating exchange rates in order to lessen the risk of large current account deficits resulting from an erosion of trade competitiveness or easy access to foreign capital. While it is understandable that everyone should see analogies between the Thai and Mexican crises, the fact is that they reflected quite different problems. The Mexican crisis resulted from the country running a large current account deficit financed primarily by securitised capital inflows during a period of political instability and sharply rising US interest rates. The Thai crisis resulted from the low quality of the country's banking supervision and the ineffectiveness of the government's response to a sharp deterioration in the quality of domestic bank credit at a time when global liquidity conditions were benign. If one compares the different background factors to the Thai and Mexican crises, it is not difficult to see how dangerous it is to generalise about exchange rate policy solely on the basis of current account deficits.

First, Thailand has a much higher domestic rate of savings and investment than Mexico. In recent years, the Thai savings rate has averaged close to 40%, compared with 16–18% in Mexico and only 20% in Thailand itself during the early 1980s. As a result, Thailand was never as dependent upon foreign capital as Mexico to support a high level of investment. Thailand ran a large external deficit because it had an abundance of foreign capital available at low interest rates, not because of a structural savings shortfall.

Second, Thailand enjoyed a much higher level of foreign exchange reserves in both absolute terms and relative to imports during the recent crisis than Mexico two years ago. Thailand's reserves were three times as large as its current account deficit during 1996, whereas Mexico's reserves were below the current account deficit projected for 1995. The Thai current account deficit rose sharply during 1996 because export growth had slowed in response to the weakness of the G7 industrial countries and an inventory adjustment in the global electronics industry which now accounts for a large share of East Asia's exports. The electronics and related industries sector accounts for around half of the exports of Singapore and Malaysia, two-fifths of the Philippines', and one-fifth of Thailand's. But since Thailand was trying to restrain its domestic consumption, import demand also was slowing and there was no shortage of foreign exchange to finance its capital needs.

Third, Thailand's source of capital inflows during the first half of the 1990s was profoundly different from Mexico's. In the years after the Bush administration and President Salinas agreed to promote the North American Free Trade Agreement (NAFTA), Mexico financed over two-thirds of its external deficit by selling equities and bonds to foreign investors, especially in the United States. During this period, Mexico was a beneficiary of both the general upsurge of investor interest in the concept of emerging markets and the special focus on NAFTA as an engine for economic transformation of the country itself. Mexico's dependence upon securitised capital inflows made its capital account vulnerable to potential news shocks, such as the assassinations which killed two prominent politicians during 1994, as well as to rising US interest rates. When a country is running a large external deficit financed by stock and bond sales, it simply cannot afford a prolonged period of either bad political news or economic uncertainty. In 1994, Mexico suffered from both, despite the commitment of the newly elected Zedillo government to maintaining the economic policies inherited from the Salinas era.

Thailand, by contrast, financed a much larger share of its external deficit through FDI and bank lending. Portfolio investment accounted for only 14.4% of its capital inflows during 1994, 1995 and the first half of 1996, compared with 64% for Mexico during the period 1990–4. Mexico enjoyed more FDI during these periods (23% of all capital inflows) than Thailand (6.4% of capital inflows), but the major difference in the two countries' capital accounts was the role of bank lending. Thailand financed 61% of its external deficit through bank loans during the period 1994–6, compared with 6% for Mexico during the period 1990–4. Thailand had established new international banking facilities during the early 1990s which had encouraged aggressive lending by foreign banks in dollars. Thai companies were anxious to borrow in dollars because the interest rate yield on such loans was about half the rate on domestic baht denominated loans and they perceived that the baht would never be devalued. As Thailand was enjoying boom-like growth, foreign banks did not apply rigorous quality standards to the loans and thus helped to set the stage for significant misallocation of capital, especially in the commercial real estate sector. It was the low quality of the commercial bank lending, not Thailand's current account deficit, which set the stage for the 1997 exchange rate crisis. As it became apparent that non-performing loans in the banks and finance companies would rise to a level equal to 20–30% of the country's GDP (gross domestic product), foreign investors sold Thai securities and international banks became more concerned about their credit exposure. Thailand delayed an exchange rate adjustment by imposing exchange controls on non-resident owners of Thai bahts and by recycling liquidity from other Asian central banks. But such a policy was not sustainable for long because it pushed up interest rates at a time when the banking system was confronting a sharp rise in the stock of non-performing loans and foreign banks were being asked to roll over a large volume of short-maturity dollar-denominated bank loans. The Thai government had been reluctant to devalue because the Thai corporate sector had borrowed nearly US$60 billion from foreign banks during the previous four years, but the imposition of exchange controls was creating such large distortions in the country's financial markets that it had to seek an alternative policy. Ironically, Thailand would have faced a much less serious adjustment problem if it had permitted the baht to fluctuate in a wider range during the period when the boom in dollar lending was occurring. The introduction of some exchange rate uncertainty would have caused Thai companies to reduce their dollar borrowing or hedge it more carefully. A more flexible currency policy also would have enhanced the ability of Thailand to cope with large fluctuations in the dollar/yen exchange rate, but trade competitiveness was not as serious a problem for the economy as the overleveraging in foreign currency debt.

The common thread linking the Mexican and Thai crises has been the poor quality of bank supervision in both countries. In the period before the peso and baht devaluations, there had been a sharp rise in the stock of non-performing bank loans in both countries which limited the freedom of central banks to pursue restrictive monetary policies in order to defend their exchange rates. Mexico's bank asset problems had resulted from the country's nationalisation of the banking sector during the 1982 debt crisis. As a result of government ownership, their loan books reflected a weak credit culture for private lending at a time when the new owners were anxious to expand the balance sheets in order to justify the high prices they had paid for their shares when the banks were denationalised during 1991. In the 1980s the Mexican banks had primarily financed large government deficits. After privatisation, they had expanded lending aggressively to households for both homes and consumer durables, despite the fact that Mexico does not provide much legal protection to creditors of the household sector. As a result, the level of non-performing loans was already at 8% before the peso crisis. In the case of Thailand, there had been a significant expansion of lending to both households and property developers. The stock of non-performing loans in the financial system was widely estimated to be equal to 15–20% of assets before the crisis, and the recession will probably cause it to rise even further. If there had been better supervision of bank credit quality during the period of rapid lending growth, both Mexico and Thailand would have had more policy options for defending their exchange rates.

The Mexican crisis encouraged discussion of bank supervision and its secondary effects on exchange rate stability, but the Asian credit boom was so mature by 1995 that it was too late for Mexico's experience to have any impact on bank lending in the region. What now remains to be seen is whether countries which are using exchange rate targets as policy anchors will become more effective at supervising their banking systems and preventing their exchange rate regimes from encouraging overleveraging in foreign currency debt.

One of the most interesting test cases of bank supervision under a fixed exchange rate system will probably be Estonia. The country introduced one of the most market-oriented economic reform programs in the world after receiving independence from the Soviet Union in 1991. It abolished all tariffs, slashed marginal income tax rates, reduced public spending to 25% of GDP, and pegged its currency to the deutschmark through a currency board modelled on Hong Kong's. The currency board has been very effective at stabilising the exchange rate, reducing inflation in the tradable goods sector, and helping to lay the foundation for a healthy banking system.

But as a result of Estonia's success in stabilising its economy and financial system, commercial bank lending has tripled during the past three years and over 80% of the loans have been denominated in foreign currencies, especially the deutschmark. The stock of non-performing loans is still low (2.4%, compared with 7.1% in 1993), but security analysts project a doubling of loan losses during 1998. While the projected increase in non-performing loans is not alarming, it does raise questions as to whether Estonia will have effective bank regulatory policies to prevent its exchange rate link to the deutschmark from encouraging excessive lending for speculative purposes, such as real estate development and equity purchases in the country's booming stock market. The central bank recently imposed higher capital–asset ratios and reserve requirements on the country's commercial banks in order to slow lending, but it is unclear if such policies will be adequate by themselves to restrain speculative lending in an economy which enjoys as much investor optimism as Estonia. It will probably be the first country from the former Soviet Union to join the European Union and is overdue for an upgrade in its credit rating. Since Estonia's current account deficit has shifted from a small surplus in 1993 to a deficit exceeding 10% of GNP (gross national product) during 1996 and 1997, the kroon could come under selling pressure if investors start to perceive that the banking system has asset quality problems comparable to other countries whose fixed exchange rate regimes encouraged overly aggressive foreign currency bank lending.

CAUSES OF CONTAGION

The scope of the 'contagion' in the recent East Asia financial crisis is provoking a far-reaching debate about the character of the global financial system in the post cold war world. As Alan Greenspan often comments in speeches, developments in computer and communications technology have profoundly altered the magnitude and volatility of global capital flows by reducing the cost of trading. The development of derivatives and other highly levered financial instruments has also encouraged a proliferation of aggressive financial intermediaries, such as hedge funds and bank proprietary trading departments, which are programmed to move large pools of capital quickly between different financial markets in order to exploit both buying and selling opportunities. The IMF estimates that there is now close to US$100 billion in such intermediaries and that they have the capacity to leverage their assets five to ten times. The hedge funds did not create the East Asian financial crisis, but they magnified the selling pressure which caused some Asian governments to abandon their fixed exchange rate regimes. The decision to float then unleashed a torrent of hedging by heavily indebted Asian companies. Asia's commercial bank lenders further reinforced the crisis by curtailing credit access for many corporations in the region. In fact, the great surprise of the crisis has been the volatility of capital flows through syndicated bank lending. In the case of Korea, foreign commercial bank lending has been more unpredictable than mutual fund-driven capital flows to Mexico during the mid-1990s.

When Mexico experienced a sudden collapse of the peso in late 1994 and early 1995, it was not difficult to rationalise what had happened. Mexico had been financing a large current account deficit (8% of GDP) by selling short-maturity Treasury bills and equities to US mutual funds during a period when the Federal Reserve was doubling the level of US short-term interest rates and when confidence within Mexico itself had been rocked by two political assassinations. When a new president took office, who did not have the benefit of a finance minister with a long history of speaking to international fund managers, confidence eroded so quickly that the country's foreign exchange reserves were exhausted within a few weeks. The great question still lingering in the background to the 1997 crisis is how the widely acknowledged real estate lending problems of Thailand's banks could produce so much financial contagion that the devaluation of the baht was followed by currency crises or financial market instability in all the ASEAN countries, Taiwan, Hong Kong, Korea, Estonia, Russia and Brazil.

There were few leading indicators of crisis, such as rising interest rates in the G7 countries, or a sudden suspension of capital flows to developing countries, after the baht devaluation in July. On the contrary, the Bank for International Settlements reports that bank lending to Asia rose to a record peak of US$14.1 billion during the third quarter of 1997. There was a small contraction of bank lending to Thailand during that quarter but other countries continued to expand their borrowing. Korea also sold US$4 billion of international bonds, compared with US$3.2 billion during the second quarter. As recently as August, some Korean forecasters were concerned that liberalisation of the country's restrictions on capital inflows might even encourage won appreciation during late 1997. In the run-up to the IMF meeting in Hong Kong during September, most analysts perceived that ASEAN would experience a growth slowdown because of currency depreciation, rising interest rates and bank caution, but no one expected the baht devaluation to evolve into a global crisis encompassing most emerging markets.

The last great episode of transnational financial contagion was the failure of the Creditanstalt bank in Austria during 1931. The crisis began when Creditanstalt had a difficult time rolling over its liabilities because of depositor concern about the Austrian economy and the bank's non-performing loans. There were attempts by the Bank for International Settlements to support Creditanstalt, but they were conditional upon the Austrian government fulfilling certain conditions which it could not satisfy. After Creditanstalt shut its doors, there were runs on banks in Hungary, Poland, Czechoslovakia and Germany. The Hoover administration in Washington tried to slow the run on German banks by proposing a debt moratorium, over the protests of the French government. But despite the attempts at policy cooperation between the United States and Europe, the crisis spread to sterling. The pound came under such severe selling pressure that the British government felt compelled to raise taxes in the midst of the Great Depression in order to restore investor confidence. But such austerity was unable to revive confidence because it triggered a political crisis which split the ruling Labour Party and encouraged a mutiny by the Royal Navy over proposed pay cuts. As investor confidence collapsed, the British government was forced to float the pound and let it decline by over 20% against the US dollar gold price four months after the Creditanstalt crisis began. In his memoirs, Herbert Hoover spoke of the 1931 events in terms not dissimilar to policymakers describing the financial contagion of 1997. He said that gold and short-term credit 'behaved like a loose cannon on the deck of the world in a tempest tossed era'.

The devaluation of the pound in 1931 did not stem directly from the banking crisis in Austria. It emerged from a series of overlapping crises which cumulatively undermined investor confidence in national economic policies and institutions. In retrospect, it can be seen that the 1997 financial contagion has followed a similar course. The magnitude of the contagion has resulted from investors re-evaluating their perceptions of risk in response to a series of events which cumulatively revealed new information about the vulnerability of particular countries and international institutions and about the character of the global financial system itself.

The Thai devaluation caused investors to focus on the large current account deficits and dollar liabilities of the ASEAN countries, so investors sold all the currencies in the region. When Thailand and Malaysia let their currencies depreciate, their corporate sectors reinforced the selling pressure on the local currencies by rushing to hedge dollar liabilities. Indonesia also startled investors and local corporations by floating its exchange rate despite the fact that it already had much wider target bands than other Asian countries. The Indonesia decision to float confirmed to investors that ASEAN had descended onto the slippery slope of a competitive devaluation process which might become uncontrollable.

The announcement of the IMF program for Thailand briefly boosted confidence because it was a broad-based multilateral effort encompassing many countries in the region, including China. But, in retrospect, it also exposed an emerging power vacuum in the region. The United States did not play any role in the program because the Treasury was still constrained by the restrictions on the use of its exchange stabilisation fund imposed by the Congress in the aftermath of the Mexican crisis. Japan also provided only US$4 billion despite its large direct investment and bank lending exposure to Thailand. In the months before the baht devaluation, some Japanese officials had suggested that they intended to play a much larger role in promoting regional financial stability through both bilateral and multilateral assistance.

The next event which rocked investor confidence was Taiwan's decision to allow its currency to float down in mid-October. Taiwan has such a large stock of foreign exchange reserves that few investors perceived that it would have to let the currency depreciate. As a result, its devaluation immediately encouraged heavy selling of the Hong Kong dollar and Korean won. Hong Kong defended its currency by letting interest rates rise. The selling pressure on the won only reinforced Korea's problem in rolling over its large stock of dollar-denominated foreign bank loans. Indonesia then announced an IMF program, which boosted investor confidence temporarily, especially as it was reinforced by currency intervention on behalf of the rupiah from Singapore and Japan. The US Treasury was also able to play a role in the IMF program for Indonesia because of the expiration of congressional restrictions on the use of the exchange stabilisation fund and the impact of global stock market volatility on congressional attitudes towards helping Asian countries. But the benefits of the Indonesian aid program were soon offset by reports of a sharp deterioration in the health of President Soeharto. Indonesia's wealthy Chinese business leaders have long benefited from their close relationship to the Soeharto family and thus moved capital offshore when concerns about his health became serious. The Soeharto family itself also moved several billion dollars offshore during late 1997. Meanwhile, the run on Korea's banks by global creditors was forcing them to sell foreign securities in order to boost liquidity. As Korean banks had large holdings of Russian treasury bills and Brady bonds, their financing problems generated immediate liquidity contagion effects on the securities in which they had invested. The collapse of the won also intensified investor concerns about the risk of a new wave of competitive devaluations throughout Asia. Since Japan was struggling with both a recession and a banking crisis, practically everyone perceived the yen to be vulnerable to a competitive devaluation by Korea. As Korea also competes directly with Taiwan in many industrial sectors, investors naturally extrapolated won depreciation into a further reason to sell the currencies of Greater China, including both the Taiwan and Hong Kong dollars. Ironically, the only pillar of stability in the whole East Asian region has been China itself. As it has a non-convertible currency, the hedge funds could not sell its currency on a large scale, while the government maintains tight controls on the movement of funds through its capital account. China's domestic banking system has a large stock of non-performing loans to state enterprises, but, since they are denominated in yuan, they can be dealt with through domestic monetary policy. China has only US$32.6 billion of foreign currency loans to its local corporations and about US$22 billion are spread over 50 different companies, including some with exposure to foreign exchange earnings from transportation services.

It is easy to identify turning points in the evolution of the crisis which might have influenced investors and altered the outcomes. If Japan had provided Thailand with US$10 billion rather than US$4 billion, investors might have perceived it as a stronger regional leader capable of altering outcomes in several countries.

The failure of Japan to effectively address its banking crisis also magnified the funding problems of the Asian countries with large dollar debts. At the end of 1996, Japanese banks had US$119 billion of loans to countries in the region, compared with US$42 billion for German banks, US$38 billion for French banks, US$34 billion for US banks, and US$26 billion for British banks. The capital adequacy problems of Japanese banks have set in motion a credit crunch within Japan which has had spillover effects on its foreign lending as well. If the government had moved more quickly to bolster its balance sheets through preferred stock purchases or some form of debt reconstruction program, it might not have slashed credit flows to Korea and other countries as abruptly as it did during the autumn of 1997. The Bank of Japan pumped huge amounts of liquidity into the financial system during the closing weeks of 1997, but it came too late to rescue the banks from investor perceptions of insolvency which then magnified their capital adequacy problems by further depressing the value of the Tokyo stock market.

The Ministry of Finance has issued reports claiming that Japanese banks have only about 27 trillion yen of non-performing loans, but a recent audit by government examiners acknowledged that the potential stock of problem loans could be as large as 79 trillion yen. The combination of problem loans and falling equity prices is forcing Japanese banks to retrench their lending all over the world and, in the case of the United States, to sell retail subsidiaries which they have been developing for several decades. Korea has been especially vulnerable to the Japanese banking crisis because Japanese banks were sympathetic to the country's economic development model and loaned heavily to Korean *chaebol*. The Japanese government's de facto credit rating agency, the Japan Center for International Finance, even gave Korea one of its highest credit ratings for any developing country. In June 1997, it rated Korea as a B+ credit, compared with C- for Brazil, C for Indonesia, the Philippines and India, C- for Thailand and B for Malaysia. Korea's decision to implement Japan's economic development model with Japanese bank lending at a time when that model was being abandoned within Japan itself created multiple risks for the Korean economy. Its high level of investment contributed to a capacity glut in highly cyclical industries, which depressed export prices at the same time as the financial contagion was reducing access to foreign bank lending. Just as the Great Depression of the

1930s began with agricultural price deflation for commodity-producing countries on the periphery of the world economy, so the Asian slump of 1997 resulted in part from capacity gluts caused by overinvestment in sectors manufacturing semiconductors and other electronic components.

The US government has tried to play a pragmatic role in the crisis by promoting the IMF as the dominant agency for providing financial assistance to troubled countries and imposing economic restructuring programs on them. When some Asian countries proposed the creation of an Asian monetary fund to complement the role of the IMF, the United States tried to discourage the development of any institution which might conceivably compete with it. Yet, the United States itself has not been able to bolster the IMF's capital because of congressional opposition to the New Agreement to Borrow, the proposal to expand the IMF's capital by US$47 billion which was announced by the major industrial countries in January. The desire of the US government to play a dominant role in the crisis through its influence over the IMF, without providing any new funding, did little to bolster investor confidence. It demonstrated yet again that there was a financial power vacuum in the Asia region quite different from the situation which had prevailed in Latin America at the time of the Mexican crisis in 1995.

The Asian countries also contributed to the severity of the crisis by responding too slowly to evidence of mismanagement in their banking systems and dollar overleveraging in their corporate sectors. Instead of reacting to their currency weakness in a cool and logical fashion, as did the Mexican and Argentine governments during the 1995 peso crisis, some politicians engaged in witch hunts, attacking foreign speculators such as the New York hedge funds. The prime minister of Malaysia was the most destructive player in this game of scapegoating. If he had remained silent, the currencies of ASEAN would probably have declined less precipitously.

As with the contagion crisis of 1931, the East Asian crisis of 1997 did not stem from a single factor. It was the by-product of several different factors interacting together, including speculative lending excesses within several Asian economies, the decadence of the Japanese banking system, the increasing isolationism of the US Congress, the propensity towards overshooting in the high-technology financial markets of the late twentieth century, and the arrogance and venality of political leadership in Asian countries which had been among the major beneficiaries of surplus global liquidity flowing to emerging markets during the early 1990s. There was no simple way for policymakers to cope with the contagion effects of such divergent factors converging simultaneously. They responded through a series of ad hoc programs, developed on a country basis as the crisis spread. But the scope of the crisis has been so global that the debate about its consequences will not end with a few IMF economic restructuring programs. In 1998 and after, there will be a far-reaching debate about the whole character of the post cold war financial system and whether it has created a propensity for overshooting in capital flows and financial market behaviour which requires new forms of regulatory supervision.

MEXICO AS A ROLE MODEL FOR ASIA

The Mexican economy enjoyed a spectacular recovery from the financial collapse and recession which followed the peso devaluation of late 1994. After contracting by 6.2% during 1995, output growth revived to 5.2% during 1996 and 7.4% during 1997. The current account deficit fell from US$29.7 billion during 1994 to only US$1.6 billion during 1995 as a result of exports increasing 33% while imports declined by nearly 13%. After contracting by 12.8% during 1995, domestic demand grew by 6.2% during 1996 and 9% during 1997. The unemployment rate should also return to its pre-1995 level of 3.6% during 1998, after rising to 6.3% during 1995.

The Mexican economy was far better positioned for recovery from the 1995 crisis than it had been at the time of the 1982 debt default. First, the movement into GATT (General Agreement on Tariffs and Trade) and NAFTA had already set the stage for a significant restructuring of the economy away from import substitution to exports. As a result, the non-oil export share of GDP shot up to nearly 30% during the mid-1990s, compared with numbers below 5% during the mid-1980s.

Second, Mexico's ability to avoid default permitted it to regain access to global financial markets far more quickly than had been possible during the 1980s. Mexico was able to re-enter the security markets only six months after the 1994 peso devaluation, whereas the 1982 default had kept it out of the market for nearly seven years.

Third, the political consensus in favour of NAFTA and globalisation remained so firm in Mexico, despite the 1994–5 crisis, that foreign companies did not curtail their investment in the country. The level of FDI should rise to US$12 billion in 1998, from US$2–3 billion per annum during the late 1980s. Foreign portfolio capital also returned to Mexico's equity market after the crisis and helped to push the market to new highs during 1997.

Fourth, Mexico moved decisively to stabilise its banking system through a combination of government intervention and relaxation of barriers to foreign investment in the financial services sector. Only three of the nineteen banks which were privatised during 1991 still have their same managements. Some were taken over by the government, while several were sold to foreign financial institutions from the United States, Britain, Canada and Spain. Foreign-controlled banks now account for nearly one-third of bank assets. The government intervention in the banking system was expensive. The government formed an agency to purchase troubled loans and it currently has about US$65 billion of assets on its balance sheet. The banks will retain some residual liability for the cost of the rescue program but most of the burden will be borne by Mexican taxpayers. There has been great criticism of the bailout program in the Mexican Congress but the government has defended its strategy on the grounds that the only alternative would have been renationalisation of the banks. The problem for the economy is that the banks have attempted to rebuild their capital through extraordinarily high levels of real interest rates on new loans, while lending policies have become so cautious that many firms are suffering from a credit crunch.

The Mexican government was able to respond decisively to the 1995 peso crisis in part because of the PRI's long-standing dominance of the country's political system, but the crisis reinforced the other trends already underway encouraging political liberalisation. The reliance upon the IMF and the US Treasury for emergency funding intensified the pressure on the Mexican government to continue the liberalisation program which had begun during the Salinas years. This process culminated in a victory for Mexico's opposition parties in the elections for both the Mexican Congress and the office of Mayor of Mexico City during the summer of 1997. Such an electoral outcome would have been regarded as inconceivable in the era before NAFTA and confirmed that the liberalisation process set in motion by NAFTA could not stop with the commercial marketplace.

It is difficult to imagine the economies of East Asia experiencing as rapid a recovery from their crisis as Mexico enjoyed during 1996 and 1997. They have inherited a much greater problem with external dollar liabilities than Mexico faced three years ago. They also depend upon intraregional trade for almost 60% of their exports and the regional marketplace will remain weak for at least another 12–18 months. There is also a much greater risk of political instability in some Asian countries than was the case with Mexico in 1995. President Soeharto of Indonesia has resigned and it is unclear who will assume the presidency when the country finally has a free election. The election of the new Korean president coincided with the financial crisis and he enjoys broad popular support, but he does not control the parliament and the trade union movement could be far more disruptive of his reform program than were Mexico's unions. The economic crisis in Indonesia has also unleashed a wave of ethnic hostility towards the Chinese which could depress the confidence of both domestic and foreign investors on a much greater scale than did Mexico's problems with the Chiapas insurgency in 1995.

What remains to be seen is whether the length and severity of the Asian recession will jeopardise the transition, which was already occurring before the crisis, towards more open and democratic political systems. The situation in each country is quite different. Korea's crisis probably helped to elect Kim Dae-jung and he has responded to it by embracing the IMF–American proposals for more economic liberalisation. In Thailand, the crisis helped to promote the campaign for constitutional reforms designed to reduce the influence of bribery and corrupt rural politicians in the government. The parliament also elected a new prime minister in November 1997 from the pro-reform Democratic party whose election defeat in 1995 had helped to set the stage for the crisis. In the case of Indonesia, the economic crisis destroyed the credibility of the Soeharto government and has set in motion political changes which might not otherwise have occurred for another generation. But the risk is high that such a rapid transition to multi-party competitive democracy could promote populism and anti-Chinese bigotry on a scale which Indonesia has not experienced since the Sukarno years. In such a scenario, the economy would continue to deteriorate and produce such widespread social instability that there would be no realistic alternative to military rule.

The fact that Asia has decided to respond to the economic crisis through further liberalisation rather than a siege economy model is less surprising than it was in the case of Mexico. In the modern era, the countries of East Asia have been major beneficiaries of the growth of world trade and the development of global financial markets. Mexico, by contrast, had a relatively closed economy until the late 1980s and has had a checkered history as a capital importer. The theme of resisting American imperialism has also been a more prominent feature of Mexican political history than of East Asia's. The resilience of the support for NAFTA and the open economy model in Mexico is therefore a powerful confirmation of how far intellectual attitudes have evolved in developing countries since the end of the cold war. There was little support in Mexico for a return to the closed economy, despite the fact that the country experienced a sudden economic collapse which devastated the middle class and undermined the promises of the political elite. It is possible that Mexico's presidential election in the year 2000 will produce a greater test for the open economy model than has occurred so far, but the fact that no serious contender is proposing to overturn NAFTA suggests that the basic thrust of the reforms will endure irrespective of the outcome.

The resilience of the support for the open economy in Mexico and Asia's traditional success with exports suggests that the reforms now being imposed by the IMF in countries such as Korea will also endure. There may be a political reaction at some point to foreign takeovers of major companies and the cost of bank bailouts but, as with Mexico, there is broad acceptance of the policy changes designed to promote more open and transparent financial systems.

Ironically, the great controversy about the role of the IMF in the current crisis has been in the US Congress, not in the East Asian countries actually implementing IMF programs. There is a remarkable coalition of left-wing Democrats and conservative Republicans who oppose new funding for the IMF on the grounds that it primarily protects bankers, not ordinary people, and that the existence of the IMF creates moral hazard risks which encourage irresponsible credit policies at banks. The end of the cold war has also lessened public support for the United States playing as active an international role as it did previously. If the US Congress refuses to provide new capital for the IMF, it is unclear how the organisation will respond to future financial crises. The United States will not want to lose the veto power which goes with its 18% shareholding by permitting other countries to expand their capital positions. There is great political resistance to the IMF borrowing directly from the markets on the grounds that such an action would reduce its democratic accountability.

As a result of these constraints, it is possible that the IMF's funding problems could revive a debate about the feasibility of regional monetary funds to complement its resources. The Japanese vice minister of finance, Mr Eisuke Sakakibara, had proposed such a fund during the autumn of 1997 but it had been dismissed by the US government on the grounds that it could undermine the authority of the IMF. Yet, if the US government is unable to provide adequate funding for the IMF, there could be renewed support for regional funds. The countries of East Asia do not have as large a surplus of foreign exchange reserves as they enjoyed before the recent crisis, but the level of reserves is so high in Japan, China, Singapore, Hong Kong and Taiwan that the countries of the region could produce a credible fund if they had the desire to cooperate in such a fashion. Such a fund would then open the door to East Asia having more influence over the content and implementation of IMF programs than any other region of the world.

The East Asian crisis unfolded so quickly and with so little warning, compared with the history of Latin America's financial crises, that it would be risky to make definitive forecasts about its long-run consequences until the region can actually see the first signs of recovery. But on the basis of the reaction so far, it is possible to draw some tentative conclusions. First, the region will continue to embrace the model of an open economy. As a result, the IMF reforms will set the stage for the introduction of far more open and transparent financial systems than existed previously. There will also be a significant expansion of the role of foreign financial institutions in most countries because of the need to obtain new capital. As with Mexico and Argentina since 1995, changes in foreign market share which might have occurred over 20 years could be compressed into two or three years.

Second, the introduction of more open and transparent financial systems should improve the allocation of capital and encourage a higher level of corporate profitability. The aging of Asia's population and the rise of pension funds would have set the stage for greater emphasis on shareholder accountability and profitability over the long term, but the crisis will accelerate the speed of this transition. In the case of Korea, the level of FDI is also likely to rise from only 3–4% of GDP to at least 20–25% of GDP. Such a large rise in the level of FDI will help to make the Korean economy far more open and will represent a significant break with the Japanese development model which has dominated government economic policy in the modern era. In Japan, FDI is still less than 1% of GDP and has been a major contributing factor to the trade tensions with other countries.

Third, the crisis will create the risk of social and political turmoil by boosting unemployment and by reversing some of the substantial increases in wealth of the indigenous (non-Chinese) people which had occurred since the 1970s. The governments of the region will therefore have to complement the movement towards more open and competitive financial systems with increased spending on unemployment insurance and welfare. If Asian corporations can no longer afford to guarantee full employment because of more demanding shareholders, governments will have to compensate through expanded welfare programs.

Fourth, the crisis in East Asia has demonstrated that a potential balance of power vacuum exists in the region. The United States was slow to respond to the Thailand crisis because of congressional criticism of the Mexico rescue package of 1995. Japan provided far more assistance for the second tier of funding in the three IMF programs than the United States did (US$19 billion, compared with US$8 billion), but the crisis in its own economy and banking system has crippled its ability to play a credible leadership role. As the scope of the crisis became more apparent, the Clinton administration moved more decisively to provide aid and to organise IMF rescue programs, but it did not enjoy the full support of the US Congress. As a result, it is unclear if the IMF will be able to obtain adequate capital to cope with future crises. The constraints on American power suggest that East Asia may want to go further than Latin America has so far gone in developing regional strategies for sharing foreign exchange reserves and recycling liquidity during periods of financial tension. The problems which the IMF has encountered in establishing conditionality terms for aid suggests that such cooperation will not be easy, but if American isolationism cripples the multilateral institutions there may be no alternative.

Aside from the US Congress, the other political wildcard in the East Asia crisis is China. It has so far earned great international and regional applause by adhering to a stable exchange rate and by promising to stimulate its economy through expanded spending on infrastructure. But with the government's emphasis on structural reform through privatisation likely to boost unemployment, it is unclear how long China will be willing to maintain a stable currency. It also has mixed views about regional monetary cooperation. It made small contributions to the IMF programs but opposed the Japanese proposal for a regional monetary fund because of fears that Japan would probably dominate it. China will inevitably challenge any proposal which appears likely to promote Japanese hegemony, even if the alternative is increased power for organisations which depend primarily upon US leadership, such as the IMF. China will also resist any proposal for regional financial cooperation which encompasses Taiwan. The Chinese apprehension about Japan and the opposition to Taiwan suggest that the process of regional monetary cooperation will probably evolve incrementally. The IMF will probably continue to play a dominant role, but it may compensate for capital inadequacy by promoting programs which have a larger tier of second-line financing from countries in the region, such as Japan, Singapore, Australia and China.

The Latin American nations have such a long history of working with the IMF that they have had few discussions about regional monetary cooperation. But with the Mercosur countries now debating the feasibility of a regional central bank, it is not inconceivable that there could be more emphasis on regional monetary cooperation, including recycling foreign exchange reserves during periods of crisis. The aid program for Mexico in 1995 included some regional contributions and it would not be difficult to imagine Argentina providing help to Brazil if it experiences another currency crisis. But since Latin America has only modest foreign exchange reserves, investors will not regard regional cooperation as a credible alternative to the IMF during the next few years.

The major risk to the countries of East Asia remaining supporters of the open economy model will be the world business cycle. Will the Japanese economy remain in recession and thus dampen their export potential? Will the easy monetary policy which the United States is pursuing to help East Asia produce a bubble economy followed by a stock market crash and recession before the region can recover? Will Europe fail to recover from high unemployment because of structural economic rigidities colliding with the loss of interest rate and exchange rate autonomy resulting from monetary union?

The countries of East Asia became important growth locomotives in the world economy during the 1980s. As they accounted for half of all world output growth and two-thirds of global capital investment in the years immediately preceding the crisis, their downturns are both depressing commodity prices and creating capacity gluts in steel, petrochemicals, shipbuilding, autos, and semiconductors and other electronic goods. The losses which portfolio managers and banks have experienced in East Asia have also depressed capital flows to all emerging market economies and thus produced stock market corrections in Latin America and Eastern Europe, not just Asia. The weakness of commodity prices has encouraged selling pressures as well against the currencies of resource-oriented economies such as Russia, South Africa and Australia.

The G7 central banks understand the risks posed by the East Asia slump. They have decided to keep interest rates stable despite falling unemployment in the United States and increasing signs of recovery in Europe. The bias towards easy monetary policy in the United States has helped to trigger further gains in the equity market and such strong growth of domestic consumption that deterioration of the trade account has not prevented total output growth from exceeding 4%. The buoyant financial markets in North America and Europe have also helped to create an appetite for speculative investment in the depressed equity markets of East Asia. Several firms have announced the establishment of large Asia-recovery funds to help troubled companies to recapitalise themselves. In the case of Thailand, the two leading banks have already raised nearly US$2 billion from such investors, while a Thai steel company was able to recapitalise itself through the sale of a convertible bond.

The problem is the magnitude of the debt overhang in East Asia, compared with the pool of speculative capital available for corporate restructuring from foreign investors. The ratios of external debt to GDP in East Asia today exceed Latin America's during the early 1980s. In 1997, they were 114% in Indonesia, 97% in Thailand, 91% in the Philippines, 62% in Korea and 53% in Malaysia, compared with 79% in Argentina, 52% in Mexico and 35% in Brazil during 1982. In contrast to Latin America, most of this debt is in the private sector, not governments and state enterprises. As a result of exchange rate depreciation and recession, there will still have to be a significant write-down of corporate debt in Korea, Indonesia, Thailand and Malaysia, while governments will probably have to absorb a large share of the cost of restructuring domestic banks. Bank analysts estimate that the stock of bad loans in the banks is equal to 51% of GDP in Korea, 48% in Thailand, 27% in Indonesia and 19% in Malaysia. The cost of rescuing banks from such a large stock of bad debt will fall primarily on the public sector and thus cause government expenditures to rise at a time when tax receipts are suffering from the recession. As most Asian countries have low ratios of public debt to GDP, they should have few problems financing the bank rescues, but, as with Mexico, the scope of the bad debt problem will inhibit private sector lending and domestic consumption for several years.

The critical element of the adjustment process which G7 central banks will not be able to control is the large swings which will have to occur in their countries' trade accounts. The United States and Europe understand that they will have to permit their trade balances to deteriorate during 1998 because of the Asian slump. In the case of the United States, it could be argued that the expanding trade deficit is actually benign because it is helping to restrain inflationary pressure in a full employment economy. But if the US economy slows during 1999 and after, there could be more complaints about the large size of the US trade deficit. The Latin American debt crisis of the early 1980s also increased the US trade deficit but more through lost export sales than increased import competition. The Latin American nations depended heavily upon commodity production and thus did not respond to their country's currency depreciation through increased exports of manufactured goods. East Asia, by contrast, will be exporting manufactured goods aggressively because of the collapse which has occurred in its domestic consumption.

The isolationist spirit now apparent in the US Congress has not yet produced an upsurge of support for protectionist trade legislation, but such a danger could develop if the US economy slows sharply and unemployment increases. The odds of such a downturn are not high during 1998 because the East Asia crisis is restraining inflationary pressures and allowing monetary policy to remain expansionary. The greater risk in the United States is that the easy monetary policy designed to help Asia could produce a bubble economy followed by a crash in 1999 or 2000. There are increasing signs of speculative excesses in the US equity market and real estate market. The capitalisation of the US equity market has risen to nearly 140% of GDP, the highest ratio ever recorded in US history. (The previous high was 82% in 1929.) The price/earnings multiple of the market has risen close to 30, despite the fact that the United States is now in the eighth year of a business cycle and vulnerable to a squeeze on corporate profit margins. Commercial real estate prices rose at double-digit levels during both 1996 and 1997, while sales of new homes are at the highest level in several years. Meanwhile, the population of share owners has risen to nearly 70 million and the mutual fund industry now has larger assets (US$5 trillion) than the banking system. If there were to be a sudden large correction in the US equity market, it would have a greater impact on household wealth and confidence than any other bear market of the modern era. It would probably also depress business investment by raising the cost of capital at a time when profit margins are starting to erode.

The stock market has become such an important factor that future economic historians may someday argue that the 1990s was an age of rotating bubbles, in which Japan and East Asia developed bubble economies in response to the declining US dollar and easy domestic monetary policy, with the Federal Reserve then having to imitate in order to help compensate for the financial consequences of the Asian bubbles imploding.

At this point there is no way to predict whether the Federal Reserve and other G7 central banks will be able to fine-tune soft deflations of overvalued equity markets. The only great certainty is that monetary policy will have to remain expansionary and run risks on the side of ease in order to help East Asia recover from the structural problems with corporate debt and overinvestment which resulted from the lending boom of the early 1990s. The policies which the IMF and the US Treasury have imposed upon East Asia will ultimately create the preconditions for economic recovery and the emergence of much stronger financial systems in the region than existed previously. But these policies cannot work in isolation or without external assistance. They will have to be supported by a steadily expanding global economy through the early years of the twenty-first century.

Part VI

Policy implications

17 The role of prudential regulation

George Fane

INTRODUCTION

This chapter discusses the prudential regulation of financial institutions in Indonesia, Malaysia and Thailand (henceforth 'the ASEAN3') in light of the financial crises of 1997–8. All three countries implemented elaborate systems of prudential controls well before the onset of the crises. In Thailand and Indonesia the controls clearly proved to be inadequate. In comparison, Malaysia's financial system appears to have been relatively robust. However, its crisis is not yet over, and the suspicion that the authorities may have papered over major problems has not yet been disproved.[1]

It is clear that financial collapses played an important part in the recent slump in real growth in Asia. This chapter does not try to determine whether deposit guarantees and inadequate prudential controls were amongst the main exogenous causal factors, or just part of the transmission mechanism; rather, its more limited objective is to provide a brief overview of the techniques of prudential regulation and their weaknesses, to describe the main controls used in the three countries discussed and how they performed in the crisis, and finally to derive the lessons of this experience for prudential regulation.

TECHNIQUES OF PRUDENTIAL REGULATION

Even if they are not fully understood, the apparent importance of such phenomena as contagion and panics demonstrates that excessive risk-taking by financial institutions may impose external costs on other firms. Given this, a case can be made that the provision of financial safety nets, backed by prudential regulations to limit moral hazard, is the best way to limit such costs. To make this latter case it is necessary to argue that the combined effect of safety nets and prudential regulations is to make the financial system stronger, not weaker. The validity of this view is subject to considerable doubt.

Most governments provide financial institutions with two safety nets: last resort lending and bailouts for depositors in banks that become insolvent. Since banks only benefit from safety nets if they get into difficulty, these policies are contingent subsidies to risk-taking. They therefore generate moral hazard: if taxpayers bear some of the costs of failure, banks that take large risks can attract deposits from more prudent banks while offering much smaller premiums on deposit interest rates than would otherwise be needed. With safety nets in place, competition for deposits therefore forces banks to hold excessively risky asset portfolios; in addition, they have an incentive to be too highly geared, so as to raise the proportion of their investments that is financed by guaranteed deposits. To limit moral hazard, prudential controls must be imposed when safety nets are provided.

The question as to whether the adverse effects of the moral hazard induced by safety nets outweigh the caution induced by prudential regulations must be approached on a case-by-case basis, since the answer presumably depends on the design and implementation of both the safety nets and the prudential regulations. It is at least very interesting that, even in industrialised countries, banks appear to take risks in excess of those taken by other firms; for example, US banks are of the order of ten times as highly geared as manufacturing companies.[2] Such very high gearing would not arise in the absence of safety nets, since depositors would then exercise the prudence for which regulators are now responsible. Capital–assets ratios of US banks averaged 30% to 35% in the late nineteenth century and 20% in 1910, before the creation of the Federal Reserve System. Partly as a result of this market-induced prudence, losses to depositors at all US commercial banks in the period 1865–1933 – before the introduction of compulsory deposit insurance, but including the bank failures of the Great Depression – averaged a trivial 21 cents per year per $100 of deposits (Benston et al. 1986: 63–4).

In addition to being highly geared, banks take risks by borrowing short to lend long; indeed, it is often asserted that this is in the nature of banks' business, although it would be more accurate to say that such a high-risk strategy is natural for a business most of whose liabilities are guaranteed by taxpayers.

In the final section of the chapter, it will be argued that bailouts for depositors are probably inevitable in the case of locally incorporated financial institutions, but not in the case of local branches of international banks. The policy implications of this proposition for both the supervision and opening of the banking sector to foreign competition are also discussed. In practice, the protection of domestic banks in the ASEAN3 has been pervasive and, to the limited extent that they have been allowed to compete at all, international banks have usually been forced to set up locally incorporated subsidiaries. Therefore, little is lost by assuming, as I shall assume until the final section, that all financial institutions must be locally incorporated.

The assumption that explicit or implicit deposit guarantees of locally incorporated institutions are a fact of life, rather than something for policymakers to adopt or reject, combined with the temporary assumption that non-locally incorporated banks are largely excluded, yields very straightforward implications for prudential regulation: there is then an overwhelming case for such regulation, and the policy problem is reduced to finding the prudential controls that will best reduce moral hazard and fraud. Until the final section, this chapter is restricted by these simplifying assumptions.

The main tools of prudential regulation are minimum ratios of capital to assets – or to risk-weighted assets, as recommended by the Basle Convention on capital adequacy; limits on lending to individual borrowers; limits on lending to 'related' firms (that is, firms controlled by the same owners, or managers, as the lending bank); minimum ratios of reserves to deposits; limits on exposure to currency and interest rate risks; and compulsory disclosure of performance in relation to these criteria.

Minimum capital–assets ratios (CARs) are the best way to check moral hazard. They have the same rationale as the deductible, or 'excess', amounts which private insurance companies usually require as a way of limiting the moral hazard problems that arise in any insurance contract: full deposit insurance is equivalent to asset insurance, subject to the insurer being liable only for the excess of total losses over capital. Similarly, setting a minimum required reserve ratio against bank deposits could play the role of the basic premium in a private insurance contract: if the interest rate paid by the central bank on required reserves is less than the interbank interest rate, the effective payment by each commercial bank to the central bank, per dollar of deposits insured – in effect, the 'premium' per dollar of insurance cover – is the difference between the interest rate in the interbank market and the interest rate on required reserves, multiplied by the ratio of required reserves to deposits. A combination of CARs and required reserve ratios could therefore roughly replicate a private insurance contract, and so the commonly made assertion that reserve requirements are a distorting tax on banking is therefore only valid to the extent that they exceed what can be justified as the cost of providing deposit insurance. In practice, Southeast Asian countries have not used reserve requirements in this way, but rather as a way of shifting the cost of sterilising capital inflows from central to commercial banks (McLeod 1998a: 24–5).

The problems potentially created when banks lend to related firms should perhaps be classified as problems of fraud, rather than moral hazard. Fraud aside, lending to a related firm is not any more intrinsically risky than lending to any other single borrower; in fact, the problems of asymmetric information, which arise because borrowers have an incentive to conceal risks from lenders, are likely to be less serious in the case of lending to related borrowers than in other cases. The special problem created when banks lend to related firms is that the owners and managers may try to disguise fraud as bad luck. In the most blatant case, a bank can transfer deposits to a related borrower under the pretence that the transfer is a loan, even though there is actually no expectation that the 'loan' will be repaid.

At the very least, this makes the bank's true capital less than it appears to be, and deposits are therefore correspondingly more risky than they appear to be. A similar, but less blatant, fraud arises if owners and managers give loans to related firms on more favourable terms than those on which they lend to others. The risk that bank 'lending' to related firms may be fraudulent arises even in the absence of guarantees for depositors; in the presence of such guarantees, supervisors need to guard against possible fraud, since depositors need no longer be concerned about whether 'loans' are repaid or not.

If adequate limits on lending to related firms are in place to control fraud, if capital requirements are adequate to control moral hazard, and if disclosure rules are also in place, then the profit motive provides incentives for banks to take adequate prudential measures, without the need for supervision of other aspects of their operations. Supervisors should therefore concentrate on these three essentials, rather than trying to control all aspects of banks' behaviour. Given the inevitable informational advantage of managers over supervisors, the attempt to control all aspects of banks' behaviour is, in any case, probably doomed to failure.

The use of minimum capital–assets ratios has three potential weaknesses. First, measured capital adequacy responds only with long lags to true capital adequacy. If the probability that a loan will be repaid falls, a bank's true capital falls immediately by the same amount as the fall in the present value of expected loan repayments. However, reported capital usually declines much more slowly: in the absence of new equity issues, a bank's reported capital only changes when its accounts are presented, and this may happen only every three or six months. In terms of financial crises, these are long delays. In industrialised countries, central banks may demand to be kept informed about changes in non-performing loans on a monthly, or even weekly, basis. But having up-to-the-minute information on what loans have been classified as non-performing may not serve any great purpose, particularly in developing countries, because in practice there are often delays of several quarters between loan repayments falling into arrears and banks having to classify the loans as non-performing, and therefore to make provisions for them. Second, enforcing capital requirements when banks get into financial difficulties can worsen a panic among depositors and other creditors. Third, enforcing capital requirements can cause banks to try to conceal non-performing loans by rolling them over. This increases the moral hazard created by deposit insurance: as a bank's true capital falls towards zero, it has less and less to lose from excessive risk-taking.

To minimise these weaknesses, capital adequacy must be high in normal times. Tight rules on loss-provisioning and loan classification are also required, and regulators must act quickly to insist that, if an institution's measured capital adequacy falls below the minimum, it must restore its CAR to the required level, or merge with a stronger institution, or be closed down. To restore its CAR, it must either cut back on lending, or inject new equity – which often involves offering new shares to stronger banks, domestic or foreign, at a discounted price.

THE SEQUENCING OF FINANCIAL SECTOR REFORMS

In all three countries discussed here, there has been a substantial tightening of the kinds of controls listed above as being 'prudential', and a substantial deregulation of other financial sector controls such as interest rate ceilings, quotas on minimum lending to 'priority' sectors, and restrictions on new entry and setting up new bank branches.

In the last few years, there has been some partial reregulation of the financial systems in Indonesia and Malaysia and, despite the overall trend towards deregulation of non-prudential controls, domestic banks have always been heavily protected from foreign competition. For example, until recently, each of the 21 foreign banks licensed to operate in Thailand was allowed to open only one branch with a licence to accept local currency deposits; in addition, these branches were severely restricted in the volume of lending they could undertake. Within the last year, these regulations have been somewhat relaxed as a result of commitments under the World Trade Organisation's General Agreement on Trade in Services (GATS), but the number of branches permitted to foreign banks remains very small compared with the number that locally incorporated banks may operate.

In Indonesia, the main banking deregulation reforms occurred in 1983 and 1988. The 1983 package removed lending ceilings on all banks, and most direct controls on interest rates at the state banks; the 1988 package reduced the required reserve ratio from 15% to 2% of deposits, removed most restrictions on setting up new branches, and allowed the entry of new banks other than wholly foreign-owned banks (McLeod 1998a).

After the collapse of Bank Duta in 1990, Indonesia began to make its prudential regulations much more extensive: 599 pages of new regulations were introduced in February 1991. The strategy for extending prudential controls had four main components: the setting of minimum prudential standards; the establishment by the central bank, Bank Indonesia, of a task force to identify and gradually reduce the extent of bad and doubtful loans; the introduction of a system for grading banks according to their 'soundness'; and the establishment of an early warning system under which each bank had to make monthly reports to Bank Indonesia of the values of 45 financial ratios, and to report all individual loans in excess of the equivalent of US$15,000 (Hendrobudiyanto 1994: 164).

Minimum prudential standards were established in relation to several criteria, of which the most important was the phased introduction of the requirement that banks comply with the Basle standard that capital be at least 8% of risk-weighted assets. To help the state banks increase their capital adequacy, new capital was injected using both World Bank loans and funds provided by the government. Minimum standards for asset quality (as measured by the ratio of total earning assets to doubtful and poor loans, and by the proportion of provisions against losses on doubtful and poor loans) were also imposed, and limits were set on lending to related firms and to individual borrowers.

Financial crises in Thailand in 1979 and 1983 provided the spur for attempts in each of those years to overhaul its system of prudential regulation. Further attempts were made to tighten the prudential regulation of banks and finance companies in 1985 (Cole 1995: 244, 250; Johnston 1991).

Since the 1990s, the government has been trying to establish Bangkok as a regional financial centre; the cornerstone of this strategy was its establishment of the Bangkok International Banking Facility in March 1993. A necessary condition for the success of the facility was the removal of ceilings on bank interest rates and bank lending. This provided the stimulus for deregulation of the Thai financial system in the mid-1990s.

In Malaysia, most interest rate controls were initially removed in 1978, but they were reinstated in 1983. Prudential controls were tightened in the period 1983–7 and were in place before the partial relaxation of non-prudential controls in 1987 (Cole 1995: 243, 250). However, Malaysia's financial system remains relatively tightly regulated: there are still some restrictions on interest rates; there are still quantitative minima for lending to 'priority' sectors, such as the indigenous (*Bumiputera*) community, small and medium-sized businesses, and owner-occupied housing; and there are still quantitative ceilings on hire-purchase lending. At the same time, lending for 'productive' purposes is encouraged by moral suasion, backed up by the requirement that financial institutions have to submit credit plans to the central bank, Bank Negara Malaysia (BNM), and by the provision of telephone hotlines, so that those who wish to borrow for such purposes can complain to BNM if their loan applications are refused.

The sequencing of financial reforms in Indonesia was in the opposite order to that usually recommended: the financial sector was deregulated in the 1980s, before the tightening of prudential controls in the 1990s. In contrast, as pointed out by Cole (1995), the sequencing adopted by Thailand followed conventional wisdom: prudential regulations were strengthened before controls over the financial sector were relaxed. The sequencing of reforms in Malaysia after 1983 was similar to that in Thailand, except that Malaysia retained more financial controls.

The large capital inflows of the 1990s led to the introduction, or reintroduction, of several regulations, most of which were at least partly prudential, despite not being among the traditional group of regulations listed above. For example, in April 1997 Malaysia set ceilings on lending to finance the purchase of shares: not more than 15% of all loans by any bank or finance company may be made for the purpose of financing the purchase of shares or unit trusts; for merchant banks, the limit is 20%. Similarly, a limit of 20% was set on the proportion of total loans that financial institutions may devote to the property sector. In Indonesia and Malaysia, controls on bank borrowing from abroad were also imposed, and required reserve ratios were raised.

CAPITAL ADEQUACY AND PROVISIONING

During the 1990s all three countries gradually phased in compliance with the convention that the capital to risk-weighted assets ratio should be at least 8%; however, lax rules for making provisions for non-performing loans have meant that the CAR requirement has really been much less stringent than in the G10 countries. Following the crises of 1997–8, all three have also announced plans to introduce much stricter rules on making provisions for non-performing loans; and in some instances CARs are to be increased.

Before the crisis, Indonesian banks reported CARs well in excess of the 8% minimum. In March 1994, the foreign and joint venture banks had the highest average capital adequacy ratios, at 15.6%; for private banks, the average was 10.8%; and for state banks, 9.8% (Hendrobudiyanto 1994: 160). The figure for state banks has little meaning because, whatever the government may once have said about not guaranteeing deposits, most people have always believed that deposits at state banks are effectively backed by the fiscal power of the government. This belief was justified by the government's handling of the occasional banking difficulties of the 1990s, and reinforced by the issuance of an explicit government guarantee to all banks at the peak of the financial crisis in January 1998. However, since Bank Indonesia used not to disclose information on the CARs of individual banks, the averages for the broad categories of institutions may have concealed CARs of less than 8% for some institutions.

Capital adequacy regulations in Thailand are being amended in three ways: first, new and much stricter rules governing provisioning for non-performing and doubtful loans are to be phased in by the end of 2000. The new provisioning rules have been copied from those used in the United States. Some of the Thai banks already make provisions against losses, using systems almost as strict as those that will become compulsory, but, for others, provisioning will have to be increased by a factor of five or six. Second, the Bank of Thailand (BOT) will in future disclose the capital adequacy information reported to it by individual institutions. Third, the CAR is to be raised from 8% to 8.5% for banks, and to 10% for finance companies.

Malaysia is also adopting US conventions for classifying loans and providing for losses, and the minimum CAR, currently 8% for both banks and finance companies, is to be raised to 8.5% for banks; for finance companies, it is to rise to 10% by the end of 1999. Malaysia began publicly disclosing prudential information on individual banks in 1998; all banks must now disclose their CARs and the extent of their non-performing loans on a quarterly basis. In March 1998, all banks and finance companies, with the exception of Sime Bank, were reported to have had more than the minimum 8% CAR. Sime Bank had a reported CAR of only 2.9% at the end of 1997; it was allowed to continue operating while plans were being made to merge it with a stronger bank.

In addition, BNM now requires banks and finance companies to do a monthly 'stress test', which simulates the effects on their capital adequacy of various adverse shocks. In March 1998, four financial institutions had CARs which would fall below 8% under some of the simulated shocks. The test is an early warning device; only if actual shocks drove a bank's capital adequacy below 8% would it be given deadlines by which to acquire new capital, merge with stronger banks, or be closed down.

RESERVE AND LIQUIDITY RATIOS

Reserve ratios in the ASEAN3 were relaxed in the initial deregulation process, and then raised in the 1990s when the central banks began to shift the costs of sterilising capital inflows onto commercial banks.

The 1988 Indonesian banking reforms reduced the required reserve ratio – which had been 15% of 'current' liabilities, or about 10–11% of all deposits – to only 2% of all deposits (McLeod 1998a: 13). To reduce the costs to Bank Indonesia of sterilising capital inflows, the required reserve ratio was raised to 3% of deposits in February 1996; at the same time, cash-on-hand was excluded from what the banks could count as 'reserves'. Since cash-on-hand formerly made up just over half of reserves, this redefinition by itself roughly doubled the burden of the requirement. In April 1997, the reserve ratio was further increased to 5% (McLeod 1998a: 25).

From June 1996 onwards, Thai banks were required to hold reserves at the BOT equal to 7% against all new short-term borrowings from abroad. The result was that the reserve and liquidity requirement that had previously applied only to domestic deposits was henceforth applied in a more onerous form to foreign borrowing: it applied to all short-term foreign borrowing, not merely deposits; and, in the case of foreign borrowing, the whole 7% had to be in the form of non-interest-bearing baht-denominated deposits at the BOT, whereas for domestic deposits only 2% had to be held in such accounts, since 2.5% could be held as cash-on-hand, and 2.5% as short-term government securities.

Nevertheless, since it does not apply to all foreign borrowings but only to those made by banks, Thailand's reserve and liquidity requirement is not really a capital control, despite its superficial similarity to the type of capital control – once widely used, and still applied in Chile – that requires a non-interest-bearing deposit to be placed at the central bank against all capital inflows other than foreign direct investment. In response to the capital out-flow and tight credit conditions of 1997, the 7% reserve and liquidity requirement was reduced to 6%.

IMPLEMENTATION

Indonesia's prudential regulations proved inadequate, partly because of inadequate enforcement and partly because they were too complex, and failed to focus on the fundamentals. This latter criticism can be illustrated by the system Bank Indonesia used in judging the soundness of commercial banks, which is modelled on the 'CAMEL' criteria – 'Capital', 'Asset quality', 'Management', 'Earnings', and 'Liquidity' – used for judging bank soundness in the United States. Points are allocated to each bank in accordance with its performance on various criteria of soundness, according to an elaborate system described by Habir (1994). One of the main criteria is capital adequacy, but there is no marginal reward for having capital in excess of 10% of total risk-weighted assets, nor any marginal penalty for capital below zero. This has bizarre implications: although a bank with negative capital would be liable to be closed down on that ground alone, its soundness rating could in principle be inside the top category if it scored maximum points on all other tests.

Some of the criteria for measured soundness probably *reduce* true soundness: for example, points are awarded for having a high share of export-oriented loans in total loans, and another criterion awards points for lending to small businesses.[3] If governments wish to subsidise exporters or small businesses, they should at least not do so by encouraging, or forcing, banks to treat loans to these groups on more favourable terms than other loans.

The new prudential regulations introduced in Indonesia in May 1993 imposed a phased reduction in the permitted ratio of bank lending to firms in the same group; the existing limit of 50% of bank capital was to be reduced to 35% by December 1995, and then to 20% by March 1997. However, these regulations seem to have been widely flouted: for example, an investigation by Bank Indonesia in 1993 found that six of the seven state banks had violated the legal lending limits (Fane 1994: 30). It was subsequently reported that, at June 1995, there were six banks with loans to related firms that were more than 200% of the bank's own capital, 23 banks for which the ratio was over 100%, and 42 for which it was over the 50% limit that applied at that time (*Infobank* 1995: 26). Montgomery (1997: 13) reports that in April 1996, according to Bank Indonesia, there were fifteen banks that failed to meet the 8% CAR, 41 that did not comply with legal lending limits, and twelve foreign exchange banks that exceeded the limits on foreign exchange exposure.

GUARANTEES AND EXIT RULES

The worsening financial circumstances of 1997–8 led to the reinforcement of government guarantees to financial institutions. In some cases, formal deposit guarantees replaced informal ones; in others, formal guarantees were issued even though governments had previously insisted that they were not liable for losses to depositors. And, in some cases, guarantees were extended not only to depositors, but also to other creditors.

Even before the baht was allowed to depreciate on 2 July 1997, the rise in interest rates and the collapse of the real estate and stock markets had reduced the capital adequacy of ten finance companies below the minimum required level; this had caused the BOT to demand in March 1997 that these finance companies acquire new capital. Far from being able to improve their capital adequacy, these and other finance companies suffered from further increases in non-performing loans, and the authorities suspended sixteen finance companies in June.

In an attempt to prevent a collapse of confidence in the financial system in the wake of the June closures, the Thai government announced that no other finance companies were in danger of being suspended, and that depositors in the sixteen closed companies would be allowed to exchange their promissory notes for certificates of deposit at a government-owned bank, but with delays during which they would receive interest at somewhat below market rates. Non-deposit creditors in these sixteen institutions were not bailed out by the government; however, in some cases the remaining assets were sufficient to repay at least part of the amounts due to them.

In August 1997, another 42 finance companies were closed; depositors in these institutions were fully bailed out, and non-deposit creditors were partially bailed out. In addition, a general guarantee was issued which promised that in future the government would fully bail out both depositors and other creditors. In December 1997, two of the 58 suspended finance companies were allowed to reopen, while the other 56 were permanently closed.

In the second half of 1997, the pressure of deposit withdrawals from the Thai financial system switched from the finance companies to the banks, and the BOT accordingly provided large last-resort loans from the FIDF (Financial Institutions Development Fund) to the commercial banks. In December 1997 and January 1998, the BOT eventually took over the management, and part of the equity, of three small banks that were in particularly serious difficulties, thus bringing to four the number of banks taken over by the FIDF.[4]

Like Thailand, Indonesia has never had a compulsory deposit insurance scheme, although the government formally guaranteed deposits at the state banks until December 1989. In the period 1983–8 private domestic banks (other than foreign and joint venture banks) offered deposit interest rates that averaged 1.6% per year above those paid by the state banks. Following the removal of the government's formal guarantee of state bank deposits in 1989, the interest premium on deposits at private banks fell only slightly to an average of 1.5% in the period 1989–92 (Marshall 1994: 194).

The fact that the fall in the interest rate differential was so small appears to have reflected a belief that the government would in practice always come to the aid of state banks, formal guarantee or not, whereas depositors at private banks – or at least the holders of large deposits at private banks – could not necessarily count on the government to bail them out in the event of bank failures. The treatment of depositors in the occasional Indonesian bank failures in the early and mid-1990s was consistent with these expectations.

In November 1997, the government closed sixteen small private banks. These closures caused an abrupt loss of confidence in the banking system, partly because Indonesia had no form of deposit insurance or general deposit guarantee, and partly because – in the absence of clearly stated criteria for the closures, and in the absence of disclosure of information on the capital adequacy and other relevant prudential data for individual banks – there was great uncertainty about which banks might be closed next. Although some of the closed banks were insolvent, others were not and appear to have been closed because they had breached the rules on lending to related companies. Since such breaches had been widespread, the uncertainty caused by closing a few of the offending banks should not have been surprising. At the end of January 1998, the government tried to restore confidence by issuing a general guarantee of all deposits and other liabilities (except equity and subordinated debt) at domestically incorporated banks; however, repayment of foreign currency deposits was guaranteed only in rupiah.

In April 1998, another seven small banks were closed, and a further seven larger ones were taken over by the Indonesian Bank Restructuring Agency, which had been set up in February 1998 to oversee the restructuring or liquidation of weak banks.

In Malaysia, the general guarantee issued in 1998 did not extend beyond depositors; but in Thailand and Indonesia, the general guarantees that were issued in response to the crisis applied not only to depositors, but also to non-deposit creditors. These guarantees also reversed the earlier claims by these latter governments that they were not liable for losses suffered by depositors.

FORCED MERGERS

In all three countries, the authorities are trying to force small and medium-sized institutions to merge. In Malaysia small institutions have been given deadlines by which they must either find partners or increase their capital to specified minimum levels; those which fail to meet these minimum levels will be closed down. The increases in minimum size are very substantial: for finance companies, minimum capital is to be raised by a factor of 120 from its current level of RM5 million to RM600 million by the end of 2000.

To encourage the larger institutions to take over smaller ones, Malaysia also provides two further merger incentives. First, institutions that acquire others have been given guarantees that the government will compensate them for losses that result from deterioration of assets in the institution being taken over. The guarantees are subject to various conditions: the acquiring institutions must exercise due diligence; the guarantees apply only to losses incurred in the first twelve months after a merger, and only to losses in excess of those that could have been anticipated, as determined in reviews by international accounting firms (BNM 1998b). Second, Malaysia has introduced a two-tier system of regulations: 'tier one' banks are given privileges denied to 'tier two' banks, and to qualify for tier one status a bank must be large and must also have a high rating according to a series of CAMEL-type tests. One of the privileges of being a tier one bank is the right to accept foreign currency deposits. A similar distinction between tier one and tier two institutions also applies to merchant banks and finance companies. A phased program has been announced to increase the minimum absolute amounts of capital that banks, merchant banks and finance companies must have in order to qualify as tier one institutions. BNM anticipates that its merger program will reduce the number of finance companies from 39 at present to about ten.

Before the bank closures during the crisis, there were about 240 banks in Indonesia. In October 1996, the biggest five owned 39% of all assets, and the biggest ten owned 58% (Djiwandono 1997: 337). Plans for mergers of both state and private banks were announced in January (*Asian Wall Street Journal*, 2–3 and 20 January 1998). In 1998 the government raised the minimum capital requirement for all banks to Rp1,000 billion. This is a twentyfold increase since 1996, when the minimum was only Rp50 billion.[5]

There seems to be no evidence that large financial institutions are necessarily safer than small ones. But it is certainly more convenient for a central bank to have to supervise a few big institutions rather than many little ones. The best way to deal with this problem would be for each bank to pay a supervision fee, set by a schedule which took account of size. Relative to such an arrangement, forced mergers are a very blunt instrument.

LESSONS FROM THE CRISIS

Strengthening prudential regulation is not a matter of imposing more controls, but of focusing on what really matters. The prudential reform that is most needed in the ASEAN3 – and in other developing countries too – is to raise CARs. In Hong Kong, the consolidated capital adequacy ratio for all locally incorporated institutions was about 17.7% at the end of September 1996 (Hong Kong Monetary Authority 1997: 2). In the United States, the average capital adequacy ratio of banks with soundness ratings in the three highest of five CAMEL categories is between 16% and 20% (Roulier 1997: 453). Given the difficulties facing supervisors, the risks to which financial systems in developing countries are exposed, and the enormous losses to which financial collapses can contribute, an appropriate CAR for countries like Indonesia, Malaysia and Thailand might be 20%. Even at this level, banks would still be very highly geared relative to almost all other businesses.

High CARs must be backed by tight rules on classifying doubtful loans and making adequate provisions against them. The ASEAN3 applied excessively lax rules for classifying loans as doubtful or non-performing. While the detailed rules varied from country to country and were very complex, the scope for lags is illustrated by the fact that, in each country, accountants were legally able in certain circumstances to avoid the need to make loss provisions until loan repayments were in arrears by over twelve months. Recent reforms had tightened these rules. The minimum CAR was supposed to allow supervisors to suspend institutions before capital became negative but, because CARs were too low and because loan classification and provisioning rules were too lax, this buffer proved inadequate in the case of several banks in Thailand and Indonesia, and in the case of most of Thailand's finance companies.

The case for prudential controls was part of the conventional wisdom for a long time, and as a consequence detailed controls were set up in all Southeast Asian countries long before the crisis of 1997–8. Commentators such as Cole (1995: 251), Djiwandono (1997), Browne (1997: 349–52) and Montgomery (1997: 4) expressed at least guarded praise for the controls themselves, subject to reservations about the effectiveness of their implementation. It turned out that there had been a chasm between the controls that existed on paper and those that were actually implemented, as the widespread flouting of the prudential regulations had demonstrated even before the crisis occurred.

However, even if they had been fully enforced, it is unlikely that Indonesia's prudential controls would have saved its financial sector; the scattergun approach to supervision, with its massive reporting requirements and inadequate emphasis on capital adequacy, would probably not have been enough to withstand the shock of the more than threefold increase in the ratio of the nominal exchange rate to the consumer price index which occurred between July 1997 and January 1998.[6] Such a shock might have been resisted if CARs had been much higher, if bankruptcy laws had worked better (so that banks could have forced the liquidation of defaulting creditors), and if the financial sector's asset portfolio had not been almost totally concentrated on the domestic economy – and therefore vulnerable to an economy-wide shock.[7] These possibilities are discussed in more detail below.

The events of 1997–8 demonstrated a familiar weakness of all regulations: markets can partially circumvent prudential regulations by moving regulated activities into alternative, unregulated channels. For example, risks that banks are prohibited from taking can be taken by other firms, and if banks lend to these firms they end up being exposed, at least in part, to the risks from which the prudential regulations were supposed to protect them.

The most important example of this in the ASEAN3 was foreign exchange risk. The rules to limit the foreign currency exposure of banks and finance companies that applied in each country largely achieved their immediate objectives: although financial institutions accepted foreign currency deposits and borrowed in foreign currencies offshore, most of them avoided having large foreign currency exposure because they made matching foreign currency loans to domestic firms. While this greatly limited the foreign currency exposure of the supervised institutions, it did so only by replacing it with credit risk: when the nominal and real exchange rates depreciated by large amounts, many of the domestic firms to which banks and finance companies had lent could not repay their loans.

The situation described above was particularly relevant in Thailand. In Indonesia and Malaysia, regulations not only limited the taking of open positions in foreign currencies, but also directly limited offshore borrowing by banks. To circumvent these regulations, domestic firms borrowed directly from offshore banks in foreign currencies, and some also borrowed from domestic banks in domestic currency. In addition, banks accepted foreign currency deposits, which financed foreign currency lending to domestic firms. In short, banks were exposed to borrowers who were themselves exposed to the risk of real exchange rate depreciation. When the real exchange rate collapsed, their bad loans proliferated. The important point is that banks whose loans are concentrated on a single economy are vulnerable to any large movement in its real exchange rate: even though the losses some firms and households suffer when there is a change in the relative prices of traded and non-traded goods must be matched by equal gains for others, banks lose if the changes are large enough to make some of the losers insolvent.[8]

The problems that result from the shifting of risk-taking activities – such as uncovered foreign borrowing – from financial institutions to other companies have been greatly exacerbated by ineffective bankruptcy laws. These problems are highlighted by the very different treatment of financial and other institutions in cases of insolvency. Financial institutions that incur large losses and are unable to attract new equity are liable to be quickly closed and liquidated by the government; indeed, one purpose of capital adequacy and exit rules is to try to ensure that this happens well before their capital becomes negative. In contrast, when other companies become technically insolvent, they generally manage to survive in a limbo in which ineffective bankruptcy laws prevent them from being seized by their creditors, which are often domestic or foreign financial institutions.

The difficulty of collecting debts obviously weakens the financial system and, since technically insolvent companies find it very hard to obtain the working capital they need to operate, another result has been a slump in real output and employment. Thailand has just introduced a new bankruptcy law, and Indonesia plans to do so. These new laws may help, but optimism would be misplaced: the main problem with the old laws appears to have been the reluctance, or inability, of the courts to enforce them.

The failure of the elaborate controls that were in place in Thailand and Indonesia raises the question whether efforts to tighten prudential regulations should be increased or abandoned. In my view, this question is largely answered by the fact that even those governments that claim not to guarantee deposits, and that manage to resist bailing out depositors when just one or a few institutions fail, have ended up by guaranteeing all deposits in locally incorporated institutions when they are faced by widespread financial panics. Indonesia and Thailand extended guarantees not merely to depositors but also to other creditors. Nor is it hard to understand why financial crises cause governments to reverse their pretence in normal times that deposits are not guaranteed: since even the seemingly most secure governments have short time horizons, they grasp at any means of alleviating an immediate crisis, even if the cost is to add to moral hazard and to weaken the financial system in the long run.

Because guarantees have been formalised, and are now applied not only to depositors but also to other creditors, the problems of moral hazard are now even greater than before the crisis. In these circumstances, there is an even greater need than before for effective prudential controls.

However, even in the recent crises, deposits at banks that are not locally incorporated have not been guaranteed. This suggests a case for facilitating the growth of a two-tier banking system. One tier would consist of branches of international banks that would not be locally incorporated, whose deposits would not be guaranteed, and which would be locally supervised only to the extent that entry by such institutions would be at the discretion of the government. The second tier would consist of domestically incorporated banks, which would be subject to domestic supervision, and whose deposits would be guaranteed by the government. These banks might be wholly locally owned, or they might be subsidiaries of international banks. In exchange for the privilege of having their deposits guaranteed by the government, they would be subject both to high CARs and to minimum reserve ratios. The reserve ratios for each bank should be set to make the interest foregone equal to the expected cost to the government of guaranteeing its deposits. The reserve ratio for each bank would ideally depend on its reputation, its CAR, and other measures of its riskiness. In practice, in a world in which official probity cannot be assured, a generally applied ratio equal to the average expected cost of guaranteeing deposits would be more suitable.

Because the pressures to protect their domestic banking systems from foreign competition are very powerful, it is most unlikely that the two-tier system proposed above would be adopted by any of the ASEAN3. However, some of them may well end up with a somewhat similar, though superficially different, outcome. During the last year, the protection of domestic financial institutions from foreign competition has been somewhat relaxed in each country. This has happened partly as a result of commitments under the GATS, and partly because deteriorating capital adequacy has forced banks and regulators to accept injections of foreign equity to help recapitalise weak banking systems and introduce foreign expertise. In Indonesia, the ownership restrictions that applied to domestic banks have been abolished, while those in Thailand and Malaysia have been substantially relaxed.

Given the importance of reputation in banking, the effects of allowing the major international banks to set up locally incorporated subsidiaries is probably very similar to those of allowing them to set up local branches. The capital of a branch is identical to that of the global parent; in the case of a subsidiary, the situation is nominally different, but is really quite similar in practice under the plausible assumption that the parent is willing to bear very large losses rather than risk its good reputation by allowing the subsidiary to fail. Provided that prudential regulations do not impose excessive reporting costs, and focus only on a few important criteria that major international banks generally satisfy anyway, it will not much matter whether international banks are subject to these requirements or not. The model to copy here is New Zealand, where the only prudential controls are CARs, limits on lending to related firms, and strict disclosure rules (Brash 1997).

A major advantage of admitting international banks is that doing so would help protect the local banking systems from their vulnerability to economy-wide shocks. In all countries in Southeast Asia except Hong Kong and Singapore, weak and inward-looking domestic banks have been sheltered from competition from the major international banks, which not only usually have higher capital adequacy ratios, but also have globally diversified portfolios rather than portfolios that are concentrated on a single economy. The lack of global diversification of assets has made Asia's financial systems vulnerable to economy-wide shocks, such as a fall in the terms of trade or a depreciation of the real exchange rate. When adverse economy-wide shocks materialised in 1997–8, the financial systems suffered much more than they would have done if banks had held internationally diversified portfolios.

Governments have long been aware of the fact that protection of some domestic manufacturing industries effectively taxes other sectors, particularly export sectors. Since the 1980s, most governments have therefore been reducing the tariff and non-tariff barriers to trade in goods. The disasters of 1997–8 have shown that sheltering a weak and inward-looking domestic finance sector can impose even greater costs on the rest of the economy than protection of steel, plastics or engineering.

NOTES

1   For evidence of such suspicions, see the predictions of impending bank failures in Malaysia by the President of Thomson BankWatch (*Nation* 8 April 1998), and a report in the *Asian Wall Street Journal* on the same day that President Mahathir had said that he 'would rather support Malaysia's beleaguered banks than allow failures or permit foreigners to take over local institutions'.
2   The average debt to equity ratio was 2.1 for all industries in the United States in 1985, and 1.2 for manufacturing. For commercial banks the ratio was 11 (Dewatripont and Tirole 1994: 23). The ratio of total debt to equity could well be 20 or more for a bank with tier one capital equal to 6% of risk-weighted assets.
3   Habir (1994: 181) notes that some (but probably not many) banks may have relaxed their lending standards on small business loans in order to meet the small business lending criterion.
4   The Bangkok Bank of Commerce had been taken over in 1994.
5   For foreign exchange banks, the increase came in two steps: from Rp50 billion to Rp150 billion in 1996, and then to Rp1,000 billion in 1998. For other banks, the whole increase occurred in 1998.
6   Between July 1997 and January 1998, the exchange rate (Rp/$) rose from 2,518 to 9,663; the CPI (April 1988 – March 1989 = 100) rose from 195.8 to 226.2. The ratio therefore rose by a factor of 3.32.
7   In February 1997, foreign assets were just 4.6% of total assets of the commercial banks (Bank Indonesia 1997: 14).
8   Banks are of course even more vulnerable to a terms-of-trade deterioration, since it would directly damage the whole economy in aggregate.

18 Exchange rate regimes for the future

Alan A. Walters

PLUS ÇA CHANGE

Many years ago, Peter (now Lord) Bauer and I argued (Bauer and Walters 1975) that the great mistakes which have been made in thinking about, as well as applying, economic policy have not been due to the manifest complexities of fashionable economic models; quite the contrary. From our survey we found that the most egregious errors were due to the neglect of the most simple principles of economics. An example: in the late 1940s and early 1950s, the vast majority of the economics profession asserted that there was, and always would be, a 'dollar problem'. (The only prominent exceptions were Milton Friedman, Gottfried Harberler and Egon Sohnen.) Indeed, Sir John Hicks, Oxford's most distinguished economist, devoted his inaugural lecture for the Drummond Chair to that proposition. He said that the dollar shortage was basically due to the fact that all countries wanted the goods produced in America but Americans had no need for foreign-produced goods, ergo the dollar problem. Other luminaries, such as Charles Kindleberger, Sir Donald MacDougal and Tomas (later Lord) Balogh, joined in this view of the seeming permanence of the dollar shortage. Formally, the dollar shortage was endorsed in 1944 by the scarce currency clause of Bretton Woods. (I wish I could explain the reasons for the ignoring of simple principles of economics. Much of the neglect was probably due to the fashionable ideas of central economic planning of these years. The widespread condemnation by the economics profession of the now legendary Erhard–Adenauer reforms of 1947 illustrated the hostile attitudes to free markets and their results. This, however, is unfinished business.)

In the event, however, in those Bretton Woods days, by the 1960s if not earlier the dollar shortage had been transformed into a dollar glut. The Volkswagens rolling into the docks of Baltimore were the physical manifestation of this turnaround. Contrary to the *obiter dicta* of Hicks et al., America did want Beetles and the like from Europe and Sonys from Japan. The great minds in the profession soon recovered their poise in analysing the new phenomena. Following the legendary political orators in Orwell's

1984, glut replaced shortage. What they had missed out of their reflections on the dollar shortage was the fact that monetary and fiscal policy had a considerable, indeed a dominating, effect on the balance of payments, both on current and capital accounts, and therefore on the 'shortages' of currencies in the pegged exchange rate system. To give the profession its due, much of the analysis in the late 1960s and early 1970s did have dominant monetary and fiscal causation.

The theme of this chapter is that governments and central bankers have not merely erred on occasion but have systematically ignored simple logic and manifest evidence. The dollar problem, both shortage and glut, the demise of the babes of Bretton Woods, the euro-snake, the various crises of the ERM (exchange rate mechanism) , the 'tequila' crash: they are all of a piece. And the recent demise of the exchange rate pegs of East Asia is no different.

The basic conclusion for policy is that governments and central banks had best make up their minds. Either they can institute a freely floating exchange rate, whereby they can run a discretionary or rule-based monetary policy, or they can have an absolutely fixed exchange rate system and succumb to the monetary policy of the currency or currencies to which the domestic currency has been fixed. Both are feasible in open capital and trade market systems. What is incompatible with open capital markets is pegged exchange rate systems.

The incompatibility of pegged exchange rates with open capital markets derives basically from the fact that pegged rates are neither fish nor fowl, although they often appear as creepy-crawly pegs. The grandiose description is that they are 'fixed but flexible'. If there developed a 'fundamental disequilibrium' or a persistent imbalance, then the peg could, usually by some multilateral agreement, be moved. Thus pegged exchange rates are emphatically not 'fixed' – by which I mean that there is no provision for movement: they remain at par.

In what follows I shall generally be considering 'pure' systems – such as a pure (or alternatively a free) float. I define this as requiring government to abstain from any policy designed to influence the exchange rate. This does not exclude a George Soros from moving the floating rate if he wants to venture that much money. The free float is only a government 'hands-off'. Similarly, absolutely fixed exchange rates are a pure case. In practice, there is always a wobble around the central parity. And there is always the possibility of governments jettisoning the fixed rate, as in Britain's departure from gold in 1931.

In order to provide institutional support for the fixity of fixed rates, an increasing number of monetary authorities are setting up currency boards. These, in their pure state, merely require the board to swap currency notes (not deposits and so on) at a fixed rate. As we shall see, the transparency of this operation is meant to ensure that everyone can see and understand the simple operation of currency exchange at the fixed parity; there are no hidden agendas. Again, however, it is necessary to say that currency boards in practice are never absolutely pure; all compromise to some degree in order to ameliorate the supposedly harsh discipline of the pure board.

THE PERVERSITIES OF THE PEG

First let us consider the critical weakness, even perversity, of the pegged system. I begin with the existence of the world's international currency: the US dollar. The countries of Southeast Asia generally pegged their currencies to the dollar. (Some allowed the yen and other currencies some role, but we ignore that throughout.) Being small relative to the United States, the Southeast Asian countries knew that, whatever the vicissitudes of their economies, they would have little or no effect on the United States; Alan Greenspan would not react to the policies of the Bank of Thailand.

The baht has long had a peg on the US dollar. In the 1960s and early 1970s, the baht was 20 to the dollar. (Since the currency was commonly called the tickel, the jingle was 'a nickel and tickel'.) However, by 1997, the baht had slipped from 20 to 25 to the dollar (now a tickel was only four US cents). Although there were at times considerable strains on the earlier peg at 20, it was possible to maintain it, partly because of the fact that there were effective exchange controls and partly because, in those years, there was very little international movement of private capital. The vast majority of capital movements were inter-governmental and, at least in principle, not devoted to upsetting exchange rate pegs.

But during the 1980s there was a massive increase in private capital movements, and they came to dominate – by an order of magnitude – the official movements of the World Bank, the International Monetary Fund and governments. Thailand reduced the barriers to international capital movements, and at the same time carried out various reforms that, with cheap capital from the West, led to the tiger-like growth that has been so much admired. The peg at 25 was thought by many to be virtually an exchange rate guarantee. At the same time, however, Thailand's rate of inflation of around 7% exceeded the 2% rate of the United States. So let us now explore the consequences of this peg.

Let us start with some simple assumptions, which illustrate some important relationships. Suppose we begin the analysis with the real interest rate the same in Thailand as on Wall Street (in practice, of course, Thai rates would be higher because of country risk, but I shall ignore this for the time being), with the nominal rate in Thailand 10% and that in New York 5%. Now we need to specify the length of time over which the exchange rate guarantee is valid. In the real world the timing is uncertain, but I shall assume for simplicity that there is a fully credible guarantee that it will be one year before the peg is adjusted. If so, then this is an invitation to short-term capital (less than a year in maturity) to flow from the United States into Thailand, because the spread over T-bills of 364 days or less is 5%.

This flow of capital will give rise to a fall in Thai interest rates unless it is fully sterilised. But sterilisation is a mug's game: it involves issuing domestic bills (i.e. borrowing) at high interest rates on the domestic market to acquire low-yielding US dollars, and it cannot go on and on. The effect of capital inflow, therefore, must be to reduce interest rates, so that Thai real interest rates become lower than those in the United States.

Pursuing the argument to the extreme, the import of short-term capital will go on until nominal interest rates in Thailand are the same as those in the United States, that is, 5%. This will imply negative real interest rates in inflationary Thailand – precisely the opposite of the policy needed to fight Thailand's inflation.

So far we have traced the effect in terms of interest rates. This is an approach with some verisimilitude, since virtually all central banks control interest rates through operations in the money market. Alternatively, if one is a Friedmanite, one may couch the argument in terms of the quantity of money. The flow of funds into Thailand, only partly sterilised, will flood into the banking system and so increase the money supply – again exactly the opposite of the policy required to subdue inflation and 'converge', as the Europeans would say, on the United States.

In our case, where there is certainty, the peg will be moved on the 365th day. To restore the *status quo ante*, the baht needs to depreciate in one fell swoop by the inflation differential – that is, 5%. If we suppose it does this – that the baht peg goes to 26.25 – the process will not stop, however. The economy will not rest comfortably in a stable equilibrium, and the differential inflation rate will start the cycle all over again. It will repeat, with the incipient rise in Thai inflation looming as the monetary effects filter through to prices (and output, which we leave out of this account).

One may raise the question: is there any hope of a stable equilibrium? The obvious case is where there is complete convergence of inflation rates. Then the capital flows may not be driven by interest rate differentials. But such a case does not give a stable self-correcting system. Any departure from the equality of inflation rates will send capital movements going again. The equality-of-inflation equilibrium is a knife edge, and no place to shelter from the wave of capital.

Of course, in a complex real world, these simple relationships are affected by changing knowledge and expectations, and above all by uncertainty about official interest rate and exchange rate policy.

An important real-world characteristic of pegged rates is that they have been notoriously sticky, at least in the period after World War II. In particular, monetary authorities have hung on to overvalued exchange rates and caused untold damage to their domestic economies, inducing mass unemployment and considerable dislocation. The best documented case is the

United Kingdom under Harold Wilson's government. The government's economic advisers, including the most influential Lord Kaldor, were strongly in favour of devaluation after the election in 1964. Wilson, however, with the most macho arguments, put the country through the wringer until 1967 when, he claims, the gnomes of Zurich – that is, capital flows – forced the fall of the pound. A similar episode occurred with the entry of Britain into the ERM, formally in 1990 but informally earlier. The Major government hung on to the Dm2.95 central value until George Soros and his ilk overwhelmed sterling. This obduracy was very costly.

From my direct observation, I adduce that politicians and central bankers are very reluctant to move the peg – a particular pegged rate acquires the status of a totem, a kind of seal of virility. Macho attitudes towards the exchange rate are common. Devaluation is presented as a great failure – a political and economic and almost a spiritual decline. This attitude is the opposite of that which prevailed from 1931 to 1939, when competitive devaluation and 'beggar-thy-neighbour' policies were followed enthusiastically. Indeed, one of the concerns at Bretton Woods was to avoid competitive devaluations. Those involved need not have worried. Uncompetitive overvaluations are the bane of post-World War II policies.

There are alternative explanations for the ubiquitous failure of pegged exchange rates. It has been argued that, since pegged exchange rates require that external stability dominate domestic conditions, pegged rates could not survive the spread of universal suffrage and the welfare state. The electorate insisted that the domestic requirement of full employment be given priority over external stability. I must say, however, that I find the evidence of these political causes less convincing than the capital mobility argument advanced above. There are many cases of countries that manifestly are not noticeably democratic in their complexion succumbing to capital movements. But this is also unfinished business and cannot be pursued further here.

FIXED RATES AND CURRENCY BOARDS

The distinction between a pegged rate and a fixed rate is subtle but important. Pegged rates are admitted to be movable – like pegs in a board. The conditions under which they will be moved, such as 'fundamental disequilibrium', are sometimes built into the agreement. The Bretton Woods system and the European Monetary System imagined that pegs would be moved only with agreement of the parties and under specified 'disequilibrium' conditions. In effect, however, pegs are moved or abandoned when capital flows threaten to overwhelm them.

Fixed exchange rates must have some way of dealing with this capital flight, otherwise they drift into being mere pegs. Only if there are obvious institutional arrangements for dealing with capital flows will it be possible to get the advantages of the fixed rate system. Historically there have been various attempts to have fixed rates by operating exchange controls – or more recently by taxing international flows (Chile, Tobin taxes, and so on). All such methods are bound to be interventionist and to distort the free flow of capital.

The basic problem is to convince the market that, when pressure is on the exchange rate, there is automatic adjustment of domestic monetary policy designed to relieve that pressure. The specie-flow mechanism of the old gold standard is a well-known adjustment mechanism that, in theory, subordinated domestic monetary policy to the exigencies of a fixed exchange rate. As gold flowed out, the domestic money supply automatically contracted and brought deflationary pressure, which helped restore purchasing power parity.

In the currency board system in its pure form, the board is set up to maintain the exchange rate with the reserve currency (usually the US dollar). The assets of the board are then relatively liquid US dollar reserves. The liabilities are the note and coin issue and the net worth of the board. The important point is that no currency notes are issued against domestic assets, since the currency board is either precluded from holding such assets or, if it does hold them, it cannot issue currency against them. In short, overwhelmingly the currency board assets are US dollars and its liabilities the domestic note and coin issue.

To illustrate the operation of a currency board, I shall call the domestic currency the rupiah. The sole purpose of the currency board is to exchange dollar currency notes against rupiah currency notes, in both directions, at a fixed rate (say, 10,000 rupiah to the US dollar). Although it is possible to have a small spread to cover administrative costs, in the main countries that have adopted the system, such as Hong Kong, there is no spread and the exchange goes both ways at HK$7.8 to the greenback.

Note that, strictly, only currency is exchanged through the board. One cannot demand that the board take deposits nor can the board supply deposits instead of currency. However, through arbitrage, the rate of exchange of deposits will always be very near that of the currency board.

Similarly, granted total confidence that the currency board will continue, rates of interest will be very near those in the United States. If Indonesia were to introduce a currency-based system in which there were total confidence, Indonesia would be presented with futures, options and swap markets very similar to (in pure terms, the same as) those in the United States – all in rupiah, because the rupiah would be as good as the US dollar. I need not dwell on the advantages of Indonesia having access to such deep and liquid markets. One of the mysteries of the currency board system is that it does induce in the populace and the markets a surprisingly high degree of confidence in its operation. No doubt the structure of the board, and particularly its transparency and guarantee, are the sources of this confidence. But as is well known, and as Keynes pointed out in the General Theory, confidence is one of the most important ingredients in monetary policy – indeed, in markets generally. Unfortunately, however, we have no way of analysing it, no way of seeing how confidence interacts, builds up and erodes. All we can record is the fact that it seems that, in all cases, even analysts who are generally opposed to currency boards have detected this burgeoning of confidence.

But we must return to the equilibrating mechanism. As mentioned above, this is none other than the price-specie-flow mechanism identified by David Hume in 1750. Suppose there is some shock, such as an inflation in tradable goods prices relative to the United States; then the deficit on the current account will increase. In financing this increased deficit, interest rates will rise relative to those in the United States. These higher interest rates, associated with a contraction in the money supply, will exert deflationary pressure on prices, thus making exports and import substitutes more competitive. And so, with exports increasing and imports decreasing, we return to the *status quo ante*.

The strict requirement of the currency board contrasts sharply with the footloose and fancy-free circumstances of central banks. A run on the rupiah would automatically reduce the money supply and domestic credit. Central banks faced with such circumstances have had the option, which in the developing world has rarely been resisted, of issuing currency and deposits against domestic assets in an attempt to prevent interest rates from rising. This may work for a short time, but ultimately the growth of the money supply will add to, rather than reduce, inflation.

A pure currency board is the extreme case of a monetary policy by rule: the monetary authorities have no discretion. As the demand for greenbacks increases, they must reduce domestic currency as they supply dollars to the market. The quantity of domestic money is determined entirely by demand.

Another feature of the currency board is that, again automatically, it induces macroeconomic discipline. A currency board cannot lend to the government. It is prohibited from acquiring domestic assets, so it cannot finance a fiscal deficit of the public sector. To cover its borrowing requirements, the government must resort to issuing bonds, either in rupiah or in other currencies. It is worth remarking that one of the main reasons for the switch from currency board to central bank, which occurred in the post-colonial period, was that the fiscal straitjacket inhibited national plans for vast public spending. We are all, I think, rather better informed now.

CURRENCY BOARDS IN PRACTICE

The acid test is: how do currency boards perform in practice – compared, of course, with central banks? The issue has been discussed recently in Ghosh et al. (1998). It must be noted that none of the currency boards reviewed was a 'pure' system in the sense discussed above. Some authorities try to massage interest rates, others operate on a marginal basis, and so on. But all preserve a fixed exchange rate and are a close approximation to a currency board system. The authors conclude as follows: 'Currency boards are indeed associated with better inflation performance, even allowing for the potential endogeneity of the choice of regime. Perhaps more surprisingly, this better inflation performance is accompanied by higher output growth.'

Perhaps the most important evidence on the efficacy of currency boards is in a recent study by the World Bank of the reactions of Mexico with its central bank and Argentina with its currency board to the exigencies of the tequila crisis in 1994–5. In response to the flight of capital, the Mexican authorities rapidly inflated domestic credit as a substitute for international credit; the Argentine authorities contained credit as the dollarisation proceeded. The inflation in Argentina was stopped in its tracks, but in Mexico a sharp increase in inflation ensued. Since the currency board system was installed in 1991, Argentina, which for decades had languished in the low-growth league, had enjoyed a very large increase in its growth rate – to about 6.5–7.5%. No such growth renaissance had appeared in Mexico. This comparison is a single swallow and does not make a summer. But after the kerfuffle in East Asia is over, we shall be able to compare the Hong Kong experience with those countries which pegged their exchange rates.

I do not think that we can yet claim the currency board as the ultimate fix. We cannot assert that we have discovered the economic elixir that can be relied upon to deliver high growth and low inflation. And one needs to keep in mind that the reserve currency has to behave itself – as the US dollar has done in the 1980s and 1990s – which, it may be claimed, has provided a benign climate for currency boards. Long may that continue.

19 Long-term implications for developing countries

Hadi Soesastro

INTRODUCTION

With a record of sustained high growth over several decades, East Asia became the place where developing countries looked for inspiration and advice, and tested policies to improve their economic performance. Many lessons have been drawn from the pooled experience of successful East Asian economies. The World Bank's study on *The East Asian Miracle* (1993) highlighted the key role of public policy in explaining that success. Today, instead of turning their attention away from East Asia because of the crisis, developing countries may find the region an even more relevant place from which to learn about mistakes that should not be repeated. After being lulled into complacency by remarkable economic performance, East Asia has received a necessary wake-up call. Understanding what went wrong is often a better teacher than knowing what was right. How developing countries assess East Asia's overall experience will definitely have an effect on their own development policies and orientation and their long-term strategies.

Crisis is in the eye of the beholder. Take the case of Indonesia, for instance. In April 1998 when students throughout the country began to step up their demonstrations, they demanded that President Soeharto make an end to nepotism, cronyism and corruption, which in their view were the main sources of the crisis. A month later they demanded the resignation of the president for being unable to resolve the crisis and, even, for being the source of the problem itself. At one time he stated that the crisis was not as severe as portrayed by the foreign media; at another time he called it a calamity and appealed for patience in resolving it. The crisis, he pointed out, had not been anticipated and it showed that Indonesia's 'economic resilience' was weaker than it was believed to be. No specifics were given about the economy's weaknesses, but the statement seemed to acknowledge the fact that Indonesia's policy regime failed to create a robust and shock-proof economy that was able to withstand the volatile movements of international capital. With the assistance of the International Monetary Fund (IMF) in resolving the crisis, the government of Indonesia finally settled on a 117-point reform program, which is wide-ranging and includes measures to dismantle monopolies that have been sanctioned by the president.

Views on the financial crisis in East Asia from non-affected countries outside the region also differ widely. One needs to bear in mind that informed views from the United States could have a significant influence on the way the crisis unfolds and on the efforts to resolve it. According to US Secretary of the Treasury, Rubin, the Asian crisis has demonstrated how badly flawed financial sectors in a few developing countries, and inadequate risk assessment by international creditors and investors, can have a significant impact on countries around the globe. To address this problem, he suggests a plan that has three major elements: first, the provision of better information through improved disclosure and transparency; second, the strengthening of financial systems; and, third, the avoidance of moral hazard by creating mechanisms to ensure that creditors and investors more fully bear the consequences of their decisions (*Australian Financial Review* 14 April 1998). Paul Volcker is of the opinion that the collapse of currencies and financial markets in Indonesia, Korea and Thailand does not signify an Asian crisis. Rather, it is 'only the latest, and most dramatic, episode in a series of events that raise some basic questions about global finance and its implications for economic development' (*Washington Post* 1998). In his view, technical fixes are not adequate. Instead, there needs to be a reform of the financial system on a global scale and the IMF is the only vehicle the world has to bring consensus and legitimacy to this reform. George Shultz, on the other hand, proposes that the IMF be dismantled because it has contributed to the crisis in East Asia. In his view, the IMF has encouraged investors and bankers to take imprudent risks by providing taxpayers' money to bail them out (*Washington Post* 1998).

The financial crisis in East Asia, as is often the case with a crisis, has taken on a dynamic of its own. It is this dynamic development that influences the policy framework to deal with, and the policy conclusions drawn from, the crisis. Three kinds of assessment will be influential. They are not mutually exclusive, and relate to one another as they are linked to the process of understanding the causes, the cures and the consequences of the crisis. The first type of assessment involves what may be termed 'lessons learned': what were the main causes of the crisis and could it have been predicted? The situation is still unfolding and lessons continue to accumulate as new sources of the crisis are uncovered and new theories about it are espoused. The second kind of assessment relates to the 'actual experience' of the affected countries in overcoming the crisis. Like the unfolding of the situation itself, the process of recovery is perhaps also characterised by multiple equilibria. In view of the complexity of the problem, economic policy measures that are introduced at each point in time may be successful only if supported by a host of other measures (social or political) that are perceived by the public and the markets as necessary. The third type of assessment has to do with the state of affairs *and* the state of mind when the crisis is finally over. How will affected countries assess the state of their post-crisis economy, either with reference to their stated or implicit national aspirations and goals or relative to the state of the rest of the world? At this juncture one can, at best, only speculate about the conditions that would prevail in the first years of the next millennium; that is the time when the affected countries are expected to come out of the crisis.

However tempting it may have been for some governments of affected countries to put the blame on 'contagion' or 'conspiracy', the crisis cannot be pinpointed to a single source. It is important, therefore, that it be examined from various perspectives. It is not the purpose of this chapter to review the variety of perceptions of political leaders or governments and the growing literature of academic writings on the crisis. Different lessons have been drawn from the situation in East Asia. Lessons are useful if they lead to specific policy conclusions or recommendations.

The various views and analyses to date can be clustered into three main themes. The first theme focuses on issues of financial fragility and the impact of volatile capital movements. Policy recommendations range from issues that are more or less of a technical nature, namely ways and means to strengthen prudential regulation and supervision of financial institutions, to those that involve complex policy choices regarding a country's exchange rate regime and external payment system. The second theme stresses the importance of institutional development and institutional arrangements, either in the domestic context of enhancing governance practices and procedures or involving regional initiatives (regional surveillance mechanism) or multilateral, global cooperation (coordinated controls on short-term capital flows). The third theme addresses the issue of long-term growth strategy. Some suggestions point to the adequacy of making incremental changes to the prevailing development strategy, but others argue for the need for a totally new development paradigm. In each cluster, the issues range from those of 'low politics' to those of 'high politics'. In examining the long-term implications of the crisis for developing countries, it may be necessary to address some of the 'high politics' issues.

This chapter cannot address all of these issues but will focus on two policy questions that are of direct relevance to the formulation of long-term strategies for developing countries. The first question relates to the challenges of globalisation. The crisis has shown that maintaining macroeconomic stability has become much more difficult in a globalised world. The issue here is not whether or not to open up, and it involves much more than the proper sequencing of the liberalisation process. The issue is how to maintain a *workable and credible commitment to open economic policies*. 'Workable' means that the respective countries feel comfortable and confident in making and keeping the commitment. 'Credible' means that outsiders feel confident that the commitment will be kept.

Thus far, the affected countries have not reversed their basic international orientation, and there has not been a clear trend towards major policy reversals in the developing world. However, to some extent, this commitment may depend on how developing countries will be able to institute policy regimes that can help them deal more effectively with temporary shocks resulting from international capital flows. The crisis in East Asia and the earlier one in Latin America show that transitory capital account shocks can create major macroeconomic disturbances and that the contagion effect is real. These pose a major challenge for developing countries since large and highly mobile international capital flows are likely to be an important feature of the world financial landscape for the foreseeable future.

The crisis in East Asia has brought a new dimension to the issue of commitment to open economic policies. As will be discussed later, a credible commitment to such policies also requires a commitment to good governance. This leads to the second policy question, which addresses the challenge of what can be termed 'grand sequencing': when should a developing country open up its political system in the process of economic development and liberalisation? In crisis-affected Indonesia today, many will argue that the origin of the crisis is as much political as it is economic in nature and, therefore, economic and political reforms will be necessary to overcome this crisis and to prevent future ones. The lack of good governance, which is seen to have brought about nepotism, cronyism and corruption, is caused by the closed political system. The main point here is that a *workable and credible commitment to good governance* has to be underpinned by political liberalisation. Yet to undertake economic and political reforms simultaneously can be highly risky. What modality can accommodate a better balance in economic and political development?

A long-term agenda for developing countries is a tall order, considering that the forces of globalisation have resulted in a compression of time as well as of space. Time is not on the side of developing countries. It has become more difficult for them to address the various issues one at a time unless a neat sequencing of the total development process is possible – a possibility often hampered by political realities. The crisis has exposed this enormous challenge. Developing countries should not shy away from it. The question is how to respond to it in an effective and meaningful way.

COMMITMENT TO OPEN ECONOMIC POLICIES

Globalisation is not a new phenomenon, but any major challenge to development is now being linked to it. Many new problems arise in a country that is in the process of opening up. Changes in the external environment can compound these problems. The Asian crisis, some observers would argue, only confirms that one cannot be sanguine about globalisation. It is inherently dangerous, risky and costly, particularly for developing countries. This asymmetrical impact results from a globalisation process that essentially moves in one direction, from the North to the South (Yusof 1998).

Developments in the global capital market have substantially eroded government controls over monetary policy, a fact that has been duly recognised. Some countries have difficulty accepting this and have opted for preserving national sovereignty. Others may see the value of the disciplining effect of an open capital account. Indonesia, for example, fully liberalised its capital account at a very early stage of its economic reconstruction in the early 1970s, to make a credible commitment to its open-door foreign investment policy. In the process, its policymakers discovered the utility of its disciplining effect and made use of it during much of the 1970s and 1980s.

The crisis, others now argue, has demonstrated that in the world of the 1990s this market disciplining effect has grown out of reasonable proportion. It needs to be recognised that external shocks today, which tend to come through the capital account, create greater macroeconomic disturbances than shocks in the past that were caused by changes in the terms of trade, which worked their way through the current account. Global capital can react so abruptly and indiscriminately, leading to a crisis and regional contagion. It has punished misbehaviour or a wrong policy harshly. What does this mean for policy? How should developing countries react to this development? From a political perspective, Tan (1998) argued that this development represents a power shift from elected governments to speculators, bond traders and fund managers, and that Malaysian Prime Minister Mahathir's visceral reaction to financier George Soros epitomises this painful shift. Tan thought that this development was bound to have significant geopolitical implications, but he failed to offer likely scenarios. In the immediate aftermath of the attack on Malaysia's currency, Mahathir campaigned for multilateral efforts to control speculative movements of capital. He pointed to the immorality of such activities that could cause great damage to an economy that is fundamentally sound. Mahathir has not gone beyond this suggestion.

The issue of capital controls has become a discussion item in various policy fora. Governments from industrialised countries have rejected the idea of coordinated controls of capital flows. Rubin's three-pronged plan mentioned earlier has set the preferred policy direction. The essence of this plan is the strengthening of financial systems through the establishment of global standards, supported by surveillance to be carried out by the IMF and the World Bank. Joseph Stiglitz, chief economist at the World Bank, recommended temporary controls on capital inflows. He argued that the force of vast international flows, especially of short-term capital, might overpower a well-managed but small economy. Controls, along with domestic reforms and greater disclosure, could help reduce the frequency and magnitude of shocks (Stiglitz 1998). To strengthen his argument, Stiglitz made two additional points. First, the net benefit of short-term capital is small or even negative; it is not as valuable as foreign direct investment, which brings with it technology and training. Also, when the savings rate is already high and when marginal investment is misallocated, additional short-term capital flows increase the vulnerability of the economy. Finally, the net benefit is further reduced when the reserves set aside to protect against the volatility of this type of capital are taken into account. Second, together with solid fundamentals and a sound financial system, capital controls may be the reason that Chile has been relatively unaffected by the 'tequila effect' of the Mexican crisis. Chile instituted three types of controls. First, 30% of all non-equity capital flowing into the country must be deposited interest-free at the central bank for one year. Second, only if rated as high as Chile's government bonds by two bond-rating agencies can Chilean firms and banks borrow from the international capital markets. Third, any foreign money coming into Chile must stay in the country for at least one year (*Economist* 1998).

The issue of controls and regulations of capital inflows will remain controversial. There is doubt that such regulations can be effective. Unless a very highly regulated financial system is introduced, there will always be loopholes. It is also not plausible or sensible to put in place a system that totally and permanently isolates the economy from fluctuations in international capital flows. Furthermore, there is the danger that capital controls will be used to insulate misguided economic policies from market discipline or to delay much-needed reform. A country that has already liberalised its capital account, such as Indonesia, cannot take a step backwards without jeopardising the credibility of its overall commitment to open economic policies. At the onset of the crisis in Indonesia, the need for some capital controls was considered but soon abandoned. Countries that are in the process of opening up should not experiment lightly with introducing capital controls, as this may send the wrong signals to the outside world. When Mahathir suggested the need for, and in fact introduced, some capital controls in dealing with the crisis, this only worsened the situation and sent the currency and the stock market further down.

It is a matter for empirical research whether Chile was unaffected by the Mexican crisis primarily because of its capital controls or because of many other factors. It may well be the case, as suggested by Gavin et al. (1996), that Chile's success lies in its ability to satisfy some form of exchange rate commitment. The Mexican crisis followed the devaluation of the peso. The effect of being forced to abandon a regime that proved to be unsustainable can be very destabilising. The crisis in Thailand and its extension to other economies followed the devaluation of the baht in early July 1997. The affected countries have also been forced to abandon policies of pegging their exchange rates to a basket of currencies in which the dollar weighed heavily. They have learnt the hard way that their old exchange rate policies were not viable. The realisation that it is important to have an exchange rate system consistent with an open capital account has led the crisis-affected countries to adopt floating exchange rates. It is believed that the crisis could have been prevented if they had allowed their currencies to float freely much earlier. This would have resulted in a reduction of domestic interest rates and an appreciation of the currency in response to the large inflows of capital, resulting in an increased current account deficit and a slowing-down of capital inflows.

Yet, in a sense, these Southeast Asian countries and many other developing countries are not fully comfortable with a floating exchange rate. There have been suggestions that sooner or later they may want to adopt a managed float, a flexible system which allows for some intervention. In this case, macroeconomic adjustment to changes in capital flows would depend on the degree of sterilisation. Greater sterilisation would tend to postpone the adjustment. Others suggest that many developing countries lack the discipline to maintain a credible commitment to a free float.

A fixed exchange regime has its attraction as a means of enforcing commitment by the monetary authority to a stable and non-inflationary policy by reducing the scope for discretion in setting monetary policy. Yet the issue here is whether the commitment to the fixed exchange rate itself is sufficiently strong. Garnaut (1998) has described the conditions under which a commitment to a fixed exchange regime can be undermined. The problem arises not only in the wake of a sudden large outflow of capital but also as a result of large capital inflows. In the latter case, net inflows will result in an immediate accumulation of reserves. Without complete sterilisation this will generate an increase in the domestic monetary base. The increase in liquidity will reduce domestic interest rates and result in an expansion of bank credit. The increase in domestic consumption and investment may result in an economic boom, accompanied by an appreciation of the real exchange rate. Conventional wisdom suggests that a government would have to adopt a policy of fiscal contraction in order to limit the expansionary impact of large or sudden capital inflows. The case study on Thailand in this volume shows that the boom can suddenly end, precipitating a crisis.

In the case of a shock caused by a sudden outflow, a sharp monetary contraction and a forceful fiscal response can sustain the fixed exchange regime. The first requirement suggests the importance of a strong domestic financial system. Monetary contraction brings about high interest rates and results in a cutback of domestic credits. Difficulties on the part of corporations to service their debt can create a banking crisis. The need for fiscal contraction as well is derived from a sharp reduction in the availability of non-inflationary financing of fiscal deficits. It is interesting to note that fiscal contraction appears to be the appropriate response to both a sudden capital inflow and a sudden capital outflow. Fiscal contraction often proves to be politically difficult in response to a sudden outflow of capital. The point here is that it is not easy to maintain discipline and coherence in policymaking.

It would be logical to expect that, in a world of highly mobile capital flows, the appropriate exchange rate regime would be one that could most effectively insulate the economy from an external shock. No strong consensus has emerged from the Latin American experience on the insulating properties of fixed or flexible exchange rates (Gavin et al. 1996). The recent experience in East Asia points to the same conclusion. Singapore has a managed float exchange rate policy and Hong Kong has adopted the currency board system. Both have not been seriously affected by the crisis. After all, what is important may not be the exchange regime as such but the credibility of the commitment to maintaining it. Both Singapore and Hong Kong have sizeable reserves and they have strong and open financial systems. As Frenkel (1996) put it, insulation from external shock should not be the objective of exchange rate policy. Also, an exchange rate system that will save a country from policy mistakes has not been invented. He proposed that the real issue is the adoption of an exchange rate regime that is most conducive to discipline in policymaking. This depends, according to Frenkel, on the nature of a country's institutions, on its policymakers, on its history and on the state of the inflation cycle: 'the danger is that in deciding on an exchange rate regime, policymakers will always think the grass on the other side is greener and will endlessly move back and forth between flexibility and fixity and thus fail to confront the real issue, which is how to establish discipline in policy making' (1996: 106–7). Discipline in policymaking should include coherence in policymaking. The case study on Indonesia in this volume shows that the viability of the exchange rate policy has been undermined by a lack of policy coherence.

Credibility is the keyword. This is not just a matter of macroeconomic policy but of the overall strategy of economic reform. Thus far, governments in the crisis-affected countries have not reversed their overall strategy of economic growth and development. All of them support the view that commitment to open economic policies is also critical for their recovery. The IMF-supported reforms in Indonesia, Korea and Thailand contain substantial structural reforms that will reinforce those commitments. Although Malaysia did not resort to the IMF for financial assistance, it has undertaken consultations with the IMF and has adopted a similar program, but with targets and a timetable that it wants to determine by itself. Malaysia has gone quite far in liberalising its current account, but it has been cautious in opening up its financial sector and its capital account. It may exercise greater caution now but is not likely to close in.

In their efforts to recapitalise the banks, Indonesia and Thailand have amended their regulations to allow unlimited foreign ownership. Most large banks in Indonesia are technically bankrupt and those in Thailand are severely distressed. Malaysia's banking system is also encountering some problems, and there may be greater urgency for Malaysia to relax the 30% limit to foreign ownership of banks. Indonesia and Thailand have no immediate alternative. To begin to stabilise the currency and the economy, they must urgently rehabilitate the financial sector and work out a solution to the problem of short-term private debt. Pragmatism will dictate that they will have to accept a return of foreign capital, largely through 'buy ins' of banks and corporations at bargain prices rather than through bailouts. Takeovers and acquisitions, rather than green-field investments, will be the name of the game. Most of the capital is expected to come from the US and Europe, plus some from Singapore and Hong Kong.

There may be greater public resistance in Thailand and Indonesia to accepting this (Vatikiotis 1998). However, with confidence in the government and domestic corporations being as low as it currently is, an increased involvement of foreign enterprises is welcome in Indonesia, if only because of perceptions of superior governance practices. This may be a misguided view, but the issue of good governance has caught the attention of the Indonesian public much more than ever before and has overshadowed all other factors that appear to be responsible for the crisis and are important for the recovery.

New, green-field foreign direct investment will be needed in the recovery process. A widely open door foreign investment policy has been an integral part of the open economic policies of Southeast Asian countries. They have opted for an internationally oriented strategy, with the objective to sustain growth and to accelerate the catching-up process. Since the 1980s, when most Southeast Asian economies abandoned their export promotion strategies to embark on full trade liberalisation, they have gone beyond the point of no return in their liberalisation. The policy of export promotion that predated trade liberalisation was perhaps a correct sequencing. It stimulated exports but did little to improve the economy's overall efficiency. The international environment during the Uruguay Round of multilateral trade negotiations also helped to end the East Asian strategy of 'double-distortion', namely that of maintaining economic inefficiencies caused by high import barriers but compensating them with subsidies and other facilities to promote export growth.

Indonesia and Malaysia initially committed themselves to open economic policies as a matter of necessity as they saw a rapid dwindling of oil revenues. But reforms in Thailand and the Philippines in the 1980s were not driven by any sense of crisis. Instead they instituted significant reforms during good times, possibly because resistance to liberalisation was weaker under improved economic conditions (Bowie and Unger 1997). But once on the track of liberalisation, all four countries elected to stay on course. An important underpinning of this commitment is the adoption of this same strategy by all ASEAN (Association of South East Asian Nations) economies, thus creating strong demonstration effects and a dynamic environment of competitive liberalisation. In the case of Korea, the extremely strong motivation to become a modern, industrialised economy that is on par with Japan appears to be the factor behind its global ambitions.

Support from within the ASEAN economies for a firm commitment to open economic policies will be important for the process of recovery. A second-track forum of ASEAN–ISIS (Institute for Strategic and International Studies) in March 1998 stressed that the recovery, reform and reinvention of Southeast Asian economies would require increased marketisation and continued large inflows of foreign direct investment (ASEAN–ISIS 1998). Garnaut (1998) has raised the possibility that this commitment may not survive recovery. Two factors can influence the strength of the policy commitment after the recovery. The first is the recovery process itself, which, if it goes smoothly, can further strengthen the commitment. The more fragile and difficult the process, the weaker will be the confidence in what can be achieved. Any new shock to the economy can rapidly produce a new round of panic that can result in a rapid regression of confidence in the system. The actual experience of the recovery process will exert great influence on the national psychology. Its consequences cannot be predicted, but a nationalist backlash is not improbable.

All affected countries have begun the recovery process, which is expected to last for at least two to three years. Much can happen during that painful period. So far, Korea and Thailand have produced encouraging signals, but the Indonesian recovery process remains troublesome. A continuing economic meltdown in Indonesia could have important regional implications. Having secured IMF support, Korea and Thailand should be able to insulate themselves to some extent from this effect, but other countries are more vulnerable. The Indonesian crisis is no longer solely a financial crisis but has been compounded by a political crisis. It remains to be seen to what extent the situation can be contained. The country's deep financial crisis resulted from a process of multiple equilibria involving contagion, panic and mishandling (Radelet and Sachs 1998b). Its recovery process is likely to be one of multiple equilibria as well. Failure to produce visible political reforms, alongside implementation of economic reforms, will result in a stagnation of the process or even an economic setback. Events in Indonesia in May 1998 clearly illustrate this challenge.

The second factor influencing the strength of commitment relates to developments in the political field. A change of government makes it easier for crisis countries to introduce reforms without having to make concessions to vested interests that grew out of the patronage system under the previous government. This is an important factor in their recovery. An equally important factor is the enthusiasm with which new governments usually look to the future. They can begin to take the steps necessary to meet the challenges that they face and to make use of the opportunities that present themselves when the economy recovers.

What are the main challenges? East Asian countries will experience a new round of competition among regional economies: competition for export markets and for foreign investment. China, and perhaps India, will be the leading drivers in this new race. What constitutes competitiveness? The World Economic Forum (WEF) has greatly influenced government and business perceptions of a nation's competitiveness through the annual publication of its competitive indices (see, for instance, World Economic Forum 1997). The indices are made up of eight clusters of structural characteristics: (a) openness to international trade and finance; (b) the role of government budgets and regulation; (c) the development of financial markets; (d) the quality of infrastructure; (e) the quality of technology; (f) the quality of business management; (g) labour market flexibility and human resources development; and (h) the quality of the judiciary and political institutions. The main point is that competitiveness appears to be signified not only by policies but also by institutions that promote and sustain long-term growth. In his cursory examination, Tan (1998) detected that, among East Asian economies, the three countries that have been hit hardest by the recent crisis – Indonesia, Korea and Thailand – have indeed experienced a gradual deterioration in their international competitiveness (as measured by the WEF competitive index) over the past five years. In Thailand and Korea, real appreciation of the currency has been a factor in this decline, but in all three countries institutional weaknesses are thought to have been an important cause.

The concept of competitiveness, as employed by the WEF, implies an active role by the government, in such areas as raising the level of technology, nationwide and at the firm level. The development of national systems of innovation to facilitate the process of creation and diffusion of new technologies requires active government involvement, if only at the initial stages. There has always been a strong temptation, however, on the part of many governments to actively engage in the industrialisation drive. A commitment to open economic policies, which is an important element in the competitiveness index, may now exercise a greater constraint on what governments can do.

COMMITMENT TO GOOD GOVERNANCE

A great deal of the analysis of the causes of the crisis has pointed to institutional weaknesses and deficiencies in many East Asian economies, which may not have been apparent before (McMullen 1997). These countries have been successful in encouraging high savings and investment, entrepreneurship and market activity, without the establishment of formal property rights, rule of law, and a capable and clean civil service. This has been the case because new and large opportunities and incentives have been created by the introduction of major reforms. Indonesia in the mid-1960s and China in the late 1970s illustrate this point well.

To varying degrees, East Asian countries have failed to meet subsequent institutional challenges. As market activities expand and become more complex, formal provisions for good governance by a government ensure a continuation of economic growth and an improved distribution of the fruits of development. The crisis has greatly exposed the consequences of weak formal provision of good governance, particularly the concentration of economic activities and growth around a patronage system that benefits only 'insiders'. Such a system produces an increasingly unsatisfactory outcome over time, in terms of distribution of the fruits of development as well as the sense of fairness and justice on the part of the citizens. McMullen has argued that, in most societies, there is a need at a fairly early point in the growth process to institute formal rule of law, property rights, enforcement of contracts, fair adjudication of disputes, a competent civil service and other characteristics of good governance, in the public sector. These need to be complemented by good corporate governance, such as transparency, disclosure, accounting standards, responsibilities of corporate directors and executives, and shareholders' rights. It also covers relationships between government officials and corporations, including the allocation of financial resources and the evenhanded enforcement of laws and regulations.

For many developing countries, making a commitment to good governance would appear to be a tall order. It is indeed not an easy task, but there needs to be a clear understanding of its critical importance in managing a society that becomes increasingly more complex as a result of economic growth. After they are properly identified and defined, the principles of good governance should be placed on the nation's development agenda. It may not be necessary to develop them simultaneously and it also may not be advisable to immediately set the highest standards. Of importance is steady progress towards higher standards over time. Equally important is their firm implementation and enforcement. Indonesia, for example, has introduced since the early 1990s a series of laws designed to improve corporate governance. The Corporate Law of 1995 has quite high standards, similar to those practised in advanced industrialised countries, but it is of little use if not enforced. A more modest law but fully enforced would have made a significant contribution to establishing the habit of good corporate governance. Many developing societies continue to have weak enforcement mechanisms and a poor quality judiciary. This is an important element of public policy that was overlooked in the World Bank's 'East Asian miracle' study (1993).

A reassessment of the 'miracle' study in light of the crisis has underlined the importance of adherence to macroeconomic fundamentals, which was one of the study's main conclusions. It suggests, however, that the concept of 'fundamentals' that is more appropriate for a high growth strategy will have to be broadened to include the quality of the legal system, regulatory capacity, and intercountry cooperation. This broadened concept, called 'augmented fundamentals' (World Bank 1997a), has yet to explicitly include the broader range of good governance policies, procedures and practices. It would be useful if the World Bank were to put issues of good governance on the agenda of the international community. The World Economic Forum is already doing so, and together they could help raise the awareness of governments on the importance of good governance. But, in the final analysis, good governance must result from efforts within the society itself. It cannot be imposed through the use of external pressures. Asia Pacific after the crisis could be the place for the development of regional and international cooperation agendas that address these issues. There is definitely a role here for APEC (Asia Pacific Economic Cooperation).

It is a significant development that intercountry cooperation is seen as an important element in the augmented fundamentals. Intercountry, regional or multilateral cooperation processes are important avenues for socialising such concepts as good governance. More importantly, the exchange of views can result in greater understanding of the need for standards or benchmarks that may vary according to particular, specified conditions. The crisis has only begun to call the attention of various regional and international fora to this new dimension of cooperation in a globalised world. Initiatives taken to date have been modest. The so-called Manila Framework of November 1997, drafted by finance and central bank deputies from some APEC economies, now known as the Manila Group, focuses on more immediate tasks to contain the crisis through the development of a regional surveillance mechanism.[1] It also establishes an approach for rescuing affected economies and for containing crises that relies primarily on the role of multilateral financial institutions. These suggestions were further developed in the follow-up meeting of the Manila Group in Tokyo in March 1998. The IMF and the Asian Development Bank have been drawn in to provide the framework for the surveillance. It may not have been immediately obvious to participating governments that a regional surveillance mechanism can only function effectively if it is supported by a commonly accepted set of standards or benchmarks. It is on the basis of those standards that governments can legitimately 'interfere' in the policies of another country.

This regional mechanism could become the forerunner of the international surveillance mechanism that has been proposed by the US Secretary of the Treasury. The objective is to ensure that country risk premiums are more accurately based. It would substantially expand the types of economic and financial data made available, including foreign exchange exposure and the maturity structure of public and private debt. It also would formulate minimum world standards for banking systems, accounting methods, bankruptcy regimes and corporate governance. These standards would not be made compulsory; however, countries failing to meet the standards for either information flow or financial regulation would suffer because wide publicity would ensure that this would be factored into market assessments. The plan is to entrust the surveillance to a joint venture between the IMF and the World Bank. It is questionable, though, whether their constitutions could allow them to effectively undertake this task.

In Southeast Asia, ASEAN has begun with non-controversial initiatives, such as the use of regional currencies to finance intraregional trade. In December 1997, ASEAN finance ministers decided to launch a process which includes a wide range of activities, such as a general exchange of notes on practical experience, monitoring and surveillance. In the context of the

Manila Group, the ASEAN process is thought to function as a caucus. If implemented effectively, it will transform ASEAN into a different kind of regional organisation. The second-track forum of ASEAN–ISIS anticipated this development. It reiterated the suggestion that the time may have come for ASEAN to be ready to put aside its sacred principle of non-interference. It has been an embarrassment to ASEAN that it has performed poorly in dealing with such important regional issues as the financial crisis and the haze problem caused by forest fires. It recognises that it must institute fundamental political and institutional changes in order to stay relevant. This means that ASEAN member states must become 'more comfortable with constructive and discreet comments on each other's policies, especially those which impinge negatively on neighbours' (ASEAN–ISIS 1998). It will not be easy to convince ASEAN governments that the principle of 'constructive involvement' should now replace the more familiar one of non-interference.

However, short of accepting this, ASEAN cannot consider the desirability of engaging members in greater macroeconomic coordination and policy harmonisation. The contagion of the 1997 crisis is likely to haunt ASEAN members for a long time, and this may have a favourable effect on their cooperation. Not all developing countries are in this fortunate situation.

The crisis has firmly placed the issue of good governance on the national agenda of the affected countries, especially in Southeast Asia. The second-track ASEAN–ISIS forum suggested that good governance should be at the top of the list of tasks in the recovery, reform and reinvention of Southeast Asia. It is a prerequisite for sound macroeconomic policies. The strengthening of institutions of checks and balances in states' systems is therefore critical, as is the maintenance of social stability and peace (ASEAN–ISIS 1998). Good governance implies that authority is based on the rule of law, its policies are transparent and it is accountable to the society, and it also must be based on institutions and not on the wishes of persons. Last but not least, it should adhere to the principle that everyone is equal before the law (Wanandi 1998).

The important policy question is how governments can be induced to make a workable and credible commitment to good governance. The immediate follow-up question is whether good governance can be promoted only in a democratic setting. Singapore and Hong Kong immediately come to mind as examples of where it can be present in a non-democratic environment. Are they models for East Asia to emulate? Good governance in these two economies is clearly manifested, first and foremost, in their clean civil administration of government, based on stringent rule of law laid down by the British. The good news is that good governance is a possibility in the region, although no local word for it exists as yet in most East Asian societies. The bad news is that both Singapore and Hong Kong are likely to be exceptions, by virtue of being city-states. Their geopolitical situation may also provide an explanation. It is difficult to imagine that, in other East Asian countries, good governance can be promoted in the absence of democratic developments because in these more diverse societies there is a greater need for flexibility and participatory processes. Even a 'soft' authoritarian system cannot accommodate this need.

Governments in many East Asian economies have taken the view that political development should follow economic development. This will guarantee that political development does not create an obstacle for economic development. The basic assumption here is that political development creates instability. Many governing elites have used this assumption as a justification for postponing political reforms. It should be recognised that economic development may also create discrepancies and inequalities initially, which can be destabilising as well. Greater participatory processes that result from an opening of the political system can help alleviate the problems created by economic discrepancies. Political development should therefore go hand-in-hand with economic development. The need for good governance at a relatively early stage in the economic growth process suggests that political development and democratisation must be introduced earlier rather than later.

Political development must be a gradual process. A 'big bang' approach to political reform can be disastrous, as shown in the case of the Soviet Union. Democratisation should be a process that produces a form of democracy that suits the members of the community. The Jeffersonian or Westminster model is not for every society to adopt. Even in continental Europe there are many variants of democracy. It is clear, however, that democracy has to be built on strong civil societies. Democracy is only a form, manifested in such practices as elections, separation of powers, and a party system. Its substance is guaranteed by the presence of a strong civil society (Wanandi 1998).

How far and how fast political change should be pursued in the East Asian countries will depend on each country's history, tradition and stage of development. The Korean model of opening up the political system only after a certain level of economic development has been achieved can no longer be applied in much of Southeast Asia today. The crisis has pointed to the need to hasten the process of political development. One wonders, however, whether there is indeed an observable relationship between economic and political development, or between economic and political liberalisation, and what that relationship is.

Crouch and Morley (1993) developed the argument that there is a kind of dynamic comprising three distinct but interrelated processes in which, initially, economic growth drives social mobilisation, then social mobilisation drives political mobilisation, and finally political mobilisation drives regime change. The initial process is characterised by improvements in the quality of factors of production, the accumulation of capital and the upgrading of technologies, which are usually initiated by the state. The state therefore plays a dominant role in economic development. This does not necessarily lead to the creation of an authoritarian state, but it tends to strengthen the state vis-à-vis society. However, the process of economic development will bring about changes in the social order and in ideas that lead to a process of social mobilisation that centres on the urban, educated middle class and the industrial working class. This process stimulates a growing awareness of group identity and interests, which encourages the development of politically active organisations and of political parties that establish deeper roots in society partly through links with those new organisations. The dynamics of this process centre on a rivalry between members of civil society and agencies of the state in controlling these organisations. The success of either the state or the society in this political mobilisation defines the regime's structure. If the state is predominant, it enhances its own autonomous influence, moving the regime in a more authoritarian direction. If it is civil society that controls and enhances its relative power, the regime is driven in the direction of liberalisation. A more or less stable balance between the two may result in a quasi-democratic system.

As the economy expands and becomes more complex, the state will introduce various economic reforms to maintain itself in authority, but it will not undertake political reforms. But sooner or later a decisive shift will occur in the balance of power between state and society. When this happens, society will demand and secure, whether by negotiation or violence, movement towards democratic transformation of the political system. Crouch and Morley (1993) suggested that the impact of economic growth on political systems in East Asia by and large corresponds to the above pattern. Yet they observed that economic growth does not drive the state to give up its power gradually as society gains strength. The cases of Korea and Taiwan show that the pressures for political change had been intensifying since the 1950s, but it was not until they approached the threshold of advanced status that political transformation began to materialise.

In view of observable exceptions to the overall pattern of political change, such as the case of Singapore on the one hand and the Philippines on the other, Crouch and Morley listed a number of factors that appear to have an influence on the outcomes of the process: geographic factors, such as size and internal regional tensions; social factors, such as the inherited class structure and communalism; and political factors, such as political institutions and elite cohesion, plus political culture and the external environment. It is perhaps changes in the external environment that will create greater pressures for change. As economies open up and the process of globalisation accelerates, individuals, communities or societies tend to feel more insecure and therefore demand greater participation in the political process in order to ensure that their security and interests are protected.

The process of democratisation and political development involves trial and error, and some instability is inherent in it, which is why it should be undertaken in a gradual fashion. The process must also be based on some consensus: in most East Asian economies there is already a critical middle-class mass that can form the basis for creating consensus and for initiating the process of democratisation.

The 'grand sequencing' issue is, after all, perhaps not a matter of dramatic choices. Economic development and political development can go in tandem and reinforce each other, if an orderly process can be allowed to take place. The concern is that political development can be highly unpredictable and, once the dam is broken, the water will immediately flood the area. This metaphor, however, would only apply if no consensus has been attempted and society's aspirations cannot find their outlet. This being the case, an anarchical situation obtains, that is, when the dam breaks. Forming the consensus is an ongoing effort. It can be likened to opening the dam bit by bit. How far and how fast this process should go is a matter that cannot be engineered in advance. They are matters to be settled within the process itself.

Most East Asian countries experience enormous obstacles in consensus building. The governing elite tend to hold back the process, while the emerging middle class wants it to go faster. It has been most unfortunate that the elite often oppose the demand for faster development by branding it as being influenced by Western values. They then come up with counter suggestions based on a more appropriate set of supposedly Asian values in defence of their unwillingness to move. Some East Asian leaders have used 'Asian values' as justification for imposing a more paternalistic and repressive political system. In reality, there is no common set of values, because of Asia's great diversity. In fact, some of the principles and concepts that are claimed as Asian values are universal and have much in common with Victorian values, which were present in the West at an earlier time. Differences in values often reflect different stages of development (Wanandi 1998).

Moreover, it can also be observed that values are changing everywhere, caused by the spread of universal education, technological innovations and, like or not, globalisation. Some convergence of values is definitely taking place today. This is happening rapidly before our eyes in the Asia Pacific region. This is good for the region and for the world. There will always be nationalistic resistance to the process of convergence. The fact that Singapore and Hong Kong practise good governance can only suggest that it is not an alien concept to Asians; 'Asian values' cannot be used to discount it. Good governance is what all societies long for. Genuine efforts at democratisation and a firm political will are important to institute and develop good governance. A democratic environment is necessary to underpin a workable and credible commitment to good governance.

CONCLUSION

The above discussion can only lead to the humbling realisation, especially for some East Asian leaders, that as societies in Asia become more complex due to successful economic development they cannot ignore some basic values and principles for organising society that were hitherto identified as Western.

This realisation is important for developing countries in making the necessary commitment to sustaining their long-term growth. A commitment to sound policies to ensure macroeconomic stability is a prerequisite for economic development and growth. The recent crisis has shown how critical this commitment is to preventing such a situation or to overcoming it. Most East Asian economies have consciously made a commitment to open economic policy as the basis of their growth strategy. This commitment is likely to survive the Asian crisis, but it can no longer be credible without a similar commitment to good governance, hence political development and democratisation.

It is unfortunate that it needs a crisis, which has caused so many hardships and a major economic setback, to bring this message home. Yet Asia is perhaps still fortunate because, in another part of the world at an earlier time, it took a big war to deliver this same message.

NOTE

1   The Manila Group consists of representatives from Australia, Brunei Darussalam, Canada, People's Republic of China, Hong Kong SAR of China, Indonesia, Japan, Korea, Malaysia, New Zealand, the Philippines, Singapore, Thailand, and the United States.

Part VII

Reflections on
the crisis

20 The new era of financial fragility

Ross H. McLeod

WHAT HAS CHANGED?

A review of the country case studies in this book suggests that there is something to be gained from thinking in terms of two polar extremes of balance of payments crises. I shall refer to these as 'old-style' and 'new-style' crises. The old-style crisis originates in the current account, and is typically brought on by the emergence of relatively high inflation or adverse terms of trade shifts, which create a gap between the current account deficit and capital inflow. In such circumstances, given a pegged exchange rate and a reluctance on the part of governments to allow the money supply to fall and interest rates to rise, reserves decline continuously,[1] eventually attracting the attention of both speculators and those with unhedged exchange rate risks; at this stage the crisis begins to involve the capital account as well. The decline in reserves then accelerates, eventually forcing a devaluation.[2] If sufficiently large, this puts an end to the problem, providing that fiscal and monetary policies are adjusted as necessary in cases where they have been the initial source of disequilibrium. (The successful resolution of the payments disequilibrium may leave other problems in its wake, but experience seems to indicate that the feared consequences of devaluations usually turn out to have been greatly exaggerated.)

New-style crises originate in the capital account rather than the current account. Three features distinguish them from old-style crises. First, they can occur with great suddenness, despite the absence of any significant prior shift in readily observable economic variables. The only obvious explanation for this is a sudden and wide-ranging change in risk perceptions that induces economic entities to attempt to modify significantly their exposure to risk. Second, the magnitude of the impact (on reserves, the exchange rate and/or interest rates) may be dramatic. This reflects both the emergence of a huge pool of internationally mobile, risk-sensitive financial capital during the last decade or so,[3] and the corresponding (and closely related) reduction in the cost of shifting funds from one country to another. Third, the warning signs are far less clear for new-style than for old-style crises. Falling (rising) prices for a country's major exports (imports) are readily observable, as are increasing current account deficits, large budget deficits, excessive money growth, high inflation and falling international reserves. But, although we can observe at least some risk premia in the financial markets, we have no obvious means of monitoring *potential changes* in risk perceptions, much less of predicting the magnitude of their impact should they occur.[4] To put it another way, we only know there has been a change in risk perceptions when this has already had its impact in the financial markets, and we only get an idea as to how great this change has been when we can observe the magnitude of its impact.

In contrast to old-style crises, new-style crises can occur without any additive spillover effect to the current account.[5] In a pegged exchange rate regime, liquidity tightens as money is used to purchase foreign exchange; this should have a negative impact on aggregate demand, resulting in increased net exports. If the exchange rate is floating, depreciation will raise competitiveness, again leading to increased net exports. In a hybrid regime, if the currency is allowed to depreciate somewhat, but interest rates are raised in order to prevent this going too far, both of these effects will be seen. On the other hand, if money is allowed to increase, they will tend to offset each other.

The outlook in relation to the current account becomes less optimistic, however, when we consider the possibility of negative feedback on risk perceptions. If the initial disturbance is strong enough to cause a significant devaluation, or a big jump in interest rates, this will add to the perception of increased risk in holding claims over firms and banks that previously had large exchange rate or interest rate risk exposures. If the banking sector then begins to look shaky, the availability to it of funds may decline suddenly. Firms – including exporters – may not be able to obtain working capital, and exports again may fail to grow, despite the stimulus from depreciation. Moreover, if several countries experience a new-style crisis simultaneously, as has been the case in East Asia, the picture becomes much more complicated. If each is important to the others as an export market or as a competitor in markets elsewhere, the export response in all countries may again be weak, and the impact on their current accounts of reduced aggregate demand and exchange rate depreciation will be muted.

In reality, there may be no cases that are purely old-style or new-style. In the East Asian crisis, different countries are ranged along the spectrum between the two extremes (and some have avoided both kinds of crisis). Of the countries considered in this book, Indonesia seems closest to the new-style extreme, while Thailand – the first domino to fall – combines elements of both. Nevertheless, outlining these polar extremes is a useful heuristic device, because it suggests the possibility that different policy responses may be appropriate to each case, and that it will be necessary to focus on different things than previously if new-style crises are to be avoided, or their destructiveness minimised, in the future.

The sections that follow build on these basic ideas.

THE CRISIS AS A FAILURE OF RISK MANAGEMENT

Risk management may be thought of as the art of avoiding nasty surprises. The East Asian crisis – seen against the backdrop of many years of seemingly solid economic performance and, with very few exceptions, the failure to foresee it, much less to imagine how severe it could be – certainly comes into the 'nasty surprise' category. To differing degrees in the countries of the region a state of euphoria existed, in which investors and governments failed to recognise the magnitude of the risks that existed and to manage those risks adequately.[6] This made certain countries highly vulnerable to a financial crisis – like the *Titanic* steaming confidently across the North Atlantic, oblivious to the proximity of icebergs, and complacent about its capacity to absorb a collision with one.

Various categories of risk were important in different degrees in the countries studied here, including: exchange rate risk (the risk posed by adverse exchange rate movements for unhedged borrowers and investors); investment risk (the risk of low or negative returns from poorly conceived, badly managed and speculative investments); bank sector risk (the risk of loss for depositors at banks that were themselves exposed to risks of various kinds); policy risk (the risk of harmful misjudgments by policymakers when responding to changing economic circumstances); and, in some countries, political risk (the risk that political developments could bring adverse policy changes, a breakdown of social stability, a loss of political protection for privileged firms, and so on). Political risk was overwhelmingly important in Indonesia, but much less so elsewhere.

'Financial risks' are those that arise from holding assets and liabilities, by virtue of uncertainty as to their future values in view of the various categories of risk just mentioned. Such risks are inescapable aspects of doing business and accumulating wealth (saving), and they contributed strongly to initiating the crisis that emerged in 1997. In so far as financial assets tend to proliferate, and their aggregate value to grow far more quickly than the value of output and the physical capital stock as countries develop (Goldsmith 1969), it may be conjectured that financial risks might also tend to grow rather rapidly. Indeed Warr (Chapter 3) and Athukorala (Chapter 5) can be interpreted as arguing implicitly along these lines – the former drawing attention to the rapid growth of financial assets held by foreign investors, and the latter to the rapid growth of banking assets (as reflected in the growth of deposits), in the fast developing Thai and Malaysian economies. Market processes develop mechanisms for dealing with financial risks;[7] but government policies may hinder them, as will be discussed shortly.

A fundamental distinguishing characteristic of financial risk is that the act of insuring or seeking protection against an adverse movement in the price of an asset or liability tends to cause this price to move in the same direction as that which is feared. Of particular relevance in the present context is that, if an expectation that the currency will depreciate takes hold, those who have borrowed in foreign currencies will want to buy such currencies, in order to repay immediately or to ensure they will not be affected later by the expected depreciation. At the same time, those who are holding assets denominated in the local currency will want to liquidate them and use the proceeds to buy foreign exchange. Finally, there will be other entities who, although not initially exposed to such risks, see the opportunity for profit in others' potential misfortune. If these entities form a strong view as to the likely direction of future movement in financial asset prices, they will deliberately seek an exposure from which they will gain if their prediction turns out to be correct.

The impact of the actions of all of these parties – if there is no central bank intervention, or if the central bank is overwhelmed by the demand for foreign exchange – will be to cause the expected depreciation to occur. Likewise in the case of a run on a bank, the withdrawal of deposits on a large scale and in a short period is likely to hasten its collapse, in turn resulting in a loss of value of the remaining deposits.

With these ideas in mond, 'financial panic' may be described as an episode in which large numbers of economic entities suddenly change their financial behaviour (i.e. try to modify significantly their portfolios of assets and liabilities) simply because they observe other entities doing so. This is often described as 'herd behaviour', but it is not necessarily irrational, given the cost of quickly acquiring better information about the assets and liabilities in question. Thus, when a herd of zebra suddenly run off in the same direction, it may be because one of them saw a lion approaching; the zebra who stays put because it has not yet seen the lion with its own eyes runs the risk of going from needing a meal to being one. And, to round out the analogy, the vulture that does not follow its flock is likely to miss out on the free meal of lion leftovers that one of its companions has spotted.

The precondition for a financial panic to occur – that is, of vulnerability to crisis – is a set of circumstances in which economic entities are aware of the possibility of changes in the prices of assets and liabilities but are not insured against such changes (or, in the case of speculators, deliberately exposed to them). Then, when they see some indication that the occurrence which concerns them might be about to happen, they act in a manner that amplifies any initial disturbance. All are aware that, unless they are among the first to hedge a newly perceived risk (or to take a speculative position), the opportunity to avoid the loss (or enjoy the gain) may quickly disappear.

In such circumstances, when hidden risks come to light, or when the probability of losses or their magnitude is perceived to increase, the rush to hedge the risk, and to speculate, hastens the very change in asset and liability values that is of concern; McKibbin (Chapter 14) incorporates such an occurrence in a general equilibrium modelling framework. This would appear to be a large part of the East Asia crisis story. In Thailand, people began to lose confidence in the US dollar peg for the baht, given the rapidly declining export growth and outlook, growing concerns about the prospects of listed companies, and a mounting excess supply of real estate. Thus investors, both foreign and domestic, were beginning to shift funds to other countries where investment opportunities seemed more promising, putting pressure on reserves. Speculators eventually saw what was going on, and the peg to the dollar was soon tested and broken.

This had elements of, but was something more than, an old-style balance of payments crisis. Both export and import growth were very volatile, making it difficult to interpret the state of the current account in the months leading up to the crisis. International reserves, although declining, seemed adequate (in terms of their equivalence in months of imports); it was learned subsequently, however, that the bulk of reserves had been sold forward by the central bank. The extent to which Thailand's crisis originated in the current account in the old-style sense, or was a new-style crisis precipitated by concerns about a much wider range of issues concerning the domestic economy as well, is therefore not clear. In Indonesia's case, however, the initial disturbance seems to have been almost entirely in the capital account (Chapter 2). Inflation was falling, there had been no marked deterioration in the current account, and reserves had been increasing. But the sudden float and devaluation of the baht in neighbouring Thailand, and then the ringgit in Malaysia, triggered a re-evaluation of risk exposures of all kinds which, in turn, brought on precisely the changes in asset and liability values that investors feared.

The first such re-evaluation in Indonesia related to exchange rate risk. Private sector foreign debt was of the order of US$70 billion, 83% of it unhedged; a further US$27 billion in foreign currency loans had been obtained from domestic banks. Borrowers began to rush to buy dollars in early July 1997, as did domestic and foreign entities holding rupiah-denominated deposits and other financial assets. Large unrealised losses were incurred by those who had borrowed offshore to finance investment in the non-tradables sector, especially property; if the companies in question were listed, selling pressure began to force the share prices down, and it is probable that some of the sale proceeds were converted to dollars. The focus of concern soon widened to encompass the banks. They were exposed to property and, even if not directly exposed to exchange rate risk, many of their borrowers were, which meant that the banks faced much larger credit risks than previously imagined. Concerned depositors began to withdraw funds; deposit rates had to be increased to staunch the flow, but lending rates could not be raised because large parts of the corporate sector were already technically insolvent.

Policy risk also came into play. The government, in its own way, became caught up in the panic, and reacted in a way that added the threat of a downturn in economic activity. It imposed a drastic liquidity squeeze, and soon announced plans to cut its own spending. It confirmed fears about the banks by closing a number of them. Political risk became important, too.

The government began to show obvious signs of internal conflict, partly because a new cabinet was due to be formed, and a new vice-president elected, within a few months. With each of President Soeharto's successive five-year terms of office it became increasingly likely that the incumbent vice-president would become the next president, raising enormous concerns about the potential impact of this inevitable transition. Backsliding in relation to reforms adopted by agreement with the International Monetary Fund (IMF) became apparent, increasing the risk that Indonesia would lose the high degree of international support it had enjoyed for the previous three decades. Eventually, the ethnic Chinese community began to be treated as scapegoats, with military leaders pointedly requesting them to repatriate funds they had sent offshore. Another aspect of risk had to be re-evaluated, with the memory of anti-Chinese rioting associated with the parliamentary elections a year earlier still fresh, and darker memories from longer in the past always in the background.[8]

For brevity, the discussion above has dealt with just two of the case study countries, in order to highlight the distinction between the origins of the crisis in Indonesia – and, perhaps less obviously, Thailand – and the old-style balance of payments crises for which the means of prevention and the appropriate policy responses are well known. The fundamental lesson to be drawn is that risk matters. It is necessary to be aware of risk, to manage it with care, and to have a clear plan of action for occasions when disturbances do occur; the achievements of decades of development may unravel at an alarming speed otherwise. The possibility of rapid, large-scale movement of financial capital across international borders needs to be taken as given, and choices need to be made as to macroeconomic and financial sector policies that will do most to enhance the resilience of economies in the face of these movements. In particular, there is now an urgent need to ensure that government policy does not add to risk but diminishes it. These issues are addressed in the remainder of this chapter.

Financial sector policies

If financial risk is at the heart of new-style balance of payments crises, this raises important policy issues in relation to the process of financial reform. In countries in which significant deregulation of banks and other financial institutions had occurred – of which Indonesia is the prime example – this was followed by rapid expansion of their financial systems, and this has often been blamed as an important element in the crisis. Indeed, it is hard to believe that banks and non-bank intermediaries could pay sufficient attention to the risks involved in expanding their loan portfolios so rapidly.[9] It would be wrong to conclude, however, that financial deregulation should be reversed in the countries that have already moved in this direction and avoided by those yet to do so.

Financial system weakness prior to the crisis was a characteristic not only of countries where reform was well advanced, but was a problem in countries where there was still much scope for reform, including Japan (Chapter 12) and Korea (Chapter 4), for example. And in some countries as yet largely unscathed by the crisis, such as China (Chapter 6) and Vietnam (Chapter 7), there was (and remains) an urgent need for reform, because the existing financial sector does not do a good job of allocating financial resources. The writer remains in favour of financial reforms that give a much stronger role to market mechanisms, therefore. Many observers have come to the same conclusion, but add the proviso that reform must be preceded by a building up of the system of prudential regulation and supervision. This will be more easily said than done. The art of financial system supervision cannot be learned merely from textbooks or in the classroom; many of the requisite skills will only be learned from experience, and it is unlikely that the necessary regulatory and supervisory capacity can be created in advance of introducing policy reforms.

There is certainly a fundamental problem that needs to be confronted. As Fane (Chapter 17) argues, people do tend to see financial institutions, especially banks, as being guaranteed by governments – implicitly, if not explicitly. The experience of the crisis shows that this belief is well founded, by and large, despite earlier government protestations to the contrary: governments have indeed stepped in to prevent losses to depositors and other creditors. This being the case, Fane would appear to be correct in arguing that this provides a strong case for government intervention in finance, the essence of which must be to ensure that the shifting of risk from banks' owners to the general public is minimised. The reform of prudential regulation can and should proceed immediately, and it should certainly be an integral part of moves to deregulate financial systems that have been heavily controlled in the past. The removal of barriers to entry, branching, interest rate controls and credit ceilings is likely to unleash a strong latent demand for banking services, creating the prospect of high returns for institutions. It is essential that the rush to establish market share be tempered by the credible threat of substantial losses to shareholders if mistakes are made.

Effective prudential regulation needs to be tightly focused. In Indonesia, by contrast, the central bank brought in a vast array of prudential regulations in 1991. It seemed clear at the time – and it has been demonstrated by subsequent events – that the regulators had no real sense of what was important: by listing countless aspects of bank management to monitor, they succeeded in monitoring nothing effectively – but at great cost.[10]

One thing the crisis has demonstrated is that the authorities need not restrict themselves to using local expertise in the monitoring process. The new Indonesian Bank Restructuring Agency is making use of foreign accounting and auditing firms to get a clearer understanding of the true financial condition of Indonesian banks (Johnston 1998). There is every reason for continuing to make use of expertise more readily available in foreign firms than in the domestic supervisory bureaucracy; other countries would do well to study this initiative.

As Fane notes, the most fundamental issue is capital adequacy. Ultimately, if the banks have sufficient capital, their owners will have a strong interest in sound management – including risk management – and this will do more than anything else to protect the interests of depositors and taxpayers. He argues in favour of much higher capital adequacy ratios (i.e. ratios of capital to assets). The writer supports this recommendation, but would broaden it – in particular, to require specific attention to foreign exchange exposures.

Indonesia had a regulated maximum of 25% for the 'net open position' (NOP) of banks, defined as the ratio of net foreign currency-denominated assets to capital. In retrospect, this was far too high. A bank with a NOP of this size would have its capital entirely wiped out if the cost of foreign currency increased by a factor of five, as occurred in Indonesia between July 1997 and January 1998. Fluctuations in bank capital ought to be kept far smaller than this in conceivable circumstances: a maximum NOP of 2.5% would seem closer to the required order of magnitude than 25%. Given our concerns about the government as guarantor, banks should not be in the business of taking on large foreign exchange exposures, nor do they need to do so in order to meet customer requirements. Provided they are permitted to borrow and to place funds offshore,[11] they can meet their customers' demands for foreign currency loans and deposit instruments.

It is not much use to have these kinds of requirements, all of which relate to capital adequacy, if capital is not measured accurately. Fane points out that, in at least some of the East Asian countries, lags between loan repayments falling into arrears and the eventual reporting of charges against bank capital resulting from provisioning for possible losses were far too long. In these days of computerised management information systems and flighty capital movements, this is an unnecessary and dangerous shortcoming.

There is an interesting contrast here with the manner in which risk is managed in markets such as the futures markets. Futures trading is done 'on margin'. In other words, investors need put up only a small amount of their own capital in order to be able to hold futures contracts much greater in value. By leveraging in this manner, there is the possibility of enormous profits if the underlying price moves in the right direction. But there is also the possibility of enormous losses if the price moves in the opposite direction. To protect the counter-party to each contract, therefore, the managers of futures exchanges require additional margin deposits to be made by the investor, sufficient to cover the entire (unrealised) loss, whenever there is an adverse price movement. This requirement operates on a very short time horizon: calls to margin might be required on the same day, or at least the following day. Consideration might be given to requiring that the process of provisioning for losses in banks approach this kind of standard.[12] This would have the effect of requiring banks to have higher levels of capital, which is precisely what is needed in order to make financial systems more resilient in the future.[13]

Fane also draws attention to the desirability of permitting foreign banks to operate freely in competition with domestic banks. Protectionist sentiment in many countries has prevented much relaxation in this area, even when other reforms have gone ahead (Athukorala, in Chapter 5). But it is important to note that governments in the troubled countries have not needed to call on public funds to bail out any of the foreign banks during the crisis. The same was true in Australia's earlier limited banking crisis in the early 1990s; foreign banks were in fact the biggest losers (as Gruen et al. point out in Chapter 13), but their parents covered the losses without cost to Australian depositors or taxpayers. Likewise, the collapse of Barings Bank in 1995 as a result of speculative activities in its Singapore office imposed considerable losses on its shareholders, but caused little harm to Singapore other than a loss of face for the supervisory authorities (D'Ingeo 1996).

Exchange rate risk

Growing fears of devaluation have been at the heart of the sudden change in risk perceptions in East Asia. Concerns about banks were initially mitigated by government promises of the safety of deposits (although later they began to play an important role in some countries), whereas assurances regarding exchange rate stability most likely were regarded as expressions of policy intentions rather than firm commitments.

Indonesians remained highly sensitive to the possibility of devaluation, notwithstanding the country's high and increasing reserves, because of lasting memories of the three large devaluations during 1978–86 and the psychological scars of hyperinflation during the mid-1960s – which so devalued the old currency that a new one had to be introduced. This sensitivity was apparent in the large differential between domestic and foreign interest rates, far in excess of both officially targeted depreciation and recorded depreciation over the previous decade. It was manifested also in relatively frequent bursts of speculation against the currency, driven by the flimsiest of rumours.

And yet there were enormous unhedged exchange rate risk exposures in Indonesia and in the other crisis countries: in retrospect, a gross failure of risk management. It would be wrong to conclude, however, that this was a case of market failure, to which the appropriate response would be to impose various kinds of controls on private sector behaviour. Those who believe in markets do not argue that mistakes are never made, but that properly functioning markets penalise those who make them. They also argue that government intervention is often the real cause of problems that are blamed on market mechanisms. We turn now, therefore, to consider whether, and how, the present crisis may have been initiated by inappropriate government policies.

In various chapters of this book, attention is drawn to the state of business euphoria that existed in countries that had been growing rapidly for many years. In less heady times, bankers and other funds managers sensibly adopt the attitude that they need to be persuaded to part with funds by way of well-researched business proposals, offers of solid security, and a willingness on the part of applicants to put a substantial amount of their own funds at risk in the venture to be financed. When an economy has been racing ahead for years on end, however, there is a strong tendency for those same bankers and financiers to become aggressive salesmen, almost begging businesses to take funds off their hands. All too often, collateral is in the form of real estate valued on the basis of extrapolated recent upward trends in property prices, and projects of all kinds are financed on very high gearing ratios.

The 'euphoria' or, more precisely, the lack of attention to risk, in the years preceding the crisis related not only to the inherent viability of projects themselves,[14] but also to aspects such as the cost of finance and the quality of security for loans. In particular, the exchange rate risk was often ignored. The problem with exchange rate policy in the long period leading up to the crisis was that its very success in maintaining stable rates (or rates of depreciation) against the dollar encouraged the belief that governments could guarantee such stability. In the days before new-style crises, governments could make these promises and live up to them, provided they managed monetary policy properly (which in turn also required responsible fiscal policy). In this new era of financial fragility, this is no longer the case.[15] The mobility of the large pool of global financial capital has rendered such promises barely credible in countries without capital controls, especially in those that rely relatively heavily on foreign capital (other than direct investment) and where banks have mobilised large volumes of deposits.

At the same time, the credibility of government promises about the safety of deposits in banks is also rightly called into question in this new era. The mobile pool of financial capital so often mentioned in this book includes funds mobilised by domestic financial systems, which can easily contribute strongly to new-style crises[16] – and compound them further, if there is a sudden loss of confidence in domestic banks. The volume of funds held in banks in the developing countries of East Asia had grown far larger prior to the crisis than in the old-style crisis days.[17] As total bank assets increase relative to the size of the economy, the credibility of government guarantees of bank deposits is likely to decline (in the absence of measures to strengthen banks' resilience). In Indonesia, for example, the outer bound of the government's contingent liability by virtue of its implicit guarantee of bank deposits grew more than threefold in the decade to June 1997, from 16% to 50% of gross domestic product (GDP). The current crisis clearly demonstrates that risk exposures of such magnitude can have devastating implications for the budget. It is essential, therefore, that they be managed consciously, rather than simply assuming – or hoping – that the guarantee will never need to be honoured.

Taking this line of thought further, it is worth asking to what extent the large exchange rate risk exposures that interacted with increased risk perceptions to spark the present crisis would have emerged in the absence of government promises (explicit and implicit) about the safety of banks or, more realistically, if banking regulations had required banks to have much higher levels of capital relative to risk assets and exchange rate exposures. Presumably it would have been much less. If banks' shareholders had borne much more of the risks relative to governments and depositors, they could have been expected to require such exposures – direct and indirect – to be kept much smaller.

In short, it seems reasonable to argue that governments themselves contributed greatly to the emergence of the East Asian crisis, by following policies that encouraged complacency in relation to risk management on the part of the private sector.

THE HANDLING OF THE CRISIS

Macroeconomic policy responses

The main policy weaknesses that appear to have created the preconditions for financial panic have been discussed. The next aspect of risk management that needs to be considered is the preparedness of governments to respond appropriately to sudden and unexpected financial disturbances. A major part of the explanation as to why the crisis became so much more severe in some countries than in others is to be found, not in what was happening prior to the initial disturbances, but in the manner in which governments reacted to the sudden emergence of speculation against, and the decline of, their currencies.

Should they have reacted at all? The question may seem ingenuous: after all, several of the countries studied in this book have suffered greatly as a result of the disruption to their economies, and it seems natural to imagine that their suffering would have been considerably worse in the absence of government measures to ameliorate the crisis. The notion of 'doing nothing' is a nonsense, of course: what is really at issue is whether governments would have done better to maintain the previous settings of macroeconomic policy, rather than to adjust them in light of the disturbance. No government maintained the previous settings in their entirety, but some came much closer to doing so than others. And the countries that have fared worst seem to be those in which governments themselves were caught up in the panic, and implemented a range of poorly chosen policies as a result.

The question of altering policy settings was of less importance in the countries that maintained controls on their capital account, since freedom of capital movement is a precondition for new-style crises. Accordingly, the discussion in this section focuses on the more open economies facing actual or potential capital outflow and exchange rate depreciation. In the case of Hong Kong, throughout the crisis the government's exchange rate policy has been to 'do nothing', and this has given us the opportunity to witness the operation of a currency board system under conditions of extreme stress. Some observers have argued that this system has been found wanting because of the dramatic surge in interest rates that resulted from speculation against the Hong Kong dollar in October 1997, but that is not the relevant consideration. Proponents of currency boards argue precisely that it is better to have a fixed exchange rate and to live with some interest rate volatility (Walters, in Chapter 18). It is natural to view with horror the jump in interest rates to almost 300% in October as a result of the sudden decline in base money as entities sold the domestic currency (Cheng et al., in Chapter 10). Upon more sober reflection, however, it can be seen that only the overnight rate attained such giddy heights, and that this extreme surge had run its course within a few days; rates remained higher than usual for some time thereafter, but circumstances were also anything but usual. Nevertheless, Hong Kong's growth turned negative for the first time in thirteen years in the first quarter of 1998, so it cannot be said that the government's policy response has provided a painless path through the crisis.

The Taiwanese government's response can also be characterised as mainly passive. The government had adopted a floating exchange rate regime a decade earlier (Kuo and Liu, in Chapter 11) and, although it was by no means a clean float, the government was quick to allow the currency to depreciate when market sentiment moved in that direction in the latter half of 1997. Of all the 'open' Asian countries considered here, Taiwan seems to have incurred the least damage from the crisis. At the other extreme from these two cases, Indonesia's government has adopted a far more activist response, implementing a wide array of policy changes – some of its own volition, some as a response to pressure from the IMF – yet its economy certainly has suffered far more than any other. Clearly, then, it is important to consider whether an activist approach was called for and, if so, what it should have encompassed.

The most fundamental objective of macroeconomic policymaking is to maximise the economic welfare of the general public. Whatever else, this requires governments to do all they can to keep resources of both labour and capital fully employed.[18] Broadly speaking, there is no reason why even large changes in asset prices, resulting from changed expectations, should lead to unemployment. A stock market crash, for example, has no physical implications: the real assets underlying company shares are still in place. It is physically possible, then, to maintain output at previous levels – and there is every reason why this should be the aim of government policy. The same is true of a currency crash affecting firms with foreign currency liabilities.

Two problems arise in such circumstances, however, that may need to be dealt with. First, there is a wealth loss on the part of those whose assets have just been devalued, or whose liabilities have just increased; this is likely to have a negative impact on consumption. But our experience of the 1987 share market crash suggests that this did not turn out to be the great disaster predicted by many at that time. World economic growth was not seriously affected – certainly not on the scale of the disruptions seen recently in East Asia. It is easy to suggest plausible reasons why this was so. First, the individuals concerned may simply have chosen not to reduce consumption, but to reduce the expected value of assets to be bequeathed to their heirs. Second, to the extent they felt it necessary to respond by reducing their own consumption, this could be spread over many years into the future. Finally, governments responded sensibly by loosening monetary policy to some extent. For all these reasons, the overall impact on aggregate demand was slight, and a large surge in unemployment was avoided.

Second, there is the problem of the banks' reaction. If there are significant falls in share or property prices, or significant increases in firms' debt burdens, the value of collateral available to support bank lending declines accordingly. Banks will therefore want to cut back on lending, other things being equal. At the same time, however, to the extent consumer demand declines because of the wealth effect, the inflow of deposits to banks should increase. These two effects tend to counteract each other, and there may be little change in the level of spending financed by bank loans (assuming no tightening of monetary policy by the government). The issue of how best to handle troubled banks will be discussed shortly.

Provided that banks have not been too heavily involved in lending secured by shares, there is no inevitability about a crash in the share market having major implications for economic activity.[19] Property crashes are more problematical, since property is widely used as collateral by banks and other financial institutions. Exactly analogous problems arise when banks become heavily exposed to entities with large foreign currency liabilities if the exchange rate depreciates significantly. In both cases, however, it is important to emphasise that these are financial, not physical, losses.

From the point of view of its owner, a property crash that halves the value of a building, or an exchange rate decline that doubles the burden of debt, may seem little different from a fire which causes damage that will cost as much to repair. From a broader perspective, however, the real level of services output from the building need not decline at all in the first two cases (although the price of such services will need to do so), whereas it necessarily declines in the third. Changes in the value of assets and liabilities affect national wealth and its distribution among individuals, but they need not cause the level of production of goods and services to fall if prices are sufficiently flexible. There is little or nothing a government can do to offset reductions in national wealth that result from changes in financial asset and liability values (although it can certainly affect the distributional impact); what it must see as its objective, therefore, is to ensure that the output of goods and services does not fall unnecessarily. If price flexibility is lacking, this may require some loosening of fiscal and monetary policies.

This is the main feature that distinguishes the 1987 stock market crash from that which occurred in 1929. And it is an important feature distinguishing the countries that have suffered most greatly from those that have been affected relatively little by the East Asian crisis. Although this has been the result of a currency crash rather than (or leading to) a stock market crash, it makes little difference whether wealth declines as a result of a fall in the value of assets or a rise in the value of liabilities. In both circumstances governments need, if anything, to err on the side of boosting demand, not adding to its decline. In East Asia in 1997, governments tended to respond to the initial decline of their currencies, not by loosening, but by tightening, fiscal and monetary policy. In some cases, there was a doctrinaire belief in the inherent desirability of balanced budgets, which overrode any sympathy policymakers may have had for the anti-cyclical demand management approach recommended by Keynes. If tax revenues were falling because of private sector wealth reduction, therefore, government spending would need to be cut commensurately. This was certainly the government's view in Indonesia, for example (Chapter 2), and it appears to have been an important factor contributing to the negative growth recorded in Malaysia (Chapter 5) and Hong Kong (Chapter 10) in the March quarter of 1998. In addition, there was a view that currency and share markets would react adversely to anything other than fiscal austerity.

Concern about the current account was also a key consideration. The balance of payments was suddenly in deficit, and a common view was that this called for adjustment on the imports side, in order to prevent further depreciation (Chapter 2; Chapter 5). Cutting government spending was therefore seen as desirable because it would reduce the demand for imports both directly and indirectly (through the negative multiplier effect on private sector spending). Finally, tightening liquidity in order to push up interest rates and thus stem, or reverse, the outflow of capital was often thought necessary.

All of this was precisely the reverse of what was required if economies were to remain fully employed. An alternative approach would have been to allow the budget to go into deficit (so that the economy would benefit from the automatic stabilising mechanism under which taxes and other revenues fall as incomes fall), and (for non-currency board countries) to allow the exchange rate to depreciate even further (thus allowing the market mechanism to determine the accommodating changes in spending and importing made necessary by the sudden outflow of capital).[20] While a modest increase in base money growth would also have been appropriate, most of the monetary impact of the budget deficit – including that part of the deficit resulting from the cost of government guarantees of bank deposits – would have needed to be offset by issuing bonds or central bank certificates, and perhaps by selling off some international reserves.

An important implication of the shift from old-style to new-style balance of payments crises is that, if the IMF is to have any useful role to play, it will need to be very different from previously. In the past, putting an end to a balance of payments crisis typically required a devaluation and a politically difficult tightening of fiscal and monetary discipline. The near exhaustion of reserves during the crisis allowed the IMF to come in with the offer of loans that would provide temporary liquidity during the wait for export recovery, conditional on the government making the necessary macroeconomic policy adjustments.

In new-style crises, it is not export recovery that is awaited, but a recovery of confidence. It seems most unlikely that the financial resources the IMF can make available to governments that choose to support their currencies when under speculative attack will increase as rapidly as the global pool of capital available for undertaking such speculation.[21] In short, the old approach will become increasingly less feasible, and the IMF will need to reinvent itself if it is to remain relevant. This may mean shifting to a role more akin to that of a 'management consultant' when brought in to assist governments in times of economic crisis, away from that of stern disciplinarian seeking to impose its will on policymakers.

Finance sector policy responses

The treatment of weak financial institutions in the context of the unfolding crisis has also been important. At a superficial level, Thailand and Indonesia followed a similar course. In both countries, huge amounts of public funds have been poured into troubled financial institutions. Moreover, a number of institutions were closed abruptly in both countries early on. In Thailand's case there have been subsequent runs on non-bank financial institutions and banks, but the side effects of the closures seem to have been considerably less disruptive than in Indonesia, where they had a devastating impact, causing a run on most of the private domestic banks and eventually almost paralysing the banking system. It is important to account for this difference. The risk of failures amongst financial institutions will always be present – and will be immeasurably higher in the midst of a financial crisis – and good risk management practice requires planning for, and therefore understanding of, such contingencies.

After the first group of bank closures in Indonesia was announced at the end of October 1997, it quickly became common knowledge that the number closed reflected a compromise between the government and the IMF: it could just as easily have been forty as the actual sixteen. This made depositors concerned about the condition of the remaining banks, and led to large-scale withdrawals in the ensuing weeks – notwithstanding the government's promise to cover the claims of all depositors up to a maximum of Rp20 million, and its assurances that no other banks would be closed.[22] Deposits migrated to state banks and to foreign banks, but it was not practicable for either group to take over the private banks' borrowers, so the wheels of finance began to seize up.

In Thailand, many more financial institutions were closed down than in Indonesia, but they were not banks. They were finance companies that were not part of the payments system: they drew the bulk of their funding from the wholesale market in the form of promissory notes and bills of exchange, rather than individuals' deposits, and they were not in the business of providing working capital finance to the business sector. Unlike in Indonesia, therefore, their closure did not have significant implications for the banking system.

Creditors of enterprises that default must always weigh the relative merits of forcing bankruptcy and the cessation of activity, on the one hand, and installing new management in the hope that the ultimate loss will be less severe if operations are continued, on the other. In a context in which a government effectively guarantees banks' liabilities, it is in the same position as such creditors when any bank fails, and it is not clear that any good purpose is served by closing down troubled banks rather than keeping them going under new management.[23] Closing a bank requires its employees to be dismissed – most of them having been in no way responsible for the bank's troubles – yet its deposit and lending customers must still be serviced. Shifting customers to other banks involves considerable disruption.

It is essential, of course, to turn off the tap if government funds are being wasted, but the basic issue is whether the bank in question can cover its variable costs if it continues to operate, not the size of losses it may have accumulated in the past. The question is especially important in conditions of systemic crisis, where not just a single institution is in trouble, but many. In the Indonesian case, the banking law gave the government power to replace a bank's management, and to explore various avenues for replenishing lost capital. At a later date, banks taken over in this manner could have been sold as going concerns, or their assets progressively sold off and their deposit business transferred to other institutions; the closure of banks without any warning seems in retrospect to have been unnecessary and counterproductive.

CONCLUSION

In this chapter it has been argued that the world has entered a new era of financial fragility. This new era has been ushered in by a huge and growing pool of highly mobile financial capital – including funds mobilised by rapidly expanding banking and financial systems in many developing countries – and by the global trend to openness in regard to capital flows. These factors provide the preconditions for new-style balance of payments crises that demand different policy responses from old-style ones.

The new-style crises are driven by changes in risk perceptions, and efforts to prevent them must be guided by the principle of avoiding policies that inadvertently encourage private sector actors to be complacent in relation to financial risk. In respect of exchange rate risk exposures, such complacency might be discouraged by adopting genuinely flexible exchange rates, or by aiming for stability relative to a genuinely diversified basket of foreign currencies rather than just the US dollar (which would amount to flexibility of rates against any single currency in which borrowing might be undertaken). But perhaps the most promising possibility involves increasing significantly the amount of capital shareholders of financial institutions have at stake relative to the size of those institutions' activities. The notion underlying such policy reforms is the axiom that capitalism does not work well if only the gains resulting from business decisions accrue to the investors who make them, and not the losses.

New-style crises also require a quite different policy response. Except if countries have adopted the currency board system, exchange rates should be permitted to be market determined, against a backdrop of steady or slightly more expansionary fiscal and monetary policy settings. The remedy for old-style crises – devaluation, accompanied by fiscal and monetary tightening – is entirely inappropriate. The notion that it is sensible to 'do nothing' in the face of a new-style crisis clearly will take time to be accepted by governments but, like first-time bungee jumpers, they will eventually come to realise that although the value of currencies may plunge and bounce alarmingly, ultimately their equilibrium values will depend on how carefully their quantity is managed.

NOTES

The writer is deeply indebted to George Fane for many helpful suggestions.

1   Alternatively, offshore borrowing by the government to prevent reserves from falling may result in a continuous decline in the government's net foreign assets.
2   Krugman (1998c) refers to this as the 'canonical', or first-generation, crisis model.
3   An important part of this phenomenon is the growing importance of securitised finance relative to bank loans. Bank finance is much more stable because of the need for banks to maintain long-term relationships with their borrowers. Securitised finance does not rely on such relationships: shares, bonds, commercial paper and the like are issued, and later traded, in impersonal markets.
4   Current attempts to find reliable indicators of vulnerability to currency crises

can be thought of as seeking to monitor potential changes in risk perceptions. In the opinion of the writer, such efforts will probably come to little: the risks are so diverse and subject to change in relative importance that this amounts to shooting at an impossibly fast-moving target.

5   The 'new-style' crisis description is in the same mould as the 'second-generation' models discussed in Krugman (1998c).

6   No doubt they were encouraged by applause from the many champions and supporters of East Asia – this writer included – and the World Bank's proclamation of 'The East Asian Miracle' (1993).

7   For example, stock markets, mutual funds, banks, life insurance and pensions providers all facilitate the diversification of financial risk; derivatives markets permit financial risks to be hedged.

8   The ethnic Chinese suffered greatly in the aftermath of the attempted coup in 1965.

9   It should not be presumed that Indonesian banks were bankrupt, or that generally they were heading in this direction, prior to the huge depreciation of the rupiah. The level of non-performing loans was high for banks as a whole, but these were much more heavily concentrated amongst the state banks than private banks; there is little hard evidence to show that problem loans were running out of control in the latter.

10 The central bank's move to implement an 'enhanced credit monitoring system' capable of reporting on loans down to a value of only US$15,000 is an indication of its inability to focus on what really mattered in this field (Hendrobudiyanto 1994: 164).

11 Curiously, this was not the case in Indonesia.

12 This would complement, rather than replace, the practice of adjusting loss provisions on a case-by-case basis when management becomes aware of changes in the borrower's business prospects, the value of collateral assets, and so on.

13 One issue here is that, if banks face much more stringent controls of this type than hitherto, there is a danger that other kinds of institution will spring up that will not be subject to the banking regulations. The most appropriate solution to this problem would be to define a 'bank' as any institution that 'collects deposits from the general public'; the authorities could be given a good deal of discretion in determining what constituted such deposits.

14 As implied by the demand for their output, required initial investment outlays, the cost of non-financial inputs, and so on.

15 In the special case of currency board countries, the promise is much more credible.

16 The Mexican crisis of 1994 was driven to a much greater extent by residents shifting funds offshore than by foreigners repatriating capital (Folkerts-Landau et al. 1995: 7).

17 Broad money growth at rates of the order of 20% per annum in many countries gives some indication of the increasing scale of banking activity (Table 1.8).

18 Except that, if the variable social cost of keeping an enterprise operational exceeds the marginal social benefit of doing so, it would be appropriate to close it down.

19 Japan appears to be the only one of our case study countries where this has been a serious problem.

20 A genuinely floating exchange rate has the advantage that it does not 'offer

speculators an easy target' since the government is not committed to defending any particular exchange rate (Krugman 1998c).

21 This is an extension of Krugman's (1998c) observation that the European currency crises of 1992–3 'demonstrated the near-irrelevance of foreign exchange reserves in a world of high capital mobility'. Recall that the IMF could pledge only US$10 billion to assist Indonesia in November 1997; Indonesia's reserves themselves were more than twice that amount (Chapter 2).

22 This lack of credibility was a clear indication of public consciousness of what was referred to earlier as political risk.

23 The writer owes this point to George Fane.

21 Economic lessons

Ross Garnaut

This chapter returns to the questions raised in the opening pages of the book. What lessons can we draw from the experience of East Asia and its near neighbours through the shocks of 1997 and 1998 about avoiding, managing and recovering from financial crisis?

The contagion across East Asia continued through June 1998. Falling economic activity and currency depreciation are leading to progressive reduction of imports, in one economy after another, accumulating to an implosion of intraregional trade and an intensification of contractionary pressures. So the lessons presented in this chapter are in the nature of a trial balance. The later parts of this chapter present some views on management of the international transmission of crisis. A final balance sheet may draw stronger lessons on these matters.

SIGNS OF PROBLEMS

There were indications of what McLeod (Chapter 20) calls 'old-style' financial problems in advance of crisis in what became the 'troubled economies': appreciation of the real exchange rate; slowing export growth measured in international currency; and a high (Thailand and Malaysia) or rapidly rising (Korea) deficit in the current account of the balance of payments. These factors raised the possibility that the maintenance of economic stability might require policy adjustment – an appropriate combination of reduction in domestic expenditure and the real exchange rate – at least temporarily slowing economic growth. The indications were less, and less obvious, in Indonesia.

An appreciation of the real exchange rate is not in itself a definitive indicator of the need for policy adjustment. Real appreciation can be associated with mature economic success, as the accumulation of capital and increases in the productivity with which labour and capital are employed make labour scarce and raise wages, and both force and facilitate structural change into more capital-intensive and technologically sophisticated production and exports. In these favourable circumstances, continuing real exchange rate appreciation can be associated with economic stability and sustained strong growth, as the earlier experience of Japan, Taiwan, Hong Kong, Singapore and Korea attests.

However, there were two reasons to be concerned about the appreciation of the real exchange rate in the mid-1990s in Thailand, Malaysia and Korea (and, to a lesser extent, Indonesia). In none of these countries had the development of economic structure yet proceeded so far that large real exchange rate appreciations were consistent with both continued strong growth in output and reasonable balance in external payments. Warr emphasises this point in his discussion of Thailand (Chapter 3). The second reason for concern was that the appreciations after 1995 were large and sudden, as East Asian currencies followed the strong dollar.

Unlike in Japan from the early 1960s and Taiwan, Hong Kong, Korea and Singapore after 1985, the troubled economies' appreciating real exchange rates after 1995 were associated with substantial current account deficits. Nevertheless, the troubled countries were not typical candidates for old-style balance of payments crises, because current account deficits were not being driven by public deficits. Rather, the deficits were being apparently comfortably covered by private capital inflow. This inflow was helping to sustain the high growth that was, in turn, reflected in the current account deficits. As became clear in 1997, the capital inflow was highly volatile, going into reverse in Thailand as market participants recognised the possibility of an old-style crisis forcing a change in the exchange rate. Crisis, when it came in Thailand, took the form of a new-style capital account reaction to old-style imbalances (McLeod, Chapter 20).

With an open capital account and internationally mobile capital, an economy can experience a sudden increase in net capital outflow even if it has neither a large current account deficit nor any recent history of one. This was the case with the speculative outflow against the Hong Kong dollar after the floating of the Thai baht. It is an important part of the Indonesian story, where domestic capital flight appears to have been quantitatively more important to the crisis than the repatriation of foreign capital.

Does the presence of large current account deficits provide any guide to the need for policy adjustment in the modern world of open capital accounts and internationally mobile capital? Foreign capital in its nature tends to be highly mobile internationally; domestic capital is mobile to varying and, on average, lesser degrees. Direct foreign investment is less mobile in the short term than portfolio investment, long-term debt less mobile than short-term debt. An economy with a continuing history of large current account deficits financed by more volatile forms of private capital inflow tends to be more vulnerable to financial crisis. Thailand especially, but also Malaysia and Korea, had these signs of vulnerability in high degree in 1997.

The crisis began in Thailand because that economy had symptoms of old-style crisis together with vulnerability to sudden, large-scale reversal of capital inflow. Other economies with these characteristics were soon in trouble as they were tested by contagion, particularly Malaysia and Korea, and more weakly the Philippines. Indonesia had less susceptibility to old-style crisis but exceptional vulnerability to domestic capital flight. As contagion struck, the weakness of financial institutions and regulatory systems became a key determinant of the extent of economic loss. The Philippines fared reasonably well on this score as well as on the criterion of vulnerability to capital flight. Thailand, Korea, Indonesia and, to a lesser extent, Malaysia were marked as candidates for major economic dislocation.

The extraordinary collapse of the Indonesian economy cannot be explained without reference to an additional factor: incoherence in the political and policy response, leading to uncertainty, higher risk premia and, after the emergence of political instability, doubts about the security of contractual and other property rights.

LESSONS FOR AVOIDING FINANCIAL CRISIS

The first lesson from the East Asian crisis is that some old economic wisdom about the business cycle in industrial economies is relevant to rapidly growing East Asian economies. The euphoria of a long boom creates risks to economic stability, and the risks can be crystallised negatively by the emergence of old-style macroeconomic imbalances.

The psychology of a long boom was important to the emergence of large banking and other financial sector problems. It was also important to the emergence of macroeconomic imbalance. In what became the four troubled economies, a decade of unbroken rapid growth had encouraged the taking of risks and expanded the gamblers' access to resources. Markets went too far in their optimism, as reflected in unrealistically high asset values. The correction when it came was also associated with overshooting in expectations and values.

Perhaps the main lesson here is for the private sector. Investors and lenders are now highly sensitive to the danger of boom psychology, as they are after every crash. For this reason, East Asian economies will not soon experience another boom with a high speculative element in the style of the mid-1990s. But, as in all other episodes of boom and crash, the lessons will gradually recede from private memories.

The main lesson for public management relates to choice of exchange rate regime in open economies in the contemporary world of internationally mobile capital. The East Asian developing economies with open capital accounts had no effective means of adjusting policy to counter the imbalances emerging from the long boom. (The Chinese authorities, with controls on external capital flows still in place, had different options. Their timely fiscal and monetary adjustment in 1995 saw China well on the way to low inflation and external payments stabilisation before the crisis hit East Asia.)

The adjustable pegs against the US dollar in all of the troubled economies, and also in the Philippines, Vietnam and China, contributed to declining competitiveness after 1995, lifting East Asian currency values with the US dollar. The monetary authorities in several of the troubled economies sought to ease inflationary pressures by tightening monetary policy. Higher interest rates and an apparently fixed exchange rate were an attractive combination for international investors. Higher capital inflow was a short-term consequence, offsetting the monetary tightening.

The US dollar was peculiarly unsuitable as an exchange rate peg in the period of its appreciation against most currencies and the large associated lift in value against the yen. The adjustable peg would have led to more moderate real appreciation in Southeast Asia and Korea after 1995, if it had been against a basket of major currencies in which the US dollar was less dominant. Such a basket would be a better choice than the dollar alone if there were to be a return to pegged exchange rates. But the basic problems of the system would remain.

The established exchange rate systems were unsuitable to the circumstances of the mid-1990s, but were there obviously more suitable alternatives? How would freely floating rates, or rates fixed rigidly within a currency board system, have responded to the pressures?

Freely floating rates would at first have generated uncomfortable outcomes. It is likely that they would have tended to appreciate in the heady boom conditions, attractive to capital inflow, in the years immediately before the crisis. It is likely that we would have seen, for a while, even larger nominal effective appreciation of the Indonesian rupiah, the Thai baht, the Malaysian ringgit and the Korean won, as the yen weakened against the dollar in 1995 and 1996. This would have taken the edge off the boom and eased domestic inflationary pressures. It would not immediately have led to a lower real exchange rate – rather, the reverse. But it is likely that, by avoiding the heights of boom, the inevitable later downward reassessments of East Asian investment opportunities would have led to nominal and real depreciation with less risk of crisis. This is broadly what happened in Western Pacific economies with more flexible exchange rates, notably Australia, Singapore and Taiwan.

The freely floating rate is no panacea. The larger real exchange rate appreciation of the boom period would have been seen to choke off some opportunities for growth, and would have been much criticised by firms producing tradable goods. The subsequent depreciation is likely to have been large – the more so since floating rates typically overshoot in adjustment to new circumstances. This would have placed strains on domestic enterprises that were exposed to foreign debt. While the floating rate would have encouraged firms to cover the exchange risk of their external liabilities, it is likely that time and unhappy experience would be needed for the lessons to be learned well. The Australian case (Chapter 13) highlights the process of learning associated with the bedding down of a freely floating rate.

How would economies have fared through the mid-1990s if they had been operating rigidly fixed exchange rates within currency board systems?

Like a floating rate, a currency board system in the years preceding the crisis may have led temporarily to an exacerbation of real exchange rate appreciation – in this case through greater short-term monetary expansion and domestic inflation, as in Hong Kong (Chapter 10). The rise in domestic relative to international costs would gradually have diminished growth and expectations of growth. It may have brought on some of the costs of boom conditions earlier, and it probably would have brought the boom to an earlier end. When the change of sentiment about prospects for investment came, it would not have been so large or sudden, if only because it would not have been exacerbated by such severe anxiety about the exchange rate itself. The change of sentiment when it came would still have been associated with capital outflow, monetary contraction, deflation and pressures for recession – just as it was in practice in Hong Kong.

The economic effects of a currency board system in these circumstances would have depended on the extent of price and structural flexibility in the domestic economy. Where there was a high degree of flexibility, as in Hong Kong, the adjustment would have been relatively smooth and only temporarily painful. But, in economies with price and structural rigidity, the monetary contraction would have generated a long period of recession.

A few East Asian economies other than Hong Kong may have the price and structural flexibility to make a currency board system work at reasonable cost (Walters, Chapter 18). Thailand might be one, having experienced falling prices and costs and rapid shifts of resources into the tradables industries in the year after the onset of crisis.

Perhaps a strong commitment to a fixed exchange rate against an appropriate basket of non-inflationary currencies, supported by commitments to manage domestic demand consistently with the exchange rate regime, is China's best bet for macroeconomic stability, pending the development of institutions that allow delivery of stability through steady monetary growth and appropriately flexible interest rates. The Chinese authorities' credibility in sustaining such a regime will have been enhanced if they are able to sustain the yuan exchange rate against the dollar through the crisis.

In the immediate aftermath of crisis, pegged but adjustable exchange rates in the pre-crisis style have been discredited. Floating rates rule by default in mid-1998, but people in the troubled economies, and in particular Indonesia, are not happy with the outcome. They are likely to become steadier floating rates over time, as market participants learn the modalities of the new regime, and strengthen their capacity to manage their relationships to it. As financial stability returns, the authorities in some countries will consider a return to fixed rates. One or more may have the flexibility to join Hong Kong in a currency board-type system. Others would be wise to stick with the floating rates.

There are lessons for the management of the capital account in the recent experience. While open capital accounts facilitated the emergence of economic instability, the appropriate response is to facilitate the effective integration of domestic into international capital markets by strengthening financial institutions and their supervision.

The reductions in transaction costs of international capital movements, and the associated expansion of capital flows, contributed to the speed with which crisis came to East Asia and to the severity of the dislocation in 1997. These developments are the other side of the coin to expanded opportunities for rapid economic development. Inevitably, the crisis has raised questions about the desirability of open capital accounts, and the conditions that must be met if open capital accounts are to be compatible with economic stability.

The cases of China (Chapter 6), Vietnam (Chapter 7) and India (Chapter 8) suggest that capital controls assisted the management of shocks from financial crisis in some Asian economies. In China, and to a lesser extent in India, the macroeconomic fundamentals were favourable to macroeconomic stability in any case. It may be that capital controls inhibited the emergence of inflationary boom conditions in China prior to the crisis in Southeast Asia and Korea, although this would not seem to have been decisive.

The Chinese monetary authorities have responded to crisis elsewhere in the East Asian region by attenuating their timetable for capital account convertibility and accelerating domestic financial reform in advance of the eventual opening of the capital account. While it would be costly to economic development, and in any case futile, for China to retreat forever from capital account convertibility, its increased caution in the late 1990s would seem to be soundly based. It is a lesson of the crisis that the strengthening of financial institutions should proceed on an early timetable, in advance of complete convertibility on capital account.

Vietnam faces more difficult macroeconomic fundamentals, amongst other things requiring high levels of capital inflow – higher than in any of the troubled economies – to cover the current account deficit. It is having difficulty in attracting the required investment in the aftermath of crisis elsewhere in Southeast Asia and in Korea, and has tightened controls on trade and current payments. This approach will be very damaging to development if it persists for long. Vietnam's weak economic fundamentals require conventional adjustment of the exchange rate and expenditure, followed by more urgent attention to structural reform, including financial reform to support eventual capital account liberalisation.

In the troubled economies, while there is no enthusiasm for the consequences of increased capital mobility in the aftermath of crisis, there is no determined movement to close the capital account. There is reluctant recognition that there can be no turning back the clock. Attention is appropriately focused on domestic financial reform to reduce the costs of instability in international capital flows.

What are the particular lessons for the development of a financial system that can deliver stability in modern economies that are open to international capital flows?

The pervasive presence of government safety nets of various kinds creates a role for prudential regulation (Fane, Chapter 17). Prudential regulation will be more effective if it has simple objectives: most importantly, accuracy, honesty and transparency in financial reporting; the avoidance of related party and other potentially non-commercial transactions; and the maintenance of relatively high ratios of capital to risk-weighted assets. For developing economies, the ratio of capital to assets needs to be rather higher than the norm for developed countries. The most important feature of effective prudential regulation is the enforcement of the rules, and simplicity contributes to effective enforcement. If the rules of the financial marketplace are sound, a competitive environment strengthens financial institutions, and openness to foreign competition in banking can contribute special strengths by allowing the spreading of risks across national borders.

The experience of weakness in financial systems carries lessons for industry policy. Intertwined with the financial sector problems, state-directed credit and resource allocation more generally introduce major risks to economic stability and development. The dirigiste models of industrial policy, notably the Korean chaebol model which was becoming more prominent in Chinese discussion, have been discredited by the crisis. The open, competitive models of industry policy have been strengthened, for the time being at least.

More generally, the crisis has provided a clearer perspective on the economic costs of corruption in government–business relations. Grand corruption had been endemic in some East Asian economies prior to the crisis, influencing resource allocation on a large scale and blocking first-best economic policies. While some economic analysts maintained consistently that this was a drag on economic performance, it was not an easily argued or readily accepted case in the days of sustained rapid growth and talk of the East Asian 'miracle'. The crisis has laid bare the costs of conflict of interest in government decisions affecting business. This will not end corruption, but there will be less force in arguments that grand corruption is harmless to growth.

LESSONS FOR THE MANAGEMENT OF CRISIS

The quality and coherence of the policy response is of central importance to the severity of crisis. This is perhaps the most important lesson for the management of crisis in the recent experience.

Amongst the five economies most at risk at the onset of crisis, the Philippines was favoured by early policy coherence in response. Indonesia was damaged by incoherence and policy error, exacerbated by confidence-sapping conflict between the Indonesian government and Washington-based international agencies. Thailand and Korea corrected unsteady initial policy responses after changes in government, in Korea at fortuitously timed presidential elections. Malaysia's substantive policy response was mixed but broadly appropriate, but its impact was damaged by discordance in public presentation. The latter weakness may cause the eventual cost of the crisis to Malaysia to be as severe as in any economy other than Indonesia.

I would draw a closely related lesson. There is no doubt that reform of the financial sector and the removal of structural weakness in other areas are essential for avoidance of crisis. But in the midst of crisis, augmenting the policy agenda with structural reform issues that are not crucial to economic recovery can severely overload political systems. In Indonesia, this was one reason for incoherence in the implementation of reform programs agreed with the International Monetary Fund (IMF), and eventually for the political instability that greatly complicated the process of recovery. Nellor (Chapter 15) argues persuasively that, in the absence of comprehensive reform, it would not have been possible to restore investors' confidence in the crisis economies. Certainly there would be large gains through confidence and other effects if it were possible to implement far-reaching reform successfully in the midst of crisis. Korea seems to be achieving gains of this kind in mid-1998, although even in Korea's favourable political circumstances the pace of reform has lagged behind early announcements. There are limits to the capacity of political systems to handle change. The cost of overloading the political system is at best the loss of credibility by the authorities. At worst, overloading leads to breakdown of the political system, and this comes to outweigh all other influences on economic development.

What are the lessons for the conduct of fiscal and monetary policy? These lessons are still emerging. In the first six months of crisis, the fiscal and monetary authorities of the troubled economies and their IMF advisers applied variations on the standard prescriptions for old-style financial crisis: budget surpluses and higher interest rates.

Whatever the merits of this approach, it was a mistake to enter commitments to fiscal contraction that could not be fulfilled. The first Letters of Intent to the IMF of Thailand, Indonesia and Korea provided for budget surpluses. These targets were later abandoned, as descent into recession cut government revenues far more than originally anticipated, and as the fiscal impact of financial sector rehabilitation increased. However reassuring to the markets the commitments to budget surpluses might have been if they had been honoured, any gains were overwhelmed by increased uncertainty and risk premia as the targets were modified. In Indonesia, the failure of the January 6 budget to deliver the 1% budget surplus was an important factor in adverse market reaction to Indonesian policy, and in the immediately following collapse of the rupiah.

Nellor (Chapter 15) describes the IMF's fiscal policy approach as one of allowing the automatic stabilisers to work – allowing the budget deficit to grow as recession reduced revenues and increased expenditure. Within the IMF definition of automatic stabilisation, new measures were to offset the fiscal costs of financial sector rehabilitation. This intention would seem to be broadly appropriate, although the unexpected depth of recession and disinflation suggests that it may have been excessively austere to attempt the recoupment of all new financial sector expenditures. However, it is not easy to reconcile the initial targets for budget surpluses with an intention to let the automatic stabilisers work. Rather, this approach seems to have emerged over time, as the depth of the downturn in economic activity became apparent.

The most obvious lesson for monetary policy from the first six months of crisis is that, whatever the average rate of monetary growth that is judged to be appropriate, as near as possible to steady application of that rate is desirable. Again, the Indonesian case provides the clearest negative lessons, with extremes of high monetary growth as central bank funds were pumped into ailing financial institutions, and then sudden and large increases in interest rates.

There is no denying the difficulty of managing monetary policy in these circumstances – of judging an appropriate rate of monetary growth, and then delivering steadily the desired expansion. Large shifts in relative prices and rates of growth of economic parameters changed established relationships between money supply and expenditure. Worse, they changed them differently for different measures of money. But, for all the difficulty, the extreme instability of money growth was both unnecessary and highly undesirable.

What have we learned about the appropriate rate of monetary expansion in the circumstances of the troubled economies? In mid-1998 we know that output declined, and current account deficits turned into surplus, far faster and further than anticipated in the early months of crisis.

Inflation as measured by the broad price indexes increased in the troubled economies, in Indonesia dramatically. But the inflation was mainly associated with the direct effect of exchange rate depreciation on the prices of tradable goods and services. Money wages for many categories of labour, and prices for non-tradable goods and services, rose hardly at all and in many cases fell. After the large currency depreciation, money growth at the pre-crisis rates was going to place downward pressure on the prices of labour and non-tradable goods and services. It was going to force a large reduction in output pending the falls in domestic prices. There has been impressive downward flexibility in wages and non-tradable prices through the crisis, but nowhere are price adjustments fast enough to avoid deep and prolonged recession at pre-crisis rates of monetary growth. From these perspectives, it seems that on average, a higher rate of monetary expansion through the crisis would have been desirable.

The main motive for high interest rates was to limit the extent of currency depreciation. Amongst other things, the IMF wished to limit the adjustment costs imposed on the world outside East Asia (Nellor, Chapter 15). The rest of the world would have to absorb the huge increase in net exports deriving from the depreciation of East Asian currencies.

Certainly, it is a matter of concern that any acceleration of monetary expansion may prompt further currency depreciation, and so impose further adjustment costs on the East Asian economies and the rest of the world. The extent of any such depreciation would depend on the balance of confidence effects affecting risk premia applied by investors of internationally mobile capital – the negative perceptions of increased exchange rate pressure and risk, and the positive perceptions from possible stabilisation of domestic economic activity. These are matters of judgment, where the relevant facts vary from country to country. But one year on from the floating of the Thai baht, recognising all the risks of faster monetary expansion, it seems that the more common error of the authorities was in the direction of restrictive monetary conditions.

It would, of course, be safer if domestic monetary expansion could be balanced by increased capital inflow, so avoiding increased downward pressure on the floating exchange rates. In the second quarter of 1998, Korea, Thailand and Malaysia made foreign bond issues to finance some fiscal expansion. Indonesia did not have access to international bond markets in the same way. By June 1998 there was active discussion of increased official international grant and loan funding, which would seem to be an essential underpinning for Indonesian stabilisation and recovery.

On monetary policy outside the troubled economies, Japan is a special case of great importance for recovery elsewhere in the region. The banking system's heavy burden of non-performing loans (Horiuchi, Chapter 12) has dragged down economic performance throughout the 1990s, and has been an important motive for exceptionally low interest rates. Japan, uniquely, appears to have descended into a liquidity trap in the mid-1990s, where the later rounds of reductions in interest rates appeared to have little stimulative effect on domestic investment or consumption. Easy money has, however, had important effects on encouraging portfolio capital outflow and yen depreciation, and therefore has reduced import growth and pressure for outward direct foreign investment. This set of outcomes after 1995 played a role in the origins of crisis. Its continuation in 1998 is a drag on recovery in East Asia. A Japanese recovery policy focused first of all on rehabilitation of the banking system, and with greater emphasis on fiscal and less on monetary expansion, would be more favourable for the regional and international economies, and ultimately for Japan.

LESSONS RELATED TO INTERNATIONAL SPILLOVERS

International spillovers, or contagion, have been a characteristic of the East Asian crisis. In Chapter 1, it was noted that contagion had had three elements. The first two elements were important to the initial spread of crisis through East Asia. These were modelled by McKibbin (Chapter 14) as an increase in risk premia on investment. The third element of contagion is the diminished opportunities for gains from trade with, and investment in and by, regional economic partners. This third element became more important as the crisis proceeded, forcing a large contraction of imports in one East Asian economy after another following exchange rate depreciation and expenditure reduction. This channel of contagion was powerful because, by the mid-1990s, East Asia provided markets for more than half of the exports of East Asian developing economies (Figure 1.5), and over the decade to 1996 the large majority of the growth in exports. It is now clear that this third element represents an important difference from the Latin American financial crises (Hale, Chapter 16), substantially complicating the challenge of regional recovery.

Kindleberger (1973) demonstrated the mutually reinforcing cycle of intensifying global depression and trade contraction between 1929 and 1932, as the dollar value of international trade fell rapidly for several years. In East Asia, there was an implosion of international and especially intraregional trade in the year after the Thai baht devaluation, by early 1998 encompassing Japan, and by May 1998 a contraction in Chinese international trade as well. By mid-1998, the continued decline of total East Asian imports was a drag on recovery throughout the region. The contraction of intra-East Asian trade meant that the large expansion of net exports required by the troubled economies' recovery strategies had to be focused overwhelmingly in North America and Europe.

The presence of external costs from financial crisis in a single country introduces the possibility that global efficiency could be raised by international cooperation. International cooperation to reduce the negative impact of one country's crisis on others can take several forms. In practice it has mainly comprised the provision of international capital, technical assistance in economic policymaking and reform, and political support and pressure to undertake productive reform against domestic resistance. More generally, international cooperation can strengthen confidence in the crisis economies that the international economic environment will be supportive of an outward-oriented development strategy, and in the international community confidence that the troubled economies' recovery strategy is soundly based.

The costs of crisis in one country extend throughout the international economy. However, they are concentrated most strongly amongst the crisis economies' major partners for trade and investment. Usually, and in East Asia, this means that external costs are concentrated in a troubled economy's own region. This suggests that there is scope for regional alongside global cooperation, with the former contributing disproportionately to support of recovery. To the extent that regional economies understand better the institutions and political economy of a troubled country, the case for regional alongside global cooperation is the stronger.

Realisation of the importance of the international transmission of depression led to the establishment in the 1940s of the current institutional framework of international economic cooperation, including the IMF and the General Agreement on Tariffs and Trade (predecessor of the World Trade Organisation). Unlike Western Europe and North America, the East Asian (or, more broadly, Western Pacific) region does not have a strong institutional framework for cooperation to avoid transmission of economic crisis. On trade matters, Asia Pacific Economic Cooperation (APEC), joining the Western Pacific to North America, Peru and Chile, provides a framework supportive of the maintenance of open trade and investment, and a forum for high-level discussion of regional issues of major importance.

Within the Western Pacific, an informal regional forum comprising the central bank governors of eleven economies (EMEAP, Executive Meeting of East Asia and Pacific Central Banks) has provided established channels for discussion of regional monetary cooperation. In the lead-up to the Vancouver meeting of APEC leaders in late 1997, an Asian Surveillance Group (ASG) brought together finance secretaries and central bank governors from Western Pacific APEC members plus the United States and Canada. The ASG met in April 1998 to discuss the financial crisis in preparation for the meeting of APEC finance ministers, and in June in Tokyo at the time of the G7 finance ministers' meeting on Japanese economic stabilisation and recovery. A Japanese proposal, as the crisis was breaking in 1997, for an Asia Fund was stillborn when the United States with some Western Pacific support baulked at the absence of explicit institutional linkage with IMF programs.

How has the international cooperative framework performed through the crisis? There was prompt movement towards putting together an assistance package for Thailand in August 1997, with the IMF playing a central role and drawing on the EMEAP framework to augment financial contributions from regional sources. Early commitments by regional economies – Japan, Australia, Singapore, China and Hong Kong – allowed a substantial funding facility to be put together without US participation. The commitments of funds and associated technical support for financial sector rehabilitation were helpful to early exchange rate stabilisation and to progress on systemic reform. There was also worthwhile success in stabilising exchange rates and the first steps in systemic reform on the basis of IMF-led packages in Korea, after a shaky start, and after a new president was elected late in 1997.

The success of international support for stabilisation and structural reform in Indonesia has been more problematical. Only US$4 billion of the US$38 billion international support package had been disbursed by June 1998. An extraordinarily ambitious program of structural reform, extending well beyond the financial sector, had become tangled in domestic politics and had few concrete achievements to its credit.

Support for financial sector reform from the IMF and informally through

Western Pacific central banks has been helpful to managing regional contagion beyond the three countries with IMF crisis packages, notably in
Malaysia, the Philippines and China. More broadly, the international community has been slow to come to grips with the scale of regional and,
potentially, global spillovers from the crisis.

The third element of contagion operates through three main mechanisms. One is the increase in net exports in troubled economies associated
with crisis and recovery. This requires trading partners to accept increased
net imports, with associated adjustment costs. A second is the contraction
in the scale of the troubled economies' trade, especially imports reducing
gains from trade and specialisation in the rest of the world. The third is the
reduced profitability of established international investment in the troubled
economies and diminished opportunity for gains from new international
investment in and from the troubled economies.

International adjustment to increases in net exports from East Asia is an
inevitable consequence of crisis. The adjustment strains are less the more
rapidly and the higher the level at which economic activity stabilises and
then returns to growth in the troubled economies, increasing their attractiveness to new private capital inflow and moderating the current account
surpluses that emerged in the response to crisis. In the terms of McKibbin
(Chapter 14), the reversal of the increase in risk premia that helped to precipitate the crisis allows a return to more normal patterns of net exports.

The contraction of opportunities for trade and specialisation is the most
important ongoing mechanism of contagion. It can only be arrested by an
appropriate combination of stabilisation of activity and the exchange rate.
A lower exchange rate may not be associated with lower total imports if it
emerges from a package of policies that contributes to an earlier stabilisation and return to growth of real economic activity.

What means are available to arrest the continuing downward spiral in
East Asian imports and intraregional trade in mid-1998? It is important
that East Asian economies, and others to which East Asia is connected by
intensive trade and investment, set macroeconomic policies to maintain
economic growth. The exchange rate depreciations that have occurred in
the Philippines (Chapter 9), Singapore (Chapter 10), Taiwan (Chapter 11)
and Australia (Chapter 13) can be part of a set of responses that helps to
maintain growth and to avoid unnecessarily large contraction of output, if
they are accompanied by appropriate rates of monetary expansion. The policy settings of China and especially of Japan are of greatest quantitative importance, simply because of their economic size. China and Japan share the
rest of the region's interest in arresting the downward spiral in regional production and trade. And the rest of the region, and the international community, have a large interest in China and Japan managing their own affairs
in ways that minimise their own contributions to trade and especially import contraction.

It has already been noted that China entered the crisis with its macroeconomy in a strong position to absorb a shock. Its maintenance of the dollar peg and the efforts to maintain output growth through fiscal and later monetary expansion have suited the circumstances of the Chinese economy in 1997 and 1998. They have also suited regional economic conditions. China has received a foreign policy benefit from acting consistently with regional interest. Discussion of these matters in regional fora and in presidential meetings with the United States has heightened recognition of this benefit and placed some constraint on China taking domestic policy actions that would reverse these gains.

Japan has been deeply embedded in the institutional structure of global and regional economic cooperation for much longer than China. It has played the largest role as aid donor to developing East Asia and financier to each of the three IMF packages. With Australia, Japan was one of only two countries to join in assistance to Thailand, Indonesia and Korea. It has, however, struggled to bring the requirements of regional economic recovery effectively to account in its choice of domestic policy settings. The long paralysis on banking reform and an inappropriate mix of fiscal and monetary policy contributed to the yen and recession crisis of June 1998, and helped to precipitate the joint US–Japanese intervention in the foreign exchange market to arrest the slide in the dollar value of the yen. Following a stock market correction in the United States that some attributed to uncertainty about the Japanese economy, and warnings from the Chinese authorities that they would not be able to hold the yuan–dollar peg indefinitely if the yen continued to slide, the United States combined participation in joint intervention with pressure for changes in domestic economic policy. This was a measure of the weakness of established regional and global institutions for monetary cooperation: major steps in regional cooperation were revealed still to depend on the leadership of the United States, directly and through the IMF.

The stabilisation and reversal of the downward spiral in output and trade is going to require success in Japanese and Chinese stabilisation efforts. The arrest of decline in Indonesia is going to need a larger international effort, backing domestic monetary and fiscal expansion with international liquidity. Indonesian economic stability is too far from the centre of US interests for that country to play a leading role in the provision of finance. Neither is the IMF in a financial position to deliver much more than has been committed but delayed in disbursement. Any large effort would need to be led from East Asia, and only Japan and the Asian Development Bank supported by Japan have the financial resources to play the leading role. Here, too, international pressure and exhortation will be required for Japan to take action with large positive implications for the region. At first sight paradoxically, on these issues it may be easier for Japan to exercise leadership in international than in domestic policy, simply because the political economy constraints on policy choice are less severe.

Recovery in East Asia will introduce strains into the international trading system. The United States will be called upon to accept without protectionist response current account deficits of unprecedented dimension. A decade ago, the trading system would have been unlikely to accommodate stress on this scale. Since then, there has been a substantial strengthening of both the global and the regional framework for maintaining open trade – the former through the completion and bedding down of the Uruguay Round and the World Trade Organisation, the latter through the intensification of regional discussion of trade issues in APEC. The United States, in a period of domestic and international success and self-confidence, is being asked to bear a major burden of adjustment at a favourable time.

The preservation of the necessary environment of open trade cannot be taken for granted. In this context, the establishment of momentum in a new round of global trade negotiations, and the maintenance of commitment to free and open trade within APEC, may turn out to be the conditions for early return to strong growth in East Asia.

GRAND SEQUENCING

The book raises bigger questions about the relationship between economic policy and reform, and political reform. This relationship is a factor in every financial crisis, but is of special importance in East Asia in the 1990s. The contrast between the smooth transition to a new political leadership in Korea and Thailand, able to implement stabilisation policies and reforms unencumbered by past loyalties, and the policy and political paralysis in Indonesia underscores the point.

Soesastro (Chapter 19) argues that political reform, incorporating elements of democratisation, is an essential accompaniment of financial stabilisation and reform. Alongside our analysis of the optimal sequencing of elements of economic reform, there is a larger sequencing, embodying political reform. These issues are much debated in the course of the East Asian financial crisis. How the debate unfolds will depend a great deal on the path of recovery in East Asia in the period ahead.

It is likely that open and competitive political systems in Korea and Thailand will be strengthened by the crisis, so long as the reform policies being implemented now by new governments generate recovery within a reasonable time frame. This outcome is less likely in Indonesia. There, success, if it comes within a small number of years, will be associated with a larger range of policy interpretation. It is likely that the post-mortems in Indonesia will be allocating blame as much as, or more than, credit. The danger is that, in a rather confusing popular drawing of conclusions, the market solutions will be discredited as much as the misjudgments that so greatly exacerbated the crisis.

References

Aoki, Masahiko (1994) 'Monitoring characteristics of the main bank system: an analytical and developmental view', in Masahiko Aoki and Hugh Patrick (eds) *The Japanese Main Bank System: Its Relevancy for Developing and Transforming Economies*, New York: Oxford University Press, 109–41.

Aoki, Masahiko, Hugh Patrick and Paul Sheard (1994) 'The Japanese main bank system: an introductory overview', in Masahiko Aoki and Hugh Patrick (eds) *The Japanese Main Bank System: Its Relevancy for Developing and Transforming Economies*, New York: Oxford University Press, 3–50.

Asia Pacific Economics Group (APEG) (1996) *Asia Pacific Profiles 1996*, Canberra: Asia Pacific Economics Group, Australian National University.

—— (1997) *Asia Pacific Profiles 1997*, Hong Kong: Financial Times Newsletters and Management Reports.

—— (1998) *Asia Pacific Profiles 1998*, Singapore: Financial Times Finance Asia Pacific.

Association of South East Asian Nations (ASEAN) – Institute for Strategic and International Studies (ISIS) (1998) 'The future of ASEAN', highlights of discussion, Eighth South East Asia Forum, ASEAN–ISIS, Kuala Lumpur, 14–17 March.

Athukorala, Prema-chandra (1997) 'Malaysia', in APEG, *Asia Pacific Economic Profiles 1997*, Hong Kong: Financial Times Newsletters and Management Reports, 203–31.

—— (1998) 'Malaysia: the macroeconomy', in Colin Barlow (ed.) *Modern Malaysia in the Global Economy: Political and Social Changes into the 21st Century*, Aldershot: Edward Elgar, ch. 2 (forthcoming).

Athukorala, Prema-chandra and Peter G. Warr (1998) 'Vulnerability to a financial crisis: the Asian experience', unpublished manuscript, Economics Division, Research School of Pacific and Asian Studies, Australian National University, Canberra.

Australian Financial Review (AFR) (1986) 'Maddern sends the super case back to the marketplace', 27 June, 1.

—— (1986) 'Maddern hands employers a wedge', editorial, 27 June, 14.

—— (1986) 'London overshoots on Australia', 18 August, 36.

—— (1986) 'Mr Keating's remarkable budget', editorial, 20 August, 1.

—— (1986) 'Favourable first impressions but doubts about the targets', 20 August, 4.

—— (1986) 'Market qualms may force even tougher decisions', 21 August, 1.

Bagnoli, P., W. McKibbin and P. Wilcoxen (1996) 'Future projections and structural change', in N. Nakicenovic, W. Nordhaus, R. Richels and F. Toth (eds) *Climate Change: Integrating Economics and Policy*, Austria: International Institute for Applied Systems Analysis, 181–206.

Bangkok Post (1995) *Year-end Economic Review*, Bangkok: Bangkok Post Publishing Company.

—— (1996) *Year-end Economic Review*, Bangkok: Bangkok Post Publishing Company.

Bank for International Settlements (BIS) (1988) *International Convergence of Capital Measurement and Capital Standards (Cooke Report)*, Basle: Committe on Banking Regulations and Supervisory Practices, BIS.

—— (1996) *Annual Report*, Basle: H. Boehm.

—— (1998) *International Banking and Financial Market Developments*, February, Basle: Bank for International Settlements.

Bank Indonesia (1997) *Indonesian Financial Statistics*, March, Indonesia: Bank Indonesia.

Bank Negara Malaysia (BNM) (1994) *Money and Banking in Malaysia*, Kuala Lumpur: BNM.

—— (1998a) *Annual Report of the Board of Directors for the Year Ended 31 December 1997*, Kuala Lumpur: BNM.

—— (1998b) 'Press statement on stabilisation package for the financial sector', 25 March, Kuala Lumpur: BNM.

Bauer, Peter and Alan Walters (1975) 'The dollar problem', *Lloyds Bank Review*, April, London: Lloyds Bank.

Bautista, E. (1992) 'A study on Philippine monetary and banking policies', *Working Paper Series*, 91, Manila: Philippine Institute for Development Studies.

Benston, George J., Robert A. Eisenbeis, Paul M. Horvitz, Edward J. Kane and George G. Kaufman (1986) *Perspectives on Safe & Sound Banking: Past, Present, and Future*, Cambridge, Mass. and London: Massachusetts Institute of Technology Press.

Bhagwati, J. (1993) *India in Transition: Freeing the Economy*, London: Oxford University Press.

Binhadi and Paul Meek (1992) 'Implementing monetary policy', in Anne Booth (ed.) *The Oil Boom and After: Indonesian Economic Policy and Performance in the Soeharto Era*, Singapore: Oxford University Press, 102–31.

Boot, Arnoud W.A. (1992) 'Why hang on to losers?: divestitures and takeovers', *Journal of Finance*, 47: 1401–23.

Bowie, Alasdair and Danny Unger (1997) *The Politics of Open Economies*, Cambridge: Cambridge University Press.

Brash, Donald T. (1997) 'Banking soundness and the role of the market', in

Charles Enoch and John H. Green (eds) *Banking Soundness and Monetary Policy: Issues and Experiences in the Global Economy*, Washington DC: IMF, ch. 16.

Browne, Christopher (1997) 'Comments', in Charles Enoch and John H. Green (eds) *Banking Soundness and Monetary Policy: Issues and Experiences in the Global Economy*, Washington DC: IMF, 349–52.

Calvo, Guillermo A. (1995) 'Varieties of capital-market crises', *Center for International Economics Working Paper 15*, College Park: University of Maryland.

Campbell, J.K. (chairman) (1981) *Australian Financial System: Final Report of the Committee of Inquiry*, Canberra: Australian Government Publishing Service.

Caprio, Gerard, Izak Atiyas and James A. Hanson (eds) (1996) *Financial Reform: Theory and Experience*, Cambridge: Cambridge University Press.

Chan, Kenneth S. and Kee-Jin Ngiam (1996) 'Currency speculation and the optimum control of bank lending in Singapore dollars: a case for partial liberalization', *IMF Working Paper 96/95*, Washington DC: IMF.

China Daily (1998) 'Economy grows, no inflation', 25 April.

—— (1998) 'Foreign investment edges up despite Asian turmoil', 20 May.

—— (1998) 'New issue of treasury bonds just for banks', 14 May.

—— (1998) 'Report on implementation of the central and local budgets for 1997 and on the draft central and local budgets for 1998', 24 March.

—— (1998) 'Textiles get more rebate points', 23 February.

China Statistical Publisher (1997) *Statistical Yearbook of China*, Beijing: China Statistical Publisher.

Claessens, S. and T. Glaessner (1998) *Internationalization of Financial Services in East Asia*, Washington DC: World Bank (forthcoming).

Cole, David C. (1995) 'Financial sector development in Southeast Asia', in Shahid N. Zahid (ed.) *Financial Sector Development in Asia*, Oxford and New York: Oxford University Press, 223–60.

Cole, David C. and Betty F. Slade (1996) *Building a Modern Financial System: the Indonesian Experience*, Cambridge: Cambridge University Press.

Conroy, F. (1997) 'Discussion: managing credit risk – an overview', in B. Gray and C. Cassidy (eds) *Credit Risk in Banking*, Sydney: Reserve Bank of Australia, 22.

Corden, W. M. (1984) 'Booming sector and Dutch disease economics: a survey', *Oxford Economic Papers*, 36: 359–80.

Corsetti, Giancarlo, Paolo Pesenti and Nouriel Roubini (1998) 'What caused the Asian currency and financial crisis?', March, <http://www.stern.nyu. edu/~nroubini/asia/AsianCrisi.pdf> (accessed 11 June 1998).

Council for Economic Planning and Development (CEPD) (various years) *Taiwan Statistical Data Book*, Taipei: Republic of China.

Crouch, Harold and James W. Morley (1993) 'The dynamics of political change', in James W. Morley (ed.) *Driven by Growth: Political Change in the Asia-Pacific Region*, New York: M.E. Sharpe Inc, 277–309.

Datastream International (Australia) Pty Ltd (1998) *Datastream*, on-line service, London: Datastream International.

Dewatripont, Mathias and Jean Tirole (1994), *The Prudential Regulation of Banks*, Cambridge, Mass.: Massachusetts Institute of Technology Press.

Diaz-Alejandro, Carlos F. (1965) *Exchange Rate Devaluation in a Semi-Industrialized Country: The Experience of Argentina, 1955–61*, Cambridge, Mass.: Massachusetts Institute of Technology Press.

D'Ingeo, Magda (1996) 'Can consumers rely on the Bank of England?', Which? Ltd, <http://www.which.net/nonsub/cacampaigns/cpr/sep1996cpr/boe/contents.html> (accessed 20 June 1998).

Dixon, Peter B. and B.R. Parmenter (1987) 'Australia's real exchange rate: 1985 to 1900', working paper, Melbourne: Institute of Applied Economic and Social Research, University of Melbourne.

Djiwandono, J. Soedradjad (1997) 'The banking sector in an emerging market: the case of Indonesia', in Charles Enoch and John H. Green (eds) *Banking Soundness and Monetary Policy: Issues and Experiences in the Global Economy*, Washington DC: IMF, ch. 15.

Dornbusch, Rudiger (1997) 'A Thai–Mexico primer: lessons for outmanoeuvring a financial meltdown', *International Economy*, September/October, 20–3 and 55.

Dornbusch, Rudiger, Ilan Goldfajn and Rodrigo O. Valdes (1995) 'Currency crises and collapses', *Brookings Papers on Economic Activity*, 2: 219–93.

Duncan, R., Satish Chand, Bryan Graham, Tony Lawson and Rod Duncan (1998) 'Exchange rate policy in Papua New Guinea', mimeo, Canberra: National Centre for Development Studies, Australian National University.

Dziobek, Claudia and Ceyla Pazarbasioglu (1997) 'Lessons from systemic bank restructuring: a survey of 24 countries', *IMF Working Paper 97/161*, Washington DC: IMF.

Economist (1998) 'Of take-offs and tempests', 14 March.

Enoch, Charles and John H. Green (eds) (1997) *Banking Soundness and Monetary Policy: Issues and Experiences in the Global Economy*, Washington DC: IMF.

Ethier, Wilfred J. (1995) *Modern International Economics*, 3rd edn, New York: W.W. Norton.

Fane, George (1994) 'Survey of recent developments', *Bulletin of Indonesian Economic Studies*, April, 30(1): 3–38.

Fleming, J. Marcus (1962) 'Domestic financial policies under fixed and flexible exchange rates', *IMF Staff Papers*, 9, Washington DC: IMF, 369–79.

Folkerts-Landau, David, Takatoshi Ito, et al. (1995) *International Capital Markets: Developments, Prospects, and Policy Issues*, Washington DC: International Monetary Fund.

Foreign Policy Bulletin (*FPB*) (1997) 'SE Asia currency crisis focus of IMF/World Bank annual meeting', excerpts from statements by Malaysian Prime Minister Mahathir Mohamad, George Soros and Michel Camdessus, 8(6): 24–33.

Frankel, Jeffrey A. (1984) 'The yen-dollar agreement: liberalizing Japanese capital markets', *Policy Analyses in International Economics*, 9, Washington DC: Institute for International Economics.

Frenkel, Jacob (1996) 'Conclusion to Part II', in Ricardo Hausmann and Liliana Rojas-Suarez (eds) *Volatile Capital Flows*, Washington DC: Inter-American

Development Bank, 105–7.

Gagnon, J., P. Masson and W. McKibbin (1996) 'German unification: what have we learned from multi-country models?', *Economic Modelling*, 13(4): 467–98.

Galbis, V. (1993) 'High interest rates under financial liberalization: is there a problem?', *IMF Working Paper 93/17*, Washington DC: IMF.

Garnaut, Ross (1998) 'The financial crisis: a watershed in economic thought about East Asia', *Asian Pacific Economic Literature*, May, 12(1): 1–11.

Gavin, Michael, Ricardo Hausmann and Leonardo Leiderman (1996) 'The macroeconomics of capital flows to Latin America: experience and policy issues', in Ricardo Hausmann and Liliana Rojas-Suarez (eds) *Volatile Capital Flows*, Washington DC: Inter-American Development Bank, 1–40.

Ghosh, Atish R., Anne Marie Gulde and Holger C. Wolf (1998) 'Currency boards: the ultimate fix', *IMF Working Paper 98/8*, Washington DC: IMF.

Glick, R. and R. Moreno (1994) 'Capital flows and monetary policy in East Asia', *Working Paper PB94-08*, San Francisco: Centre for Pacific Basin Monetary and Economic Studies, Economic Research Department, Federal Reserve Bank of San Francisco.

Goldfajn, Ilan and Rodrigo O. Valdes (1997a) 'Capital flows and the twin crises: the role of liquidity', *IMF Working Paper 97/87*, Washington DC: IMF.

—— (1997b) 'Are currency crises predictable?', *IMF Working Paper 97/159*, Washington DC: IMF.

Goldsmith, R.W. (1969) *Financial Structure and Development*, New Haven, Conn.: Yale University Press.

Gomez, Edmund T. and K.S. Jomo (1997) *Malaysia's Political Economy: Politics, Patronage and Profits*, Cambridge: Cambridge University Press.

Greenspan, Alan (1998) *Humphrey-Hawkins Report*, 24 February, <http://www. bog.frb.fed.us/boarddocs/hh/9802Report.htm> (accessed 16 June 1998).

Grenville, S.A. (1991) 'The evolution of financial deregulation', in Ian MacFarlane (ed.) *The Deregulation of Financial Intermediaries*, Sydney: Reserve Bank of Australia, 3–35.

—— (1998) 'The Asian economic crisis', *Reserve Bank of Australia Bulletin*, Sydney: Reserve Bank of Australia, April, 9–20.

Gruen, D., B. Gray and G. Stevens (1998) 'A tale of two crises: Australia's experience in the 1980s and 1990s', paper for the East Asia in Crisis: From Being a Miracle to Needing One? conference, Economics Division, Research School of Pacific and Asian Studies, Australian National University, Canberra, 4–5 May.

Habir, Manggi (1994) 'Bank soundness requirements: a commercial bank perspective', in Ross H. McLeod (ed.) *Indonesia Assessment 1994: Finance as a Key Sector in Indonesia's Economic Development*, Canberra: Research School of Pacific and Asian Studies, Australian National University and Singapore: Institute of Southeast Asian Studies, ch. 10.

Haggard, Stephan and Susan Collins (1994) 'The political economy of adjustment', in Stephan Haggard, Richard Cooper, Susan Collins, Choongsoo Kim and Sung-Tae Ro (eds) *Macroeconomic Policy and Adjustment in Korea, 1970–1990*, Cambridge, Mass.: Harvard University Press.

Hellman, Thomas, Kevin Murdock and Joseph E. Stiglitz (1997) 'Financial restraint: toward a new paradigm', in Masahiko Aoki, Hyung-Ki Kim and Masahiro Okuno-Fujiwara (eds) *The Role of Government in East Asian Economic Development: Comparative Institutional Analysis*, New York: Oxford University Press, 163–207.

Henderson, Callum (1998) *Asia Falling: Making Sense of the Asian Currency Crisis and Its Aftermath*, Singapore: McGraw-Hill.

Hendrobudiyanto (1994) 'Bank soundness requirements: a central bank perspective', in Ross H. McLeod (ed.) *Indonesia Assessment 1994: Finance as a Key Sector in Indonesia's Economic Development*, Canberra: Research School of Pacific and Asian Studies, Australian National University and Singapore: Institute of Southeast Asian Studies, ch. 9.

Hiebert, Murray (1998) 'Big isn't beautiful', *Far Eastern Economic Review*, 5 March, 44–6.

Hoagland, Jim (1998) 'Which way for the IMF?', *Washington Post*, 10 May.

Hobday, Michael (1995) *Innovation in East Asia*, UK: Edward Elgar.

Holloway, Nigel (1997) 'All together now: needed banking standards for a volatile region', *Far Eastern Economic Review*, 22 May, 83–4.

Hong Kong Monetary Authority (1997) 'Approach to supervision', 30 April, <http://www.info.gov.hk/hkma/banking/app_sup.html> (accessed 30 April 1998).

Horiuchi, Akiyoshi (1996) 'An evaluation of Japanese financial liberalization: a case study of corporate bond markets,' in Takatoshi Ito and Anne O. Krueger (eds) *Financial Deregulation and Integration in East Asia*, Chicago: University of Chicago Press, 167–91.

Horiuchi, Akiyoshi and Katsutoshi Shimizu (1998) 'Did *amakudari* undermine the effectiveness of regulatory monitoring in Japan?', *Discussion Paper 98F-10*, April, Tokyo: Research Institute for the Japanese Economy.

Huh, Chan, and Sun Bae Kim (1994) 'Financial regulation and banking sector performance: a comparison of bad loan problems in Japan and Korea', *Economic Review*, San Francisco: Federal Reserve Bank of San Francisco, 2: 18–29.

Infobank (1995) Issue 190, October, Jakarta.

Intal, P. and G. Llanto (1998) 'Financial reform and development in the Philippines, 1980–1997: imperatives, performance and challenges', *Discussion Paper 98:2*, Manila: Philippine Institute for Development Studies.

Intal, P. and E. Medalla (1998) 'The East Asian crisis and Philippine sustainable development', paper for the Forum on the Asian Financial Crisis and Sustainable Development, Sixth Session of the United Nations Commission on Sustainable Development, ECOSOC Chamber, UN Headquarters, New York, 22 April.

International Monetary Fund (IMF) (1969) *Articles of Agreement*, Washington DC: IMF.

—— (1996) *Thailand: The Road to Sustained Growth*, Washington DC: IMF.

—— (1997a) *Annual Report 1996*, Washington DC: IMF.

—— (1997b) 'Press release No. 97/55', <http://www.imf.org/external/np/sec/pr/ 1997/pr97ind.htm> (accessed 11 June 1998).

—— (1997c) *World Economic Outlook*, December, Washington DC: IMF.

—— (1997d) 'World economic outlook: interim assessment', *World Economic and Financial Surveys*, Washington DC: IMF.

—— (1998a) 'IMF concludes Article IV consultation with Singapore', *Press Information Notice 98/19*, 16 March, Washington DC: IMF.

—— (1998b) *World Economic Outlook*, April, Washington DC: IMF.

—— (1998c) *World Economic Outlook*, May, Washington DC: IMF.

—— (1998d) *International Financial Statistics*, Washington DC: IMF.

Jager, Henk (1997) 'The South East Asian currency crisis: lessons to be learned from Europe and Latin America', paper for the Roundtable Discussion on the Exchange Rate Bubbles and Crisis: a Case of the Tequila Phenomenon in South East Asia, Philippine Institute for Development Studies and Philippine Economic Society, Manila, 25 November.

Johnston, Colin (1998) 'Survey of recent developments', *Bulletin of Indonesian Economic Studies*, August, 34(2): 3–57.

Johnston, R. Barry (1991) 'Distressed financial institutions in Thailand: structural weaknesses, support operations, and economic consequences', in V. Sundarajan and Tomas J.T. Balino (eds) *Banking Crises: Cases and Issues*, Washington DC: IMF, ch. 5.

Jomo, K.S. (1998) 'Financial liberalisation, crises and Malaysian policy responses', mimeo, Kuala Lumpur: Economics Department, University of Malaya.

Jorgenson, D.W. and P.J. Wilcoxen (1990) 'Environmental regulation and US economic growth', *Rand Journal*, 21(2): 314–40.

Joshi, Vijay and Ian Little (1994) *India: Macroeconomics and Political Economy 1964–1991*, Washington DC: World Bank.

—— (1996) *India's Economic Reforms: 1991–2001*, Oxford: Oxford University Press.

Kaminsky, Graciela, Saul Lizondo and Carmen M. Reinhart (1997a) 'Leading indicators of currency crises', *IMF Working Paper 97/79*, Washington DC: IMF.

—— (1997b) 'Leading indicators of currency crises', *Working Papers in International Economics*, 36, College Park: Centre for International Economics, University of Maryland.

Keeley, Michael C. (1990) 'Deposit insurance, risk, and market power in banking', *American Economic Review*, 80: 1183–1200.

Khoman, Sirilaksana (1993) 'Education policy' in P.G. Warr (ed.) *The Thai Economy in Transition*, Cambridge: Cambridge University Press, 325–54.

Kindleberger, Charles P. (1973) *The World in Depression, 1929–1939*, London: Allen Lane.

—— (1989) *Manias, Panics and Crashes: A History of Financial Crises*, New York: Basic Books.

—— (1992) 'Financial crises', in Peter Newman, Murray Milgate and John

Eatwell (eds) *The New Palgrave Dictionary of Money and Finance*, London: Macmillan, 46–7.

Klein, Benjamin and Keith B. Leffler (1981) 'The role of market forces in assuring contractual performance', *Journal of Political Economy*, 89: 615–41.

Kokko, A. (1997) *Managing the Transition to Free Trade: Vietnamese Trade Policy for the 21st Century*, Hanoi: Embassy of Sweden.

Krugman, Paul R. (1979) 'A model of balance of payments crises', *Journal of Money, Credit and Banking*, 11: 311–25.

—— (1994) 'The myth of Asia's miracle', *Foreign Affairs*, November/December, 62–78.

—— (1998a) 'What happened to Asia?', January, <http://web.mit.edu/krugman/www/disinter.html>, (accessed 11 February 1998).

—— (1998b) 'Fire-sale FDI', February, <http://web.mit.edu/krugman/www>, (accessed 11 February 1998).

—— (1998c) 'Currency crises', <http://web.mit.edu/krugman/www/crises.html> (accessed 27 March 1998).

Laya, J.C. (1982) *A Crisis of Confidence and Other Papers*, Manila: Central Bank of Philippines.

Lee, H.L. (1998) answer to parliamentary question, 19 February, <http://www.mas.gov.sg/speeches/parliament4-c.htm> (accessed 21 April 1998).

—— (1998) answer to parliamentary question, 20 April, <http://www.mas.gov.sg/speeches/parliamentary_200498a-c.htm> (accessed 21 April 1998).

Lee, Peter (1998) 'Korea stares into the abyss', *Euromoney*, March, <http://www.emwl.com/contents/publications/euromoney/em.98> (accessed 11 June 1998).

Leiderman, Leonardo and Alfredo E. Thorne (1996) 'The Mexican crisis and its aftermath: what are the main lessons?', in Guillermo A. Calvo, Morris Goldstein and Eduardo Hochreiter (eds) *Private Capital Flows to Emerging Markets after the Mexican Crisis,* Washington DC: Institute for International Economics, 1–43.

Leung, E.S. (1995) 'Exchange rate regimes and outward-looking growth', in R. Garnaut, E. Grilli and J. Riedel (eds) *Sustaining Export Oriented Development: Ideas from East Asia*, Hong Kong: Cambridge University Press, 151–91.

—— (1996) 'Capital flows, monetary policy and exchange rates in the Asian region', *Working Paper 96:2*, Canberra: Economics Division, Research School of Pacific and Asian Studies, Australian National University.

—— (1997) 'Financial deregulation and trade expansion', in D. Robertson (ed.) *East Asian Trade after the Uruguay Round*, United Kingdom: Cambridge University Press, 78–97.

—— (1998) 'State-owned enterprise reform and competitive markets in Vietnam', paper for the Understanding the Decline of China's State Sector: Reform Experience and Future Direction conference, Australian National University, February.

Leung, E.S. and T.T. Vo (1996) 'Vietnam in the 1980's: price reforms and stabilisation', *Banca Nazionale del Lavoro Quarterly Review*, June, 197: 187–207.

Li, Kang, Wu Tianxin, Wu Meiping and Qian Hua (1998) 'The East Asia financial crisis and virtuous developments of the security market in China', *Securities Market Herald*, 2(67): 4–17.

Lindgren, Carl-Johan, Gillian Garcia and Matthew I. Saal (1996) *Bank Soundness and Macroeconomic Policy*, Washington DC: International Monetary Fund.

Little, Ian, Richard Cooper, Max Corden and Sarath Rajapatirana (1994) *Boom, Crisis and Adjustment: The Macreconomic Experience of Developing Countries*, New York: Oxford University Press.

Liu, L., M. Noland, S. Robinson and Zhi Wang (1998) 'Asian competitive devaluations', *Institute for International Economics Working Paper 98/2*, Washington DC: Institute for International Economics.

Mackenzie, George (1996) 'Quasi fiscal operations of public financial institutions', *IMF Occasional Paper 142*, Washington DC: IMF.

Mallon, R. (1997) 'Achieving greater equity between private and state enterprises', presentation to MPI – Asian Development Bank Enterprise Reform Workshop, October.

Marshall, Kathryn G. (1994) 'The case against deposit insurance in Indonesia', in Ross H. McLeod (ed.) *Indonesia Assessment 1994: Finance as a Key Sector in Indonesia's Economic Development*, Canberra: Research School of Pacific and Asian Studies, Australian National University and Singapore: Institute of Southeast Asian Studies, ch. 11.

Masson, Paul R. (1998) 'Contagion: monsoonal effects, spillovers, and jumps between multiple equilibria', unpublished paper, IMF, Washington DC.

Mathieson, Donald J. and Liliana Rojas-Suarez (1992) 'Liberalization of the capital account: experiences and issues', *IMF Working Paper 92/46*, Washington DC: IMF.

McKibbin, W.J. (1994) 'Dynamic adjustment to regional integration: Europe 1992 and NAFTA', *Journal of the Japanese and International Economies*, 8(4): 422–53.

—— (1996) 'Quantifying APEC trade liberalization: a dynamic analysis', *Working Paper in Trade and Development 1*, Canberra: Economics Division, Research School of Pacific and Asian Studies, Australian National University.

—— (1997) 'Some global consequences of financial market liberalization in the Asia Pacific region', paper for the EMBA Investment Liberalisation and Financial Reform in the Asia–Pacific Region conference, Sydney, 29–31 August.

—— (1998) 'The crisis in Asia: an empirical assessment', *Brookings Discussion Paper in International Economics 136*, Washington DC: Brookings Institution.

McKibbin, W.J. and J. Sachs (1991) *Global Linkages: Macroeconomic Interdependence and Co-operation in the World Economy*, Washington DC: Brookings Institution.

McKibbin, W. and P. Wilcoxen (1995) 'The theoretical and empirical structure of the G-Cubed model', *Brookings Discussion Paper in International Economics 119*, Washington DC: Brookings Institution.

—— (1997) 'Macroeconomic volatility in general equilibrium', mimeo, Canberra: Economics Division, Research School of Pacific and Asian Studies, Australian National University and Austin: University of Texas.

McKinnon, R. and H. Pill (1994) 'Credible liberalizations and international capital flows: the over-borrowing syndrome', paper for the Fifth Annual East Asian Seminar on Economics, Singapore.

McLeod, Ross H. (1994a) 'Indonesia's foreign debt', in Ross H. McLeod (ed.) *Indonesia Assessment 1994: Finance as a Key Sector in Indonesia's Economic Development*, Canberra: Research School of Pacific and Asian Studies, Australian National University and Singapore: Institute of Southeast Asian Studies, ch. 15.

—— (ed.) (1994b) *Indonesia Assessment 1994: Finance as a Key Sector in Indonesia's Development*, Research School of Pacific and Asian Studies, Australian National University and Singapore: Institute of Southeast Asian Studies.

—— (1996) 'Indonesian foreign debt: a comment', *Bulletin of Indonesian Economic Studies*, August, 32(2): 119–31.

—— (1997a) 'Explaining chronic inflation in Indonesia', *Journal of Development Studies*, February, 33(3): 392–410.

—— (1997b) 'Survey of recent developments', *Bulletin of Indonesian Economic Studies*, April, 33(1): 3–43.

—— (1997c) 'Policy conflicts in Indonesia: the impact of the current account deficit target on growth, equity and stability', *ASEAN Economic Bulletin*, July, 14(1): 32–45.

—— (1997d) 'Postscript to the survey of recent developments: on causes and cures for the rupiah crisis', *Bulletin of Indonesian Economic Studies*, December, 33(3): 35–52.

—— (1998a) 'Control and competition: banking deregulation and regulation in Indonesia', *Journal of the Asia–Pacific Economy* (forthcoming).

—— (1998b) 'From crisis to cataclysm?: the mismanagement of Indonesia's economic ailments', *World Economy* (forthcoming).

—— (1998c) 'Paradise lost: the pernicious impact of exchange rate policy on Indonesia's banking system', paper for the Vietnam and the Region: Asia-Pacific Experiences and Vietnam's Economic Policy Directions conference, Economics Division, Research School of Pacific and Asian Studies, Australian National University, 20–1 April.

—— (1998d) 'Indonesia', in Asia Pacific Economics Group (APEG) *Asia Pacific Profiles 1998*, Singapore: F.T. Finance Asia Pacific, 210–1.

McMullen, Neil (1997) 'Institutional challenge in economic growth', paper for the Sustaining Economic Growth in Indonesia: a Framework for the Twenty-first Century conference, USAID, ACAES and LPEM–UI, Jakarta, 17–18 December.

Medalla, E. (1997) 'Trade and industrial policy beyond 2000: an assessment of the Philippine economy', draft report submitted to the Philippine Institute for Development Studies, Manila, 9 December.

Mishkin, F.S. (1996) 'Understanding financial crises: a developing country perspective', in M. Bruno and B. Pleskovic (eds) *Annual World Bank Conference on Development Economics 1996*, Washington DC: World Bank, 29–68.

Mo, Jongryon and Chung-in Moon (1998) 'Democracy and the origins of the 1997 Korean economic crisis', in Chung-in Moon and Jongryon Mo (eds) *Democracy and the Korean Economy* (forthcoming).

Monetary Authority of Singapore (MAS)(1997) *Monthly Statistical Bulletin*, various months, <http://www.mas.gov.sg> (accessed 24 April 1998).

—— (1998) *Monthly Statistical Bulletin*, various months, <http//www.mas.gov.sg> (accessed 24 April 1998).

Montes, M.F. (1998) 'The currency crisis in Southeast Asia: update', mimeo, Singapore: Institute of Southeast Asian Studies

Montgomery, John (1997) 'The Indonesian financial system: its contribution to economic performance, and key policy issues', *IMF Working Paper 97/45*, April, Washington DC: IMF.

Moreno, R. (1998) 'Asia's financial crisis: lessons and policy responses', paper for the Vietnam and the Region: Asia-Pacific Experiences and Vietnam's Economic Policy Directions conference, Economics Division, Research School of Pacific and Asian Studies, Australian National University, 20–1 April.

Mundell, Robert A. (1962) 'Capital mobility and stabilization policy under fixed and flexible exchange rates', *Canadian Journal of Economics and Political Science*, 29: 475–87.

Nascimento, J.C. (1991) 'Crisis in the financial sector and the authorities' reaction: the Philippines', in V. Sundararajan and T. Balino (eds) *Banking Crises: Causes and Issues*, Washington DC: IMF.

Newman, Peter, Murray Milgate and John Eatwell (eds) (1992) *The New Palgrave Dictionary of Money and Finance*, London: Macmillan.

Ngo Huy Duc (1998) 'Dollarization in Vietnam and its economic implications', unpublished PhD thesis, National Centre for Development Studies, Australian National University.

Nickell, Stephen, Daphne Nicolitsas and Neil Dryden (1997) 'What makes firms perform well?' *European Economic Review*, 41: 783–96.

Noerhadi, D. Cyril (1994) 'The role of the Indonesian capital market', in Ross H. McLeod (ed.) *Indonesia Assessment 1994: Finance as a Key Sector in Indonesia's Economic Development*, Canberra: Research School of Pacific and Asian Studies, Australian National University and Singapore: Institute of Southeast Asian Studies, ch. 12.

Obstfeld, Maurice (1986) 'Rational and self-fulfilling balance-of-payments crises', *American Economic Review* 76: 72–81.

—— (1994a) 'The logic of currency crises', *Cahiers Economiques et Monetaires*, 43: 189–213.

—— (1994b) 'The logic of currency crises', *NBER Working Paper 4640*, Cambridge, Mass.: National Bureau of Economic Research.

Oksenberg, Michel C., Michael D. Swaine and Danial C. Lynch (1997) *The Chinese Future*, Los Angeles: Pacific Council on International Policy and Santa Monica: Rand Centre for Asia-Pacific Policy.

O'Mara, L.P. (1987) 'The medium term outlook for the real exchange rate and real interest rates', paper for the Policy Forum on Exchange Rates and Interest

Rates: Where to Now?, ACT Branch, Australian Agricultural Economics Society, Canberra, 30 September.

Organisation for Economic Cooperation and Development (OECD) (1994) *OECD Economic Survey – Korea*, Paris: OECD.

—— (1996) *OECD Economic Survey – Korea*, Paris: OECD.

—— (1998) *OECD Economic Outlook*, Paris: OECD.

Park, Y.C. (1991) 'Financial repression and liberalization', in L.B. Krause and K. Kihwan (eds) *Liberalization in the Process of Economic Development*, California: University of California Press.

Radelet, S. and J. Sachs (1998a) 'Understanding the East Asian financial crisis', mimeo, Cambridge, Mass.: Harvard Institute for International Development.

—— (1998b) 'The onset of the East Asian financial crisis', 10 February, <http://www.hiid.harvard.edu/pub/other/eaonset.pdf> (accessed 10 February 1998).

Reserve Bank of India (RBI) (1997) *The Annual Report on the Working of the Reserve Bank of India*, New Delhi: Government of India.

Robinson, David, Yangho Byeon and Ranjit Teja (1991) 'Thailand: adjusting to success, current policy issues', *Occasional Paper 85*, Washington, DC: IMF.

Roubini, N. (1998) 'The case against currency boards: debunking 10 myths about the benefits of currency boards', February, <http://www.stern.nyu.edu/~nroubini/asia/AsiaHomepage.html#currency board> (accessed 27 May 1998).

Roulier, Richard P. (1997) 'Governance issues and banking system soundness', in Charles Enoch and John H. Green (eds) *Banking Soundness and Monetary Policy: Issues and Experiences in the Global Economy*, Washington DC: IMF, ch. 20.

Sachs, Jeffrey D., Aaron Tornell and Andres Velasco (1996) 'Financial crises in emerging markets: the lessons from 1995', *Brookings Papers on Economic Activity*, 1: 147–215.

Shand, R.T. (ed.) (1998) *Economic Liberalisation in South Asia*, Delhi: Macmillan (forthcoming).

Soesastro, M. Hadi (1998) 'Survey of recent developments', *Bulletin of Indonesian Economic Studies*, April, 34(1): 3–54.

Soesastro, M. Hadi and Peter Drysdale (1990) 'Survey of recent developments', *Bulletin of Indonesian Economic Studies*, December, 26(3): 3–44.

Song, Inwon (1998) 'Korean banks' responses to the strengthening of capital adequacy requirements', *Pacific Basin Working Paper 98/1*, San Francisco: Federal Reserve Bank of San Francisco.

Song, Ligang (1998) 'Understanding the rapid expansion of China's foreign trade', paper for the APEC and Its Impact on the Chinese Economy conference, Australia Japan Research Centre, Australian National University, Canberra, 16 February.

South China Morning Post (1998) 'IMF, ratings agency worry about banking in Singapore', 18 March.

Stiglitz, J. (1989) 'Financial markets and development', *Oxford Review of Economic Policy*, 5(4): 59–68.

—— (1998) 'Boats, planes, and capital flows', *Financial Times*, 25 March.

Stiglitz, J. and A. Weiss (1981) 'Credit rationing in markets with imperfect information', *American Economic Review*, 71(3): 393–410.

Stolper, W.F. and P.A. Samuelson (1941) 'Protection and real wages', *Review of Economic Studies*, 1: 35–68.

Takeda, Masahiko and Phillip Turner (1992), 'The liberalization of Japan's financial markets: some major themes', *BIS Economic Papers*, 34.

Tan, E. (1997) 'Effects of the five per cent uniform tariff', *Discussion Paper 97/17*, Manila: Philippine Institute for Development Studies.

Tan, Kong Yam (1998) 'The regional economic crisis: looking at the lessons', paper for the Eighth South East Asia Forum, ASEAN–ISIS, Kuala Lumpur, 14–17 March.

Taylor, John B. (1993) *Macroeconomic Policy in a World Economy*, New York: W.W. Norton.

Thomson BankWatch Inc. (1997) *BankWatch*, various pages, <http://www.bankwatch.com> (accessed 11 June 1998).

Tsang, Donald (1998), budget speech, 18 February, <http://www.info.gov.hk/fb/bdgt98/english/eindex.htm> (accessed 27 May 1998).

Tsang, Shu-ki (1997) 'Attack at the safe haven: whither Hong Kong's currency board system?', *BRC Papers on China*, December, Hong Kong: Business Research Centre, School of Business, Hong Kong Baptist University.

Vatikiotis, Michael (1998) 'Fund under fire', *Far Eastern Economic Review*, 14 May.

Villanueva, D. and A. Mirakhor (1990) 'Strategies for Financial Reforms: interest rate policies, stabilization, and bank supervision in developing countries', *IMF Staff Papers*, 37(2), Washington DC: IMF.

Wallis, S. (chairman) (1997) *Financial System Inquiry Final Report*, Canberra: Australian Government Publishing Service.

Walters, Alan A. (1998) 'Currency board could save Indonesia from ruin', *Scotsman*, 22 February.

Wanandi, Jusuf (1998) 'Good governance, domestic and regional stability: agenda for the future', paper for the Twelfth Asia Pacific Roundtable, Kuala Lumpur, 31 May–4 June.

Warr, Peter G. (1986) 'Indonesia's other Dutch Disease: economic effects of the petroleum boom', in J.P. Neary and S. van Wijnbergen (eds) *Natural Resources and the Macroeconomy*, Oxford: Basil Blackwell, 288–320.

—— (1993) 'The Thai economy', in P.G. Warr (ed.) *The Thai Economy in Transition*, Cambridge: Cambridge University Press, 1–80.

—— (1997) 'Thailand', in APEG (1997) *Asia Pacific Profiles 1997*, Hong Kong: Financial Times Newsletters and Management Reports, 283–305.

Warr, Peter G. and Bhanupong Nidhiprabha (1996) *Thailand's Macroeconomic Miracle: Stable Adjustment and Sustained Growth*, Washington DC: World Bank and Kuala Lumpur: Oxford University Press.

Williamson, John (1998) 'Learning from Asia's woes', paper for the Adjustment and Beyond: the Reform Experience in South Asia conference, Dhaka, 30 March–1 April.

World Bank (1993) *The East Asian Miracle*, Oxford: Oxford University Press.

—— (1994) *Vietnam: Financial Sector Review. An Agenda for Financial Sector Development*, Washington DC: World Bank.

—— (1997a) 'Rethinking the East Asian miracle', preliminary suggestions from the Office of the Chief Economist, prepared for the Second World Bank Japan Research Fair '97 Workshop, Tokyo, 12 December.

—— (1997b) *World Development Indicators 1997, CD-ROM*, Washington DC: World Bank.

—— (1997c) *Vietnam: Refining Reform for Growth*, Washington DC: World Bank.

World Economic Forum (1997) *The Global Competitiveness Report*, Geneva: World Economic Forum.

Yi, Gang and Fan Min (1997) 'Analysis of the determinants of the RMB exchange rates and its trend', *Economic Research*, 10: 26–35.

Yi, Gang and Xiao Zhao (1998) 'Searching for effective policy combinations under the multi-objectives of the economy: analysis of China's macroeconomic situation in 1998 and suggestions', unpublished report prepared by the China Centre for Economic Research, Peking University.

Yusof, Zaina A., Awang A. Hussain, Ismail Alowi, Lim Chee Sing and Sukhdave Singh (1994) 'Financial reforms in Malaysia', in Gerard Caprio, Izak Atias and James A. Hanson (eds) *Financial Reform: Theory and Evidence*, Cambridge: Cambridge University Press, 276–322.

Yusof, Zainal Aznam (1998) 'The regional economic crisis: looking at the lessons', paper for the Eighth South East Asia Forum, ASEAN–ISIS, Kuala Lumpur, 14–17 March.

Zahid, Shahid N. (ed.) (1995) *Financial Sector Development in Asia*, Oxford and New York: Oxford University Press.

Zhang, Shuguang, Zuo Dapei and Yang Fan (1998) 'Macro aggregates, financial risks and external shocks: analysis of the current macroeconomy in China', *Economic Research*, 3: 3–14.

Index